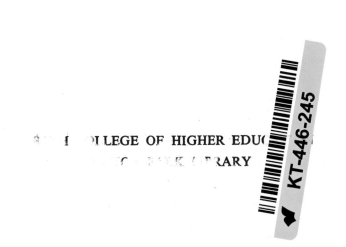

EARLY MUSIC HISTORY 11

EDITORIAL BOARD

EARLY MUSIC HISTORY 11

STUDIES IN MEDIEVAL
AND
EARLY MODERN MUSIC

Edited by

IAIN FENLON
Fellow of King's College, Cambridge

CAMBRIDGE
UNIVERSITY PRESS

Published by the Press Syndicate of the University of Cambridge
The Pitt Building, Trumpington Street, Cambridge CB2 1RP
40 West 20th Street, New York, NY 10011–4211, USA
10 Stamford Road, Oakleigh, Victoria 3166, Australia

First published 1992

Phototypeset in Baskerville by Wyvern Typesetting Ltd, Bristol
Printed in Great Britain at the University Press, Cambridge

ISSN 0261–1279

ISBN 0 521 41957 3

SUBSCRIPTIONS The subscription price to volume 11, which includes postage, is £42.00 (US $79.00 in USA and Canada) for institutions, £27.00 (US $45.00 in USA and Canada) for individuals ordering direct from the Press and certifying that the annual is for their personal use. Airmail (orders to Cambridge only) £8.00 extra. Copies of the annual for subscribers in the USA and Canada are sent by air to New York to arrive with minimum delay. Orders, which must be accompanied by payment, may be sent to a bookseller, subscription agent or direct to the publishers: Cambridge University Press, The Edinburgh Building, Shaftesbury Road, Cambridge CB2 2RU. Payment may be made by any of the following methods: cheque (payable to Cambridge University Press), UK postal order, bank draft, Post Office Giro (account no. 571 6055 GB Bootle – advise CUP of payment), international money order, UNESCO coupons, or any credit card bearing the Interbank symbol. Orders from the USA and Canada should be sent to Cambridge University Press, 40 West 20th Street, New York, NY 10011–4211, USA.

BACK VOLUMES Volumes 1–10 are available from the publisher at £40.00 ($79.00 in USA and Canada).

NOTE Each volume of *Early Music History* is now published in the year in which it is subscribed. Volume 11 is therefore published in 1992. Readers should be aware, however, that some earlier volumes have been subscribed in the year *after* the copyright and publication date given on this imprints page. Thus volume 8, the volume received by 1989 subscribers, is dated 1988 on the imprints page.

CONTENTS

v

NOTES FOR CONTRIBUTORS

Contributors should write in English, or be willing to have their articles translated. All typescripts must be double spaced *throughout*, including footnotes, bibliographies, annotated lists of manuscripts, appendixes, tables and displayed quotations. Margins should be at least 2.5 cm (1″). The 'top' (ribbon) copy of the typescript must be supplied. Scripts submitted for consideration will not normally be returned unless specifically requested.

Artwork for graphs, diagrams and music examples should be, wherever possible, submitted in a form suitable for direct reproduction, bearing in mind the maximum dimensions of the printed version: 17.5 × 11 cm (7″ × 4.5″). Photographs should be in the form of glossy black and white prints, measuring about 20.3 × 15.2 cm (8″ × 6″).

All illustrations should be on separate sheets from the text of the article and should be clearly identified with the contributor's name and the figure/example number. Their approximate position in the text should be indicated by a marginal note in the typescript. Captions should be separately typed, double spaced.

Tables should also be supplied on separate sheets, with the title typed above the body of the table.

SPELLING

English spelling, idiom and terminology should be used, e.g. bar (not measure), note (not tone), quaver (not eighth note). Where there is an option, '-ise' endings should be preferred to '-ize'.

PUNCTUATION

English punctuation practice should be followed: (1) single quotation marks, except for 'a "quote" within a quote'; (2) punctuation outside quotation marks, unless a complete sentence is quoted; (3) no comma before 'and' in a series; (4) footnote indicators follow punctuation; (5) square brackets [ ] only for interpolation in quoted matter; (6) no stop after contractions that include the last letter of a word, e.g. Dr, St, edn (but vol. and vols.).

BIBLIOGRAPHICAL REFERENCES

Authors' and editors' forenames should not be given, only initials; where possible, editors should be given for Festschriften, conference proceedings, symposia, etc. In titles, all important words in English should be capitalised; all other languages should follow prose-style capitalisation, except for journal and series titles which should follow English capitalisation. Titles of series should be included, in roman, where relevant. Journal and series volume numbers should be given in arabic, volumes of a set in roman ('vol.' will not be used). Places and dates of publication should be included but not publishers' names. Dissertation titles should be given in roman and enclosed in quotation marks. Page numbers should be preceded by 'p.' or 'pp.' in all contexts. The first citation of a bibliographical reference should include full details; subsequent citations may use the author's surname, short title and relevant page numbers only. *Ibid.* may be used, but not *op. cit.* or *loc. cit.*

ABBREVIATIONS

Abbreviations for manuscript citations, libraries, periodicals, series, etc. should not be used without explanation; after the first full citation an abbreviation may be used throughout text and notes. Standard abbreviations may be used without explanation. In the text, 'Example', 'Figure' and 'bars' should be used (not 'Ex.', 'Fig.', 'bb.'). In references to manuscripts, 'fols.' should be used (not 'ff.') and 'v' (verso) and 'r' (recto) should be typed superscript. The word for 'saint' should be spelled out or abbreviated according to language, e.g. San Andrea, S. Maria, SS. Pietro e Paolo, St Paul, St Agnes, St Denis, Ste Clothilde.

NOTE NAMES

Flats, sharps and naturals should be indicated by the conventional signs, not words. Note names should be roman and capitalised where general, e.g. C major, but should be italic and follow the Helmholtz code where specific ($C_{,,}$ C, $C\,c\,c'$ C'' C'''; c' = middle C). A simpler system may be used in discussions of repertories (e.g. chant) where different conventions are followed.

QUOTATIONS

A quotation of no more than 60 words of prose or one line of verse should be continuous within the text and enclosed in single quotation marks. Longer quotations should be displayed and quotation marks should not be used. For quotations from foreign languages, an English translation must be given in addition to the foreign-language original.

NUMBERS

Numbers below 100 should be spelled out, except page, bar, folio numbers etc., sums of money and specific quantities, e.g. 20 ducats, 45 mm. Pairs of numbers should be elided as follows: 190–1, 198–9, 198–201, 212–13. Dates should be given in the following forms: 10 January 1983, the 1980s, sixteenth century (16th century in tables and lists), sixteenth-century polyphony.

CAPITALISATION

Incipits in all language (motets, songs, etc.), and titles except in English, should be capitalised as in running prose; titles in English should have all important words capitalised, e.g. *The Pavin of Delight*. Most offices should have a lower-case initial except in official titles, e.g. 'the Lord Chancellor entered the cathedral', 'the Bishop of Salford entered the cathedral' (but 'the bishop entered the cathedral'). Names of institutions should have full (not prose-style) capitalisation, e.g. Liceo Musicale.

ITALICS

Titles and incipits of musical works in italic, but not genre titles or sections of the Mass/English Service, e.g. Kyrie, Magnificat. Italics for foreign words should be kept to a minimum; in general they should be used only for unusual words or if a word might be mistaken for English if not italicised. Titles of manuscripts should be roman in quotes, e.g. 'Rules How to Compose'. Names of institutions should be roman.

AUTHORS' CORRECTIONS

It is assumed that typescripts received for publication are in their final form. There may be an opportunity to make minor emendations at the copy-editing stage, but corrections in proof *must* be restricted to printer's and publisher's errors. Any departure from this practice will be at the discretion of the editor and the publisher, and authors may be subject to charge.

Early Music History (1992) Volume 11

BONNIE J. BLACKBURN

MUSIC AND FESTIVITIES AT THE COURT OF LEO X: A VENETIAN VIEW*

'On 1 October 1518, Cardinal Cornaro and Cardinal Pisani left Venice for Rome; they went by water to Chioggia, then set out on horseback.'[1] Thus begins the diary entry of a young Venetian patrician, Marcantonio Michiel, who was himself a member of the travelling party. Twenty-five days later they arrived in Rome, where Michiel was to stay for two years. During this period he noted in his diary both political events in Rome and news from Venice, but – unlike many diarists – he was keenly interested in art and music, and he also recorded detailed descriptions of Roman festivities. Having been brought up in Venice, with its magnificent state pageantry, he was prepared to appreciate Roman ceremonial, both civic and religious, and, with his entrée to the papal court, he was privileged to be present at private entertainments. For some of these occasions we have eye-witness accounts by other observers, but for several Michiel seems to be the only source known so far. He enlarges our picture of the music-loving pope and highlights the activities of Leo's private musicians. His reports of musical performances add new information to our meagre knowledge of early sixteenth-century instrumentation.

* Parts of this article were read in 1990 at the State University of New York at Buffalo, Stanford University, the University of California at Berkeley and the Eighteenth Medieval and Renaissance Conference at Royal Holloway and Bedford New College. The Stanford and Berkeley lectures were enlivened by spirited performances of the villotta *Bacco, Bacco* under the direction, respectively, of William Mahrt and Anthony Newcomb. I wish to thank Anthony M. Cummings for reading the article in advance of publication and drawing my attention to several documents I had overlooked.

[1] 'Adi primo ottobre 1518 si partirono di Venetia il Cardinal Cornaro et il Cardinal Pisano per Roma, et andorono per acqua a Chioza, et indi se messero à cavallo.' Venice, Biblioteca Correr, Cod. Cicogna 2848, fol. 287ᵛ. Francesco Pisani, elected on 1 July 1517, was making his first trip to Rome.

1

Michiel began his diary in 1511, at the age of twenty-seven. Born into an illustrious patrician Venetian family, he became a member of the Maggior Consilio in 1504. He was a prize pupil at the school of the famous humanist Giovanni Battista Egnazio, from whom he learned Greek and Latin. The stimulus for his diary seems to have been his voyage to Dalmatia and Corfù in 1510; his letters from that trip show that he was a keen observer, especially of antiquities, which were to become a lifelong interest. In 1512 he went to Bergamo with his father, the newly appointed *Capitanio*; there he interrupted his diary to write a description of the city in elegant Latin, published in 1532.[2]

The turning-point in Michiel's life must have been his Roman experience in 1518–20. There he gravitated towards artistic and literary pursuits; besides his Venetian acquaintances Sebastiano del Piombo and Pietro Bembo, he came to know Raphael, Jacopo Sannazaro and other artists, architects and literary figures. It was in Rome that he began to take an active interest in art, at first as connoisseur, then as patron and collector. Indeed, it is for his observations on art that he is best known today. Two of his Roman letters found their way into Marino Sanuto's famous diaries; one describes the artistic activities in which Raphael was engaged and laments his premature death.[3] In the 1520s and 1530s Michiel made extensive notes on works of art in churches and private houses in Venice, Padua, Milan and other northern Italian cities; his manuscript was discovered in the eighteenth century and published in 1800 as the work of 'un anonimo'. Subsequent editions and translations testify to the value of this work for art historians.[4] When Michiel died in 1552, he left a personal collection that included at least one Giorgione; his notes describe no fewer than fourteen paintings of that elusive figure.

[2] On Michiel's life and writings, see E. A. Cicogna, 'Intorno la vita e le opere di Marcantonio Michiel', *Memorie dell'Istituto Veneto*, 9 (Venice, 1860), pp. 359–425 (also published separately, Venice, 1861); F. Nicolini, *L'arte napoletana del Rinascimento e la lettera di Pietro Summonte a Marcantonio Michiel* (Naples, 1925); and now (with new documents) J. Fletcher, 'Marcantonio Michiel: His Friends and Collection', *The Burlington Magazine*, 123 (1981), pp. 453–67, and 'Marcantonio Michiel, "che ha veduto assai"', *ibid.*, pp. 602–8. For his collection, see Fletcher, 'Marcantonio Michiel's Collection', *Journal of the Warburg and Courtauld Institutes*, 36 (1973), pp. 382–5.
[3] M. Sanuto, *I diarii*, ed. R. Fulin *et al.*, 58 vols. (Venice, 1879–1903), xxviii, cols. 299–301 (on Carnival) and 424–6 (on Raphael).
[4] See Fletcher, 'Marcantonio Michiel: His Friends and Collection', p. 453, n. 9.

The diary itself, Cod. Cicogna 2848 in the Biblioteca Correr in Venice, has never been published, apart from the extracts on art that first appeared in Cicogna's study of 1860 and the sections on Naples printed in Nicolini's book. It is not an autograph but a copy in a clear and legible sixteenth-century hand, although the acid corrosion of the ink makes some passages difficult to read. Comprising 383 folios, it covers the years 1511 to 1545. Like many Venetian diaries and chronicles, it leans heavily towards politics. Disappointingly, it says nothing about music in Venice, although we know that Michiel's interest in music dates from his boyhood; a letter written in 1510 to one of his former schoolmates, Bertuccio Soranzo, recalls their discussions about literature, music and philosophy.[5]

It was not until Michiel had been in Rome for almost a year that he began to make more than cursory mention of Roman festivities. Carnival 1519 passed by with the laconic note: 'Carnival in Rome was very festive and cheerful because of hunts, comedies and other festivities'; in Naples, in contrast, it was melancholy because of the political situation (he had spent March in Naples).[6] In August the diary contains a long entry on the feast of the Assumption,[7] in which each merchant guild prepared a *carro* or float, making a procession, organised according to the regions of Rome, from the Campidoglio to St John Lateran, where the image of Christ, supposedly painted by St Luke for the Virgin, was removed and carried in procession through the regions back to the Campidoglio, where the senators and conservators were waiting, and thence to the church of St Adrian and then to S. Maria Maggiore, where it spent the night facing a portrait of the Virgin painted by St Luke. The image was carried back the next day, but with less pomp. Michiel remarks that this is a feast that is very dear to the Romans.

---

[5] 'tecum de litteris, de musica, de philosophia, ut solebamus, suavissime colloqui opto'; see Nicolini, *L'arte napoletana*, p. 138. Nicolini reprints the letter of Pietro Summonte of 20 March 1524, written in answer to Michiel's request for information about Neapolitan painting, sculpture and architecture. In it Summonte praises the architect Giovanni Mormando, remarking that 'questo da prima fo maestro d'organi, poi s'è convertito all'architettura e alla totale imitazione di cose antique' (pp. 172–3).

[6] 'Il carnoval in Roma fu molto festoso, et lieto per caccie, et comedie, et altre feste, che si fecero; all'incontro in Napoli malinconico per li respetti di presoni, et gelosia de Hispani.' Cod. Cicogna 2848, fol. 297[r].

[7] *Ibid.*, fols. 306[r]–307[r].

Indeed, it seems to be one of the few festivities that did not involve the guiding hand of the papal establishment.

Carnival, on the other hand, was very much subject to papal direction. While it was organised by municipal magistrates, they had to receive papal approval; on the other hand, they also received papal funding, with the result that the ten-day period of carnival was carefully programmed, with events that catered for the lowliest citizens as well as the upper reaches of the papal hierarchy. The more barbaric aspects were confined to Monte Testaccio, where carts to which pigs and bulls were attached were sent headlong down the steep incline; at the bottom the carts were smashed and the animals slaughtered by the waiting crowd (Michiel thought it a 'spectacolo veramente dilettevole, magnifico, et che molto ha de la antiqua magnificenza'[8]). Carnival involved a considerable number of races: of old men, of young men, of Jews (who were forced to run naked), of prostitutes in their underclothing, of donkeys, buffaloes and horses. Formerly these also took place on Monte Testaccio, but Pope Paul II moved them to the Via del Corso so that he could watch the finishing-line from his palace on the Piazza di Venezia. And when the papal residence moved to the Vatican, the race-course was again rerouted. Other events were bull hunts in the Piazza del Campidoglio, and the Festa di Agone, with masquerades, tournaments and processions of allegorical floats in Piazza Navona. Under Julius II and Leo X the programmes for these floats were devised by humanists, who mixed the legends of ancient Rome with the glorification of the reigning pope.[9] Michiel's account of Carnival in 1520 covers fols. 319^r–321^r, running from 12 to 21 February. He was most impressed with the races and the Festa di Agone; the theme that year was 'al proposito delle vittorie delli antiqui romani, et del stato di Roma presente', or what might be termed the Myth of Rome.

Descriptions of the Roman carnival are known from other sources as well.[10] What are much rarer are descriptions of the

---

[8]   See his letter of 23 February 1520 to Nicolò Dolfin, printed in Sanuto, *I diarii*, xxvIII, cols. 299–301. The diary entry is very similar, but does not include this last remark.

[9]   The literature on Roman carnivals is extensive. For a brief account, with references, see C. L. Stinger, *The Renaissance in Rome* (Bloomington, IN, 1985), pp. 57–9.

[10] A number of excerpts from contemporary accounts are reprinted in F. Cruciani, *Teatro nel Rinascimento: Roma 1450–1550* (Rome, 1983). See also L. Fiorani *et al.*, *Riti, ceremonie, feste e vita di popolo nella Roma dei Papi* (Bologna, 1970).

private festivities of the papal court, limited in attendance to the higher echelons of the curia, the ambassadors and visiting dignitaries, at which women were sometimes present. Michiel reports on four of these, all of which involved musical performances.

The first occurred on 1 August, the feast of St Peter in Chains. On this day in 1520 the cardinals went to the homonymous church, as was customary. Then, Michiel continues, the pope gave a dinner, but deferred the usual celebration to the following day because he was eating fish (it was a Wednesday, a fast-day); however, he had a comedy performed. The remark is surprising: what should there be about the feast of St Peter in Chains that would call for a comedy, which was normally part of carnival festivities? In fact, the feast on 1 August was not a religious but a secular – not to say pagan – one, as the next entry in Michiel's diary makes clear:

On 2 August the pope hosted a sumptuous luncheon and dinner for whichever cardinals wished to come, both all the cardinals, and many others. And after dinner he presented a musical concert, on which he spent 500 ducats, as follows. First some ten musicians, dressed in violet, performed a Bergamasque song, singing and playing in alternation with a lirone, two flutes, a lute and a clavicembalo. Then another group, dressed in yellow, performed a German song, singing and playing in alternation on trombones and cornetts. Then yet another group, dressed in pink, sang a Spanish song, playing it alternately on lironi. Then crumhorns. Then boys, who sang in the English manner. Then all the instrumentalists and singers sang and played together in twelve parts. The English sang a macaronesque 'tano', with all the words on the subject of the first day of August and Bacchus, and between one performance and the other there was a nude Bacchus, and Maestro Andrea the buffoon, who was his translator, who read a supplication for the Germans, and all of them had garlands of grape leaves, satin jackets and cloth stockings. (Appendix 1, excerpt 1)

It has long been known that Leo X employed a number of musicians in his private household.[11] In the documents they are called *cantores et musici secreti*. Their names are known from payment records, but not their specific duties. We assume that they played during meals and in the evenings, and whenever the pope wished to

---

[11]   The most extensive account is found in H.-W. Frey's article, 'Regesten zur päpstlichen Kapelle unter Leo X. und zu seiner Privatkapelle', published in instalments in *Die Musikforschung*, 8 (1955) and 9 (1956). For the private chapel, see 8, pp. 412–37, and 9, pp. 46–57, 139–56 and 411–19.

hear music – which was often, Leo X being a well-nigh insatiable listener. From Michiel's diary we learn that the *cantores et musici secreti* also put on musical shows, which required costumes and a certain degree of staging. Michiel's account for 2 August speaks of three groups of about ten musicians each, half singers and half players, plus a group of boys. It seems curious that a French chanson was not performed at this geographical extravaganza; perhaps that is what was sung in alternation with the crumhorns, in which case we need to include another ten musicians. Were there forty-five performers among Leo's chamber musicians? Only one boy is listed in the records,[12] but for August 1520 the forces numbered ten singers[13] and twenty-nine instrumentalists:

eight shawm players (*pifferi*):[14]

[12]   Petrus Pirrinus, aged fourteen in 1520; see Frey, 'Regesten' (1956), p. 50. The three 'cantores parvi' sent by Louis XII to Leo X on his election, including Hilaire Penet and Johannes Consilium, were now grown, but might have been replaced, as was their companion, Pierre de Monchiaron, in 1514; see A. Pirro, 'Leo X and Music', *The Musical Quarterly*, 21 (1935), pp. 1–16, on p. 8. Indeed, in 1518 Leo charged his legate in France, Cardinal Bibbiena, with procuring 'tre putti cantori', even specifying what voices and ages were wanted; see the exchange of letters between Cardinal Giulio de' Medici and Bibbiena discussed by A. M. Cummings in 'Giulio de' Medici's Music Books', *Early Music History*, 10 (1991), pp. 65–122, on p. 72. No boys are listed among the salaried singers. However, special payments were made to Gasparino, the chapel-singer Antonio Bidon's son, and to a 'Philippo cantarino' (24 December 1520), who lived with Bidon (3 March 1519, 25 June 1521); Frey, pp. 54–5. Boys might have been borrowed from the entourages of cardinals: on 29 September 1518 Leo gave 2 gold ducats 'a uno pucto cantore di mons. R.mo de Aragona' (*ibid.*, p. 143). On boy singers in Rome, see C. J. Reynolds, 'Rome: A City of Rich Contrast', *The Renaissance: From the 1470s to the End of the 16th Century*, ed. I. Fenlon (London, 1989), pp. 63–101, on pp. 77–80.

[13]   Andreas de Silva, Antonius Bruhier, Firminus le Clerc, Franciscus Vanelst, Jacotinus Level, Jo. Jacobus de Tarvisio, Laurentius de Bergomotiis, Simon Malle, Valentinus de la Rue and Gaspar van Weerbeke; see Frey, 'Regesten' (1955), pp. 412–14, 416–17, 422–3, 425–7, 432–7, (1956), pp. 51–2 and 55–6 (the payment to van Weerbeke may have been only a pension; he was then about seventy-five years old). Bruhier, Laurentius de Bergomotiis and Jo. Jacobus de Tarvisio had been *cantores secreti* since 1513 (*ibid.* (1955), p. 412); Andreas de Silva joined them in January 1519 (*ibid.*, p. 413), Firminus le Clerc, Franciscus Vanelst and Jacobinus Level in February of that year (*ibid.*, p. 416), Valentinus de la Rue in September 1519 (*ibid.* (1956), p. 51) and Simon Malle in June 1520 (*ibid.*).

[14]   The first five appear on a list of August 1520 (Frey (1956), p. 140, n. 94). 'Gian Jacomo piffero', also from Cesena, had formerly been a member of the Florentine Signoria's wind-band during the time when Lorenzo de' Medici, Duke of Urbino, was governor of Florence. See R. Sherr, 'Lorenzo de' Medici, Duke of Urbino, as a Patron of Music', *Renaissance Studies in Honor of Craig Hugh Smyth*, 2 vols. (Florence, 1985), I, pp. 627–38, on p. 628. The two Bartolos had originally served Cardinal Luigi d'Aragona; on his death attempts were made to engage them as well, but it was too late: the pope had already hired all five of the cardinal's wind players (and at a higher salary than Lorenzo's ambassador thought them worth); *ibid.*, p. 629. Leo had given them a gift of 150 ducats in May 1518, while they were still in the cardinal's service (Frey (1956), pp. 142–3). In

Bartholo Fiammingo piffero
Bartholo da Milano piffero
Domenico da Cesena piffero
Antonio da Cesena piffero
Giorgio Greco piffero
Jo. Jacomo piffero
Melchiore Milanese
Michele da Verona[15]
seven lutenists:[16]
Jo. Franciscus de Manfronibus
Jo. Maria Dominici Alemanus (de' Medici)
Francesco Milanese
Francesco Tertio and his three companions, who 'cantono
    con leuto'
two keyboard players:[17]

Leo's service the five were paid 177 ducats every three months, plus rent on their houses (Frey (1956), p. 57). Melchiore was hired in April 1520 (*ibid.*, p. 141).

[15] Michele da Verona joined in February 1520 (Frey (1956), p. 140, n. 94). Knud Jeppesen suggested that he is the same as Michele Pesenti da Verona, lutenist and composer; see *La frottola*, 3 vols. (Århus and Copenhagen, 1968–70), I, p. 159. Since then further information has come to light that strengthens this hypothesis. Michele was in the service of Ippolito I d'Este from 1506 to 1514, as lutenist, singer, purchaser of music and instruments and copyist; see L. Lockwood, 'Adrian Willaert and Cardinal Ippolito d'Este: New Light on Willaert's Early Career in Italy, 1515–21', *Early Music History*, 5 (1985), pp. 85–112, on pp. 99 and 112. He had a son Alberto, traceable in Ippolito's accounts in 1510–11 and 1517–20 (*ibid.*, p. 110). Another musician, 'Alexandro de pre Michele', appears in 1516–17 and 1520 (*ibid.*), and 'Janes de pre Michele (sonator de fagotto)' in 1508–10, 1512–14, 1517 (p. 111). Jeppesen suggested that he is the 'Michael presbyter et cantor' who wrote to Ippolito d'Este in 1504 and 1505 (*La frottola*, I, pp. 158–9). That the Michele da Verona in Leo's accounts is a 'piffero' might seem to speak against the identification. However, he is qualified as 'messer' and is paid the very high salary of 15 gold ducats a month; he also had additional duties, for which he was paid extra: 'duc. cinque per certe spese fe, quando ando la musica a la Manliana' in August 1520 (Frey (1956), p. 140, n. 94), and 'per alcune spese facte per N. S. per nolo de habiti nel carnevale et per far fare libri di musica per andar fora il Maggio a la Magliana et per far conciare le storte duc. octo iul. dui' in June 1521 (*ibid.*, p. 142, n. 97). He was obviously a versatile musician.

[16] Frey (1955), pp. 424–5, 427–31, (1956), pp. 56, 140. On Jo. Maria, variously called 'Dominici', 'Alemanus', 'Hebreo', 'de Medici' and 'Conte de Verrucchio', see H. C. Slim, 'Gian and Gian Maria, Some Fifteenth- and Sixteenth-Century Namesakes', *The Musical Quarterly*, 57 (1971), pp. 562–74, on pp. 563–8, and A. M. Cummings, 'Gian Maria Giudeo, Sonatore del Liuto, and the Medici', *Fontes Artis Musicae*, 38 (1991). Another four-lute ensemble, including Jo. Maria Alemanus (de' Medici), played at a banquet in Rome on 20 May 1523; see N. Pirrotta, 'Music and Cultural Tendencies in 15th-Century Italy', *Journal of the American Musicological Society*, 19 (1966), pp. 127–61, on p. 158 (citing Sanuto, *I diarii*, XXXIV, col. 216).

[17] Frey (1956), pp. 139–40. In February 1520 Sanuto notes that 'Zuan Maria dal Clavicimbano, marito di Hieronima che canta, per il suo ben sonar a Roma, il Papa li ha dato provisione e lo tien de lì' (*I diarii*, XXVIII, col. 302). Frey lists no keyboard player of this

Hieronymo de Asti ('sona de bonaccordo')
Marco Antonio da Bologna (Cavazzoni) ('sona di
   gravicembolo')
two trombonists:[18]
   Zacharia trombone
   Francesco
ten other musicians (players of string instruments?):[19]
   Andreas de Silio
   Cesar de Johanne Antonii de Tolentino
   Claudius de Alexandris
   Galeatius de Baldis
   Georgius de Parma
   Hieronimus de Ameria
   Johannes Esquinus
   Martinus
   Mathias Marilianus
   Julio Mantuano

The shawm players must have been capable of playing all the wind instruments. But Leo had also hired a Venetian virtuoso on the cornett, Jo. Maria dal Corneto, a private musician of the doge. From a note in Sanuto's diary of May 1520 we know how this was accomplished: the Venetian ambassador to the Holy See wrote that after having dined with the pope at La Magliana, just as he was leaving, Cardinal Corner requested on the pope's behalf that he prevail upon the Signoria to give 'Zuan Maria', the doge's *piffaro*, leave to come to Rome to participate in a musical occasion, 'the

---

name. It is my suspicion that Sanuto gave an incorrect name for Marc'Antonio Cavazzoni, perhaps confusing him with the other Venetian musician at Leo's court, Jo. Maria dal Corneto. Cavazzoni entered the pope's service in that same month (Frey (1956), p. 140). We know nothing of his wife, but he did have a son, Girolamo, who followed in his father's footsteps. For the most up-to-date information on the two musicians, see Oscar Mischiati's articles in the *Dizionario biografico degli italiani*.

[18] See Frey (1956), pp. 140–1. Zacharia was well enough known to have been included in Philippo Oriolo's poem 'Monte Parnaso'; see H. C. Slim, 'Musicians on Parnassus', *Studies in the Renaissance*, 12 (1965), pp. 134–63, on p. 144.

[19] See Frey (1955), pp. 413, 415–19, 424, (1956), pp. 47–8, 56–7. Galeazzo Baldi, a Bolognese, was possibly the singer Galeazzo listed in the accounts of the Cappella Giulia for Oct–Nov 1513; see A. Ducrot, 'Histoire de la Cappella Giulia au XVIᵉ siècle depuis sa fondation par Jules II (1513) jusqu'à sa restauration par Grégoire XIII (1578)', *Mélanges d'Archéologie et d'Histoire de l'École Française de Rome*, 75 (1963), pp. 179–240, 467–559, on p. 187. He had been in Leo's service before he became pope (Frey (1955), p. 412). A 'Galeazzo sonatore di liutto' served Clement VII in 1524; *ibid.* (1956), p. 144.

which, being done, would gratify the pope greatly'.[20] The doge acceded, consenting to be without the services of Zuan Maria for a whole year; Sanuto thought the matter worth noting in his diary.[21]

Thirty instrumentalists certainly sufficed for the August celebration, but there are about ten singers too few. These could easily have been provided from the singers in the papal chapel, who numbered about thirty-one in 1520.[22]

We learn a number of things from Michiel's description. The Bergamasque song, perhaps something like the villotta *Le pur morto Feragù*,[23] was accompanied by a group of instruments that recalls nothing so much as the Elizabethan broken consort: a lirone, two flutes, a lute and a keyboard instrument. That such a combination was used as early as 1520 comes as a distinct surprise. According to Howard Brown, 'in the first half of the sixteenth century, the consort principle dominated almost completely' – that is, pure consorts, instruments all of the same family.[24] Furthermore, he found that 'keyboard instruments seem to have been reserved for compositions performed by solo voices'.[25] His evidence was based on the Florentine *intermedi*, one of the best sources we have for

---

[20] '[Marco Minio] scrive, havendo disnato col Papa a la Magnana, nel partir il cardinal Corner li disse, da parte dil Papa, instasse esso Orator con la Signoria nostra fosse dato licentia a uno Zuan Maria pifaro dil Doxe aziò vengi de lì per compir certa musicha; la qual cossa facendo sarà molto grata al Papa'; *I diarii*, xxviii, col. 488. He is probably the 'Ser Zuan Maria pifaro dal corneto' who entered the Scuola di San Giovanni Evangelista in 1527; see J. E. Glixon, 'Music at the Venetian "Scuole Grandi", 1440–1540', 2 vols. (Ph.D. dissertation, Princeton University, 1979), i, p. 78.

[21] 'Per la Signoria fo dà licentia, a complacentia dil Papa, che Zuan Maria pifaro dil Doxe possi andar per uno anno a servir el Papa, lasando suo fradelo in loco suo con il suo salario'; 15 June 1520 (Sanuto, *I diarii*, xxviii, col. 618). In Rome he was paid at the high rate of 15 ducats a month from May 1520 to April 1521; Frey (1956), pp. 140–1. For other references to Jo. Maria and his playing, see Pirro, 'Leo X and Music', pp. 14–15, and Slim, 'Gian and Gian Maria', p. 570.

[22] Frey (1955), p. 199.

[23] A setting by F. P. (Francesco Patavino=Santa Croce) is in *Canzoni, frottole e capitoli, libro secondo de la croce* (1531), fols. 29ᵛ–31, and an anonymous one in the *Libro primo de la fortuna*, fol. 13. Other candidates are Paulo Scotto's *Turluru la capra e moza* (Petrucci, *Frottole* bk vii) and Rossino da Mantova's *Lirum bililirum* (*Frottole* bk ii). Pirrotta suggests that the latter and his *Perche fai, donna, el gaton* may have been used in theatrical performances; see *Music and Theatre from Poliziano to Monteverdi*, trans. K. Eales (Cambridge, 1982), pp. 67–9. The former is headed 'Un sonar de piva in fachinesco', imitating the sound of bagpipes and in Bergamasque dialect. On these and other pieces with a Bergamasque connection, with translations, see W. F. Prizer, 'Games of Venus: Secular Vocal Music in the Late Quattrocento and Early Cinquecento', *Journal of Musicology*, 9 (1991), 3–56, on pp. 47–52.

[24] H. M. Brown, *Sixteenth-Century Instrumentation: The Music for the Florentine Intermedii*, Musicological Studies and Documents 30 (n.p., 1973), p. 78.

[25] *Ibid.*, p. 25.

instrumental practice, but a body of evidence that largely falls into the second half of the century. In accounts of musical performances at banquets in Ferrara in 1529 and 1532, however, Brown found more evidence of mixed consorts, especially as a finale.[26] The harpsichord was a regular member of these groups, as was, incidentally, a trombone. Broken consorts used in the *intermedi* may have been motivated by particular circumstances of the actions or characters. The consort that Michiel describes seems to have no such motivation; it may well represent normal performance practice. The ensemble that played music between the acts of Ariosto's *I suppositi* in Rome during Carnival 1519 is similar: shawms, crumhorns, two cornetts, viols, lutes, organetto, flute and voices.[27]

Michiel consistently refers to the string instruments as *lironi*. According to the article in *The New Grove Dictionary of Musical Instruments*, the lirone is the bass counterpart to the lira da braccio, with nine to fourteen strings on the fingerboard and two to four drone strings. Because of its nearly flat bridge, it was primarily used for chordal playing. The descriptions of the lirone all date from late in the century, and its greatest popularity seems to have been in the seventeenth century.[28] The earliest known reference to a lirone in a specific performance is in the 1565 Florentine *intermedio* to *La Cofanaria*, where it accompanied a lament. Brown believes that it functioned as a foundation instrument; only one is used in the

---

[26] H. M. Brown, 'A Cook's Tour of Ferrara in 1529', *Rivista Italiana di Musicologia*, 10 (1975), pp. 216–41.

[27] 'et per ogni acto, se li intermediò una musica de pifari, de cornamusi, de dui corneti, de viole, et leuti, de l'organeto che è tanto variato de voce, che donò al Papa monsignor illustrissimo de bona memoria [Cardinal Luigi d'Aragona], et insieme vi era un flauto, et una voce che molto bene si commendò; li fu ancho un concerto de voce in musica'; from a letter of Alfonso Paolucci of 8 March 1519 to Alfonso I d'Este, reprinted in Cruciani, *Teatro nel Rinascimento*, pp. 455–7. It is not clear whether the *intermedio* consisted solely of music or also acting; the last *intermedio* was a *moresca* on 'la fabula de Gorgon'. While Leo's instrumental forces were sufficient for the 1520 performances, he did not have enough for the Ariosto *intermedio* and Cardinal Cibo wanted to borrow some from the Florentine Signoria; see the urgent requests in Sherr, 'Lorenzo de' Medici', p. 629. However, the Duke proved stubborn – until informed that 'N. S. li disidera', whereupon they were dispatched the following day. Three new *cantores secreti* had been hired in February, probably with the Carnival festivities in mind (see above, n. 13).

[28] But Atalante Migliorotti had conceived the instrument as early as 1505; in a letter written to Francesco Gonzaga he called it 'a new and unusual form of lyre': 'col mio debile ingegno, introduco nuovo, inaudito et inusitato modo di sonare, con nuova et inusitata forma di lyra, con ciò sia cosa io adgiunga corde al compimento al numero di XII, parte nel suo tempo oportuno dal piede, et parte dalla mano tastabili in perfecta et consummata consonantia'; see W. F. Prizer, 'Isabella d'Este and Lorenzo da Pavia, "Master Instrument-Maker"', *Early Music History*, 2 (1982), pp. 87–127, on p. 108.

intermedi.[29] Michiel, however, says that the Spanish song was played on lironi: there must have been four or five of them. But a bowed instrument with a flat bridge would not be suitable for playing individual polyphonic lines: viols would. Could lirone be Michiel's term for viol?

In his book *The Early History of the Viol*, Ian Woodfield cites an apt remark of David Boyden on the terminology of string instruments in the early sixteenth century: 'a treacherous quicksand ready and eager to engulf those who mistake it for *terra firma*'.[30] Indeed, bowed string instruments in the first two decades of the century were called by a bewildering variety of names: viola, viola da archo, viola da gamba, viola grande da archetto, violone grande, viola spagnola, lira, lira da braccio, lirone. According to the article in *The New Grove Dictionary of Musical Instruments*, the 'earliest known reference to the lirone is in a document of 1536 (*I-Vas*) of the Venetian religious confraternity, the Scuola di S. Giovanni Evangelista'.[31] Further references are found in the records of the Scuola di S. Rocco. Jonathan Glixon's research on the Scuole Grandi has brought to light even earlier references, in which the terms 'violone', 'lira' and 'lirone' seem to be used interchangeably. In January 1530 the Scuola dalla Misericordia hired new instrumentalists who played 'violoni over lironi';[32] four years later they are called 'sonadori de lire et violoni', though the marginal reference reads 'lironi'.[33] The distinction may be one of range; in 1541 the Scuola Grande di S. Maria della Carità accepted five 'sonadori de lironi' into its ranks, one who played 'soran', another 'basso', a third 'tenor', a fourth 'contra alto' and the last 'bassetto'.[34] It seems likely, then, that 'lirone' was a specifically Venetian term for viol, that is, viola da gamba, at least in the first half of the sixteenth century, and that it came in different sizes.[35]

---

[29] Brown, *Sixteenth-Century Instrumentation*, p. 47.
[30] I. Woodfield, *The Early History of the Viol* (Cambridge, 1984), p. 7.
[31] *The New Grove Dictionary of Musical Instruments*, ed. S. Sadie, 3 vols. (London, 1984), II, p. 529.
[32] Glixon, 'Music at the Venetian "Scuole Grandi" ', II, pp. 87–8.   [33] *Ibid.*, p. 89.
[34] *Ibid.*, p. 70. Other early references to the lirone are found in Giovan Francesco Straparola's *Le piacevoli notti*, published in 1550–3 but set in Venice about 1536, and Teofilo Folengo's *Caos del triperuno* of 1526; see C. A. Elias, 'Musical Performance in 16th-Century Italian Literature: Straparola's *Le piacevoli notti*', *Early Music*, 17 (1989), pp. 161–73, on pp. 164–5.
[35] Woodfield, *Early History*, also believes that early mentions of the lirone are 'almost certainly references to the viol' (p. 181).

It is interesting that Leo's musicians chose viols to accompany the Spanish song, for the earliest references to viols in Italy are connected with Spaniards. A newsworthy item, reported by the Mantuan ambassador, was Ascanio Sforza's sending Spanish players of 'viols almost as large as myself' from Rome to Milan to celebrate the birth of Ludovico il Moro's son Massimiliano in 1493.[36] None of Leo's *musici secreti* has a demonstrably Spanish name (perhaps Johannes Esquinus?), but there was a contingent of Spaniards in the papal chapel. Of course, by 1520 the viol was a common instrument, but the association between Spaniards and string instruments, especially in Rome, evidently remained strong.[37]

Although none of Leo's musicians appears to be German, except perhaps his favoured lutenist, Giovanni Maria de' Medici, the choice of trombones and cornetts to accompany the German song is completely in keeping with German skill as makers of wind instruments, and many of the wind players at the courts of Milan, Mantua and Ferrara were of German origin. 'Piffaro' seems to be a generic name for wind-instrument players; we know from other sources that such musicians played a variety of wind instruments.[38]

The boys who sang in the English manner are a distinct novelty. While English music was well known and much admired on the Continent in the first half of the fifteenth century, by 1470 it was thoroughly *passé*; according to Tinctoris, it suffered from 'a wretched poverty of invention'.[39] By 1520, of course, the English school was flourishing – but only in England, as far as we know. What can have been known of English music in Rome in 1520? John Hothby may have been the last English musician resident in Italy; he left Lucca for London in 1486, at the request of Henry VII, but died in 1487 on the return trip. No English singers seem to be found in any north Italian court or in the papal chapel. A lone

[36] *Ibid.*, p. 81.
[37] Keith Polk has recently argued that there is not much evidence that the Spanish viol tradition was very influential in the northern Italian courts, and that the German and native Italian viol traditions need to be taken into account. See 'Vedel and Geige – Fiddle and Viol: German String Traditions in the Fifteenth Century', *Journal of the American Musicological Society*, 42 (1989), pp. 504–46, esp. 531–7.
[38] See W. F. Prizer, 'Bernardino Piffaro e i pifferi e tromboni di Mantova: strumenti a fiato in una corte italiana', *Rivista Italiana di Musicologia*, 16 (1981), pp. 151–84, esp. 160–3.
[39] Prologue to *Proportionale musices*; see O. Strunk, *Source Readings in Music History* (New York, 1950), p. 195.

'Joannes Inglese' was a singer in the Cappella Giulia in 1526.[40] Did the Italian singers know the English style so well that they could 'cantare alla Inghlese' – or were those boys themselves English? Michiel says 'li Inglesi' sang the 'tano macharonescho'. He might simply be referring to the earlier performers, but it is not out of the question that there was a group of English choristers in Rome, perhaps in the household of an English ecclesiastic,[41] or at the English church in Rome.[42]

Two questions need answers: what does it mean to 'cantare alla inglese', and what is the 'tano macharonescho' that they sang? The latter term has eluded identification.[43] 'Macharonescho' must mean that it mixed languages, but which: English and Italian? or Latin? or even Greek, since it was about Bacchus? There is a delightful macaronic song in the Ritson manuscript, *Up I arose in verno tempore*,[44] but the words have nothing to do with Bacchus.

[40] See Ducrot, 'Histoire de la Cappella Giulia', p. 192. He must have entered the Chapel some time after 1514; all records are lost between 1514 and 1526. The Cappella Giulia regularly employed boys; a 'Johannes' was a boy singer in 1513–14 (pp. 187–8), but the name is so common that he cannot be identified securely with the adult singer Johannes of 1526.

[41] The English cardinal, Thomas Wolsey, did not reside in Rome; business was conducted through the Bishop of Worcester, who, however, was an Italian, Silvestro Gigli, as was Henry VIII's ambassador to the Holy See, Gregorio Casali. Little is known about their households, but it seems unlikely that they included many Englishmen. Before 1514 the presence of English choristers would have been more likely. Cardinal Christopher Bainbridge, who did reside in Rome, had a number of Englishmen in his household, including Richard Pace, the humanist and friend of Erasmus, who was keenly interested in music. He left Rome on the cardinal's death in 1514.

[42] There is little evidence, however, to support this notion. The English church and hospice in Rome, which flourished during the Middle Ages, serving as the centre for English pilgrims to Rome, were in a parlous state in these very years. Cardinal Bainbridge had been forced to retrench to pay the debts his predecessors had run up. Records of this period are fragmentary, but we do know that Bainbridge paid for many expenses from his own income. See D.S. Chambers, *Cardinal Bainbridge in the Court of Rome 1509 to 1514* (London, 1965), esp. pp. 78, 80 and 118–19. In 1518 Gigli warned Wolsey that the hospice was in great distress and was hardly able to bear the cost of feeding pilgrims, to say nothing of the 'evil disposed clerks, which came yearly from England to be made priests, and so by they made clandestine with false tittylls' (letter of 9 January 1518; abstract in *Letters and Papers ... Henry VIII*, II, p. 1213). On the history of the English Hospice in Rome, see vol. XXI of *The Venerabile* (Exeter, 1962), esp., for this period, Brian Newns, 'The Hospice of St Thomas and the English Crown 1474–1538', pp. 145–92.

[43] The word rarely occurs in Italian dictionaries, and always in a sense not applicable in the present case. Even dialect dictionaries of the Veneto have not been helpful. The word is clearly written, and it is hard to imagine that the copyist of Michiel's diary misread the word 'canto', which would be the most likely meaning. Anthony Newcomb made the interesting suggestion that it might be derived from the adjectival ending -*tano*, such as '(canzone) napolitano'.

[44] *Early Tudor Songs and Carols*, ed. J. Stevens, Musica Britannica 36 (London, 1975), p. 19. There are few secular macaronic songs, but many carols mix English and Latin.

However, the contemporary Venetian MS 1795–1798 has a four-part villotta, *Baco, Baco, santo idio*, that would be entirely appropriate to the occasion, which indeed seems to be a sort of 'St Bacchus day'. The song text includes the words 'Baco, Baco, col cantare, festeggiando oggi s'honori'.[45] We can imagine that the wine was flowing freely at Leo's banquet. The spectacle also pokes fun at the Germans, who were reputed to be great drinkers: Bacchus is made to present a supplication for them, which was translated by Maestro Andrea, one of Leo's favourite buffoons.

National characteristics of singing have been remarked on by several writers. Pietro Aaron quotes the common view: 'The French sing, the English jubilate, the Spaniards weep, the Germans howl and the Italians bleat like goats.'[46] This is obviously a French view, and Aaron takes justifiable exception to the denigration of Italian singers.[47] The idea that the English 'jubilate' is common to Flemish,[48] German[49] and Italian writers of the fifteenth and six-

---

[45] See F. Luisi, *Apografo miscellaneo marciano: Frottole, canzoni e madrigali con alcuni alla pavana in villanesco* (Venice, 1979), pp. 135–6. A chorus of bacchants appeared in Politian's *Orfeo*. Francesco Corteccia set to music a song that was sung and danced by four bacchants and four satyrs at the end of the comedy performed in July 1539 for the wedding of Cosimo de' Medici with Eleanor of Toledo; see Pirrotta, *Music and Theatre*, pp. 157–9. It too begins with the words 'Bacco, Bacco', continuing with the cry of the bacchants, 'e u o e'.

[46] *Lucidario in musica* (Venice, 1545), bk IV, ch. 1: 'per ritrovarsi come habbiamo detto varie lingue, & populi, conseguentemente da quelli derivano, diverse musiche, & pronontie ... sì come à Franciosi il cantare, alli Inglesi il giubilare, alli Hispagnuoli il piagnere, a Tedeschi l'urlare, Et all'Italiani il caprezzare, la qual cosa non mi si puo far a credere, che da altro proceda, che da invidia, & malignita.' His source is probably Franchinus Gaffurius's *Theorica musicae* (Milan, 1492), fol. k5: 'Anglici enim concinendo iubilant. Cantant Galici. Hyspani ploratus promunt. Germani ululatus. Italorum nonnullos ut genuenses et qui ad eorum littora resident caprizare ferunt.'

[47] In defence of the Italians, I quote the report of the performance of Lamentations at the papal chapel during Holy Week 1518: 'prima per hispanos lamentabiliter, secunda per gallicos docte, tertia per italos dulciter'; see N. Pirrotta, 'Rom', *Die Musik in Geschichte und Gegenwart*, ed. F. Blume, 14 vols. (Kassel and Basle, 1949–68 and suppls.), xI, col. 703. The report comes from the diary of the master of ceremonies, Paride de' Grassi. In Alexander VI's time the Passion was sung exclusively by the Spaniards, who, in Grassi's words, 'naturaliter cantando magis flere videntur quam vociferari'; see R. Sherr, 'The Singers of the Papal Chapel and Liturgical Ceremonies in the Early Sixteenth Century: Some Documentary Evidence', *Rome in the Renaissance: The City and the Myth*, ed. P. A. Ramsey (Binghamton, NY, 1982), pp. 249–64, on p. 263, n. 35.

[48] See the prologue to Tinctoris's *Proportionale musices*: 'Haec eis Anglici nunc, licet vulgariter iubilare, Gallici vero cantare dicantur.'

[49] Andreas Ornithoparchus: 'Hinc Angli iubilant, galli cant ... Hispani ploratus promunt: Italorum pars, qui Januensium littora inhabitant caprisare dicuntur, ceteri latrant: Germani vero: quod pudet dicere: ut lupi ullulant' (taken from Gaffurins, with acknowledgement); *Musice active micrologus* (Leipzig, 1517), fol. M2. Hermann Finck omits the English in his list: 'Germani boant: Itali balant: Hispani eiulant: Galli cantant'; *Practica musica* (Wittenberg, 1556), fol. Ssiᵛ. Even the English themselves use the

teenth centuries.[50] The Venetian ambassador to the court of Henry VIII, on hearing the king's choristers, declared that they didn't sing but jubilated: 'non cantavano ma giubilavano'.[51]

The Latin word 'jubilare' seems to have been understood by all writers as generally applicable to music. But what it meant specifically is worth investigating, if indeed it applies to the style of singing that was heard in 1520. Only the 'English' were said to perform in a certain manner; the other groups simply sang Bergamasque, German and Spanish songs. In his commentary on Psalm 46, Augustine explains 'jubilatio' as a representation of joyfulness that cannot be expressed in words ('quid est iubilatio nisi admiratio gaudii, quae verbis non potest explicari').[52] In his commentary on Psalm 99 he mentions that grape-pickers, rejoicing in the abundance of the harvest, sometimes sing in exultation, inserting into their song 'certain sounds without words in their elation and this is called *jubilatio*'.[53] The word 'jubilus' is associated with the elaborate, wordless final melisma of the Alleluia.[54] This is the

term. The fourteenth-century motet *Sub Arturo plebs* includes the words 'musicorum vero chorus odas jubilat'; see F. Ll. Harrison, ed., *Musicorum collegio: Fourteenth-Century Musicians' Motets* (Monaco, 1986), p. 27; 'odas jubilat' descends through an octave (bars 32–4).

[50] A fifteenth-century Spanish manuscript takes the saying back to antiquity: 'Diversae nationes ... diversimode sibi displicent in cantando. Graeci dicunt Latinos ut canes latrare et Latini dicunt quod Graeci gemunt sicut vulpes. Saraceni dicunt Christianos non cantare sed delirare fatentur. E converso referunt Christiani quod Saraceni voces transglutiunt et cantus in faucibus gargaricant. Asserunt Gallici quod Italici semper in crebra vocum fractione delirant. Unde illos dedignantur audire.' Quoted by N. Bridgman, 'On the Discography of Josquin and the Interpretation of his Music in Recordings', *Josquin des Prez: Proceedings of the International Josquin Festival-Conference*, ed. E. E. Lowinsky and B. J. Blackburn (London, 1976), pp. 633–41, on p. 640, from J. Handschin, 'Réflexions dangereuses sur le renouveau de la musique ancienne', *Atti del terzo congresso internazionale di musica* (Florence, 1940), p. 53.

[51] June 1515; quoted in F. Ll. Harrison, *Music in Medieval Britain* (4th edn, Buren, 1980), p. 171.

[52] *In Ps. 46*, 7 (Corpus Christianorum, Series Latina 38, p. 533, ll. 5–6). A similar explanation appears in *In Ps. 65*, 2 (*ibid.* 39, p. 833, ll. 15–18). For this and the following notes I am greatly indebted to Leofranc Holford-Strevens.

[53] 'et inter cantica quae verbis enuntiant, inserunt voces quasdam sine verbis in elatione exsultantis animi, et haec vocatur iubilatio'; *ibid.* 39, p. 1394, ll. 12–19. (The modern reader will be reminded of yodelling.) Gregory the Great echoes Augustine in emphasising the mental exultation that cannot be expressed by words but only by sound: 'iubilum vero dicimus cum tantam laetitiam corde concipimus, quantam sermonis efficacia non explemus; et tamen mentis exsultatio hoc quod sermone non explicat voce sonat'; *Moralia in Iob* 8: 88 (*ibid.* 143, p. 451, ll. 14–16). He makes a similar remark at 24: 10 (*ibid.* 143B, p. 1195, ll. 9–11).

[54] K. Schlager, 'Jubilus', *The New Grove Dictionary of Music and Musicians*, ed. S. Sadie, 20 vols. (London, 1980), IX, pp. 744–5.

meaning that would have been most familiar to Renaissance musicians. If they had wanted to consult a dictionary, however, they would have found that Hugutio (Uguccione of Pisa, d. 1210), in his *Magnae derivationes*, defines 'iubilus' as 'a clear and ringing, sonorous and joyful song. Specifically, *jubilus* is a sound confused out of joy, whence *iubilo* means to sing, to rejoice through a sound confused out of joy, to exult and be joyful.'[55]

The style of English music that most closely matches the meanings of 'jubilare' is that of the Eton Choirbook and English composers of the first decades of the sixteenth century such as William Cornysh.[56] Two aspects of this music must have struck Continental listeners: the extremely ornate melismatic lines and the high range of the boys' voices, both of which tend to make a confused jumble of the words. Michiel says that it was 'putti', or boys, who sang 'alla inglese'. The music of the Eton Choirbook is characterised by very high ranges: a'' occurs in three works,[57] b^{b}'' in five[58] and high C in three.[59] In recent years it has been argued, principally by David Wulstan, that the written pitch requires transposition upwards by a minor third.[60] The question of sounding pitch versus notated pitch is a vexed one, and it will undoubtedly continue to occupy scholars for the foreseeable future. Even without transposition the range of many of the pieces in the Eton Choirbook and other sacred English music of the time is very high – nor is transposition downwards very likely, since the compass of the five-part works is 22–3

[55] 'Hic iubilus li .i. argutus sonorus et letabundus cantus. Proprie quidem iubilus est vox confusa pre gaudio. Unde iubilo as cantare gaudere quadam voce confusa pre gaudio exultare et letari.' Quoted from Bodleian Library, MS Laud Misc. 626, fol. 91vb.

[56] At my lectures I used the *Sicut erat* of Cornysh's Magnificat for five voices, sung by the Tallis Singers, as an illustration. It begins with a duo for the two lowest voices, which gradually rises by voice-pairs until the meane and treble sing the most dazzling melismatic lines, reaching to the top of the range, whereupon all five voices unite in the Amen. The effect was all the more striking since the Tallis Singers had transposed the work up by a minor third, making the top note b^{b}''.

[57] In the edition by F. Ll. Harrison, *The Eton Choirbook*, Musica Britannica 10–12 (London, 1956–61), nos. 2, 3 and 14.

[58] *Ibid.*, nos. 10, 12, 27, 43 and 52.   [59] *Ibid.*, nos. 20, 24 and 45.

[60] D. Wulstan, 'The Problems of Pitch in Sixteenth-Century English Vocal Music', *Proceedings of the Royal Musical Association*, 93 (1966–7), pp. 97–112. For a list of various reactions to that article, and Wulstan's further publications, see D. Fallows, 'The Performing Ensembles in Josquin's Sacred Music', *Tijdschrift van de Vereniging voor Nederlandse Muziekgeschiedenis*, 35 (1985), pp. 32–64, on p. 62, n. 75. Fallows notes that the Italian ambassador was in fact remarking particularly on the bass singers ('non cantavano ma jubilavano, et *maxime* de contrabassi, che non credo al mondo sieno li pari'; cited from Sanuto, *I diarii*, xx, col. 266).

notes. From a pragmatic point of view, it would seem likely that each choir set the range according to the capabilities of the singers of the highest and lowest parts; the exact pitch may have varied from performance to performance, depending on conditions. But whatever the particular pitch of this music, it is clear that the very high soprano range is characteristic of English music of this time and exceptional in Continental music.[61] Such ranges simply were not demanded of boy singers in Italian chapels, let alone of male singers. If the 'putti' who sang at Leo X's Bacchus-day entertainment were Italian, they must have had to spend a lot of time practising the music. But what would they have sung, and who would have taught them? If they were English, they could easily have sung the music that was being performed at the royal court in 1520 under the direction of William Cornysh, who was then master of the choirboys. (Interestingly, he was also the author and organiser of, and actor in, spectacles and disguisings at the English court.)[62] But the possibility remains that the boys were Italian and that they were only making a stab at the way they thought English music sounded; after all, this was an occasion for a good deal of spoofing, not serious, polished performances.

Leo X must have had someone similar to Cornysh who produced his entertainments: the programme had to be planned, the musicians and instruments assembled and rehearsed, and costumes had to be made. Other festivities, as we shall see, involved choreography. Michiel remarks that Leo spent 500 ducats on this entertainment. To calculate what this means, some comparative figures are in order. Leo paid his musicians 6–8 ducats a month, which must have been a very decent salary; his master of ceremonies received only 5 ducats a month.[63] Cardinal Armellini spent about 266 ducats

---

[61] See the curious anonymous virelai *Helas mon tetin* in Escorial B, fol. 128ᵛ: the soprano ranges from *c'* to *c'''*. Modern edition in *The Chansonnier El Escorial IV.a.24*, ed. M. K. Hanen, 3 vols., Musicological Studies 36 (Henryville, PA, Ottawa and Binningen, 1983), III, pp. 446–9; commentary I, p. 65, and in *Anonymous Pieces in the MS El Escorial IV.a.24*, ed. E. Southern, Corpus Mensurabilis Musicae 88 (Neuhausen–Stuttgart, 1981), pp. 40–1.

[62] For this aspect of Cornysh's career, see S. Anglo, 'William Cornish in a Play, Pageants, Prison, and Politics', *Review of English Studies*, new ser., 10 (1959), pp. 347–60, and *idem*, 'The Evolution of the Early Tudor Disguising, Pageant, and Mask', *Renaissance Drama*, new ser., 1 (1968), pp. 3–44.

[63] See Frey, 'Regesten' (1956), p. 197, n. 73. However, Grassi and many of the singers had additional income from benefices, and extra payments to singers, detailed in the Sistine diaries, added considerably to their income.

a month to support his household of 100 persons, including his stables.[64] And a palace of moderate size could be rented for 200–400 ducats annually.[65] The sum of 500 ducats therefore represents an enormous expenditure, and one well worth remarking on.

As addicted as he was to worldly pleasures, Leo X was also exacting in his religious duties. All sources agree on the 'dignity, majesty and piety that he evidenced in religious ceremonies'.[66] He scrupulously fasted on Wednesdays and Fridays and heard Mass every day. Two days in the liturgical calendar had personal significance for him, 24 June, the feast of the Nativity of John the Baptist, St John being both his namesake and the patron of Florence, and 27 September, the feast of SS. Cosmas and Damian, the patron saints of the Medici family.

It was the habit of the Florentines in Rome to celebrate St John's day with horse- and buffalo-races, concluding the feast with fireworks. Leo X commemorated the day by attending Mass, and then inviting the cardinals and ambassadors to lunch in Castel Sant' Angelo. Michiel reports on the events in his diary entry for 1520:

On Sunday 24 June, the day of St John, there was Mass, and then the pope went to dine in the Castello, where many cardinals and ambassadors dined. And in the afternoon the Florentines held a horse-race from Campo de' Fiori to the papal palace for a prize of gold cloth, lined with fur, and the Archbishop of Nicosia's barbary horse won. Then there was a buffalo-race for a red cloth, which was run all the way to the Castello. And then the pope hosted a dinner, also in the Castello, where there was a musical performance by eight voices, eight lironi, seven flutes and a trombone. And then buffoons, etc. And in the evening fireworks were set off which were attached at the head of the bridge to three very tall pieces of wood, in which there was a likeness of Phaëthon falling from the chariot of the sun into the Eridanus, and his sisters converted into trees, etc. (Appendix 1, excerpt 2)

Phaëthon was the son of Phoebus, the sun god. Having persuaded his father to let him drive the sun's chariot one day, he lost control of the wild steeds. As he plunged earthward in the fiery chariot, Jupiter hurled a thunderbolt to stop his course, lest the

---

[64] P. Partner, *Renaissance Rome 1500–1559: A Portrait of a Society* (Berkeley and Los Angeles, 1976), p. 138.

[65] *Ibid.*

[66] L. Pastor, *Storia dei Papi dalla fine del medio evo*, trans. A. Mercati, IV, pt 1 (repr. Rome, 1945), p. 336.

earth be burnt. Phaëthon fell into the Eridanus, the river Po, and his sisters, mourning him, were turned into poplars. The myth was probably felt to be appropriate to the day because 24 June is the longest day of the year.

The music that evening may have been sacred or secular; in all probability it was both. Michiel does not say how many pieces were performed or by what combinations of instruments. Judging from the Bacchus-day celebration, the singers and instrumentalists performed separately, then came together in a finale. This time the more raucous instruments – the cornetts and crumhorns – were omitted; the trombone must have served as bass to the flute consort, since flutes transpose up an octave.[67]

Michiel evidently did not attend Mass that day, or else he was unaware of the singers' subversive behaviour, reported by Paride de' Grassi, the *magister caeremoniarum* under Leo X. Normally, knowing that the pope set particular store by the feast of St John, the singers put forth a special effort. In 1513, the first year of Leo X's reign, they sang the Credo in *falsobordone*, which greatly incensed the master of ceremonies, since it was contrary to tradition. He reports that it caused many to murmur, some to laugh at his evident confusion. The pope, however, wanted it thus, even though he should not have done.[68] In 1515, Grassi notes, the singers 'sang in a certain manner that was sweeter than usual'.[69] In 1520, however, he notes that they 'responded [to the celebrant] almost unwillingly'.[70] And why? Because the bishop, celebrating his first papal Mass, had neglected to give the singers a gift, as was the custom. But Grassi, foreseeing trouble with the singers, persuaded the pope to rectify the omission and give the singers something to buy themselves a drink. Grassi knew very well that Leo needed no persuasion in the matter. They shared a love of music: in 1518,

---

[67] Brown found the same practice in the Florentine *intermedi* (*Sixteenth-Century Instrumentation*, p. 66).

[68] See Appendix 2, excerpt 1. Grassi rarely refers to singing in polyphony. As Richard Sherr has remarked, he mentions it 'when something new, strange or incorrect has occurred'. For several such occasions, see Sherr, 'Singers of the Papal Chapel', pp. 255–8. Grassi evidently did not care for *falsobordone*. This is one of two occasions on which he criticised the singers for using it (see *ibid.*, p. 256 and n. 33).

[69] 'Cantores cantarunt certo modo dulciore, quam soleant.' Biblioteca Apostolica Vaticana, MS Vat. lat. 12275, fol. 136ᵛ.

[70] 'Missam cantavit episcopus Tudeanentis [*recte* Tudertinus] assistens novus, et satis laudabiliter cantavit. Sed cantores quasi aegre sibi respondebant, quia nihil eis donavit, tunc Papa autem me suadente, nescio quid eis pro bibalibus dedit.' *Ibid.*, fol. 380ʳ.

19

after Mass on St Stephen's day, the pope gave his master of ceremonies a gift of 'a very beautiful clavicembalo, or excellent monochord, which he used to have in his chambers, ... because he knew that I delighted greatly in its sound'. And, underlines Grassi, 'it was worth 100 ducats' – for him, a year and a half's salary (Appendix 2, excerpt 2).[71]

For several years, the feast of St John the Baptist was the occasion of a running battle between the pope and his master of ceremonies: Leo wanted to increase the degree of solemnity of the feast by including the Credo, but Grassi argued that it was not authorised. In 1513, the first year of Leo's papacy, the Credo was sung because the pope wanted it at all costs. In 1514, the decision to sing the Credo was made in mid-Mass, without Grassi's foreknowledge, because, he says, 'they feared I would forbid it', but the pope wanted it, and so, as Grassi reports,

it was said, although irregularly, and invalidly, nor indeed should it even be said in the basilica of St John, though it is said because of the canons' ignorance, and in another of my ceremonial books I have fully written [on this], but blessed John was born before the Creed was written, and therefore it should not be said on the feast of his nativity. (Appendix 2, excerpt 3)

In 1517, having lost the battle, Grassi merely notes that the Credo was sung.[72] In 1518, however, a brilliant idea occurred to him, one calculated to salve his conscience and gratify the pope. Noting in his diary that the pope sometimes wanted to hear sung Mass in the small chapel, where the singers participated in daily offices, sometimes in the great chapel (the Cappella Sistina) in the presence of all the cardinals and prelates, though not in full ecclesiastical garb, Grassi records the following:

Seeing this devotion of the pope, which is all the greater in him because his name is John and he is Florentine, for the Florentine nation venerates this most celebrated saint above all others, in order to gratify him I said in consistory, in the presence of the cardinals, that in former times, as was

---

[71] See also *Il diario di Leone X di Paride de Grassi*, ed. P. Delicati and M. Armellini (Rome, 1884), p. 68, for the same entry, in slightly different wording, taken from another manuscript. The edition includes only excerpts; no complete edition has as yet been published.

[72] 'Missam in die idem Episcopus cantavit ceremonijs solitis et dixit Credo...' Vat. lat. 12275, fol. 220[r].

clearly written in our ordinary ceremonial book,[73] this feast had a *cappella papale* on the Vigil and on the day itself, for there used to be both vespers, and on the day a solemn Mass celebrated by a cardinal priest, and there was also a sermon, and the Credo was not said unless the feast fell on a Sunday. Thus, since this feast is much honoured in the church, for according to the testimony of our Lord Jesus Christ, among those that are born of women no greater has arisen [Matt. 11: 11], which word even the infidels and Moors and almost all nations of all sects worship, venerate and adore on this day above all others, but we Christians omit celebrating in a *cappella papale*, which in truth is not good, it would therefore be good if there were Vigils in the presence of the pope and cardinals with their copes and also the bishops wearing copes, and also, on the day, there were an ordinary *cappella*, since at most simply the pope and cardinals are present and only the pope might be inconvenienced because of the pluvial and mitre he would wear, thus if it would please His Holiness to resume the old abandoned custom on this feast, it would be good to decree it in consistory and have a cardinal celebrate it.

The pope, upon hearing this, was quite content and, turning to the cardinals, said that he had often wondered why it was that this feast did not have an ordinary *cappella*, and indeed he thought it was because of the heat that normally prevails at this time, but, however, if it would please them to endure the heat on this day – that is Vigils, for it is not hot in the morning – that he would also be willing. And thus all responded in the affirmative, and the pope decreed that a cardinal priest from the Florentine nation should celebrate Mass; there would be no sermon, but the Creed would be said out of devotion. And thus it was established in every aspect as an ordinary *cappella* and shall be observed in future years in perpetuity, and the cardinals shall wear red copes. (Appendix 2, excerpt 4)[74]

In this manœuvre, Grassi shows himself as much the diplomat as the punctilious master of ceremonies. Can it be only coincidence that it was in this same year, 1518, that the pope gave him the beautiful clavicembalo?

---

[73] Grassi refers to his Ceremonial, Biblioteca Apostolica Vaticana, MS Vat. lat. 5634bis, fol. 344ʳ.

[74] Not until 1573 was the solemn observation revoked, to the regret of the then master of ceremonies, Francesco Mucanzio: 'Die Mercurij 24 Junij [1573] in die Sancti Joannis Baptistae non fuit celebrata missa solemnis in Capella prout tempore Pij Quinti et iampridem ex instituto seu decreto Concistoriali tempore Leonis X.ᵐⁱ fuerat ordinatum, Nam in congregatione reformationis cerimoniarum visum fuit presentibus eam omitti posse. Quod meo iudicio (cum reverentia tantorum patrum) non bene fuit resolutum, quia ut in Cerimoniali ordinario habetur, haec erat missa antiqua, et solemniter celebrari solita etiam multo ante Leonem X.ᵐ etiam cum Vesperis precedentibus, et bene. Quia inter natos mulierum non surrexit maior Jo. Baptista Quod et Paris animadvertit.' I have used the copy in Venice, Biblioteca Nazionale Marciana, MS Lat. IX.29 (=3440), fol. 7ʳ.

It is often not realised to what extent the solemnity of liturgical celebrations was subject to personal initiative. In the papal chapel it was exceptional; Father John O'Malley has observed that the tendency in the papal liturgy was to restrict rather than to expand, and that Nicholas V's institution of the feast of St Thomas Aquinas was a radical departure, not least because Nicholas wanted the Creed to be said, thus putting Thomas, a 'Confessor', into the company of the Doctors of the Church, Augustine, Ambrose, Jerome and Gregory the Great.[75] In other churches, however, and especially in collegiate churches, a person desirous of honouring his patron saint had only to create an endowment for that particular feast that would pay for the extra clergy needed to celebrate it with more solemnity. The account books of many churches, especially in the north, record such payments down to the last *denier* for the bellringer, and, not infrequently, among the persons to benefit are the singers, paid extra for singing a polyphonic Mass or a motet. The steady increase in the number of polyphonic Masses and devotional motets observable in the fifteenth and sixteenth centuries may owe its impetus in large part to individual initiative – and an ecclesiastical hierarchy only too willing to fatten its coffers.[76]

Leo X succeeded in elevating the feast of St John the Baptist over the objection, and eventual acquiescence, of his master of ceremonies. With another feast he had less trouble, in fact no trouble at all. On 23 September 1513, he simply decreed that the feast of SS. Cosmas and Damian, four days thence, would be a *cappella papale*, that is, one requiring the participation of the whole curia. When Grassi ventured to ask whether it would be a city-wide feast, that is, one in which all manual labour would be suspended, the pope replied that it would apply only to the papal palace (Appendix 2, excerpt 5). Mass that year, the first of Leo's reign, was celebrated with great pomp in the Sistine Chapel, attended by almost twenty cardinals and many prelates. Grassi reports, rather sourly, that the Credo was sung at the pope's wish, but improperly.

---

[75] 'The Feast of Thomas Aquinas in Renaissance Rome: A Neglected Document and its Import', *Rivista di Storia della Chiesa in Italia*, 35 (1981), pp. 1–27, esp. 5–7.

[76] Increasing attention has been given to this area in recent years. I cite in particular the work of Barbara Haggh; see 'Music, Liturgy, and Ceremony in Brussels, 1350–1500' (Ph.D. dissertation, University of Illinois, 1988), esp. ch. 2, and 'Itinerancy to Residency: Professional Careers and Performance Practices in 15th-Century Sacred Music', *Early Music*, 17 (1989), pp. 359–66.

Then he continues with a rare non-ceremonial observation: 'All these cardinals and prelates and many citizens and nobles, after the Mass, partook of a very festive dinner with the pope in the upper consistorial room, and during it all kinds of musicians, except trumpets and shawms, [played] and an infinite number of other things' (Appendix 2, excerpt 6).

One gains the impression that the celebration on the feast day of SS. Cosmas and Damian was Leo's equivalent of a birthday party. Cosmas and Damian were chosen as the patron saints of the Medici family because they were physicians – *medici* in Italian. (The famous Medici name Cosimo derives from Cosmas.) Cosimo il Vecchio, Leo's great-grandfather, wisely resisted making the feast a state celebration, but the chapels he founded in the major churches in Florence ensured that honour was paid to the saints. Richard Trexler has remarked that 'in this way the Medici could measure their status annually without Cosimo incurring the charge that he was impinging on the public identity'.[77] The political sensitivity of this feast was equally appreciated by his great-grandson, who celebrated it annually in Rome during the exile of the Medici, and used the occasion to separate supporters from antagonists.[78] During the time he was pope, however, the feast day seems to have been one of the great social events of the year.

In 1514, Grassi notes, the feast was celebrated with the same splendour, including a magnificent banquet attended by all cardinals and princes and an infinite number of members of the curia and Romans. The entertainment included the recitation of many Latin and Italian verses and the mock coronation of a hopelessly vain and dreadful poet, Baraballo di Gaeta, who was then paraded through Rome on the back of an elephant.[79] In other years, however, Leo went on vacation in September, taking with him all the cardinals who joined him in his passionate love of hunting. But he did not omit the celebration of the feast of SS. Cosmas and Damian: wherever he was, the singers were to be sent to him to sing Vespers and the solemn Mass.[80]

[77] R. C. Trexler, *Public Life in Renaissance Florence* (New York, 1980), p. 423.

[78] *Ibid.*, n. 16.

[79] See Pastor, *Storia dei Papi*, IV, pt 1, pp. 383–4.

[80] On Leo's love of hunting, see D. Gnoli, *La Roma di Leon X* (Milan, 1938), p. 245. In 1516 Grassi notes: 'Die Veneris xviij Septembris Papa solatij causa recessit ex urbe versus Viterbium cum aliquibus Cardinalibus venatoribus et aucupibus et similibus, et dixit

In 1519, exceptionally, Leo stayed in Rome. Michiel notes briefly in his diary that after solemn Mass, the pope invited all the cardinals and ambassadors and other prelates to a sumptuous feast, and the entertainment consisted of comedies, dances, music and actors (Appendix 1, excerpt 3).[81] The general nature of his report suggests that Michiel was not present but heard about it from his friends. Grassi, not quite reconciled to the secular nature of the celebration, notes that Leo 'had a vernacular comedy performed that was more ridiculous than moral, and he gave the singers the usual reward' (Appendix 2, excerpt 8). Several commentators have suggested that this particular comedy was Machiavelli's *Mandragola*. As we shall see, however, *La mandragola* was far more suited to the festivities in the following year.

The 'usual reward' to the singers was a twice-yearly tradition with Leo X, on the feast of SS. Cosmas and Damian and on the anniversary of his coronation.[82] From the pope's private accounts, kept by Serapica, we learn that in September 1519 Leo gave 245 ducats to his 'cantori, pifferi, trombetti, giucolatori'.[83] This is in addition to their regular salaries, which cost the pope about 300 ducats a month.[84] Leo was exceedingly generous with musicians; the Venetian ambassador remarked in 1517, perhaps with some exaggeration, that 'the pope is an excellent musician, and when he sings with someone, he gives him 100 ducats and more'.[85] His private accounts are full of payments to musicians who were not on the payroll: 25 ducats to German organists, 40 ducats to a priest who makes viols, 20 ducats to a Ferrarese boy who played the monochord, 10 ducats to a girl singer from Pistoia – to give just a small sample.[86] These are enormous sums: no wonder that musicians flocked to Rome during Leo's papacy!

According to Grassi, many persons, clergy and lay people,

---

mihi in recessu quod mitterem Cantores ad ipsum pro missa Sanctorum Cosmae et Damiani in Viterbium celebranda' (Vat. lat. 12275, fol. 177ʳ).

[81] This festivity was the occasion of the coronation of another 'archpoet', Camillo Querno, renowned more for his great appetite and capacity to hold liquor than for his verses. At the banquet, dressed up as Venus, he sang improvised verses, to which Leo X is supposed to have responded in kind. See Pastor, *Storia dei Papi*, IV, pt 1, p. 383.

[82] Frey, 'Regesten' (1956), p. 142.

[83] *Ibid.*

[84] *Ibid.*, p. 141.

[85] As reported by Marino Giorgi to the Venetian Senate, 17 March 1517 (Sanuto, *I diarii*, XXIV, col. 93).

[86] Frey, 'Regesten' (1956), pp. 142–3.

attended the festivities on the day of SS. Cosmas and Damian, but surprisingly few accounts have come down to us, compared to descriptions of the Roman carnival. One rare eye-witness report of the pope's entertainments, apart from Grassi and Michiel, is a letter of Baldassare Castiglione to Federico Gonzaga describing the event in 1520: 'The day of St Cosmas the pope held a delightful party: he invited twenty cardinals, many prelates and all the ambassadors to a splendid dinner, after which there were fifty-two musicians, all dressed as physicians, who sang and played various instruments, all together. Afterwards there was a comedy.'[87] Castiglione was not easily impressed by the pope's theatricals; he often admired the scenery more than the play, which he never describes in detail.[88] Grassi confined himself to the religious ceremony on this occasion, still grumbling that the pope insisted on having the Creed said, even though it was improper, just as it was on the feast of St John the Baptist (Appendix 2, excerpt 9).

It is Michiel who gives us a colourful report on the 1520 festivities; it was the last such occasion he could attend, since he left Rome on 7 November, and perhaps for this reason he recorded a more detailed description than usual:

On 27 September, the day of SS. Cosmas and Damian, the pope had a solemn Mass celebrated in the Sistine Chapel, as usual, and invited all the cardinals, for thirty of whom (because the elderly ones did not wish to stay) he had prepared an impressive banquet, also for many other prelates and gentlemen, in the salon of [Cardinal] Innocenzo [Cibo],[89] and after dinner he presented singing and playing, and the music was done in this manner: some fifty singers and players of various instruments, dressed as physicians, that is with a long gown, partly pink and partly violet, and red stoles, came out two by two, led by Maestro Andrea and another buffoon, dressed up like Spirone and Maestro Archangelo, the pope's physicians. They imitated them, cracking many jokes, and made everyone laugh. And there before the pope alternately they sang and played a number of pieces, and at the end all, including the first, sang some songs about physicians, and for the finale everyone sang a motet for six voices. The costumes were made at the pope's expense. After the music a vernacular comedy was

---

[87] B. Castiglione, *Le lettere*, ed. G. La Rocca, 1 (Tutte le Opere, I; Verona, 1978), no. 452, p. 609.

[88] He did admire the elaborate choreography of a *moresca* during Carnival 1521 (*ibid.*, no. 506, p. 716; the passage is also given in Cruciani, *Teatro nel Rinascimento*, pp. 491–2).

[89] The 'Sala de Innocentio' was the room where Ariosto's *I suppositi* was performed in 1519. That performance was sponsored by Cardinal Innocenzo Cibo, Leo's nephew; the 'sala' was part of his apartments in the Vatican. See Cruciani, *Teatro nel Rinascimento*, p. 450.

recited in a small room next to the large one. After the magnificent dinner, fruit of infinite sorts was handed out, especially boiled chestnuts, jujubes and pomegranates. The pope presents a ceremony in this manner every year on this day, according to the custom of his ancestors, since SS. Cosmas and Damian were physicians, and they were descended from the Medici. The night before there were six large silk tapestries on the pope's tables which were made for him in Florence in the Levantine fashion, but with our own design, and they were very beautiful. (Appendix 1, excerpt 4)

Fifty musicians dressed in physician's robes must have been quite a sight. Michiel omits mention of their headgear, a large floppy red beret, such as those worn by the saints in various paintings by Fra Angelico and other Florentine artists.[90] One wonders how the pope's two physicians reacted to seeing themselves caricatured. Arcangelo da Siena was the highest-paid professor at the university, and Bernardino Speroni was a professor at the University of Padua.[91] But if they had any acquaintance with the court, they knew that the pope was very partial to buffoonery; the proud and vain stood little chance of coming away unscathed. In the present case, the spoof was probably good-natured: Leo, who was corpulent and suffered from a painful fistula, had need of his physicians.

Michiel seems far more interested in music than he does in theatre, or perhaps he did not see the play, which took place in a small room. During the years of Leo's papacy, the court had seen, among others, productions of Cardinal Bibbiena's *Calandria* and Ariosto's *I suppositi*, both of which elicited enthusiastic reports from those privileged to attend, and not only for the plays themselves but for the scenery, designed by Baldassare Peruzzi and Raphael respectively. Many other comedies were performed, including some by an acting company from Siena, but we do not know their titles or authors.[92]

For some time it has been thought that the play performed on the feast day of SS. Cosmas and Damian in 1520 was Machiavelli's

[90] See, for example, Fra Angelico's cycle of paintings for San Marco in Florence, now dispersed between Florence, Paris, Munich and Dublin.
[91] On Arcangelo da Siena, see Pastor, *Storia dei Papi*, IV, pt 1, p. 459. On Speroni (Bernardino Speroni degli Alvarotti), see G. Pieraccini, *La Stirpe de' Medici di Cafaggiolo*, 3 vols. (2nd edn, Florence, 1947), I, p. 226.
[92] On theatrical productions during the pontificate of Leo X, see Cruciani, *Teatro*, pp. 379–492.

Mandragola. Although the year is based on a misdating of an entry in Grassi's diary – the comedy that he characterised as 'more ridiculous than moral' took place in 1519, not 1520 – other evidence does point to 1520: in a letter to Machiavelli of 16 April 1520 from Rome, Battista della Palla reports that his comedy is ready: the actors have learnt their parts and it is sure to please.[93] Paolo Giovio stated that the comedy 'Nichia' (the name of a principal character) was first performed in Florence, and that when Leo heard about it he decided to have it done in Rome, using the same production and actors.[94] Much ink has been spilt over when the Florentine production took place (1518 and 1519 are the favoured dates), and whether the actors were Florentine or Roman. Nor is it certain when Machiavelli wrote the play: the first dated printed edition is of 1524, though an earlier manuscript source is known. To judge by Battista della Palla's remarks, it had not been performed in Rome by April 1520, and if Giovio is right that the same actors gave it in both cities, Della Palla's letter could be understood to mean that Roman actors had been rehearsing for a Florentine performance and went to Florence to present it in late April 1520. It seems reasonable to believe that the two performances were separated by several months, not one or two years, as has hitherto been assumed.[95]

To the foregoing circumstantial evidence of the dating of the Roman performance of *La mandragola* I should like to add Michiel's account of the festivities in 1520. Those who have read or seen *La mandragola* will immediately know why. The play, the first great comedy in Italian, with its witty portrayal of contemporary life and mores, was an immediate hit, and it retains the same fresh qualities today. More to the point, in the present circumstances, the plot revolves around a lovesick young man, Callimaco, who disguises himself as a doctor in order to 'treat' the inability of a virtuous young wife to conceive. Worming his way into the confidence of his intended beloved's old husband, who is remarkably gullible, Callimaco – with the aid of his friends, the wife's mother, and the

---

[93] The letter is quoted in K. Neiiendam, 'Le théâtre de la Renaissance à Rome', *Analecta Romana Instituti Danici*, 5 (1969), pp. 103–97, on p. 194, n. 204.

[94] *Ibid.*, p. 173.

[95] The performers would probably have been Francesco Cherea and his troupe, who were paid from the pope's private accounts in September, October and November 1520. Indeed, it was Cherea who took *La mandragola* to Venice in 1522. See *ibid.*, p. 174.

assistance of her confessor, Fra Timoteo – devises an elaborate ruse that ends happily for all concerned, including, we presume, Messer Nicia, the husband, whose wish for children will undoubtedly be fulfilled in due course of time. In his guise as a physician, Callimaco surely wore the same garments that were described by Michiel and that appear in paintings of the saints, and he spouts some very professional-sounding Latin when he examines the wife's urine specimen. There could hardly have been a more appropriate play on this feast day of the patron saints of physicians.

Now let us return to Michiel's report about the musical performances. As at the Bacchus-day feast in the previous month, the singers and instrumentalists performed in alternation. In August, dual performances are implied; perhaps the music was strophic, with an instrumental rendition separating the stanzas. If so, an embellished version would have been very appropriate. In September, a number of pieces were performed alternately, but Michiel does not suggest that the same music was performed vocally and instrumentally. The forces available were about the same as in August, with the instrumentalists outnumbering the singers by nearly three to one.

Judging from Michiel's descriptions, all the pope's extravaganzas had a theme and involved costumes, and at least some of the music, particularly at the end, was related to the theme. The September 1520 performance closed with some songs about physicians and a motet for six voices. Songs about physicians can be found: two song texts that would have been very appropriate (although all the settings were probably composed later than 1520, since they first appear in print in the 1540s) are *Madonna, io son un medico perfetto* and *Medici nui siamo, o donne belle*. The first was set for three voices by Costanzo Festa and published in 1543.[96] A popular text, it was also set by Hubert Naich, Bernardino Lupacchino and Francesco della Viola.[97] The words are transparently obscene

---

[96] C. Festa, *Opera omnia*, ed. A. Main and A. Seay, Corpus Mensurabilis Musicae 25 (Neuhausen–Stuttgart, 1962–78), VII, p. 1. Iain Fenlon and James Haar, following Einstein, consider it dubious; it was also printed in Eliseo Ghibellini's *Il primo libro de canzoni villanesche, alla napolitana, a tre voci* (Venice: Gardane, 1554). See Fenlon and Haar, 'Fonti e cronologia dei madrigali di Costanzo Festa', *Rivista Italiana di Musicologia*, 13 (1978), pp. 212–42, on p. 214, n. 6.

[97] For the Naich setting, see Hubert Naich, *Opera omnia*, ed. D. Harrán, Corpus Mensurabilis Musicae 94 (Neuhausen–Stuttgart, 1983), pp. 76–9; the first edition was published *c.* 1540.

(which does not make the song inappropriate for Leo's court). The other text was set by Giovanni Domenico da Nola and printed in 1541; it too is a *canzona villanesca*.[98] These texts are reminiscent of carnival songs, and it is quite possible that carnival songs are what was sung at the entertainment.[99] The German song sung at the Bacchus-day festivities might even have been one of the *canti di lanzi*, which poked fun at German mercenary soldiers, including their drinking habits.[100]

A hallmark of Leo's festivities, indeed of life at his court, is the easy intermixture of sacred and secular. The feasts of St John the Baptist and SS. Cosmas and Damian were both on the liturgical calendar and were celebrated with all the ecclesiastical pomp Leo could muster, with or without the help of his master of ceremonies. But the religious aspects of the feasts gave way to secular celebrations in the course of the day. At the end of the September 1520 festivities, however, the solemn tone returned: Michiel reports that a motet for six voices was sung. Motets on SS. Cosmas and Damian are somewhat of a rarity, let alone six-part motets. None occur in the Sistine Chapel manuscripts. A search in Florentine manuscripts turned up an anonymous setting for six voices in MS 11 of the Duomo, *Sancti tui Domine*.[101] The text seems to be a generic one for saints, but the cantus firmus carries the words 'Sancti Cosma et Damiane orate pro nobis', set to the litany melody. The possibility of its being the motet sung in 1520, however, founders on the birthdate of the composer, named as Corteccia in a concordant source; Corteccia was born in 1502.

There is, however, another six-part motet in praise of the two medical saints, of the right time and place, although also

---

[98] Modern edition in L. Cammarota, *Gian Domenico del Giovane da Nola*, 2 vols. (Rome, 1973), I, p. 121. Harrán discusses the melodic resemblances to Naich's *Madonna* in his edition, *The Anthologies of Black-Note Madrigals*, Corpus Mensurabilis Musicae 73 (Neuhausen–Stuttgart, 1978–81), I, pt 2, pp. lxxi–lxxii.

[99] See, for example, the 'Canzona delle vedove e dei medici', the 'Canzona de' medici' and 'Medici siam maestri in cerusia' (only the text survives) in C. S. Singleton, *Canti carnascialeschi del Rinascimento* (Bari, 1936), pp. 79–80, 167–8 and 424–6. A 1546 publication of *Mascharate di Lodovico Novello di più sorte et varii soggetti apropriati al carnevale* includes four-part settings of *S'alcuna è d'amor ferita che vol esser risanata* ('Da medici') and *Siam chirurghi, o buona gente, sin da India qua venuti* ('Da ciroichi').

[100] For the texts of some of these, see T. J. McGee with S. E. Mittler, 'Information on Instruments in Florentine Carnival Songs', *Early Music*, 10 (1982), pp. 452–61.

[101] Now available in a facsimile edition by F. A. D'Accone in the series Renaissance Music in Facsimile 3 (New York, 1987).

anonymous, and I am convinced that this was the work sung in 1520. The motet, *Laetare sancta mater ecclesia*, is found in the single partbook Florence, Biblioteca Nazionale Centrale, Magl. XIX, 125bis, which dates from 1530–4 and was probably copied in Florence; it is closely related to the Vallicelliana manuscript, with which it shares eleven concordances, slightly less than half its contents. Edward Lowinsky drew attention to the motet in his study on the Vallicelliana manuscript: he described it as a motet by an anonymous author written 'in celebration of the election of Pope Clement VII in 1523, in which homage is paid to the Medici family and to its official saints, St. Cosmas and St. Damianus. The text ... plays in humanist fashion on the meaning of the name *medicus*, and praises Clement de' Medici as "medicine" against the ills of the age.'[102] The text runs as follows:

Letare sancta mater ecclesia et exultate vos medicos
in honore sanctorum medicorum Cosme et Damiani
quibus spiritus sanctus tantam gratiam conferre dignatus est
ut omnem egritudinem expellerent.
Advocemus omnes
sancti Cosma et Damiane orate pro nobis.

Gaudeat Medicum nobilissima familia
que contra fidelium mortiferos morbos
Clementem medicum simul et medellam nobis contulit suavem.
Dominus conservet eum et beatum faciat eum in terra
et non tradat eum in animam inimicorum eius
et vitam celestem tribuat nobis. Amen.

(Rejoice, Holy Mother Church, and be glad, ye physicians,
in honour of the holy physicians Cosmas and Damian
on whom the Holy Ghost hath deigned to confer so much grace
that they might drive out all sickness.
Let us all call upon them:
Holy Cosmas and Damian, pray for us.

Let the most noble family of the Medici rejoice,
that against all the deadly diseases of the faithful
hath sent the physician Clement and with him healing.
The Lord preserve him and make him blessed upon the earth
and deliver him not up to the will of his enemies
and grant him heavenly life.)

---

[102] 'A Newly Discovered Sixteenth-Century Motet Manuscript at the Biblioteca Vallicelliana in Rome', *Journal of the American Musicological Society*, 3 (1950), pp. 173–232, on p. 197; reprinted in Lowinsky, *Music in the Culture of the Renaissance and Other Essays*, ed. B. J. Blackburn, 2 vols. (Chicago, 1989), ii, pp. 433–82, on p. 451.

Lowinsky assumed that the motet was written in celebration of the election of Clement VII because it is non-liturgical and names Clement in the text. However, there is nothing in the wording that refers to an election; the *prima pars* deals exclusively with SS. Cosmas and Damian, and the *secunda pars* apotheosises the Medici family and prays for the health of one in particular, Clement. But the text would fit Leo just as well, and the name could easily be substituted. Since the manuscript was copied during the pontificate of Clement VII, it is perfectly natural that his name should appear in the text. Clement probably continued Leo's celebration of the feast day of SS. Cosmas and Damian, and the performance of this motet may have become traditional.

There are two words in the text, however, which, coupled with Michiel's description of the festivities, allows us to place the composition of this work with great probability in September 1520: 'ye physicians'. The text begins 'Rejoice, Holy Mother Church, and be glad, ye physicians, in honour of the holy physicians Cosmas and Damian'. These words would be mystifying did we not know that all the participants in the programme were dressed up as physicians and two of Leo's buffoons impersonated Leo's doctors. Moreover, it is quite likely that Leo had invited the upper echelons of the entire medical community to this festivity.

The second part of the text, as Lowinsky remarked, plays on the word *medicus*: Clement (or Leo) is both a Medici and a physician who will cure the 'deadly diseases of the faithful'. The characterisation of the pope as *medicus* is not new: it was applied to Julius II and recalls St Augustine's epithet of Christ as *medicus humilis*.[103] But it has particular relevance for Leo and Clement because of their family name. Moreover, the words 'mortiferos morbos fidelium', the 'deadly diseases of the faithful', may contain a topical allusion. For nearly three years Leo had had to contend with the rapidly spreading heresy in Germany, instigated by the stubborn Augustinian monk Martin Luther. Much of the spring of 1520 was devoted to the preparation of the Bull *Exsurge Domine*, which was intended to persuade the faithful to forsake Luther. It was ready in June, and in August the papal legate was sent to Germany to publish it. The Bull did not excommunicate Luther; it gave him

---

[103] J. Sherman, *Raphael's Cartoons in the Collection of Her Majesty the Queen and the Tapestries for the Sistine Chapel* (London, 1972), pp. 72 and 50, n. 32.

and his followers sixty days in which to recant their errors. Thus, in September 1520, the pope was truly engaged in healing 'all the deadly diseases of the faithful'.

The motet, unfortunately, is anonymous, and what remains is a single part in the alto clef. It probably had a cantus firmus, perhaps on the text of the final phrase of the *prima pars*: 'Sancti Cosma et Damiane orate pro nobis'. It is tempting to speculate on the composer, though risky on the basis of a single voice. The major candidate is, of course, Andreas de Silva, who was simultaneously a singer in the papal chapel and one of Leo's *cantores secreti*, with a double salary. He is the only musician who is characterised in the documents as 'compositor noster'. Indeed, he is the composer of another motet for Leo X, *Gaude felix Florentia*, whose cantus firmus Richard Sherr has cleverly connected with the Medici coat of arms.[104] However, the voice part is dissimilar to De Silva's style and appears to be by a less skilful composer. The motet may eventually be found with an alternative text of general applicability, as is the case with De Silva's *Gaude felix Florentia*.

What lessons can we draw from Michiel's diary? That Leo lost no opportunity to show off his musicians should not surprise anyone who has read Pastor's *History of the Popes* or André Pirro's article 'Leo X and Music'. What we did not know is that he staged what were, in a sense, public concerts, although the public was restricted. Some of these events indeed were concerts, and not incidental music performed between the courses of a banquet. But others were more like a musical revue, with costumes and choreography: who would have imagined that the pope or his producer dreamt up a chorus line of fifty physicians, and two comedians cracking jokes? From Michiel's diary we learn something about what Leo's private musicians were expected to do. We also gain valuable information about early sixteenth-century instrumentation. It seems to have been quite normal for instruments and voices to perform in alternation, coming together in the finale. The broken consort, mixing

---

[104] See 'The Medici Coat of Arms in a Motet for Leo X', *Early Music*, 15 (1987), pp. 31–5. Charlet's *Vidit Dominus*, whose author Mitchell P. Brauner has convincingly identified as the papal singer Charles d'Argentil, likewise has a cantus firmus derived from the Medici coat of arms; see 'The Manuscript Verona, Accademia Filarmonica, B 218 and its Political Motets', *Studi Musicali*, 16 (1987), pp. 3–12.

strings, wind and keyboard instruments, is not a development of the later sixteenth century but was considered normal practice in 1520. Keyboard instruments were not limited to accompanying voices but took part in mixed ensembles. This will come as news to directors of early music groups, and should stimulate experiments with varied ensembles. Now and then directors like to plan their programmes around a theme; this too has venerable antecedents, though it can rarely be done on the lavish scale of Leo's entertainments. And as for the buffoons, we may not be as enamoured of them as Leo was, but there certainly is room to inject more levity into our concerts of Renaissance music: after all, the Renaissance was not the Age of Innocence. Let us therefore learn from one of the greatest music lovers of the epoch, Leo X.

Oxford

APPENDIX 1

Excerpts from Marcantonio Michiel's diary

(Venice, Biblioteca Correr, MS 2848)

1. A di 2 ditto [August 1520] il Papa fece disnar et cena contuose [*sic*] à quanti cardinali vi andorono, et a tutti li cardinali, et molti altri, Et doppo cena fece una musica, nella quale spese 500 ducati cioè prima forse x vestiti di pavonazzo, che cantorono, et sonorono con un lirone, duoi flauti, un liuto, et uno claocimbano alternatamente una canzone alla Bergamasca: Indi altritanti vestiti di giallo, che cantorono et sonorono tromboni et cornetti alternatim una canzone Todescha: Indi altritanti vestiti di rosato, che cantavano, et sonavano lironi alternatim una canzone spagnola. Indi pive storte: Indi putti, che cantavano alla Inghlese. Indi tutti li instrumenti et cantori insieme cantorono, et sonorono a xii. Li Inglesi cantavano uno tano macharonescho, tutte le parole erono al proposito del primo di d'Agusto, et di Bacho, et tra una musica et l'altra era uno Bacho nudo, et m.ro Andrea Buffone, che era il suo interprete, che lesse una supplicatione per li Thodeschi, et tutti haveano ghirlande di viti, li zipponi di raso, et le calze di panno etc. (fol. 337ᵛ)

2. Adi 24 ditto [June 1520] Domenica, el di de San Giovanni fu cappella et dapoi il Pontefice andò à desinare in castello, ove desinorno molti Cardinali et Ambasciatori, Et la sera li fiorentini fecero correre li barbari da campo di fiore fino al Palazo un palio di panno d'oro foderato di vari, et

Bonnie J. Blackburn

hebbelo il barbaro dell'Arcivescovo de Nicosia. Et fecero correre li buffali
il panno rosso, li quali corsero fino al castello: Et poi il Papa fece pasto la
sera pur in castello, ove fu una Musica di 8 voce, 8 lironi, et 7 fiauti, et un
trombone, Et poi buffoni, etc. Et la sera fu brusciata una girandola attac-
cata al principio del ponte à 3 legni altissimi, nella quale era finto
Phetonte cadente dal carro del sole ne leridano, et le sorelle sue convertite
in arbori, etc. (fols. 335ᵛ–336ʳ)

3. Adi 27 ditto [September 1519]. Il di di San Cosmo, et Damiano el Papa
de more familiæ et maiorum suorum in memoria di suo attavo Cosmo et
per esser stati questi santi Medici fece dire messa solemne in capella,
Invilati [*sic*] tutti li cardinali, et Ambasciatori, et altri prelati, à quali
diede anchora pasto suntuoso, et feceli representationi de comedie, balli,
et musiche et attizadori. (fol. 308ᵛ)

4. Adi 27 di settembre [1520], el giorno di San Cosmo et Damiano el
Papa fece dir messa solenne in capella consueta di Sisto, invitati tutti li
cardinali, a 30. delli quali, perche li vecchij non volsero restare el fece
pasto solenne, et à moltissimi altri Prelati, et gentilhuomini in sala de
Innocentio, et doppo desinare fece cantare, et sonare, et fu una musica in
questo modo, che ben 50 tra cantori, et sonatori di diversi instrumenti,
vestiti da Medici, cioè con veste parte di rosato, et parte pavonazze
longhe, et stole rosse vennero à due à due guidati da m.ʳᵒ Andrea buffone,
et un'altro stravestiti dal Spirone, et M.ʳᵒ Archangelo medici del Papa i
quali contrafacendo li ditti, et dicendo molte cose facete fecero rider
ogn'uno. Et ivi avanti il Papa alternatim et cantorono, et sonorono piu
man di musiche, et alla fine tutti insieme li primi alcune canzoni à proposito di Medici, et in fine tutti uno mottetto à 6. Et le veste erono fatte à
spese dal Papa. Dopo la Musica fu recitata una comedia vulgare in una
sala picchola accosto la grande. Doppo il pasto mag.ᶜᵒ furono date frutte
d'infinite sorte, Et massime castagne lesse, zizole, et pomigranati. Laqual
solennità in questa guisa il Papa la fa ogni anno in tal giorno, secondo la
usanza delli suoi maggiori, per esser stati San Cosmo et Damiano Medici,
et essi esser discesi da Medici. La vigilia fu vesporo privato, et pochi vi
andorono. Nel giorno del pasto sopra le tavole del Papa erono 6 tappeti
grandi di seta fatti fare per lui à Fiorenza secondo el lavoro levantino, ma
con disegno nostrano, che erono bellissimi. (fols. 340ᵛ–341ʳ)

34

APPENDIX 2

Excerpts from the diary of Paride de' Grassi*

(Biblioteca Apostolica Vaticana, MS Vat. lat. 12275)

1. Credo quod non debuit dici fuit sic omnino volente papa dictum, et male quia Cantores nescientes regulas ceremoniarum prepararunt cantum per falsum bordonum sic appellatum et multi murmurarunt: aliqui riserunt de nostra quasi ignorantia, sed papa sic voluit quod non debuit velle. (fol. 50^v)

2. Hodie mihi Papa pro mantia donavit pulcherrimum clavotimbalum [*sic*] sive Monocordium optimum, quod ipsemet in sua camera tenere solitus erat, valoris centum ducatorum. Hoc autem dixit se libenter fecisse, quia intellexit me multum in tali sono delectari prout in veritate delector. (fols. 306^{r-v})

3. Finito Evangelio socius petijt à Papa an vellet ut diceretur Credo, et hoc fecit me nesciente, quia timuit forsan ne ego contradicerem, prout in veritate contradixissem, quia regulariter Credo non debet dici hodie sed persuasit Pape talia forte non cogitanti ut cantaretur, et sic Papa annuit quod diceretur prout dictum fuit quamquam irregulariter, et nulliter, quinimmo in ipsamet basilica sancti Joannis dici non debet, licet dicatur ex ignorantia canonicorum, et ego in alio meo cerimoniali libro plene scripsi, nam beatus Joannes natus est antequam simbolum factum esset, et ideo in nativitate eius dici non debet. (fols. 118^v–119^r)

4. Unde ego videns istam devotionem Papae quae eo maior in ipso est quo ipse Joannes vocatur et florentinus nam natio Florentina hunc sanctum celeberrimum veneratur preter ceteros ut gratificarer Papa, dixi in consistorio Audientibus Cardinalibus quod antiquitus sic clare scriptum est in libro nostro ceremoniali ordinario hoc festum habeat cappellam Papalem in Virgilia et in die nam et vespere esse solebant, et in die missa solemnis quam celebrabat presbiter cardinalis et etiam faciebat sermo et credo, non dicebatur nisi festum caderet in dominica itaque cum hoc festum sit celebre in ecclesia, nam testimonio ipsius Domini nostri Hiesu christi, inter natos mulierum non surrexit maior: quod verbum etiam infideles et mauri et ferre [*sic*] omnes nationes omnium sectarum hanc die

---

* There are multiple versions of Grassi's diaries. For a complete list, see P. Salmon, *Les manuscrits liturgiques latins de la Bibliothèque Vaticane*, III: *Ordines Romani, pontificaux, rituels, cérémoniaux*, Studi e Testi 260 (Vatican City, 1970).

pre ceteris colunt, venerantur, et adorant: nos vero christiani omittimus celebrare in cappella Papali, quod in veritate non bene est bene igitur esset ut in vigilia vespere presente Papa et Cardinalibus cum cappis et etiam prelatis cappatis: ac etiam in die fieret cappella ordinaria ex quo omnino Papa et Cardinales simpliciter adsunt et solus Papa ex hoc gravari posset propter pluviale et mitram quam gestat: itaque si sue sanctitati placeret revocare antiquam intermissam consuetudinem de isto festo bonum esset quod consistorialiter decernat et mandet uni cardinali celebret et Papa hoc intellecto contentus fuit satis et conversus ad Cardinales dixit se sepe admiratum de hoc fuisse [quo]d hoc festum non habuisset capellam ordinariam, et quidem credidit fuisse propter calores qui hoc tempore vigent: si tamen placeret eis tollerare calores pro ista die vz. vigilia, nam in mane diei non essent calores quod etiam sibi placeret: et sic omnes per verbum placet responderunt et papa imposuit quod unus presbiter Cardinalis de natione florentina cantaret missam: sed non fiat sermo et dicatur credo: propter devotionem et sic factum est in omnibus et per omnia sicut in Cappella ordinaria et fiet sequentibus annis in perpetuum et Cardinales erunt in cappis rubeis. (fols. 296^{r-v})

5. Antequam Pontifex ad consistorium hodiernum de quo supra veniret vocatis ad se Cardinalibus statuit quod sanctorum Cosme et Damiani dies esset perpetuo inter festa palatij et cum a me inquireretur an etiam festivicaretur per urbem: ita ut omnia opera servilia Urbis etiam mecanica cessarent, non placuit sed solum quod esset festum palatij et mihi mandavit ut omnibus iudicibus et officialibus Urbis intimarem quod et feci et sic ipsa die S. Cosme et Damiani non fuit habita cancellaria et clausa sunt fora ac officia cessarunt. (fols. 63^v–64^r)

6. ... et cantatum est sic volente Papa Symbolum quod non debuit et in fine data est indulgentia plenaria: Omnes hi Cardinales ac Prelati ac cives nobilesque multi post missam festivissime cum Papa in aula superiori consistoriali fecerunt prandium et intra illud omne genus musicorum preter tubas tybiasque et alia huiusmodi infinita. (fol. 64^v)

7. ... in die similiter solennis missa est habita eodem modo ut prius, et eisdem cerimonijs in presentia Pape et cardinalium ac principum, et ut alias omnia facta sunt, nisi quod in fine Papa non solum indulgentiam plenarium concessit, sed etiam addidit pro omnibus hac die cappellam istam visitantibus, et post hec dedit epulum omnibus cardinalibus, et principibus, et infinitis Curialibus, ac Romanis solenne: post quod recitata sunt multa festiviter carmina latina et vulgaria, et creatus Poeta quidam ... [*sic*] quem curia semper pendentem opinata est, et nunc recognovit eum stultum, et fatuum. (fol. 125^r)

8. ... post missam dedit Papa prandium omnibus cardinalibus, qui voluerunt ibi manere, et post prandium fecit recitari comediam vulgarem potius ridiculam quam moralem, et donavit cantoribus iocalia solita. (fols. 361ᵛ–362ʳ)

9. Et cum ego petijsse quid de credo, sive simbolo placeret, dixit licet regulariter dici non debeat, sicut nec etiam in festo sancti Jo. Baptistae, tamen voluit quod in utroque festo dicatur, et quod sic toto tempore suo ordinarem, quod diceretur. (fol. 383ᵛ)

Early Music History (1992) Volume 11

M. JENNIFER BLOXAM

'LA CONTENANCE ITALIENNE': THE MOTETS ON *BEATA ES MARIA* BY COMPÈRE, OBRECHT AND BRUMEL*

Musicians have recognised distinct national styles of musical composition and performance for centuries, and even today our understanding of the development of musical style in virtually every

* Different versions of this article were delivered at the fifty-fourth annual meeting of the American Musicological Society in Baltimore, November 1988, and at the Nineteenth Medieval and Renaissance Music Conference in Oxford, July 1991. The author is indebted to Professors Anthony Cummings, Paula Higgins, Patrick Macey, William Prizer and Craig Wright for their many valuable suggestions, as well as to Jerry Call, Archivist for the Musicological Archives for Renaissance Manuscript Studies of the University of Illinois at Urbana–Champaign, for his generous assistance.

   The manuscripts of polyphony cited in the text are abbreviated according to the sigla used in the *Census-Catalogue of Manuscript Sources of Polyphonic Music 1400–1550*, 5 vols., Renaissance Manuscript Studies 1 (Neuhausen–Stuttgart, 1979–88):

BolC Q15 – Bologna, Civico Museo Bibliografico Musicale, MS Q15 (*olim* 37)
BolU 2216 – Bologna, Biblioteca Universitaria, MS 2216
CapePL 3.b.12 – Cape Town, South African Public Library, MS Grey 3.b.12
FlorBN Magl. 112bis – Florence, Biblioteca Nazionale Centrale, MS Magliabechi 112bis
FlorBN Panc. 27 – Florence, Biblioteca Nazionale Centrale, MS Panciatichi 27
MilD 1 – Milan, Archivio della Veneranda Fabbrica del Duomo, Sezione Musicale, Librone 1 (*olim* 2269)
MilD 3 – Milan, Archivio della Veneranda Fabbrica del Duomo, Sezione Musicale, Librone 3 (*olim* 2267)
MilD 4 – Milan, Archivio della Veneranda Fabbrica del Duomo, Sezione Musicale, Librone 4 (*olim* 2266)
MunBS 3154 – Munich, Bayerische Staatsbibliothek, Musiksammlung, Musica Manuscripta 3154
PavU 361 – Pavia, Biblioteca Universitaria, MS Aldini 361 (*olim* 130.A.26)
PerBC 431 – Perugia, Biblioteca Comunale Augusta, MS 431 (G.20)
RomeC 2856 – Rome, Biblioteca Casanatense, MS 2856
SienBC K.I.2 – Siena, Biblioteca Comunale degli Intronati, MS K.I.2
TarazC 2 – Tarazona, Archivio Capitular de la Catedral, MS 2
ToleBC 13 – Toledo, Biblioteca Capitular de la Catedral Metropolitana, MS B.13
ToleBC 21 – Toledo, Biblioteca Capitular de la Catedral Metropolitana, MS B.21
TrentC 87 – Trent, Museo Provinciale d'Arte, Castello del Buon Consiglio, MS 87
VatS 15 – Vatican City, Biblioteca Apostolica Vaticana, MS Cappella Sistina 15
VatS 42 – Vatican City, Biblioteca Apostolica Vaticana, MS Cappella Sistina 42
VenBN 7554 – Venice, Biblioteca Nazionale Marciana, MS 7554 (*olim* Italiana IX, 145)

period rests in large part on observations of the contact and melding of national idioms. From the suppression and absorption of Gallic chant by Roman plainsong during the time of Charlemagne, through the wedding of French, Italian and German styles accomplished by Bach, to the joining of north Indian classical musical elements with modern avant-garde music by Philip Glass and other minimalist composers, our telling of music history is in large part analysis of a continuing process of musical colonialisation.

Accounts of fifteenth-century music and musical style today manifest just such an interest in the confluence of national styles. In the thirteenth and fourteenth centuries, the hegemony of French musical culture remained largely unchallenged and untouched by neighbouring nations enthralled by it. The central musical language developed by medieval French musicians changed profoundly, however, over the course of the fifteenth century, and explanations for this transformation of style were sought, even as they occurred, in the influence of other national styles. Perhaps the best-known contemporary witness to such exposure is the poet Martin Le Franc, whose phrase 'la contenance angloise' (the English guise) has come to signal an English impact on Continental musicians of Dufay's generation.[1] Although many have been led by Reese's translation of Le Franc's verses to attribute the more euphonious harmony of early fifteenth-century Continental composers to their new acquaintance with English music, the precise nature of English influence during the first half of the century remains enigmatic.[2] That English music made an impression on French composers cannot be denied, but, as David Fallows has pointed out, the process of assimilation was probably both more subtle and more gradual than previously thought.[3]

But the English cannot take sole responsibility for new developments in fifteenth-century musical style. Certain key aspects of the transformation of French and Franco-Flemish composition during this period are today routinely credited to the indigenous music of

[1] This phrase occurs in Le Franc's poem *Le champion des dames*, written between *c*. 1438 and 1442, and entered the mainstream of modern musicological scholarship through the translation by Gustave Reese in *Music in the Renaissance* (New York, 1954), pp. 12–13.

[2] For an insightful critique of commonly held assumptions about *la contenance angloise*, see D. Fallows, 'The Contenance Angloise: English Influence on Continental Composers of the Fifteenth Century', *Renaissance Studies*, 1 (1987), pp. 189–208.

[3] *Ibid.*, p. 194.

quattrocento Italy, in particular the genre of the lauda spirituale. Increasing use of homophonic textures and a greater concern for the vertical harmonic conception as well as sensitivity to clarity of text and its proper declamation are widely regarded as the reflection of 'la contenance italienne' – the Italian face – on the intricate, linear polyphony of northern composers during the century. Although no delighted poet immortalised this union – hence this author's paraphrase of Le Franc – there can be little doubt that the burgeoning presence of northern musicians in Italy that began with Ciconia and his generation and reached its peak in Josquin's lifetime greatly facilitated a cross-fertilisation between northern and southern composition, with important consequences in both arenas. It is the impact of Italian style on northern composers, however, that will be the focus of this inquiry.

The process of the assimilation of 'la contenance italienne' by transalpine musicians cannot be charted here; it is certainly a longer and more complicated development than has been previously acknowledged, extending from Ciconia through Dufay to Josquin and encompassing not only laude and frottole but also the refined secular music of the late Italian trecento and early fifteenth-century Italian motets and mass movements.[4] This article offers a re-examination of only one aspect of Italian influence on northern composers, that exerted by the popular song of religious praise called the lauda, and focuses primarily, though not exclusively, on the latter half of the century.

While most scholars agree on the significance of northern contact with the lauda, they have disagreed about when and how this interaction occurred. Helmut Osthoff maintained that the process of synthesis began in Milan during the 1470s, when Josquin, Compère and Weerbeke together shared exposure to the southern musical climate at the Sforza court.[5] Lowinsky, however, argued that four-voice laude, the presumed primary models for northern

---

[4] For an investigation addressing aspects of Italian influence on northern composition in the first half of the fifteenth century, see W. Arlt, 'Musik und Text im Liedsatz franko-flämischer Italienfahrer der ersten Hälfte des 15. Jahrhunderts', *Schweizer Jahrbuch für Musikwissenschaft*, 1 (1981), pp. 23–69. A useful overview of the reciprocal influences between north and south in the first decades of the century remains Reese, *Music in the Renaissance*, pp. 10–33.

[5] H. Osthoff, *Josquin Desprez*, 2 vols. (Tutzing, 1962–5), I, pp. 127–8. It should be noted that Josquin had arrived in Milan by 1459.

emulation, did not emerge until the 1490s, and that the Italian influence apparent in Josquin's generation must therefore date from no earlier than the last decade of the fifteenth century.[6] Contrafacted portions from homorhythmic, syllabic motets by Josquin and Weerbeke included in Petrucci's *Laude libro secondo* of 1508 (RISM 1508[3]) bolstered the notion of a causal relationship between the rise of the four-voice lauda style and the appearance of such pervasively homophonic compositions as Josquin's *Tu solus qui facis mirabilia*.

In the most recent contribution to the debate surrounding the contact between northern and Italian style, Jonathan Glixon has suggested that laude exerted little if any impact on the musical style of northern composers.[7] Two points are cited in support of this thesis: first, that what should be regarded as the true style of the polyphonic lauda (simple note-against-note pieces in two or three parts) was quite unlike that of the motets composed by Netherlanders in Italy, and was moreover unlikely to be encountered in the courtly and ecclesiastical circles in which the northern musicians working in Italy moved; and secondly, that the four-voice lauda as exemplified in Petrucci's collections not only developed too late to have influenced northern composers but was also in large part a derivative genre that borrowed the style of the frottola and motet.

Several observations will help to clarify the murky waters of this debate. First, the notion that northerners were deprived of exposure to the music of the laude by virtue of their more sophisticated milieu must be dispelled immediately. *Laudesi* companies in cities throughout northern Italy held their numerous devotions at chapels maintained in a city's churches, and frequent processions through city streets exposed the entire population to this music.[8] Instructions to the cathedral choir of Florence confirm their performance of laude for evening devotions in a certain chapel of the

---

[6]   E. E. Lowinsky, 'Scholarship in the Renaissance', *Renaissance News*, 16 (1963), pp. 260–1.

[7]   J. Glixon, 'The Polyphonic Laude of Innocentius Dammonis', *The Journal of Musicology*, 7 (1990), pp. 40–1.

[8]   See B. Wilson, 'Music and Merchants: The Laudesi Companies of Republican Florence, ca. 1270–1494' (Ph.D. dissertation, Indiana University, 1987), esp. pp. 65–130. William F. Prizer, in a paper entitled 'Court Piety, Popular Piety: The Lauda in Renaissance Mantua' delivered at the annual meeting of the American Musicological Society in Chicago, November 1991, emphasises processions as occasions at which court culture and the artisan culture met, with important consequences for music in both spheres. I am grateful to Professor Prizer for sharing this paper with me.

church, a practice that must have been duplicated by other Italian church choirs.[9] And laude were a regular component in the *rappresentazioni sacre* staged by numerous Italian courts and churches.[10] Northern musicians, whether active at church or court, could hardly have avoided hearing laude.

Secondly, the four-voice lauda, in its simplest homophonic style, certainly developed earlier than the 1490s; indeed, four-part laude are evident as early as *c.* 1430, as witnessed by the anonymous four-voice setting of the lauda *In natali Domini* in BolC Q15 (see Example 1).[11] Only the triplum of this work is unique to this setting: two identical two-voice settings in PavU 361 and BolU 2216 employ the discantus and tenor framework that forms the basis of the four-voice version in BolC Q15, while a three-part setting in TrentC 87 simply adds the contratenor voice to the discantus and tenor lines.[12]

Example 1. *In natali Domini*, BolC Q15, fols. 201ᵛ–202ʳ.

[9] F. D'Accone, 'The Musical Chapels at the Florentine Cathedral and Baptistry during the First Half of the 16th Century', *Journal of the American Musicological Society*, 24 (1971), p. 3.

[10] The use of laude at *rappresentazioni sacre* is documented in W. Osthoff, *Theatergesang und darstellende Musik in der italienischen Renaissance (15. und 16. Jahrhundert)*, Münchner Veröffentlichungen zur Musikgeschichte 14, 2 vols. (Tutzing, 1969), i, pp. 30–8.

[11] See the Inventory of BolC Q15 by G. de Van, 'Inventory of Manuscript Bologna, Liceo Musicale, Q 15 (*olim* 37)', *Musica Disciplina*, 2 (1948), pp. 246–7, in which *In natali Domini* is identified as a lauda. Margaret Bent is preparing a study of BolC Q15; a summary of the dating of the layers in the manuscript is given in 'A Contemporary Perception of Early Fifteenth-Century Style: Bologna Q15 as a Document of Scribal Editorial Initiative', *Musica Disciplina*, 41 (1987), pp. 185 and 198.

Example 1 – *cont.*

44

Example 1 – *cont.*

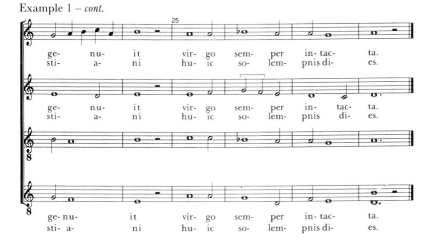

ge-   nu-   it   vir- go   sem- per   in- tac- ta.
sti-   a-   ni   hu- ic   so- lem- pnis di- es.

ge-   nu-   it   vir- go   sem- per   in-   tac- ta.
sti-   a-   ni   hu- ic   so- lem- pnis di- es.

ge- nu-   it   vir- go   sem- per   in- tac- ta.
sti- a-   ni   hu- ic   so- lem- pnis di- es.

ge- nu-   it   vir- go   sem- per   in- tac- ta.
sti- a-   ni   hu- ic   so- lem- pnis di- es.

The impression made by the resulting note-against-note syllabic settings in two, three and even four parts on northern composers in the early decades of the fifteenth century is surely evident in the appearance of such passages in the music of Ciconia, Arnold de Lantins, Lymburgia and Dufay.

Finally, past emphasis on the four-part lauda as the inspiration behind northern composers' interest in the Italian style has failed to take into account an essential feature of the lauda repertory in the fifteenth century suggested by the example of *In natali Domini* just cited. Throughout the fourteenth century, laude were virtually all monophonic, and this stock of melodies clearly continued in popular circulation throughout the fifteenth century and beyond; indeed, many polyphonic laude from the fifteenth century appear to be based on monophonic tunes.[13] An especially good example illustrating the continuum from monophony to elaborate four-voice polyphony is provided by the lauda *Verbum caro factum est*. This melody first appears in Turin, Biblioteca Nazionale Universitaria, MS Bobbiese F.I.4 (hereafter Turin F.I.4), a collection of

---

12 All extant settings of *In natali Domini* are edited in the excellent study by E. Diederichs, *Die Anfänge der mehrstimmigen Lauda vom Ende des 14. bis zur Mitte des 15. Jahrhunderts,* Münchner Veröffentlichungen zur Musikgeschichte 41 (Tutzing, 1986), pp. 324–9. Both the three- and four-voice settings of *In natali Domini* contain numerous unprepared dissonances and other crudities of part-writing probably resulting from the as yet unrefined layered process of composition here employed. The sonority of the chordal triad does, however, prevail.

13 K. Jeppesen and V. Brøndal, *Die mehrstimmige italienische Laude um 1500* (Leipzig, 1935), pp. xx–xxv.

monophonic Latin laude dating from the mid-fourteenth century.[14] During the fifteenth century this tune furnished the basis for a number of polyphonic versions, including serving as the tenor in two settings *a* 2 in VenBN 7554; as the upper line in one two-voice setting in FlorBN Panc. 27; as the tenor in five different three-voice settings, one each in BolU 2216, CapePL 3.b.12, FlorBN Magl. 112bis, FlorBN Panc. 27 and VenBN 7554; and as the discantus in three settings *a* 3, two in FlorBN Magl. 112bis and one in FlorBN Panc. 27.[15] Culminating the career of this particular long-lived lauda was its role as the tenor of two four-voice arrangements by Innocentius Dammonis, published by Petrucci in his *Lauda libro primo* of 1508.[16] The complex and thoroughly 'composed' four-voice laude exemplified in Petrucci's publications therefore represent only the final stages in a process of polyphonic elaboration that had its roots in the practice of creating new counterpoints to a well-known melody.[17]

Polyphonic adornment of a pre-existing tune is, of course, a compositional technique that also underlies northern composition of masses and motets during much of the fifteenth century. And it is clear that one avenue by which *oltremontani* arrived at their absorption of the Italian guise was through their participation in the polyphonic elaboration of indigenous Italian melodies. On their introduction to the Italian musical scene, several northern composers seized on popular songs of that country for inclusion in their secular works, the best-known examples of which are Josquin's and Compère's settings of *Scaramella fa la galla.*[18] Even the mass genre

[14] A discussion, plate and transcription of this piece are included in P. Damilano, 'Laudi latine in un antifonario bobbiese del Trecento', *Collectanea Historiae Musicae*, 3 (1963), pp. 15–57. *Verbum caro factum est* may trace its origin to the conductus *In hoc anni circulo*, as proposed by Dom A. Hughes, 'In hoc anni circulo', *The Musical Quarterly*, 60 (1974), pp. 37–45.

[15] Modern editions of the settings of *Verbum caro factum est* here mentioned are found in F. Luisi, *Laudario Giustinianeo*, 2 vols. (Venice, 1983), ɪɪ, pp. 194–211. For a critical assessment of this edition, see the review by Jonathan Glixon in *Journal of the American Musicological Society*, 41 (1988), pp. 170–9. A comparison of the variants in the monophonic tune as it appears in its many polyphonic arrangements is provided in Diederichs, *Die Anfänge der mehrstimmigen Lauda*, pp. 332–3.

[16] Modern editions of Dammonis's arrangements are found in Jeppesen, *Die mehrstimmige italienische Laude*, pp. 106–7, and Luisi, *Laudario Giustinianeo*, ɪɪ, pp. 212–20.

[17] A comparable evolution, from a fund of melodies to which counterpoints were improvised into a fully notated four-part polyphony, characterises the rise of the frottola in the latter part of the fifteenth century, as shown by William Prizer in 'The Frottola and the Unwritten Tradition', *Studi Musicali*, 15 (1986), pp. 3–37.

[18] On Josquin's italianate songs, see C. Gallico, 'Josquin's Compositions on Italian Texts

occasionally ingested secular Italian tunes: Dufay, for example, included a suspiciously folk-like tune identified as 'la vilanella' in his troped Credo 'Dic Maria'; Obrecht later based a mass on the *Scaramella* melody; and Martini may have used secular Italian songs in his *Missa 'Dio te salvi Gotterello'* and *Missa 'Io ne tengo quanto te'*.[19] These are isolated cases, however; noticeably absent are examples suggesting such a connection between the indigenous devotional songs of religious praise, the laude spirituale, and the substantial body of sacred music created by northern composers active on the Italian peninsula.

A direct link between the Italian lauda and sacred polyphony by northern composers can now be established thanks to the identification of a hitherto unknown cantus firmus in three motets by three northern composers. The works in question, *Ave Maria gratia plena* by Loyset Compère, *Beata es Maria* by Jacob Obrecht and *Beata es Maria* by Antoine Brumel, were first grouped together for discussion by Ludwig Finscher.[20] Remarking on the unusual amount of common textual and melodic materials shared by these three motets, Finscher noted that all give prominence to a particular tune presented by the tenor and associated with the following text: 'Beata es Maria virgo clemens et pia, candore vincis lilia et rosa sine spina, sanctorum melodia' (Blessed are you, Mary, gentle and holy virgin, in radiance you surpass the lilies and the thornless rose, the melody of saints). But neither Finscher nor subsequent scholars treating the music of Obrecht or Brumel have comprehended the origin of the tune.[21]

and the Frottola', *Josquin des Prez: Proceedings of the International Josquin Festival-Conference*, ed. E. E. Lowinsky and B. J. Blackburn (London, 1976), pp. 446–54. Compère's two frottolesque songs are discussed in L. Finscher, *Loyset Compère (c. 1450–1518): Life and Works*, Musicological Studies and Documents 12 (Rome, 1964), pp. 242–3.

[19] L. Lockwood, *Music in Renaissance Ferrara 1400–1505* (Cambridge, MA, 1984), pp. 233–40.
[20] Finscher, *Loyset Compère*, pp. 161–6.
[21] Johannes Wolf, in the critical notes to his edition of *Beata es Maria* by Obrecht, identified this text as the responsory for the Marian antiphon *Virgo Galilaea*, referring to *Analecta hymnica*, ed. C. Blume, G. M. Dreves and H. M. Bannister, 55 vols. (Leipzig, 1886–1922; reprint, New York, 1961), xxi, p. 182 (see *Werken van Jacob Obrecht*, ed. J. Wolf (Leipzig and Amsterdam, 1908–21; reprint 1968), vi: *Motetten*, pt 2, p. x). Barton Hudson followed Wolf's lead in his description of this text as it appears in Brumel's motet; see *Antoine Brumel: Opera omnia*, ed. B. Hudson, 6 vols., Corpus Mensurabilis Musicae 5 (n.p., 1969–72), v, p. xxx. In Finscher, *Loyset Compère*, p. 162, the melody and text are designated as the *repetitio* (refrain) of the *cantio Virgo Galilaea*, referring again to *Analecta hymnica*, xxi, p. 182. Although Finscher cites Damilano, 'Laudi latine', the article that led this author to the source of this cantus firmus, he does so without further comment.

The text *Beata es Maria* and the tune with which it appears derive from a monophonic lauda spirituale preserved today in the most important trecento collection of monophonic Latin laude, Turin F.I.4, first brought to attention by Don Piero Damilano in 1963.[22] The first 133 folios of this book contain a mid-fourteenth-century antiphoner from Bobbio, a small northern Italian town in the vicinity of Genoa; this service book follows the usage of the Benedictine monastery of S. Columbo, a house belonging to the reformist Congregation of S. Giustina. Preserved in the last fascicle are thirteen anonymous monophonic Latin laude, copied by a different but contemporaneous scribe and probably compiled at the monastery.[23] *Beata es Maria* is the sixth in this collection.[24]

Clarity and graceful simplicity are the hallmarks of this lauda, whose refrain is given in Example 2a. Syllabic text setting prevails, melodic movement is primarily conjunct and the range is modest, particularly within phrases. The heptasyllabic five-line refrain, with its AAB musical structure, and the seven-line stanzas are, however, atypical of the genre and distinctive features of this lauda.[25] Neither does the larger structure conform to the clear ballata plan characteristic of eleven of the thirteen laude contained in the manuscript: the *volta* does not duplicate the music of the *ripresa* exactly, but condenses it to two phrases.[26]

In addition to the manuscript Turin F.I.4, which is the earliest extant source of the lauda *Beata es Maria*, two fifteenth-century sources also transmit this piece. A collection of readings and prayers associated with the Benedictine order and compiled for the monastery at Melk includes the text of the lauda, albeit in a version somewhat different from that of the Turin manuscript.[27] And on an appended folio at the end of an early(?) fifteenth-century Italian

---

[22] Damilano, 'Laudi latine'.

[23] The central role in the cultivation and collection of the late medieval lauda repertory played by Benedictine establishments in Italy, specifically those belonging to the Congregation of S. Giustina, is explored by G. Cattin, 'Tradizione e tendenze innovatrici nella normativa e nella pratica liturgico-musicale della Congregazione de S. Giustina', *Benedictina*, 17 (1970), pp. 254–99.

[24] A plate of the lauda *Beata es Maria* is found in Damilano, 'Laudi latine', tavola III.

[25] *Ibid.*, pp. 20–1.

[26] See the transcription of this lauda in Damilano, 'Laudi latine', p. 50.

[27] Melk, Stiftsbibliothek, MS 1087 (*olim* 932), p. 110. The text of the refrain matches that of Turin K.I.2, but the order of stanzas is shuffled and some lines changed, stanza 4 is omitted and two verses are added.

Example 2

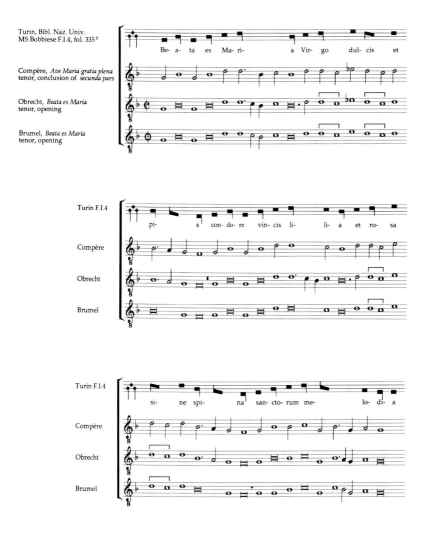

missal, whose calendar establishes its Benedictine origin, appears a
variant reading of the melody and a different order of the six
stanzas.[28] *Beata es Maria* clearly enjoyed a rather long life.

[28] Naples, Biblioteca Nazionale, MS VI.G.3, fol. 275[r]. The version of the tune preserved
herein omits the phrase 'sanctorum melodia' and shows considerable disagreement in
pitch content.

That three *oltremontani* – the Fleming Obrecht, and the French-men Compère and Brumel – each composed a motet based in part on the text and melody of the same lauda is indeed intriguing, and invites a fresh investigation of the relation of these works to one another. Reconstructing the strands of the web that binds these and other related motets by these composers together suggests not only dates and places of origin for the works in question, but also pro-vides a particularly focused perspective on one phase in the syn-thesis of Netherlandish and Italian musical styles in the latter half of the fifteenth century.

Ave Maria gratia plena was Compère's best-known and most widely distributed motet, surviving in one print and eleven manuscripts spanning about seventy years and four countries (see Table 1), thus rivalling Josquin's *Ave Maria ... virgo serena* in popularity.[29] The pan-European fascination with the Blessed Virgin that burgeoned in the late Middle Ages, and the concomitant plethora of liturgical and devotional services in her honour, accounts in part for the appeal of these and numerous other motets and masses in praise of the Blessed Virgin.[30] Also germane to the renown of Compère's *Ave Maria* are its uncomplicated style, suited for singers of only modest abilities (the tenor, for example, recites on one pitch for the first twenty-two *tacti*), and the general laudatory content of its text, appropriate for a host of purposes.

A medley of Marian texts and tunes combine in this motet (see Table 2). Compère commences his piece with the text of the famous all-purpose prayer to the Virgin, 'Ave Maria gratia plena', or 'Hail Mary, full of grace' (see Example 3a).[31] The cantus firmus, placed in the altus, proves to be the opening couplet from the great sequence *Ave Maria gratia plena*, whose tune Compère apparently

---

[29] See the edition in *Loyset Compère: Opera omnia*, ed. L. Finscher, 5 vols., Corpus Mensu-rabilis Musicae 15 (Rome, 1958–72), iv, pp. 8–10.

[30] Suggested by Finscher, *Loyset Compère*, p. 161.

[31] Although the Marian prayer 'Ave Maria gratia plena' was universally known and employed in a wide variety of liturgical and devotional functions (see J. Leclercq, 'Ave Maria', *Dictionnaire d'archéologie chrétienne et de liturgie*, 15 vols. (Paris, 1907–50), x/2, pp. 2043–62), Compère's inspiration for the selection of this particular prayer may have derived from the lauda spirituale genre. This text was a favourite among northern Italian composers of polyphonic Latin laude; for example, Petrucci's *Laude libro primo* (Venice, 1508) and *Laude libro secondo* (Venice, 1507/8) together include no fewer than ten settings of the 'Ave Maria' prayer, making it by far the most popular single text in these publications.

Table 1   Ave Maria gratia plena *by Loyset Compère: sources*

Sources	Provenance/Date[a]
Barcelona, Biblioteca Central, MS 454	Spain, late 15th–early 16th century, with later additions
Berlin, Staatsbibliothek Preussischer Kulturbesitz, MS Mus. 40021 (*olim* Z 21)	Leipzig?/Torgau?, *c.* 1485–1500[b]
Milan, Archivio della Veneranda Fabbrica del Duomo, Sezione Musicale, Librone 3 (*olim* 2267)	Milan, *c.* 1500
Siena, Biblioteca Comunale degli Intronati, MS K.I.2	Siena, 1481, with later additions
Tarazona, Archivio Capitular de la Catedral, MS 2	Seville?, early 16th century
Toledo, Biblioteca Capitular de la Catedral Metropolitana, MS B.21	Toledo, 1549
Vatican City, Biblioteca Apostolica Vaticana, MS Chigi C VIII 234	Brussels/Mechlin, *c.* 1498–1503, with later additions[c]
Vatican City, Biblioteca Apostolica Vaticana, MS Cappella Sistina 15	Rome, *c.* 1495–1500
Verona, Biblioteca Capitolare, MS DCCLVIII	Verona, *c.* 1500
Warsaw, Biblioteka Uniwersytecka, Oddzial Zbiorów Muzycznych. MS. Mf. 2016 (*olim* Rps. Mus.58)	Silesia or Bohemia, *c.* 1500
Wrocław (Breslau), Biblioteka Uniwersytecka, Oddzial Rekopisów. MS I-F-428	Frankfurt an der Oder?, *c.* 1510–30, perhaps *c.* 1516
Motetti A (RISM 1502[1])	Venice: Petrucci, 1505

[a]Information regarding provenance and date of manuscript sources is drawn from *Census-Catalogue of Manuscript Sources of Polyphonic Music, 1400–1550*, compiled by the University of Illinois Musicological Archives for Renaissance Manuscript Studies, Renaissance Manuscript Studies 1 (Neuhausen–Stuttgart, 1979–88).

[b]*Ave Maria gratia plena* is preserved in a layer of this manuscript dating from 1497/1500; see M. Just, *Der Mensuralkodex Mus.ms 40021 der Staatsbibliothek Preussischer Kulturbesitz Berlin* (Tutzing, 1975), i, pp. 24–49.

[c]*Ave Maria gratia plena* was added to this manuscript by a Spanish scribe after 1514. See *Census-Catalogue*, iv, p. 12.

plundered because of its textual similarity to the prayer.[32] Although the texts of the prayer and the sequence diverge after the initial

---

[32]   For an edition of the text and melody of the sequence *Ave Maria gratia plena*, see *The Utrecht Prosarium*, ed. N. de Goede, Monumenta Musica Neerlandica 6 (Amsterdam, 1965), pp. 63–4.

Table 2 *Texts of the Motets on 'Beata es Maria'*

Compère	Obrecht	Brumel
Pars I	*Pars I*	
Ave Maria, gratia plena, Dominus tecum, virgo serena, Benedicta tu in mulieribus, Et benedictus fructus ventris tui.	Beata es Maria, Virgo clemens et pia, Candore vincis lilia, Et rosa sine spina, Sanctorum melodia.	Beata es Maria, Virgo dulcis et pia, Candore vincis lilia, Et rosa sine spina, Sanctorum melodia.
Kyrie eleison. Christe eleison. Kyrie eleison.	Kyrie eleison. Christe eleison.	Kyrie eleison.
O Christe audi nos.	O Christe audi nos.	O Christe audi nos.
Sancta Maria, ora pro nobis ad Dominum.	Sancta Maria, ora pro nobis ad Dominum.	Sancta Maria, ora pro nobis ad Dominum.
O Christe audi nos.	O Christe audi nos.	O Christe audi nos.
Sancta Dei genetrix, ora pro nobis ad Dominum.		
O Christe audi nos.		
Pars II	*Pars II*	
	Superius, Altus, Bassus	
Sancte Michael, ora pro nobis ad Dominum.	Ave Maria, gratia plena, Dominus tecum, virgo serena, Benedicta tu in mulieribus, Et benedictus fructus ventris tui.	Sancte Michael, ora pro nobis.
O Christe audi nos.		
Sanctae Stephane, Ludovice, Omnes sancti angeli et archangeli Dei, orate pro nobis ad Dominum.	Sancta Maria, ora pro nobis peccatoribus.	Maria mater gratiae, Mater misericordiae, Tu nos ab hoste protege, Et hora mortis suscipe. Beata es Maria.
O Christe audi nos.	O Christe audi nos. *Tenor*	O Christe audi nos.
Sanctae Francisce, Quintine, Ludovice, Sebastiane, Raphael, Martine,	Beata es Maria, Virgo clemens et pia, Candore vincis lilia, Et rosa sine spina,	Sancte Raphael, ora pro nobis. Gloria tibi Domine,

Table 2 *continued*

Compère	Obrecht	Brumel
Omnes sancti martyres, Omnes sancti confessores.	Sanctorum melodia.	Qui natus Virgine. Cum patre et Sancto Spiritu
Omnes sancti et sanctae Dei, orate pro nobis ad Dominum.	Kyrie eleison. Christe eleison.	In sempiterna saecula. Beata es Maria.
O Christe audi nos.	O Christe audi nos.	O Christe audi nos.
Beata es Maria, Virgo dulcis et pia, Candore vincis lilia, Et rosa sine spina, Sanctorum melodia.	Sancta Maria, ora pro nobis ad Dominum.	
O Christe audi nos.	O Christe audi nos.	

couplet, the composer continued to fashion a cantus firmus from a pastiche of melodic snippets extracted from the sequence that corresponded with the text of the 'Ave Maria' prayer: thus the line 'Benedicta tu in mulieribus' is set to the tune of the opening of the second verse of the sequence, and 'Et benedictus fructus ventris tui' is sung to the melody that begins the fourth verse of the sequence.[33] And another apparent reference to a well-known melody is suggested at the outset of the motet, before the cantus firmus makes its appearance, as first the superius and then the bassus enunciates a motif strongly reminiscent of the incipit from Ockeghem's chanson *Fors seulement*.[34]

Following the conclusion of that portion of the text based on the 'Ave Maria' prayer, the composer goes on to conclude the *prima pars* with texts derived from the Litany of the Saints, beginning with invocations to the Trinity and continuing with pleas to the Blessed Virgin.[35] The *secunda pars* resumes with acclamations from the Litany, focusing in this section on appeals to various saints and

---

[33] Finscher, *Loyset Compère*, p. 162, identified the source of the cantus firmus for the opening couplet, but did not observe that the two lines following also derived their *cantus prius factus* from the sequence.

[34] I am grateful to Leeman Perkins for bringing this quotation to my attention.

[35] The development of the Litany is summarised by M. Huglo in 'Litany', *The New Grove Dictionary of Music and Musicians*, ed. S. Sadie, 20 vols. (London, 1980), XI, pp. 75–8.

building to a strong four-part homophonic cadential articulation in bars 122–4 (see Example 3b). Serving as cantus firmus for this segment of the motet is an as yet unidentified version of the tone for singing the Litany; the formulaic repetition of small melodic units

Example 3a. Compère, *Ave Maria gratia plena*, opening

Example 3a – *cont.*

Example 3b. Compère, *Ave Maria gratia plena*, conclusion (as transmitted in all sources except SienBC K.I.2)

Example 3b – *cont.*

Example 3b – *cont.*

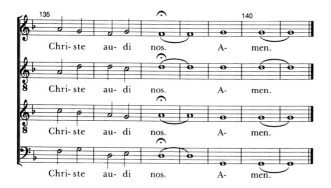

thus pervades all four voices of the composition while it is occupied with the text of the Litany.[36]

Compère concludes the *secunda pars* with a jaunty, joyous section based on the text and tune of the lauda's refrain (see Example 3b, bars 124–41). Announced by a shift from the duple metre that governs the work to this point into a lilting *tripla*, the melody of the lauda appears in the tenor, furnishing the basis for an enlivened four-part homophonic texture.[37] With the exception of a few melodic variants, which doubtless reflect a slightly different version of the lauda circulating in the fifteenth century, Compère adhered almost note for note to the lauda melody as transmitted in Turin F.I.4, interpolating only the briefest cadential extensions (see Example 2b). The rhythm to which Compère set the lauda's tune probably reflects that of the original; certainly the notation of the lauda in the Turin manuscript supports a metrical interpretation.[38]

---

[36] The numerous Litany settings from the sixteenth century tend to retain the recitational melodic character evident in the treatment of Litany texts in the later fifteenth century; see J. Roth, *Die mehrstimmigen lateinischen Litaneikompositionen des 16. Jahrhunderts*, Kölner Beiträge zur Musikforschung 14, ed. K. G. Fellerer (Regensburg, 1959), pp. 69–74.

[37] The mensuration sign indicated for those sections of Compère's *Ave Maria gratia plena* in duple metre varies between sources: SienBC K.I.2 and TarazC 2 provide C; ToleBC 21 indicates C2; and the nine remaining sources employ ₵.

[38] The rhythmic realisation of laude remains problematic; solutions range from Riemann's theory of *Vierhebigkeit*, implemented by F. Liuzzi in *La lauda e i primordi della melodia italiana* (Rome, 1934) to the 'modified mensural' system devised by H. Anglès in 'The Musical Notation and Rhythm of the Italian Lauda', *Essays in Musicology: A Birthday Offering for Willi Apel*, ed. H. Tischler (Bloomington, IN, 1966), pp. 51–60. Damilano's interpretation of the note shapes in Turin F.I.4 often results in the lilting triple metre of rhythmic mode 1 (see Damilano, 'Laudi latine', pp. 45–57); this realisation appears to be confirmed by Compère's adoption of this rhythm in *Ave Maria gratia plena*.

Ave Maria gratia plena culminates with a return to *tempus imperfectum diminutum* for a final plea, 'O Christe audi nos'. This phrase from the Litany functions as a refrain throughout the motet, bringing both *partes* of the work to a close and also articulating the meditational unfolding of the individual acclamations. Compère consistently associates this textual phrase with one melodic motif derived from the Litany tone, and although the motif is heard in both two- and four-part contexts, a musical as well as a textual refrain is effectively achieved.

Finscher has aptly described the style of this piece as 'the most "un-Netherlandish" c.f. motet imaginable, a technical tour-de-force and an experiment only partially successful'; he notes the composer's adherence to cantus firmus technique while achieving complete rhythmic integration of all pre-existent melodies into the surrounding texture, the inconsistent equation of verse metre with rhythmic motifs despite an obvious preoccupation with syllabic text declamation, and the retention of the traditional bipartite motet form that flies in the face of a text structure in three distinct sections. These features combine to suggest, as Finscher does, that *Ave Maria gratia plena* is a comparatively youthful work. Yet Finscher proposes a period for its creation between 1495 and 1500, when the composer would have been a man about fifty years old.[39]

The stylistic hallmarks of *Ave Maria gratia plena* adduced by Finscher are, however, entirely consistent with those of the *motetti missales* believed to date from Compère's first Italian sojourn. A somewhat uneasy coexistence of counterpoint and homophony, incorporation of cantus firmi in textural settings that belie their presence, texts assembled by collage and evident concern for text declamation as yet imperfectly realised are principal features that link *Ave Maria gratia plena* with this composer's first period in Italy.

Recent codicological discoveries may confirm an earlier dating for *Ave Maria gratia plena*. Two more sources for this motet have been added to the eleven known to Finscher, and one of these, SienBC K.I.2, transmits *Ave Maria gratia plena* in a layer now believed to date from 1481.[40] This Sienese manuscript thus appears

---

[39] Finscher, *Loyset Compère*, pp. 165–6. Finscher was guided in his proposed dating by *termini ad quos non* for the sources of the motet then known.

[40] F.A. D'Accone, 'A Late 15th-Century Sienese Sacred Repertory: MS K.I.2. of the Biblioteca Comunale, Siena', *Musica Disciplina*, 37 (1983), pp. 121–70. D'Accone argues that Matteo Ghai, a French scribe commissioned by the Sienese patrician Alberto de

to be the earliest surviving source for this motet, though the attribution to Compère is later and derives from three Italian sources copied *c.* 1500 and three Spanish copies from the first half of the sixteenth century (see Table 1).

One noteworthy detail concerning the transmission of *Ave Maria gratia plena* in SienBC K.I.2 has escaped notice. Although this copy of the motet is defective owing to a missing leaf, thus lacking the altus and bassus of the *prima pars* and the superius and tenor of the *secunda pars*, it is clear that the final section of the piece based on the lauda *Beata es Maria* was not included and was never intended to appear in this manuscript: the *secunda pars* ends emphatically after the Litany section with a double bar on fol. 112^r, and fol. 112^v commences an anonymous setting of the antiphon *Sub tuum praesidium* in the same hand. What is more, the setting of the invocation 'O Christe audi nos' that concludes the motet in the Sienese source differs substantially from the analogous segment in all later sources, where it immediately precedes the commencement of the lauda. In SienBC K.I.2, this final acclamation is treated to motion in breves and semibreves, whereas all later sources employ semibreves and minims; this extension of the cadence is further prolonged by the appearance of the flat-VI as the antepenultimate chord (see Example 3c). In SienBC K.I.2, bars 118–28 effect a conclusive end to the motet, comparable to the broadening of motion heard at the end of the *prima pars*. All other sources, however, transmit a version of these measures that flows smoothly into the lauda section, after which a broad cadential progression quite similar to that preserved in SienBC K.I.2 ends the piece.

Was the concluding lauda section for some reason simply omitted from SienBC K.I.2 or its exemplar, and a different, more effec-

Francesco Aringhieri, copied two collections of music, one for Vespers and the other for Mass, between February and July 1481; these were later rebound into the single volume now known as SienBC K.I.2. According to D'Accone, five other scribes added items up until the early sixteenth century, but the motet in question exists in the earlier layer in Ghai's hand. For a facsimile of this manuscript, see *Siena, Biblioteca Comunale degli Intronati, MS K.I.2*, introduction by F. A. D'Accone, Renaissance Music in Facsimile: Sources Central to the Music of the Late Fifteenth and Sixteenth Centuries 17 (New York, 1986).

D'Accone bases his hypothesis on the intersection of payment records to copyists and surviving inventories of books from the cathedral of Siena. The proposed dating is not without problems: the evidence of the watermarks remains to be assessed, and implications for the attribution and chronology of certain pieces explored (for some preliminary thoughts on one such example, *Sancti Dei omnes*, see below, n. 50).

Example 3c. Compère, *Ave Maria gratia plena*, conclusion transmitted in SienBC K.I.2 (superius and tenor reconstructed from later sources)

tive ending for the Litany portion provided? Or do the other, presumably later, sources transmit an expanded version of a motet originally conceived without the lauda section? In light of the organic character of the revision as it apparently proceeds from the earliest to the later extant sources of *Ave Maria gratia plena*, a revision that manifests a concern for the integral function of the refrain 'O Christe audi nos', the latter possibility seems far more probable.[41]

If indeed the lauda setting was a later addition to *Ave Maria gratia plena*, was Compère responsible for the version of the motet as it survives in SienBC K.I.2, or does the association with Compère stem only from the subsequent revision and expansion of the

---

[41] The preservation of an apparently earlier version of *Ave Maria gratia plena* in SienBC K.I.2 would appear to support D'Accone's dating of the manuscript.

work?[42] Although lacking attribution in this source, stylistic criteria support Compère's authorship of the main body of the motet. A passage that bears a striking similarity to the Litany invocations in *Ave Maria gratia plena* occurs in this composer's *motetti missales* cycle *Ave Domine Jesu Christe*, where at the conclusion of the *loco Offertorii* St Augustine is invoked in paired declamatory lines that recall the recitational chant of the Litany.[43] Also akin to the style of *Ave Maria gratia plena* is the motet *Ad honorem tuum, Christe*, which likewise employs material from the Litany of the Saints in a quasi-recitational manner and incorporates a refrain based on the text and melody of the plea 'Ora pro nobis' from the Litany chant.[44]

The discovery of a lauda serving as a cantus firmus in Compère's *Ave Maria gratia plena* further strengthens the case for the Italian genesis for this motet. Compère had surely arrived in Italy by 1474, for by July of that year he numbered among the singers of Galeazzo Maria Sforza, Duke of Milan; his service at the Sforza court may even date back to 1471 or before, if the singer 'Aloysio' sent by the duke to recruit singers in the north in October 1471 can be identified as the composer.[45] Compère left Milan early in 1477, shortly after the murder of the duke, and nothing more is known of his activities until February 1486, by which time he had secured employment at the French court. Not until the autumn of 1494 did he return to Italy, and then in the retinue of the invading Charles VIII.[46]

Compère was surely exposed to laude during both Italian sojourns. Indeed, one specific occasion on which he would certainly

[42] On the possibility that attributions may identify not the original composer but another composer's revision, see A. Atlas, 'Conflicting Attributions in Italian Sources of the Franco-Netherlandish Chanson, ca. 1465–ca. 1505: A Progress Report on a New Hypothesis', *Music in Medieval and Early Modern Europe: Patronage, Sources and Texts*, ed. I. Fenlon (Cambridge, 1981), pp. 249–93.

[43] See the edition by Finscher, *Loyset Compère: Opera omnia*, II, pp. 25–6.

[44] See the discussion of *Ad honorem tuum, Christe* by Finscher in *Loyset Compère*, pp. 166–71. An edition is found in Finscher, *Loyset Compère: Opera omnia*, IV, pp. 1–5. Finscher suggests a date of 1503 for this motet, on the basis of the date of its only source and the mention of Pope Julius in its text. But names invoked in motets were easily and often changed, and the style of *Ad honorem tuum, Christe*, which is most akin to that of *Ave Maria gratia plena*, strongly suggests that it is also earlier than was previously suspected.

[45] The possibility of the equation of 'Aloysio' with Compère was raised by W. F. Prizer, 'Music at the Court of the Sforza: The Birth and Death of a Musical Center', *Musica Disciplina*, 43 (1989), p. 156.

[46] The authoritative study of Compère's biography remains Finscher, *Loyset Compère*, pp. 13–23.

have heard laude sung has been chronicled. In November 1494, Charles VIII was treated to a performance of the *sacra rappresentazione* of Feo Belcari known as the *Festa de San Felice* during his visit to Florence; this production, which Compère, as a member of the king's retinue, must have attended, included the lauda *Laudate el sommo Dio*.[47] But the composer's Milanese period would have provided the richest opportunities for contact with this indigenous Italian song style. Although no extant collections of laude can be traced to Milan, it is known that Galeazzo Maria Sforza cultivated a strong interest in the music of his native country: in the early 1470s, for example, he undertook to obtain from a Venetian singer all the canzone poetry of Leonardo Giustinian (as well as 'all the others that are lovely and can be found in Venice', probably including laude), as well as the music for several canzoni 'so that one can understand the Venetian style of singing'.[48] And although their musical activities have not yet received attention, there can be little doubt that the many confraternities of *disciplinati* active in Milan included the singing of laude in their services and processions just as did similar organisations in Venice, Florence and other northern Italian cities.[49]

A number of clues combine to suggest that *Ave Maria gratia plena* is a product of Compère's years in Milan. The motet claims a Milanese concordance in MilD 3, one of the codices prepared under the supervision of Franchinus Gaffurius, *maestro di cappella* at the cathedral of Milan from 1484 until 1522. Furthermore, some pieces in SienBC K.I.2 suggest that its compiler drew in part on repertory originating in Milan: Weerbeke's *O virginum praeclara* derives from one of the composer's *motetti missales* found in MilD 1, and the other motet by Compère included in this manuscript, *O genetrix gloriosa*, appears in no fewer than three of the Milanese

---

[47] See A. Cummings, *The Politicized Muse: Medici Festivals, 1512–1537* (Princeton, NJ, forthcoming 1991), ch. 12. I am grateful to Professor Anthony Cummings for bringing this occasion to my attention, and for providing excerpts from his book prior to its publication.

[48] Prizer, 'Music at the Court of the Sforza', pp. 154–5. Galeazzo Maria Sforza also witnessed the above-mentioned *sacra rappresentazione* by Belcari during a visit to Florence in March 1471 (Cummings, *The Politicized Muse*, ch. 12); if Compère was in the duke's service then (see above, p. 61), he would probably have attended this performance.

[49] On the *disciplinati* of Milan, see P. L. Meloni, 'Topografia, diffusione e aspetti delle confraternite dei disciplinati', *Risultati e prospettive della ricerca sul movimento dei disciplinati: Convegno internazionale di studio*, Centro di Documentazione sul Movimento dei Disciplinati (Perugia, 1972), tavola III.

choirbooks.[50] Also noteworthy is the fact that the litany-motet, to which category Compère's *Ave Maria gratia plena* belongs, seems to have enjoyed a certain vogue in Milan. Indeed, Gaffurius himself cultivated the polyphonic Litany, of which four examples by him survive in the Milanese choirbooks.[51]

[50] See the list of sources for *O genetrix gloriosa* in Finscher, *Loyset Compère*, p. 46.

Another piece held in common by the Milanese choirbooks and SienBC K.I.2 is the four-voice litany-motet *Sancti Dei omnes*, currently included in the corpus of music assigned to Jean Mouton. Like Compère's *Ave Maria gratia plena*, *Sancti Dei omnes* survives both in MilD 3 and in the earliest layer of SienBC K.I.2, as well as in at least eight other sources (see the list of sources in *Josquin Desprez: Werken*, ed. A. Smijers (Amsterdam, 1951–), *Motetten* v/46, pp. xi–xiv, to which should be added SienBC K.I.2. An edition of *Sancti Dei omnes* is found therein, pp. 28–36). *Sancti Dei omnes* opens with a prevailingly homophonic and syllabic setting of the Litany invocation 'Sancti Dei omnes, orate pro nobis'; this phrase and its music are then treated as a refrain, returning four times over the course of the piece. A tendency to a recitational melodic character is also apparent, as is a concern for variety of texture achieved through the liberal use of answering duets. Although richer in melodic and rhythmic invention and more adept contrapuntally, the composer of *Sancti Dei omnes* seems to be experimenting with the same ideas that occupy Compère in *Ave Maria gratia plena*.

Sancti Dei omnes is first attributed to Mouton in VatS 42, a manuscript from the Papal Chapel copied between 1503 and 1512; the only conflicting assignment is to Josquin, occurring in ToleBC 13, a Spanish source from the mid-sixteenth century. Mouton, however, is not documented in Italy until 1515 (L. Lockwood, 'Jean Mouton and Jean Michel: French Music and Musicians in Italy, 1505–1520', *Journal of the American Musicological Society*, 32 (1979), pp. 193–217), and while he may have visited earlier, it is highly unlikely that this composer could have created such a thoroughly italianate piece as this prior to 1481, the year it was apparently entered in SienBC K.I.2, when every indication is that he was at that time a young man just beginning his career as a singer, teacher and later *maître de chapelle* at the church of Notre Dame in Nesle, outside Paris (the possibility that Mouton may have visited Italy prior to 1515 is acknowledged in Lockwood, 'Jean Mouton and Jean Michel', pp. 211–12; such a visit seems most likely to have occurred after the composer became attached to the French royal court at some time during the first decade of the sixteenth century). Moreover, the inclusion of *Sancti Dei omnes* in MilD 3 and VerBC 758 (both dated *c.* 1500) is highly suspect: neither source gives an attribution for the piece, the Veronese manuscript preserves no other work by Mouton, and none of the Milanese choirbooks transmit any other music believed to be by this composer. Both sources, however, contain a number of motets by Josquin. It can only be suggested here that *Sancti Dei omnes* may indeed be the work of Compère's colleague in Milan, the young Josquin; certainly, in their musical kinships and similar transmission histories, *Ave Maria gratia plena* and *Sancti Dei omnes* appear to derive from a common milieu. D'Accone, in 'A Late 15th-Century Sienese Sacred Repertory', pp. 144–5, foresaw the question of attribution raised by the appearance of this motet in SienBC K.I.2. Further investigation into the question of Mouton's authorship of *Sancti Dei omnes* is clearly needed, but cannot be pursued here. Worth noting, however, is the fact that at least ten motets bear conflicting attributions to Josquin and Mouton, and that the likelihood of mistaking one composer's work for the other's was acknowledged as early as 1521 by the poet Teofilo Folengo (see H. M. Brown, 'Mouton, Jean', *The New Grove Dictionary*, xii, p. 657).

[51] Litany-motets by Gaffurius include *O beate Sebastiane*, *Virgo Dei digna* and *Salve mater Salvatoris* in MilD 1, and *Solemnitas laudabilis* in the fragmentary MilD 4. The flowering of the polyphonic Litany setting during the sixteenth century is discussed in Roth, *Die mehrstimmigen lateinischen Litaneikompositionen*.

Example 4

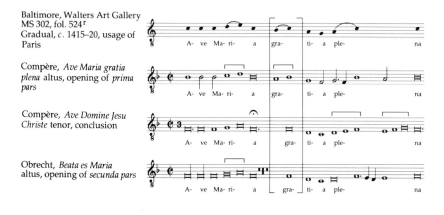

Baltimore, Walters Art Gallery
MS 302, fol. 524ʳ
Gradual, c. 1415–20, usage of
Paris

Compère, *Ave Maria gratia
plena* altus, opening of *prima
pars*

Compère, *Ave Domine Jesu
Christe* tenor, conclusion

Obrecht, *Beata es Maria*
altus, opening of *secunda pars*

Certain details transmitted in the cantus firmus and in the text of Compère's *Ave Maria gratia plena*, however, suggest the French heritage of the motet's creator. The melody of the sequence *Ave Maria gratia plena* served the composer as a cantus firmus in one other motet, the *loco Deo gratias* of the *motetti missales* cycle *Ave Domine Jesu Christe*, a composition almost certainly written while Compère was working in Milan. The version of the sequence tune here employed differs in one small but potentially significant way from the same melody as it appears in *Ave Maria gratia plena* (see Example 4). Of particular interest is the fact that the variant included in the litany-motet corresponds to the version of this sequence as sung in the usage of Paris (see the top line in Example 4), in which city Compère probably worked before his Italian sojourn. We can only speculate that the composer might have drawn on his recent memory of a familiar Parisian chant in creating the cantus firmus for a motet composed either in Milan or in anticipation of his return to France some time after the assassination of Duke Galeazzo Maria in 1476.

Another aspect of the work's transmission may hint at a French connection as well: the roster of saints to whom exhortations are directed in *Ave Maria gratia plena*, while changing from source to source, frequently includes the French martyr St Quintinus (Quentin) and/or St Ludovicus, possibly Louis, King of France.[52] These two names are fairly consistently transmitted in this motet along with those of the universally favourite intercessors Raphael, Gabriel, Francis, Martin and Nicholas; the names of other local or regional saints, apparently inserted on the initiative of local scribes, make only isolated appearances.[53] St Louis of France received little attention on the Italian peninsula, and St Quentin, while not unknown in Italy, enjoyed only minor status. Both saints, however, help to characterise the liturgical calendar of Paris, and St Quentin in particular suggests a connection to Compère in France: the composer was to obtain a canonry at the collegiate church of St Quentin by 1491, and he eventually retired there.[54] It must be noted, however, that neither Quentin nor Louis is mentioned in what appears to be the earliest source of Compère's *Ave Maria gratia plena* (SienBC K.I.2) or in the manuscript possibly closest to the provenance of the piece (MilD 3). Moreover, the mention of Ludovicus in other Italian sources might refer either to Louis of Anjou, an important Franciscan saint, or to Louis Morbioli, a late fifteenth-century Bolognese holy man whose *cultus* developed after his death in 1485 and quickly spread across northern Italy.[55] The inclusion of the French saint Quentin and possibly Louis in certain late fifteenth- and sixteenth-century sources of this motet may well signal a reintroduction of the piece to Italy after Compère's return to France; perhaps Compère, returning to Italy in 1494–5,

---

[52] Summaries of the lives of St Quentin and St Louis of France are found in *Butler's Lives of the Saints*, ed. H. Thurston and D. Attwater, 4 vols. (London, 1956), IV, pp. 229–30, and III, pp. 394–8, respectively. Ludovicus is named in TarazC 2, VatC 234, VatS 15 and VerBC 758, and St Quintinus appears in BerlS 40021, VatC 234, VerBC 758, WarU 2016, WrocU 428 and *Motetti A*. SienBC K.I.2, MilD 3 and ToleBC 21 include neither saint, and the names included in BarcBC 454 are in a cursive hand that cannot be read from microfilm.

[53] SienBC K.I.2, for example, names St Bernardine of Siena; BerlS 40021 includes St Frederick of Regensburg, WarU 2016 invokes St Lambert of Maastricht and WrocU 428 appeals to St Kilian, all three saints popular in German-speaking territories; and TarazC 2 calls on Prudentius, the Spanish Bishop of Troyes.

[54] Regarding Quentin and Louis of France in the calendar of Paris, see P. Perdrizet, *Le calendrier parisien à la fin du moyen âge* (Paris, 1933), pp. 209–12 and 246. Compère's association with the church of St Quentin is discussed in Finscher, *Loyset Compère*, pp. 16 and 19.

[55] On Louis of Anjou and Louis Morbioli, see *Butler's Lives of the Saints*, III, pp. 357–9, and IV, pp. 359–60. Of these two additional candidates for the identity of Ludovicus, Louis of Anjou appears to be more likely, especially in light of the fact that all manuscripts naming Ludovicus also appeal to Francis, the patron saint of the Franciscan order.

delivered a copy reflecting his recent French environment to the scribe of VatS 15, thereby initiating the transmission of French elements in the piece on the Italian peninsula.

The many disparate strands of evidence here woven together in order to reconstruct the chronology of Compère's *Ave Maria gratia plena* support the hypothesis that the first two sections of *Ave Maria gratia plena*, those based on the Marian prayer and the Litany, derive either from Compère's service in Milan, which appears probable, or shortly thereafter. But when did the final section based on the lauda *Beata es Maria* join the main trunk of the motet? Later sources of *Ave Maria gratia plena* reveal only that the piece existed in its final form by approximately 1495 (see Table 1), by which time the composer had already returned to France following his service in Milan, only to reappear on the Italian scene during the French invasion in 1494. Clues to the chronology of the third section of Compère's *Ave Maria gratia plena* can be gleaned through a consideration of another composition based on the lauda *Beata es Maria*, the motet by that title attributed to Jacob Obrecht.

Obrecht travelled to Italy twice during his life, both times at the behest of Duke Ercole I d'Este of Ferrara. His first visit took place in the winter of 1487–8, during a six-month leave granted by the canons of St Donatian in Bruges; he returned to Ferrara again by late summer 1504, and died there before the end of August the following year.[56] *Beata es Maria*, incorporating as it does the text and tune of a lauda and showing a marked dependence on Compère's *Ave Maria gratia plena*, probably does not predate Obrecht's first advent on the Italian musical scene.[57]

That Obrecht modelled *Beata es Maria* on *Ave Maria gratia plena* is suggested both by its textual make-up and by its choice of cantus firmi (see Table 2). At the beginning of the piece Obrecht immediately introduces the text and tune of the lauda *Beata es Maria* (see Example 5a); both the melody and the rhythm of the tenor cantus firmus employed here are almost identical with those used by Compère, even duplicating the variants noted between Compère's ver-

[56] Lockwood, *Music in Renaissance Ferrara*, pp. 162–4 and 207–10.
[57] The possibility that Obrecht may have come to know Compère's motet while in Bruges cannot be ruled out: Compère's music was circulating north of the Alps prior to the mid-1480s, and the vigorous Italian merchant community in Bruges may have furnished both a conduit and an audience for polyphony based on laude.

Example 5a. Obrecht, *Beata es Maria*, opening

sion and the tune preserved in Turin F.I.4 (see Example 2c). Obrecht then goes on to conclude the *prima pars* with texts derived from the Litany, using as tenor cantus firmus a version of the Litany tone markedly similar, in both pitch and rhythm, to that

Example 5b. Obrecht, *Beata es Maria*, opening of *secunda pars*

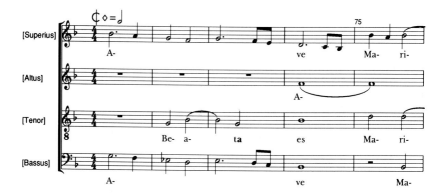

Example 5b – *cont.*

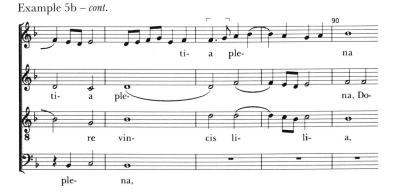

adopted by Compère. The cantus firmus of the *prima pars* is thus a combination of two separate components, the tune of the lauda's refrain and the Litany tone.

The *secunda pars* of Obrecht's motet is built on the unchanged repetition of the complete tenor from the *prima pars*, a procedure that harks back to the isorhythmic motet. Now, however, the motet becomes bitextual as the superius, altus and bassus voices enunciate the text of the prayer 'Ave Maria gratia plena' (see Example 5b). As the tenor is occupied with the melody of the lauda, the altus simultaneously intones precisely the same pastiche of melodic phrases borrowed from the sequence *Ave Maria gratia plena* assembled by Compère to carry the text of the prayer (Obrecht does not, however, incorporate the Parisian variant employed by Compère; see Example 4). This hodge-podge method of cantus firmus creation is quite foreign to Obrecht's procedure, which consistently associates a liturgical text with its correct liturgical melody.[58] And finally, the phrase 'O Christe audi nos' recurs several times in both the *prima* and *secunda partes*, and both sections culminate with all voices proclaiming this text, just as in Compère's motet. Unlike Compère, however, Obrecht does not clearly articulate this phrase as a musical refrain, choosing instead to weave it into the surrounding counterpoint.

Obrecht shows a pronounced penchant for the simultaneous combination of two or more pre-existent melodies in his sacred music; no fewer than five other motets employ this unusual tech-

[58] An excellent survey of Obrecht's cantus firmus technique is E. Sparks, *Cantus Firmus in Mass and Motet 1420–1520* (Berkeley, CA, 1963), pp. 245–311.

nique.[59] That Obrecht effected his own inimitable synthesis of precisely the three disparate elements combined in Compère's motet – the Marian prayer, the Litany and the lauda – is eloquent testimony to the fact that Obrecht must have known *Ave Maria gratia plena* in its final, three-section form.

Despite its obeisance to the materials of Compère's motet, *Beata es Maria* is in no way indebted to its model for its musical style. Obrecht's work is by comparison quite conservative, a fact already suggested by its use of slow-moving multiple cantus firmi, rigid cantus firmus design and polytextuality. The texture is dense and florid, with little imitation between parts; cadences are accomplished by the superius and tenor, and are often avoided. Chordal, declamatory passages and the lively rhythms that might suggest 'la contenance italienne' are entirely absent. In its musical style, therefore, this motet bears an unmistakable resemblance to Obrecht's other multiple cantus firmus compositions, such as the *Missa de Sancto Donatiano*, recently shown to date from Obrecht's first appointment in Bruges, extending from October 1485 to January 1491.[60] The style of *Beata es Maria* is thus entirely consistent with the proposal that the work dates from the composer's first visit to Ferrara in the winter of 1487–8.[61]

Source evidence further supports an Italian provenance for *Beata es Maria*. The motet is preserved only in Petrucci's *Motetti libro quarto* of 1505 (RISM 1505²), in which are also collected three other motets attributed to Obrecht.[62] One of these, *O beate Basili*, also survives in a Florentine manuscript of the early sixteenth century, but the other two motets, *Quis numerare queat* and *Laudes Christo redemptoris*, are unica in Petrucci's print. A brief consideration of these other compositions and of the contents of Petrucci's print in general will help place Obrecht's *Beata es Maria* in context.

[59] The other multiple cantus firmus motets by Obrecht are *O beate Basili, Homo quidam, Salve crux arbor vitae, Laudemus nunc Dominus* and *Factor orbis*. For a discussion of these compositions, see M.J. Bloxam, 'A Survey of Late Medieval Service Books from the Low Countries: Implications for Sacred Polyphony, 1460–1520' (Ph.D. dissertation, Yale University, 1987), pp. 312–66.

[60] On the date of the *Missa de Sancto Donatiano*, see R. Strohm, *Music in Late Medieval Bruges* (Oxford, 1985), pp. 146–7.

[61] The possibility that Obrecht may have composed *Beata es Maria* during the period in Bruges immediately preceding his first excursion to Italy cannot be ruled out; see above, n. 57.

[62] A useful summary of the sources of Obrecht's music is M. Picker, *Johannes Ockeghem and Jacob Obrecht: A Guide to Research*, Garland Composer Resource Manuals 13 (New York, 1988), pp. 57–87.

O beate Basili, with its polytextuality and several slow-moving cantus firmi, is an old-fashioned piece much like *Beata es Maria*.[63] This motet was certainly composed for Bruges – St Basil's relics were among the most prized treasures of the city, and the chants Obrecht employs are peculiar to the usage of Bruges.[64] In light of its style, it appears most probable that *O beate Basili*, like the *Missa de Sancto Donatiano*, dates from the composer's initial tenure in Bruges.

Quis numerare queat and *Laudes Christo redemptoris*, on the other hand, adopt a distinctly more up-to-date musical style.[65] *Laudes Christo redemptoris* relies heavily on imitation, uses non-canonic duets extensively and has several short homophonic sections, while *Quis numerare queat* emphasises chordal declamatory writing and a transparent texture in which duets also figure prominently. Most importantly, both motets do without the use of a cantus firmus. In short, these appear to be late works, markedly influenced by Italian musical style traits, and therefore are most likely to date from the last period of Obrecht's life, perhaps even from his last visit to Ferrara in 1504–5. For all three unica motets by Obrecht transmitted in Petrucci's print, therefore, an Italian connection can be construed on the basis of either style or pre-existent materials.

Indeed, Petrucci's *Motetti libro quarto* of 1505 shows a marked preference for composers with connections to northern Italy, Ferrara in particular. A statistical summary is telling: of the thirty-six attributed motets in this print, twenty-three (almost sixty-four per cent) are by composers either active at Ferrara or, like Gaspar van Weerbeke, well known there. The complexion of their only source, therefore, supports the hypothesis that Obrecht's *Beata es Maria*, *Quis numerare queat* and *Laudes Christo redemptoris* date from Obrecht's visits to Ferrara.

If *Beata es Maria* was indeed composed during Obrecht's first stay in Ferrara in 1487–8, then Compère's *Ave Maria gratia plena* had certainly assumed its ultimate form (complete with the final section

---

[63] See the edition of *O beate Basili* by Wolf in *Werken van Jacob Obrecht*, IV: *Motetten*, pt 2, pp. 85–94.

[64] The cantus firmi in *O beate Basili* are discussed in detail in M.J. Bloxam, 'Sacred Polyphony and Local Traditions of Liturgy and Plainsong: Reflections on Music by Jacob Obrecht', *Plainsong in the Age of Polyphony*, ed. T.F. Kelly (Cambridge, 1992, pp. 157–61).

[65] Obrecht's *Quis numerare queat* and *Laudes Christo redemptoris* are edited by Wolf in *Werken van Jacob Obrecht*, VIII: *Motetten*, pt 3, pp. 120–30, and IV: *Motetten*, pp. 75–84, respectively.

based on the lauda) at some time prior to February 1486, by which time Compère had left Italy for the French royal court. That the French composer's music was known at Ferrara before Obrecht's initial arrival is witnessed by the inclusion of six chansons by Compère in the Casanatense Chansonnier (RomeC 2856), copied in Ferrara c. 1479–81.[66] *Beata es Maria* thus emerges as a peculiar token of homage to a composer whose initial essays in adopting 'la contenance italienne' Obrecht may well have first encountered in Ferrara; confronted with a musical language in *Ave Maria gratia plena* quite unlike anything he had encountered in the north, Obrecht responded not by immediately attempting to emulate this novel style, but by recognising and further exploring the multiplicity of materials within Compère's motet. By seizing on the possibilities presented by Compère's cantus firmi and creating a new motet based on these, Obrecht showed himself a skilful inheritor of the centuries-old tradition of fashioning new compositions from *cantus prius facti* already employed in earlier polyphonic settings.

Another intersection between Compère and Obrecht proffers a later perspective on these two composers and their assimilation of 'la contenance italienne'. The humanistic poem *Quis numerare queat* survives solely in settings by these two composers, and, as in the case of the motets using the lauda *Beata es Maria*, Compère's effort appears to predate the version by Obrecht. As argued above, Obrecht's *Quis numerare queat*, unicum in Petrucci's *Motetti libro quarto* of 1505, probably dates from this composer's last visit to Ferrara in 1504–5. Compère's setting, on the other hand, first appears in VatS 15, a manuscript copied by a papal scribe in 1495 or shortly thereafter.[67] Compère was in the retinue of Charles VIII when the French monarch visited Rome in January 1495, and it is likely that the six compositions by Compère contained in VatS 15 were brought to Rome by the composer himself.[68] *Quis numerare queat* celebrates a peace accord recently concluded, and it seems

---

[66] See the discussion of this manuscript in Lockwood, *Music in Renaissance Ferrara*, pp. 224–6.

[67] On VatS 15, see *Census-Catalogue of Manuscript Sources of Polyphonic Music*, IV, pp. 29–30. Compère's *Quis numerare queat* is edited by Finscher in *Loyset Compère: Opera omnia*, III, pp. 9–14.

[68] This explanation for the appearance of this corpus of motets by Compère in VatS 15 was first suggested by Joshua Rifkin in 'Compère, Loyset', *The New Grove Dictionary*, IV, p. 596.

reasonable to suspect, as Finscher does, that an agreement between French and Italian forces supplied the inspiration for the motet.[69] Many treaties were struck during the French army's drive down the Italian peninsula, and one can only speculate as to which peace accord may have occasioned this piece. A logical choice, however, would be the much-celebrated concord established between Charles VIII and Pope Alexander VI, signed in Rome on 15 January 1495.[70]

Compère's *Quis numerare queat* is a five-voice motet based on the antiphon *Da pacem*, from which the fifth voice is derived canonically. Although clearly allied with the tenor motet as it coalesced in the last two decades of the fifteenth century (incorporating such old-fashioned features as a slow-moving structural cantus firmus often treated to a variety of contrapuntal manœuvres, as well as polytextuality), Compère's piece is markedly more chordal in conception, and tends to the recitational melodic and rhythmic character evinced earlier in *Ave Maria gratia plena*. *Quis numerare queat*, as set by Compère, thus achieves a carefully poised balance between the requirements of the grand tenor motet and the harmonious clarity of the polyphonic laude and frottole of Italy.

A decade later, faced with the same text, Obrecht responded with a four-voice setting, free of any pre-existent material, which attains a perfect coordination of textually induced homophony, transparent duets and motifically integrated polyphony. One phrase even calls forth a tripla section that immediately brings to mind Compère's harmonisation of the lauda in *Ave Maria gratia plena* (Example 6). Whether Obrecht knew Compère's setting of *Quis numerare queat* cannot be ascertained; certainly he makes no musical allusion to the earlier version. The two settings of this poem, although not related in the intimate way now demonstrated

---

[69] This proposal seems to find confirmation in the sources themselves: in the VatS 15 reading of *Quis numerare queat*, it is France that is exhorted to pour forth prayers, while in Petrucci's *Motetti A* it is Italy whose prayers are tendered. See Finscher, *Loyset Compère*, p. 121.

[70] On the French occupation of Italy in 1494–5, see Y. LaBande-Mailfert, *Charles VIII et son milieu (1470–1498): La jeunesse au pouvoir* (Paris, 1975), pp. 265–438. Finscher (*Loyset Compère*, p. 121) suggested the Peace of Vercelli established by Charles VIII and Ludovico il Moro in October 1495 or the French occupation of Milan in April 1500 as possible inspirations for Compère's *Quis numerare queat*, but these events postdate the composer's stay in Rome, when the six motets in VatS 15 were probably delivered to a Papal scribe.

Example 6. Obrecht, *Quis numerare queat*, excerpt from *secunda pars*

for *Ave Maria gratia plena* and *Beata es Maria*, nevertheless offer testimony to both Obrecht's and Compère's continuing interest in 'la contenance italienne', an interest sustained despite both composers' prolonged absences from its centre of cultivation.

We turn finally to the last member of the triumvirate of motets based on the lauda spirituale *Beata es Maria*, Antoine Brumel's four-voice motet *Beata es Maria*.[71] The way in which the text unfolds indicates that Brumel took as his starting-point Obrecht's motet by the same name (see Table 2), although certain essential musical differences between the two works suggest that Brumel was also familiar with Compère's setting. Like Obrecht, Brumel begins his piece with the text of the lauda, presenting its melody in the tenor voice; this cantus firmus is melodically and rhythmically almost identical with that used by Compère and Obrecht (see Example 2d). Brumel's treatment of the lauda, however, immediately evokes the final sections of Compère's *Ave Maria gratia plena* (Example 7). Following Obrecht, Brumel then continues with Litany acclamations punctuated by the refrain 'O Christe audi nos', but unlike the Netherlander Brumel seems to take Compère's lead in treating this as a structurally important musical refrain. The two five-line verses that interrupt the Litany (the sections beginning 'Maria mater gratiae' and 'Gloria tibi Domine') are unique to Brumel's setting; their use of the lauda's melody and their return to 'Beata es Maria' for the concluding line suggests that these are stanzas from an as yet unknown version of the lauda circulating around 1500. And like its two predecessors, Brumel's motet ultimately concludes with the plea 'O Christe audi nos'.

In terms of its musical style, Brumel's *Beata es Maria* inhabits a different world from that of either Obrecht or Compère, being a consummate synthesis of Franco-Flemish contrapuntal craft with the light, tuneful, rhythmically vivacious, vertically oriented Italian style of the polyphonic lauda.[72] The opening of the motet (Example 7) shows the accomplished way in which this composer absorbed the tune of the lauda into a melody-dominated, chordally conceived setting, and the ease with which he employed textural and metric contrast to differentiate discrete textual units. Brumel elected not to employ the traditional bipartite division of the northern cantus firmus motet, instead allowing the repeated textual and musical refrain of 'O Christe audi nos' to organise the piece. A highly effective contrast between duets and four-voice texture further clarifies the structure of the text, and intelligibility of text and

[71]   Brumel's *Beata es Maria* is edited by Hudson in *Antoine Brumel: Opera omnia*, v, pp. 18–21.
[72]   Finscher, *Loyset Compère*, p. 164.

Example 7. Brumel, *Beata es Maria*, opening

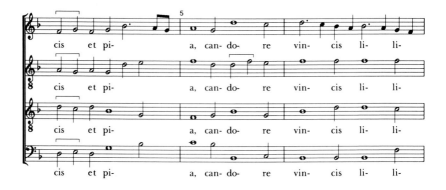

Example 7 – *cont.*

prosodically correct declamation are clearly of paramount importance.

Brumel's *Beata es Maria* is transmitted solely in Petrucci's *Motetti libro quarto* of 1505, the very source preserving the unica copies of Obrecht's *Beata es Maria*, *Quis numerare queat* and *Laudes Christo redemptoris*. The *explicit* of this print bears the date 4 June 1505, one month prior to the commencement of negotiations to recruit Brumel as *maestro di cappella* of the Ferrarese court chapel. It was not Ercole d'Este, but rather his son and heir Alfonso, who initiated these negotiations after dismissing Obrecht as *maestro di cappella* soon after Ercole's death in February 1505.[73] Alfonso's readiness to release Obrecht perhaps reflects the changing tastes of a younger generation whose interests inclined to secular music, particularly the frottola.[74] Brumel's *Beata es Maria* would certainly have demonstrated most powerfully to Duke Alfonso that the younger composer was capable of satisfying the court's appetite for music in a lighter vein, and may even have originated to serve just that purpose.

The discovery of a lauda masquerading as a cantus firmus in three motets has exposed yet another instance of Renaissance composers modelling new pieces on old, and has circumscribed the date and provenance of several pieces. Most importantly, however, the unmasking of the lauda *Beata es Maria* has opened a new perspective on the ways in which northern composers of the fifteenth century responded to the Italian musical climate. But a pressing question remains to be answered before the significance of this discovery can be fully apprehended: how exceptional are these examples? Is this group of motets on *Beata es Maria*, originating with Compère, simply another isolated example of northern musicians borrowing, directly or indirectly, from indigenous Italian genres, to be added to the handful of pieces such as the *Scaramella* settings? Or does this discovery of a lauda serving as a cantus firmus point to a more widespread way of donning 'la contenance italienne' as yet unrecognised by scholars today? To answer these questions definitively is beyond the scope of this article, but a brief

---

[73] See the recent summary of Brumel's life by Barton Hudson in 'Brumel, Antoine', *The New Grove Dictionary*, III, p. 378.

[74] Suggested by Lockwood, *Music in Renaissance Ferrara*, p. 208.

re-examination of certain key compositions strongly suggests that *Beata es Maria* was not the only lauda to furnish northern composers with the building-blocks for new music.

More than twenty years ago Sylvia Kenney observed that both Arnold de Lantins and Johannes de Lymburgia, northern composers active in Italy in the first half of the fifteenth century, apparently played a key role in the fusion of the Netherlands motet with the lauda style.[75] Both men contributed a handful of three-voice works in a decidedly chordal style, setting rhymed metrical poems of several stanzas, often in the ballata form favoured by the lauda. As yet unremarked, however, is the songlike character of certain individual voice parts whose melodic structure and rhythm echo the style of the monophonic lauda as preserved, for example, in Turin F.I.4; these melodies possess an integrity quite independent of their polyphonic settings, and may well derive from the fund of popular melodies circulating in Italy in the late Middle Ages and now largely lost to us.[76] Arnold de Lantins's three-voice *In tua memoria*, for example, reveals a tenor part whose catchy melody is constructed from the varied repetition of several strongly contoured phrases. This repetition, which is unique to this voice, recalls the lauda's tendency to repeat phrase units, a device foreign to the northern song-motet (see Example 8).[77] This composition, as well as others by Lymburgia in which the superius assumes the character of a lauda melody, survive in BolC Q15, a manuscript that also preserves five anonymous Latin and Italian laude in two to four voices.[78]

Less obvious, though still suggestive, are the choices of texts and the melodic character evident in portions of Dufay's Italian-texted compositions. *Vergene bella* sets a poem by Petrarch whose association with the lauda repertory is confirmed by its inclusion in an important source of fifteenth-century laude from the Veneto,

[75] S. Kenney, 'In Praise of the Lauda', *Aspects of Medieval and Renaissance Music: A Birthday Offering to Gustave Reese*, ed. J. LaRue (New York, 1966), pp. 495–6. See also Diederichs, *Die Anfänge der mehrstimmigen Lauda*, pp. 140–55.

[76] Diederichs suggests the possibility of *cantus prius facti* in some works by Lantins and Lymburgia; see *Die Anfänge der mehrstimmigen Lauda*, pp. 140–55.

[77] A modern edition of Arnold de Lantins's *In tua memoria* is found in C. van den Borren, ed., *Polyphonia Sacra: A Continental Miscellany of the Fifteenth Century* (University Park, PA, 1963), pp. 267–8.

[78] See the inventory of BolC Q15 by G. de Van, 'Inventory', in which each composition is identified by genre.

Example 8. Arnold de Lantins, *In tua memoria*, tenor

VenBN 7554, where the text appears in the earliest layer of this manuscript dating from *c.* 1420–40, as well as by its appearance in all authoritative sources of Leonardo Giustinian's *Laudario*.[79] Dufay's setting of *Vergene bella* cannot be called a lauda; it does not adopt the simple note-against-note style of the fifteenth-century lauda, instead assuming the character of what has been termed the song-motet or cantilena.[80] Rather, the more refined and complex construction of Dufay's *Vergene bella* seems to have made an impression on contemporary composers of laude, notably on one Frater Pauperculus, who contributed a handful of laude to VenBN 7554. His three-voice *Vergene bella gratiosa e pura* exhibits an obvious reference not only to Petrarch's poem but also to Dufay's setting of that poem; the Italian composer inverts the initial motif and fashions an opening imitation modelled directly on Dufay's piece.[81]

Connections to the lauda repertory also emerge in Dufay's ballata *Invidia nimica*, whose text could apparently also be sung to the tune of the lauda *La charne m'è nimicha*, now lost.[82] What is more, the superius melody in the *volta* section manifests the square phrasing

[79] Luisi, *Laudario Giustinianeo*, i, tavola 37, provides a list of sources containing the text *Vergene bella*; on p. 247 he notes that a fifteenth-century Roman source indicates this text could be sung to the lauda *Sacrosanta immortale et degna spina*.

[80] Arlt, 'Musik und Text', p. 56, and D. Fallows, *Dufay* (London, 1982), p. 129.

[81] See Arlt, 'Musik und Text', pp. 56–8, for a partial transcription of the lauda by Frater Pauperculus and further discussion of Dufay's *Vergene bella* and its reception as a lauda.

[82] Luisi, *Laudario Giustinianeo*, ii, p. 236. The text identified as a *cantasi come* for the lauda *La charne m'è nimicha* is 'Invidia al ciel nimicha', surely a reference to the poem set by Dufay.

Example 9. Dufay, *Invidia nimica*, opening of *volta*, superius

and rhythmic homogeneity of many lauda melodies, and is atypical of Dufay's melodic style (see Example 9).

Perhaps most intriguing is the question regarding the influence of the lauda on the *motetti missales* and other individual motets composed by Gaspar van Weerbeke, Compère, Gaffurius and others, possibly for use in the celebration of the Ambrosian liturgy in Milan.[83] Attempts to match certain textual and melodic components contained in the *motetti missales* and other presumably Milanese motets with their associated plainsong melodies have met with only occasional success, yet many portions of these works seem to communicate the presence of a *cantus prius factus*.[84] This impression is especially strong during those frequent bursts that set a rhymed, metric text in a swinging tripla, at which junctures the tenor invariably assumes the melodic character of a popular tune. Finscher first entertained the idea that such 'Italian' features might well be of Italian origin, but did not attempt to locate the suspect melodies in the repertory of Italian song.[85] With the now certain evidence that Compère did treat a lauda melody as a cantus firmus in a motet surely composed during his first sojourn in Italy, the possibility of a more extensive treatment of indigenous Italian song by northern composers invites consideration.

The motet *O genetrix gloriosa* by Compère proffers an interesting

[83] The literature concerning the *motetti missales* repertory is considerable; the most important recent contribution is L. H. Ward, 'The *Motetti Missales* Repertory Reconsidered', *Journal of the American Musicological Association*, 34 (1986), pp. 491–523, wherein earlier authors are cited. A connection between the *motetti missales* and the Ambrosian rite of Milan is generally assumed, although Jeremy Noble has argued convincingly for their more general function in conjunction with votive masses not necessarily governed by the Ambrosian liturgy; see 'The Function of Josquin's Motets', *Tijdschrift van de Vereniging voor Nederlandse Muziekgeschiedenis*, 35 (1985), pp. 17–18.

[84] The most detailed explorations of the origins of the texts and tunes employed in the *motetti missales* repertory are Finscher, *Loyset Compère*, pp. 89–117, and T. L. Noblitt, 'The Ambrosian *Motetti Missales* Repertory', *Musica Disciplina*, 22 (1968), pp. 85–93.

[85] Finscher, *Loyset Compère*, pp. 95, n. 24, and 114, n. 45.

starting-point by virtue of the fact that it, like *Ave Maria gratia plena*, numbers among the handful of compositions by Compère transmitted in SienBC K.I.2; *O genetrix gloriosa*, however, was copied not by the principal scribe but by a slightly later hand whose proposed date is *c.* 1485.[86] The italianate character of the piece was first observed by Wolfgang Stephan;[87] Finscher subsequently discussed the work as an example of a free 'Italian' motet (that is, not associated with the *motetti missales* repertory, without cantus firmus and displaying a musical style senstive to text declamation and interpretation), and argued for its creation during Compère's Milanese period.[88] Most recently, Lynn Halpern Ward has shown that *O genetrix gloriosa* belongs to the hitherto unidentified motet cycle *O admirabile commercium*, components of which are scattered within all four Milanese choirbooks.[89] Ward also argues that the so-called *secunda pars* of *O genetrix gloriosa*, beginning 'Ave virgo gloriosa', is actually a separate motet also belonging to this cycle.[90]

In its style and plan, *O genetrix gloriosa* bears an unmistakable resemblance to *Ave maria gratia plena* (see Example 10). The opening

Example 10. Compère, *O genetrix gloriosa*, excerpt

[86] For a modern edition of *O genetrix gloriosa* by Finscher, see *Loyset Compère: Opera omnia*, IV, pp. 29–30. The contributions of the second copyist to SienBC K.I.2 are summarised in D'Accone, 'A Late 15th-Century Sienese Sacred Repertory', pp. 135–43, wherein this date of copying is suggested.

[87] W. Stephan, *Die burgundisch-niederländische Motette zur Zeit Ockeghems*, Heidelberger Studien zur Musikwissenschaft 6 (Kassel, 1937; repr. 1973), pp. 68–70.

[88] Finscher, *Loyset Compère*, pp. 184–8.

[89] Ward, 'The *Motetti Missales* Repertory Reconsidered', pp. 508–15.

[90] *Ibid.*, pp. 511–12.

Example 10 – *cont.*

section in *tempus imperfectum diminutum* incorporates a modicum of imitation, tends to a thick and rather contrapuntal texture that is none the less vertically controlled, and often resorts to melismatic and unsynchronised text declamation that ignores the regularity of the poetic metre. An abrupt change of style heralds the concluding segment, a tripla section characterised by a carefully structured succession of short, homophonic phrases whose syllabically declaimed metrical text clearly dictates the musical articulation of the section. The melodic materials of this section immediately call to mind the style of the lauda as exemplified by *Beata es Maria*, and although no tune corresponding to melodies within *O genetrix gloriosa* has yet been found within the corpus of extant laude, the paired voices together present a profile of an unmistakably popular cast. This musical structure initially mirrors the poetic rhyme, resulting in a melodic repetition scheme that corresponds precisely to that of the lauda *Beata es Maria* as far as bar 24, after which three more phrase units are presented, possibly corresponding to the stanza of the unknown lauda's tune.[91]

rhyme scheme: a b a b c   a a a
musical form: A B A B C   D E F

O genetrix gloriosa, whose sources, musical styles and textual treatments all intersect with those of *Ave Maria gratia plena*, thus gives credence to the hypothesis that Compère's use of lauda melodies extended to his *motetti missales* as well. Indeed, Compère's motet cycles are replete with segments that intimate the probable presence of Italian popular song tunes disguised as cantus firmi.

The fact that only one tune from the known repertory of laude has yet surfaced in the fifteenth-century motet repertory should not surprise us: such essentially popular songs as these would have been set down in musical notation only exceptionally, as witnessed by the rarity of collections of lauda melodies as compared to the abundant compendia of lauda texts surviving from the fourteenth and fifteenth centuries.[92] Future study of the influence of indigenous Italian song on polyphonic composition of the period must

---

[91] The poetic and musical analysis of this section of *O genetrix gloriosa* is modelled on that presented by Finscher, *Loyset Compère*, p. 185.

[92] A wide selection of lauda texts in the vernacular are found in A. d'Ancona, *La poesia popolare italiana* (Livorno, 1906; repr. Bologna, 1967).

take into account these compilations of texts as well as expanding the search to include secular as well as sacred tunes.

Finally, the impact of the lauda on composers other than Compère must be assessed; especially promising are the motets and motet cycles by Weerbeke and Gaffurius. Such a project is beyond the scope of this article, but one well-known and controversial motet invites preliminary comment. *Ave Maria . . . virgo serena* by Josquin claims an even wider array of sources than Compère's motet by the same name, one of which appears to have special implications for the dating and provenance of the piece.[93] A manuscript probably copied in Innsbruck, MunBS 3154, contains this motet in a layer dated on the basis of watermark analysis to *c.* 1476.[94] Two anonymous *motetti missales* are also preserved in this source, both copied by the same scribe on the same paper used for Josquin's *Ave Maria . . . virgo serena*.[95] The motet may thus date from this composer's long tenure in Milan, lasting from July 1459 at least until the murder of Duke Galeazzo Maria Sforza in December 1476.[96]

Josquin's *Ave Maria . . . virgo serena* draws for its opening on the very sequence from which Compère (as well as Obrecht) borrowed, and then continues with a rhymed metric poem of five verses, each commencing 'Ave' and devoted to one of the joys of the Blessed Virgin. This poem, usually preserved in books of hours, originated in the fourteenth century and was widely known in France and

---

[93] See the edition by A. Smijers in *Werken van Josquin des Pres: Motetten* (Amsterdam, 1922), I/2, pp. 1–4; a partial list of sources appears on p. xiii. Additional sources are cited by Jeremy Noble in 'Josquin Desprez', *The New Grove Dictionary*, IX, p. 729.

[94] T. Noblitt, 'Die Datierung der Handschrift Mus.ms.3154 der Staatsbibliothek München', *Die Musikforschung*, 27 (1974), p. 49. Noblitt's new dating, upsetting as it does previously held assumptions about the date of Josquin's *Ave Maria . . . virgo serena*, has not gone unchallenged: Noble, in 'Josquin Desprez', p. 719, states that Noblitt's study 'rests on questionable assumptions'. As yet, however, no one has refuted Noblitt's analysis of the manuscript.

[95] See Noblitt, 'Die Datierung', in conjunction with Noblitt, 'Das Chorbuch des Nikolaus Leopold (München, Staatsbibliothek, Mus. Ms. 3154): Repertorium', *Archiv für Musikwissenschaft*, 26 (1969), pp. 169–208.

[96] The possibility of a Milanese connection is further suggested by the inclusion of *Ave Maria gratia plena* in MilD 4, one of the codices assembled by Gaffurius for Milan Cathedral. Thomas Noblitt has noted, however, that filiation study reveals the transmission of Josquin's *Ave Maria gratia plena* in MilD 4 to be contaminated and thus distant from the archetype; see his 'Textual Criticism of Selected Works Published by Petrucci', *Quellenstudien zur Musik der Renaissance I*, ed. L. Finscher, I: *Formen und Probleme der Überlieferung mehrstimmiger Musik im Zeitalter Josquins Desprez*, Wolfenbütteler Forschungen 6 (Munich, 1981), pp. 207 and 234–5.

Germany;[97] although the extent of its circulation in Italy remains to be determined, it is quite likely, considering Galeazzo Maria Sforza's francophile tendencies, that *horae* prepared in the north and containing this poem circulated at this court.[98] Furthermore, metric poems that begin each stanza with a salutation and proceed to enumerate Mary's joys were an important component of lauda poetry and music, and several of the *motetti missales* adopt poetry of this type.[99]

More interesting than the poetic structure of the motet, however, is the musical setting of its penultimate stanza. This verse is the only one treated as a tripla section and is further distinguished by the use of a canon at the fifth between superius and tenor, the tenor following the superius at the temporal interval of only one semibreve (see Example 11). The melody here treated in canon, however, shows a marked stylistic affinity with lauda tunes such as those preserved in Turin F.I.4, with short phrases of equal length, some phrase repetition, a very limited range, emphasis on iambic metre and a melodic contour featuring skips and giving prominence to triadic outlines. If this is not a melody derived from the lauda

[97] For information on the date and circulation of this poem, see F. J. Mone, *Lateinische Hymnen des Mittelalters*, 3 vols. (Freiburg, 1853–5), II, p. 5, and V. Leroquais, *Les livres d'heures manuscrits de la Bibliothèque nationale*, 3 vols. (Paris, 1927), I and II, passim. On the inclusion of accessory texts in *horae*, see R. S. Wieck, *Time Sanctified: The Book of Hours in Medieval Art and Life*, with essays by L. R. Poos, V. Reinburg and J. Plummer (New York, 1988), pp. 103–10.

[98] The preservation of nine illuminated fifteenth-century French *horae* in the Biblioteca Trivulziana in Milan lends weight to this suspicion, although none can be definitively associated with Galeazzo Maria and their contents remain to be investigated (C. Santoro, *I codici miniati della Biblioteca Trivulziana* (Milan, 1958), pp. 110–19). Also suggestive is a fifteenth-century French *hora* containing the poem set by Josquin preserved today in the Biblioteca Ambrosiana in Milan (S.P.II.162); the core of this library was assembled by Cardinal Borromeo during the late sixteenth century, and drew substantially on books once in the Sforza collection (see C. Marcora, *I libri d'ore della Biblioteca Ambrosiana* (Milan, 1973), pp. 66–71). And although *horae* were generally not included in the inventories of the Milanese ducal library, an inventory of that collection made in 1426 includes two volumes, now lost, containing prayers to the Blessed Virgin in French and Latin, both commencing with the text 'Douce dame', a poem celebrating the five joys of the Virgin (E. Pellegrin, *La bibliothèque des Visconti et des Sforza ducs de Milan, au XVe siècle*, Publications de L'Institut de Recherche et d'Histoire des Textes 5 (Paris, 1955), pp. 253–4).

[99] Prizer has drawn attention to the importance of the Joys of the Virgin in the Italian confraternities and their laude in 'Court Piety, Popular Piety'. The anonymous *motetti missale Gaude flore virginale* preserved in MunBS 3154 employs a text of this type also used in several laude, and *motetti missales* by Compère and Weerbeke also incorporate poetry with repeating acclamations (see in particular Compère's *Missa Galeazescha* and *Ave Domine Jesu Christe*, and Weerbeke's *Ave mundi Domina*).

Example 11. Josquin, *Ave Maria . . . virgo serena*, excerpt

Example 11 – *cont.*

repertory (a possibility which must be allowed), then it can only be Josquin's own adoption of 'la contenance italienne', here deployed just as earlier composers of polyphonic laude had treated favourite monophonic tunes, as the basis for a polyphonic setting in a simple homophonic style.

Italian composers seem to have recognised and appreciated the adept quotations of Italian song embedded in learned motets by their northern colleagues. In what now seems an amusing reminder that musical exchange between north and south went both ways, the sixteenth-century Italian composer Costanzo Festa skilfully wove the lauda *Verbum caro factum est* into his elaborate Christmas motet *Angelus ad pastores ait*, a work of great contrapuntal finesse that rivals the skill of any northern composer.[100] Festa signals the introduction of the lauda melody in the tenor by a sudden shift to a simple homophonic texture in a lilting tripla; these are, of course, the same cues that marked the advent of the lauda *Beata es Maria* in the motets by Compère and Brumel, and may signal the quotation of popular tunes as yet unidentified in motets throughout the fifteenth century.[101]

---

[100] This quotation in Festa's motet was identified by E. E. Lowinsky, *The Medici Codex of 1518: A Choirbook of Motets Dedicated to Lorenzo de' Medici, Duke of Urbino: Historical Introduction and Commentary*, Monuments of Renaissance Music 3 (Chicago, 1968), p. 140.

[101] W. Kirsch observes the frequency of such snippets of triple metre in the motets of this period, noting that the metrical change is often prompted by expressions of joy, hope or appeal; see 'Zur Funktion der Tripeltaktigen Abschnitte in den Motetten des Josquin-Zeitalters', *Renaissance-Studien: Helmuth Osthoff zum 80. Geburtstag*, ed. L. Finscher, Frank-

Much remains to be learned about the interplay between northern and southern music and musicians over the course of the fifteenth century, but the evidence here presented suggests that northern composers' attention to indigenous Italian melodies and their simple polyphonic settings germinated in the early decades of the century and flowered in Milan in the 1470s. Wherever future study of the question leads, it is clear that the notion of the northern composer suddenly captivated in late century by the full-blown, four-voice lauda needs refinement. Rather, it now appears that the tried and true techniques of cantus firmus composition facilitated northern adoption of 'la contenance italienne', as transalpine composers participated in the creation of polyphonic settings based on indigenous Italian tunes.

Williams College, Williamstown, Massachusetts

furter Beiträge zur Musikwissenschaft 11 (Tutzing, 1979), pp. 145–57. These sentiments are, of course, those generally expressed in the lauda repertory.

Early Music History (1992) *Volume 11*

JEANICE BROOKS

JEAN DE CASTRO, THE PENSE PARTBOOKS AND MUSICAL CULTURE IN SIXTEENTH-CENTURY LYONS*

The city of Lyons enjoyed its heyday in the sixteenth century. Favourably situated along the great trade routes connecting Italy and the north, Lyons was a busy commercial centre that saw a constant flow of goods and people through its marketplaces and fairs. Its large population was polyglot and cosmopolitan: many of its most prominent citizens were recent immigrants or members of one of the foreign 'nations' that wielded so much financial power through their connections with banks in Italy. The city boasted a flourishing book trade and an active cultural life, and its culture was in many ways as international as its citizenry. Trade links with other great economic centres of the time were often mirrored in art and music. Although artistic ties with Italian cities were perhaps the strongest, connections with Antwerp and other northern cities existed as well. A newly identified set of manuscript partbooks in the Bibliothèque Nationale is an example of one such economic and cultural link. Commissioned by a young merchant of Lyons from a composer in Antwerp, they testify to the vitality of cultural exchange along the major trade routes of the Renaissance. Furthermore, they shed new light on the careers of the copyist Jean

* I would like to thank Professors Howard Mayer Brown, Jessie Ann Owens and Richard Freedman for reading and commenting upon an earlier version of this article. My sincere gratitude is also due to M. François Lesure, for his help with archival documents, to Professor Lawrence Bernstein, for the use of several items from his magnificent microfilm collection, to Dr Frank Dobbins, for sharing his discovery of n.a.f. 1818 with me, and to Professor Henri Vanhulst, for providing much helpful information about the copyist Pollet. Finally, I owe special thanks to M. Laurent Guillo, whose knowledge of Lyonnais musical culture in the Renaissance is matched only by his generosity in sharing it with others.

Pollet, who worked at the Bavarian court with Lassus, and the Netherlands composer Jean de Castro, and provide a unique and fascinating view into the life of Justinien Pense, the patron who commissioned them.

Only the superius (f.fr. 25536) and bassus (n.a.f. 1818) of the original five partbooks (perhaps four, if the quintus part was combined with one of the others on facing pages) have as yet come to light. They are a late example of the kind of luxurious presentation manuscript often prepared in northern workshops for wealthy music patrons earlier in the century. They are copied on vellum, in a graceful humanist cursive with teardrop-shaped noteheads. The informal script and the small dimensions (305×220 mm, oblong format) are consistent with the private and secular character of most of the poetry and music the manuscripts contain. The partbooks retain their original bindings of leather – the superius tan, the bassus red – tooled on front and back with the coat of arms and motto ('Humble et courtoys') of their first owner, Justinien Pense (Figure 1; a detailed description of each partbook is provided in Appendix 1). The elaborate bindings have proved difficult to identify with a particular workshop, but they appear to have been executed in Lyons.[1] The books seem to have been assembled according to the not uncommon practice of copying a book in one city and then sending it to its ultimate destination for binding, often with the goal of matching the binding to those already owned by the person commissioning the work, for the Pense partbooks were copied not in Lyons but in Antwerp; this information is conveniently supplied on their title pages, to be discussed below.

The Pense partbooks are abundantly supplied with illuminations: each has two oval portraits, two coats of arms, three large historiated initials, one at the beginning of the first chanson in each of the three books into which each partbook is divided, and small historiated initials for the beginning of each section of all of the other pieces. The portraits at the beginning of each partbook are of

---

[1] This is the opinion of Dr Mirjam Foot, Director of Collections and Preservation of the British Library. It is shared by M. Georges Colin, Chef du Département des Collections historiques of the Bibliothèque Royal Albert Ier, Brussels, who has informed me that the floral development of the central coats of arms on the Pense partbooks is not characteristic of Flemish bindings, making it unlikely that they were executed in the Low Countries. I would like to thank Dr Foot and M. Colin for their help in attempting to identify the bindings.

Figure 1   Binding of the superius partbook, f.fr. 25536

Figure 2   Portraits in the superius partbook, f.fr. 25536, fol. 2

the same two men, each posed in the same way in both of their
portraits, but attired in differently coloured pseudo-classical dress
(Figure 2). The verso of the folio featuring the portraits is decorated
with two oval coats of arms: in both partbooks the arms on the left
are those of the Pense family (the same as that tooled on the
manuscripts' binding) (Figures 3a and 3b). In the superius partbook the arms on the right are those of the Bullioud, a powerful
bourgeois family of Lyons; in the bassus the arms on the right are
the Bullioud and Pense arms impaled, indicating a marriage
alliance between the two families.[2] The position of the coats of arms
suggests that the portrait on the left side of the preceding page is of
Pense. This hypothesis is supported by the relative age of the two
men portrayed; Pense was still a minor of about twenty years of age
when the partbooks were commissioned, and the man on the left is
obviously younger than his counterpart on the right. The man on
the right is not identified, and it is possible that the subject is the

[2]   The Pense coat of arms, still used by the Piedmontese branch of the family as late as the
first Empire, is described in E. Arnaud, *Répertoire de généalogies françaises imprimées* (Paris,
1982), III, p. 241. The Bullioud arms are described in J. Tricou, *Jetons armoriés de personna-
ges lyonnais* (Lyons, 1942), pp. 20–1. Descriptions of both sets of arms are included in the
Bullioud genealogy in F-Pn MS f.fr. 27040 (pièces originales, vol. 556).

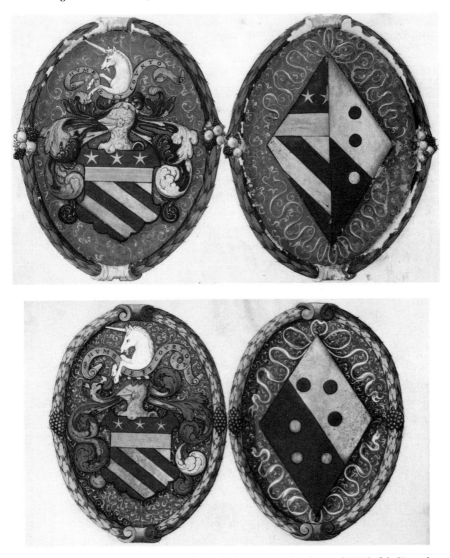

Figure 3a and 3b   Coats of arms from the bassus partbook, n.a.f. 1818, fol. 2^v, and the superius partbook, f.fr. 25536, fol. 2^v

composer Castro, although other candidates could be the copyist Pollet or the unknown illuminator of the books.

The large decorated initial of book 1 of the superius represents the Virgin, seated, with the infants Jesus and John the Baptist on her lap; that of book 2 a horizontally posed lute surrounded by pansies and leaves; and book 3 begins with a depiction of an unidentified female saint, young and simply clad, with a crown and martyr's palm (possibly a representation of Blandine, an early Christian martyr of Lyons). The small ornamented initials feature fruit, flowers, birds, insects, small dogs, rabbits and deer as well as various abstract designs. The three large historiated initials of the bassus depict, respectively, two books with an olive branch and the motto 'humble et courtoys', a lute posed vertically with a background of flowers and leaves, and a bouquet of carnations with a butterfly, a ladybird and a snail. Most of the small initials are purely decorative, on the same themes as those of the superius, but unlike the other partbook the bassus contains some illustrative initials. 'Donc o mon Dieu', for example, is supplied with a 'D' representing the Holy Spirit descending; 'Ah quantefois au son de ma guitarre' bears a tiny guitar and music book.

Each manuscript consists of three separately titled books containing twenty-two pieces by Jean de Castro for four, five and eight voices, all on French texts except for one Italian and two Latin works. Virtually all of the pieces are multi-sectional and the incipit of each section is listed separately in the tables, furnishing 120 titles in all (see Table 1). The title page of each book of both partbooks identifies the composer and the copyist and specifies that the manuscripts were copied in Antwerp in 1571; the title page of the first book of the superius, for example, reads: 'LE PREMIER LIVRE / DES CHANSONS A QUATRE / Parties, composées et mises en musique / par M. Jean de Castro // Cantus // Escriptes en Anvers par Jean Pollet Lillois demourant / audict Anvers anno 1571'.

Both partbooks contain a preface by Castro, signed in Antwerp and dated 14 March 1571 (the complete text is provided in Appendix 1). The preface leaves no doubt that the manuscripts were the result of a commission. After a short discussion of the powers and virtues of music, the composer writes: 'Now it is time for me to declare what has made me put forward this little address. It is, Monsieur, that having at your request composed and put in order three books of music, the first and second for four voices and the third for five, I wished to dedicate and present them to you...'[3]

---

[3] 'Maintenant est il temps que je declare ce quy m'a faict mettre ce petit discours en avant. C'est Monsieur qu'ayant à vostre aveu composé et mis par ordre trois livres de Musique, le premier et le second à quatre parties, et le tiers à cincq, j'ay bien voulu les vous dedier et presenter...' F-Pn f.fr. 25536, fol. 1ᵛ.

The musician honoured with this substantial order was then at the beginning of a career as one of the most frequently published composers of the late sixteenth century. Versatile and extremely prolific, he was the author of madrigals, chansons and Latin sacred and secular works for two to eight voices. Between 1569 and 1610 over thirty volumes of his music appeared in print, in Paris, Antwerp, Louvain, Frankfurt, Cologne, Düsseldorf, Douai and Venice. But in early 1571, when the Pense partbooks were signed, Castro had published only two books entirely devoted to his own music, both issued in the Low Countries, and a handful of pieces in anthologies.[4] There is no doubt that he was beginning to establish his reputation as a composer by 1571; it is equally clear, however, that he had not yet gained the international renown that he would later enjoy. No evidence exists to suggest that he was in Lyons in the late 1560s, and in fact those prefaces to his collections published between 1569 and 1580 which designate locations are signed from Antwerp. With only one exception – a 1575 volume also dedicated to Pense – they are dedicated to prominent citizens of Antwerp and Liège, indicating that the composer was probably living and working in the Low Countries when the music of the Pense partbooks was written.

The copyist Jean Pollet from Lille was also living in Antwerp in 1571, as the title pages of the manuscripts clearly state (the books were written 'en Anvers par Jean Pollet Lillois demourant audict Anvers anno 1571'). After holding posts in the mid-1550s in at least two churches in Bruges,[5] Pollet had been in the employ of the Duke

---

[4]   Six pieces by Castro appear in RISM 1569[10], the *Recueil des fleurs produictes de la divine musicque à troys parties ... second livre* (Louvain: Phalèse); for the complete contents, see H. Vanhulst, *Catalogue des éditions de musique publiées à Louvain par Pierre Phalèse et ses fils, 1545–1578* (Brussels, 1990), p. 147. RISM 1569[11], the *Recueil des fleurs produictes de la divine musicque ... tiers livre* (Louvain: Phalèse) features two works by Castro; complete contents in Vanhulst, pp. 148–9. The *Dixiesme livre de chansons à quatre parties, d'Orlande de Lassus...* (Paris: Le Roy & Ballard, RISM 1570[9]) contains one chanson by Castro which has been edited by J. Bernstein in *The Sixteenth Century Chanson*, v: *Jean de Castro* (New York, 1989); complete contents of the volume listed in F. Lesure and G. Thibault, *Bibliographie des éditions d'Adrian Le Roy et Robert Ballard (1551–1598)* (Paris, 1955), p. 142. The two prints entirely devoted to Castro's music are *Il primo libro, di madrigali, canzoni & motetti à tre voci...* (Antwerp: Veuve Jean de Laet, 1569) and the *Chansons et madrigales à quatre parties...* (Louvain: Phalèse, 1570); complete contents of the latter in Vanhulst, p. 155. None of these volumes shares any music with the Pense partbooks.

[5]   From 1555 to 1557 a Jan Pollet 'uit Rijsel' ('of Lille') filled various posts at the church of St Jacques in Bruges. A. Dewitte, 'Zangmeesters, organisten en schoolmeesters aan de Sint-Jacobparochie te Brugge 1419–1591', *Biekorf*, 72 (1971), pp. 337 and 347; see also Dewitte, 'De geestelijkheid van de Brugse Lievevrouwkerk in de 16de eeuw', *Annales de la*

of Bavaria in Munich, where he worked with Lassus in the late 1550s and through the 1560s. He was one of the principal copyists of the Munich choirbooks and a singer in the chapel. He was a poet as well, and the author of the first piece of laudatory verse devoted to Lassus to be printed with a collection of the composer's works, a long Latin poem in a 1562 motet collection published by Montanus and Neuber.[6]

In collaboration with the painter Hans Mielich, Pollet was responsible for three elaborate manuscripts commissioned by Albrecht of Bavaria, Munich Bayerische Staatsbibliothek Mus. Mss. A (2 volumes) and B. Jessie Ann Owens has identified Pollet as the copyist of another important manuscript commissioned by Albrecht, Vienna, Österreichische Nationalbibliothek Mus. Hs. 18.744, a set of partbooks containing Lassus's *Prophetiae Sibyllarum* and *Sacrae lectiones ex propheta Job*. Pollet did not sign the Vienna partbooks, and many scholars had assumed that the scribe was Lassus himself since the script used was an elegant humanist cursive, unlike the gothic script Pollet employed for the manuscripts conserved in Munich. Owens's case was based on the similarity of elements which did not change according to the script used (such as clefs, mensuration signs and custodes) and on the resemblance of the script of the Vienna partbooks to the only other known example of Pollet's humanist cursive, the index of Mus. Ms. B.[7] The Pense partbooks were signed by Pollet, and were copied in a humanist

Société d'Émulation de Bruges, 107 (1970), p. 113. Pollet seems to have worked at St Sauveur in Bruges from January to April 1559; he was dismissed for being 'incurious concerning singing and negligent in attending the Offices'; Dewitte, 'De Kapittelschool van de collegiale Sint-Salvator te Brugge 1514–1594', *Annales de la Société d'Émulation de Bruges*, 104 (1967), pp. 41 and 52. A Jan Polet who was *magister cantus* at St Gilles in Bruges in 1564–6 is identified as being from Hainaut; Dewitte is probably incorrect in assuming that he was the same man as the copyist of the Pense partbooks, since the latter Pollet was almost certainly in Bavaria by then. Dewitte, 'Zangmeesters, "schoolmeesters" en organisten aan de Sint-Gilleskerk te Brugge, ca. 1471–ca. 1570', *Biekorf*, 77 (1977), pp. 92 and 99. I would like to thank M. Henri Vanhulst for drawing Dewitte's work to my attention.

[6] H. Leuchtmann, *Orlando di Lasso* (Wiesbaden, 1976), I, pp. 264–6; the entire poem is reproduced on p. 267. On the Munich choirbooks, see J.J. Maier, *Die musikalischen Handschriften der K. Hof- und Staatsbibliothek* (Munich, 1879); manuscripts copied by Pollet are discussed on pp. 9–13, 49–51 and 89–94. See also M. Bente, *Neue Wege der Quellenkritik und die Biographie Ludwig Senfls* (Wiesbaden; 1968), pp. 18–29.

[7] *Vienna, Oesterreichische Nationalbibliothek, Musiksammlung, Mus. Hs. 18.744*, Renaissance Music in Facsimile 25 (New York, 1986), pp. vi–vii. On Pollet and Mus. Ms. B, see Owens, 'An Illuminated Manuscript of Motets by Cipriano de Rore (München, Bayerische Staatsbibliothek, Mus. Ms. B)' (Ph.D. dissertation, Princeton University, 1978).

cursive exactly matching that of the Vienna partbooks, including the idiosyncratic upper-case 'I', 'E', 'B' and 'P', and the lower-case 'g' and 'h' as well as the occasional use of 'ß' for a double 's' (Figure 4). The rediscovery of the Pense partbooks confirms Owens's hypothesis about the identity of the copyist of Vienna 18.744 and furthermore provides new information about Pollet's later career: according to Wolfgang Boetticher, Pollet left Munich some time around 1570.[8] Until now his whereabouts after his departure were unknown; the partbooks provide evidence that he was established in Antwerp by early 1571.

One of the issues about the Pense partbooks needing to be addressed is how a merchant from Lyons came to commission manuscripts copied in Antwerp and containing works written in the Low Countries by a native composer. The patron Justinien Pense[9] was the scion of one of the most important Lyonnais merchant families engaged in textile trade with Antwerp. Documents concerning their activities are, happily, extremely well preserved; for several decades the Penses relied on the services of their friend and neighbour, the notary Benoist Dutroncy, whose records are among the most complete of the sixteenth-century notarial series now housed in the Archives Départementales du Rhône. The Pense trading house has thus attracted the attention of historians interested in the economic development of Lyons during the Renaissance, although until now Justinien's role as a patron of the arts has largely been ignored.[10]

---

[8] *Orlando di Lasso und seine Zeit* (Kassel, 1958), pp. 170–1.

[9] The surname also appears as Panse, Panze or Pansa in documents from the sixteenth century.

[10] Richard Gascon's excellent article 'Lyon, marché de l'industrie des Pays-Bas au XVIe siècle et les activités commerciales de la maison Panse (1481–1580)', *Cahiers d'Histoire Publiés par les Universités de Clermont, Lyon et Grenoble*, 7/4 (1962), pp. 493–536, is a detailed study of the Pense trade with the Low Countries, and is the basis for the following summary of the family's history. See also Gascon, *Grand commerce et vie urbaine au XVIe siècle: Lyon et ses marchands*, 2 vols. (Paris, 1971); E. Coornaert, *Les Français et le commerce international à Anvers*, 2 vols. (Paris, 1961); and H.-L. and J. Baudrier, *Bibliographie lyonnaise*, 12 vols. (Lyons and Paris, 1985–1921; reprint, Paris, 1964), which all contain frequent references to the Penses. On Dutroncy, who combined his notarial activities with a remarkable career as a politician, translator and author, see J. Tricou, *Benoît Du Troncy, 1525–1530–1599, notaire, secrétaire de la ville, ligueur et écrivain lyonnais* (Lyons, 1953 [*Albums du Crocodile*, 21ᵉ année]). Dutroncy's best-known work is a satire of notarial procedure entitled *Formulaire fort recreatif de tous contractz, donations, testamens, codicilles et autres actes qui sont faicts et passez devant notaires et tesmoings* (Lyons, 1593) which he published under the pseudonym 'Bredin le Cocu'.

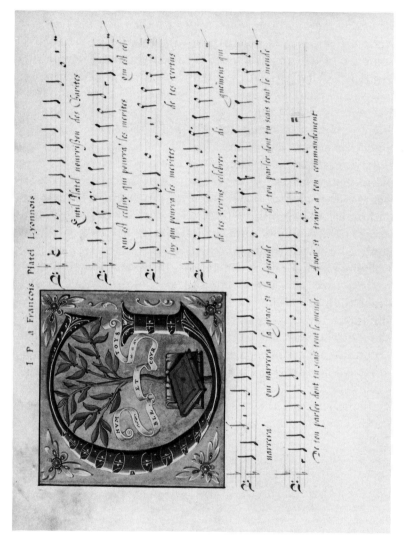

Figure 4   Jean Pollet's humanist cursive script, n.a.f. 1818, fol. 4ᵛ

The family business was founded by two brothers, Bernardin and Jerosme Pense, originally from Piedmont and naturalised as French citizens in 1481. Under the inspired direction of Jerosme, the house flourished and rapidly became one of the most important in Lyons. When Jerosme died in 1529, the business passed into the hands of his two nephews Pierre and Gerardin. It was Gerardin, Justinien's father, who brought it to its greatest prosperity, adding shops in Paris and Antwerp to the store in Lyons. He was politically active as well, serving in the Consulate of Lyons in 1540–2, 1550–2 and 1561–2. The position of his family was further consolidated by his advantageous marriage to Marguerite Pournas, daughter of a powerful spice merchant.

When Pierre Pense died in 1562, his portion of the business passed into the hands of his son Cesar, and after Gerardin's death three years later his son Justinien inherited his share of the house as well as its management. Justinien was still a minor in 1565, however, and Gerardin's will specifies that a group of guardians, including his wife Pournas and her nephew Nicolas de Vignebien, should direct the family business until Justinien came of age.[11] Their administration appears to have been successful, since in 1569 the Pense trade with Antwerp reached its zenith and the volume of merchandise they imported exceeded that of any other Lyonnais house dealing in goods from the Low Countries.[12] It seems likely that Justinien, then learning the family trade, travelled at least occasionally to Antwerp during the late 1560s; his acquaintance with Castro and his music probably dates from this period. The Pense finances were furthermore exceptionally healthy around the time the partbooks were commissioned, permitting large expenditures on luxury items such as illuminated music manuscripts.

Pense's involvement in the compilation of the manuscripts was not limited to commissioning and paying for them. He was also the

---

[11] Will of Gerardin Pense, Lyons, Archives Départementales, 3 E 579 (14 March 1565). According to the will Justinien would reach full majority at the age of twenty-five, although it is not clear which year this would be. As he was of marriageable age in 1571 but not yet twenty-five in 1570, he was probably between fifteen and twenty years old at the time of Gerardin's death. The baptismal registers of St Paul, the parish church of the Penses and one of those who archives were partially destroyed during the Protestant occupation of 1562, are missing for the years around 1550 when Justinien's birth would have been recorded.

[12] Gascon, 'Lyon, marché de l'industrie', p. 516.

author of a large number of the texts Castro set to music. Most of his poems were addressed to members of his family and to friends and teachers in Lyons, and although often poetically less than inspired they provide a fascinating glimpse at the circle frequented by a member of the wealthy Lyonnais merchant class as well as offering a view into the domestic life of the Pense family.

The most developed (and certainly the most diverting) series of texts is composed of a lengthy exchange, between Pense and his mother Pournas, that makes up over three-quarters of the *premier livre* of the manuscripts. In a set of twelve chansons, the first marked 'Margarite Pourvas [*sic*] à son filz', Pournas laments her son's lack of filial duty in consorting with an unsuitable woman by the name of Orlandine. She cannot stop him from seeing Orlandine, but it is within her power to prevent their marriage:

> Have you then truly, my son, such base cowardice,
> That you would forget one that holds you so dear,
> And set aside all of your parental ties,
> For one who can only claim to prevent your well-being,
> And no matter how much they say she is in love with you,
> Never will I permit her to become your wife.[13]

Justinien replies ('Justinien Pense à sa mere', fol. 13ᵛ) with twelve chansons describing the beauty of Orlandine, his sorrow at offending his mother and finally his decision to renounce his beloved in order to return to the maternal good graces. The cycle concludes with twelve chansons by Pournas (the first again labelled 'Margarite Pourvas à son filz', fol. 19ᵛ) celebrating her son's good sense.

There seems no reason to doubt that the poems are actually by Pense and his mother. Furthermore, the quarrel they describe did in fact take place, as a document preserved in Lyons makes clear. On 3 July 1570 Pournas swore out a *procuration*, or power of attorney, before the family notary Dutroncy empowering her nephew Vignebien to act in her name and:

to demand and require before all judges and magistrates that Justinien Pense, minor and son of the said late Sieur Gerardin Pense and of her, be

---

[13] 'As tu doncq bien mon fils, ung si lasche courage / De vouloir oublier celle qui t'ha tant cher, / Et mettre à non challoir tout le tien parentage / Pour une qui ton bien ne pretend qu'empescher, / Et combien qu'on la die estre ton amoureuse, / Jamais n'accorderay qu'elle soit ton espeuse.' F-Pn f.fr. 25536, fol. 10ᵛ. Punctuation in all texts cited from the manuscripts is mine; texts have been edited from the superius.

forbidden to contract marriage with Jeanne Orlandini, daughter of Guillaume Orlandini of the said city of Lyons. To require as well that the said Justinien Pense be detained and imprisoned in punishment for the misdemeanour committed by him of contracting the said marriage in his minority against the wishes and without the knowledge of the said constituent his mother.[14]

The *procuration* continues by specifying that Pense was not only to be arrested but to be disinherited from the succession of both his father and mother.

Pournas was availing herself of rights granted to French parents only relatively recently; earlier in the century the only requirement for legal marriage was the consent of both partners, who merely had to exchange words of consent (with or without witnesses or parental permission) to be married in the eyes of both the church and state. This sort of clandestine marriage was practised for a variety of reasons, principally by minors who were unable to obtain parental permission to marry. In 1557 Henri II issued an edict imposing penalties on minors who married without their parents' consent and declaring most such marriages null and void in civil law. Then, in its last session of 1564, the Council of Trent declared that the reading of banns and the presence of a parish priest were henceforth necessary for a marriage to be recognised by the church.[15] The older practice of clandestine marriage was difficult to root out, however, and a phrase in the text of the Pense–Pournas cycle suggests that it was this sort of marriage that Justinien attempted to make. Pournas asks her son, 'Alas, why do you wish to secretly [*clandestinement*] leave / your mother...'[16]

---

[14] '... demander et requerir pardevant tous juges et magistratz desfense estre faite à Justinien Pense filz mineur d'avec dud. feu Sr Gerardin Pense et d'elle de contracter mariage avec Jane Orlandin fille de Guill. Orlandin dud. Lyon. Requerir aussi led. Justinien Pense estre detenu et arresté prisonnier pour la punition du delit par luy commis de contracter led. mariage en sa minorité au desceu et maugré lad. constituante sa mere.' Lyons, Archives Départementales, 3 E 572 (3 July 1570). The 'Orlandine' in Pense's poetry, rather an unusual appellation, is thus explained as a diminutive of his beloved's family name. The Orlandini were a family of Florentine merchants established in Lyons; a Jean Orlandini, probably a relative of Justinien's 'Orlandine', appears on a 1571 tax list cited by Gascon, *Grand commerce*, II, p. 912.

[15] On the edict of 1557 and its legal implications, see J. de Coras, *Des mariages clandestinement et irreveramment contractés par les enfants de famille, au deceu, ou contre le gré, vouloir & consentement de leurs Peres & meres...* (Toulouse: Pierre du Puis, 1557), especially pp. 29–30. On clandestine marriages in general, see B. Gottlieb, 'The Meaning of Clandestine Marriage', *Family and Sexuality in French History*, ed. R. Wheaton and T. K. Hareven (Philadelphia, PA, 1980), pp. 49–83.

[16] F-PN f.fr. 25536, fol. 9.

It is not clear from the *procuration* whether Pense actually married Jeanne Orlandini or if he was in fact arrested. No record of a sentence passed on Pense appears in the minutes of the Sénéchaussée of Lyons for 1570, he was legally able to marry another woman in the following summer, and he did eventually inherit the family business, so it seems as if the document may have been intended as a warning, should he continue to oppose his mother's wishes. The family may have thought it wise to marry off Justinien as quickly as possible to someone more suitable than the unlucky Jeanne, for in the summer of 1571 he married eighteen-year-old Emeraude Bullioud, daughter of *maître* Pierre Bullioud, a prosperous bourgeois. This marriage probably pleased Pournas since it represented a step up the social ladder for the Penses, as the Bulliouds did not belong to the merchant class but had most of their wealth placed in land.[17]

The evidence of the *procuration* combined with that of the manuscripts themselves permits fairly accurate dating for the copying of the Pense partbooks and even for the composition of some of the poetry and music they contain. First of all, Pense could not have written the texts for the Pense–Pournas cycle until after the quarrel with his mother and the end of his relationship with Jeanne Orlandini; that is, they must have been written after the date of Pournas's *procuration*, 3 July 1570. Castro's setting of the texts must therefore date from the second half of 1570, and the copying of the partbooks could not have been done earlier than late 1570. This is confirmed by Pollet's title pages, which state that the manuscripts were copied in Antwerp in 'anno 1571'.

The coats of arms at the beginning of each partbook can help to narrow the time frame for the preparation of the partbooks still further. Both manuscripts feature the arms of the Bullioud family, and in the bassus the Pense and Bullioud arms are impaled. Impaled arms were borne by married women (normally from

<hr />

[17] The marriage contract is dated 20 July 1571, and the wedding presumably took place soon after. Lyons, Archives Départementales, BP 3665, fols. 139^v–141^v (Insinuations de la Sénéchaussée, 1571). The Bullioud family's notable history is amply documented in the manuscript genealogies of Lyons, Archives Départementales, Fonds Frecon, dossiers rouges, vol. 2, and in the genealogical series of the Bibliothèque Nationale; see particularly MSS f.fr. 29690 (Dossiers bleus, vol. 145), f.fr. 30953 (Cabinet de d'Hozier, vol. 72) and f.fr. 27040 (pièces originales, vol. 556). The latter contains extracts from the registers of the church of Ste Croix in Lyons, recording Emeraude's baptism on 8 July 1552. The hôtel Bullioud, with its celebrated gallery by Philibert Delorme (1536), is still standing at 8 rue Juiverie in Lyons.

families as illustrious as, or more so than, their husband's), who added the arms of their husband's family to their own. The arms in the bassus thus belong to Emeraude Bullioud, whom Pense married in the summer of 1571. It is unlikely that Emeraude's arms would have been included if the partbooks were copied long before the marriage, and their presence in fact suggests that the manuscripts may have been prepared as a gift for or in celebration of the wedding. The date of Castro's preface, 14 March 1571, may thus actually represent the date of the completion of the music for the Pense partbooks, and the copying and illumination could have been done between March and July. After the partbooks were finished they were apparently sent to Lyons for binding, since the covers do not resemble others made in Antwerp in the early 1570s but are tooled in a style sometimes seen in contemporary Lyonnais bindings. If the manuscripts were indeed prepared to celebrate the wedding of Justinien and Emeraude the inclusion of a set of songs on texts about another woman may seem somewhat curious. But it must be remembered that the outcome of the Orlandine affair was happy, in the eyes of Pense and his mother at least; Justinien recognises his error, is reconciled with his family and is saved by the grace of God and the prayers of his mother from falling into sin. Furthermore, Justinien's pride in his own poetry and in the musical settings by Castro that he commissioned may have outweighed any consideration of the appropriateness of the texts' content.

Justinien was not the only child of Gerardin Pense whose sentimental attachments ran counter to the wishes of the formidable Marguerite Pournas. His sister Marie, a young widow at the time of Gerardin's death, had to defy her mother in order to leave Lyons for Piedmont to marry Palemon Cacherano, a noble named by the Duke of Savoy as a senator in Turin.[18] Once again intimate details of the Pense family life found their way into the archives of the notary Dutroncy and onto the pages of the partbooks. On 7 April 1565, only a little over a month after Gerardin's death, Marie made a statement before Dutroncy to the effect that as a widow and of age

[18] This information about Cacherano is supplied by Pense's poem. F-Pn f.fr. 25536, fol. 51ᵛ. Cacherano was no doubt a relative of the Ottaviano Cacherano who wrote at least three Latin works connected with Piedmont: *Disputatio an principi christiano...* (Turin: Cravotum, 1566); *Decisiones sacri senatus Pedemontani...* (Frankfurt: Feyrabend, 1599); and *D. Octaviano Cacherani ... responsorum quae in causis arduis et illustribus...* (Turin: Societatem Concordiae, 1624).

(thus free to act as she wished) she was leaving Lyons for Piedmont to marry Cacherano; this marriage was arranged during her father's lifetime, she added, and was to her advantage as well as her family's. She attempted to procure her mother's blessing before leaving, but Pournas refused to see her, saying that 'she had heard that her daughter was so upset that she could not receive her well, fearing that she would fall herself into a similar unchecked rage and that she would argue in such a fashion that her life would be endangered'. Furthermore, Pournas found it 'fort mauvais et de pernicieuse consequence' that Marie should have taken her jewels and clothing and left their home without her permission, and she would never have believed that her beloved daughter should come to be so disobedient.[19]

Justinien apparently approved of the match, however, since the poems in the partbooks dedicated to his sister and to Cacherano are both filled with Cacherano's praise. Marie is lauded only by association, as it were; her sole accomplishment in Justinien's eyes seems to have been her marriage. The following section of the chanson dedicated to Marie is typical:

> Who is he who does not cherish
> The nobility of the Cacheranais,
> I do not esteem myself the least
> Among the ranks of the fortunate,
> Since his blood to ours
> Hymen has consented to join.[20]

One wonders if Justinien manifested so much approval as a means of protesting against his mother's meddling in his own emotional affairs.

Two other family members were honoured with chansons in the partbooks: Justinien's younger sister, Leonore, and his cousin Cesar. Pense admonishes Leonore, as yet unmarried, to employ

---

[19] '... qu'elle a sceu et entendu sad. fille estre tellement passionée qu'elle ne la pourrois veoir de bon oeil craignant de tomber de sa part en pareille demesurée passion et se contester de telle sorte qu'elle en tumbast au danger de sa vye. Et qu'elle a trouvé fort mauvais et de pernicieuse consequence que dès le jour d'hier lad. Marie soit sorty d'avec elle emporté ses bagues et hardes sans luy parler ny demander le congé et la benediction qu'elle dut chercher presentement. Et n'eusse jamais pensé que sad. fille qu'elle a eue tant chere soit venue à telle desobeissance.' Lyons, Archives Départementales, 3 E 567 (7 April 1565).

[20] 'Quy est celluy qui ne caresse / Du Cacheranais la noblesse: / Je ne m'estime au rang / Des bienheureux le moindre, / Puis qu'au sien nostre sang / Hymen a voulu joindre.' F-Pn f.fr. 25536, fol. 53ᵛ.

herself in pastimes suited to her station and gender ('joindre le livre à l'esguille / Et ensuivre la vertu . . .'); she should take great care to preserve her virtue and chastity, and should avoid listening to licentious chansons. (This presumably meant that the Pense partbooks were forbidden to Leonore, since they contain at least one piece, 'Pour blasmer le baiser', which would certainly qualify as an 'impudique chanson'.) The poem dedicated to Cesar Pense is a celebration of his friendship with Justinien and the friendship enjoyed by their fathers.

Of those outside the family to whom Pense dedicated his verse we are best informed about the mathematician Miles de Norry (Figure 5). Born about 1532 in Chartres,[21] he worked as a schoolteacher in Lyons until 1574, when he moved to Paris.[22] As well as teaching, he seems to have worked in trade (his first treatise was a business arithmetic) but no evidence exists to suggest that he was employed by the Penses. As Justinien addresses him as 'mon precepteur' at the beginning of his poem it seems likely that he was one of Norry's pupils.

Norry was a man of letters as well as a mathematician, and may have encouraged Pense in his literary endeavours. According to Du Verdier, Norry was in his youth the author of 'farces & Tragedies', although none were ever printed;[23] he contributed prefatory sonnets to the works of Courtin de Cissé and the *Poematia* of Jean Dorat, and was himself honoured with sonnets by Dorat and Jean de Baïf among others. His published works included a verse treatment of astronomy and astrology in four books and two short treatises on geometric instruments as well as his business arithmetic.[24] Natalie Zemon Davis has made a convincing case for

---

[21] According to the caption of the portrait printed in 1574 with his first published treatise Norry was then forty-two. *L'Arithmetique de Milles Denorry Gentilhomme Chartrain...* (Paris: Gilles Gorbin), unpaginated. On the *Arithmetique*, see N. Z. Davis, 'Sixteenth Century French Arithmetics on the Business Life', *Journal of the History of Ideas*, 21 (1960), pp. 18–48.

[22] Norry was in Lyons by at least 1567, when he abjured Protestantism there. Lyons, Archives Municipales GG 87, pièce 4, cited by N. Z. Davis, 'Mathematicians in the Sixteenth-Century French Academies: Some Further Evidence', *Renaissance News*, 11 (1958), p. 4. In 1572 he was taxed as a 'maistre d'ecole'. Lyons, Archives Municipales cc. 276, cited by Émile Picot, MS F-Pn n.a.f. 23532 (fichier Émile Picot, vol. 60). The privilege for the *Arithmetique* was issued in Lyons but the book was published in Paris.

[23] *Les bibliothèques françoises de La Croix du Maine et de Du Verdier* (Paris: Rigoley de Juvigny, 1773), ii, p. 139.

[24] *Les quatres premiers livres de l'Univers...* (Paris: Beys, 1589), *L'usage du compas à huict pointes...* and *L'usage du compas optique...* (both Paris: Lenocier, 1588).

Figure 5   Miles de Norry at the age of forty-two (from *L'Arithmetique de Milles Denorry Gentilhomme Chartrain*... [Paris: Gilles Gorbin, 1574])

regarding Norry as one of the mathematicians involved in Baïf's Parisian academy and its successor, the Académie du Palais.[25]

No other dedicatee left literary traces comparable to those of Norry, but the texts themselves and documents from the Dutroncy archives help to sketch in the rest of Pense's circle. The friends to whom he dedicated poems – Jacques Burnicard, François Platel,

---

[25]   'Mathematicians', pp. 3–5.

Balthazar Pecoul and Jean Jacques de Ferraris – all seem to have been, like Pense himself, members of the youngest generation of prominent merchant families of Lyons. All came from families with consular honours, boasting of at least one member who served in the Consulate of Lyons during the mid- to late sixteenth century. These families, from the wealthy merchant class and the petty nobility, formed a tightly closed social entity; they had a marked tendency to intermarry[26] and, as the partbooks demonstrate, to socialise together.

Pecoul, member of a merchant family whose name often appears in the Dutroncy registers from the 1560s, gave his age as 'trent huict ans ou environ' in a deposition in 1589, and so would have been about twenty years old – approximately the same age as Pense – in 1571.[27] Platel was the son of Claude Platel, a cloth merchant, leader of the Catholic contingent in the Consulate of Lyons and familiar of Gerardin Pense.[28] Burnicard was the son of a powerful Milanese fabric merchant of the same name, who was with Gerardin Pense and Claude Platel among the staunchest of the Catholic consuls to serve in the Lyons government during the religious troubles of the early 1560s. The elder Burnicard died in 1565, the same year as Gerardin,[29] and his business was inherited by his two sons, both minors. Jacques Burnicard the younger was apparently a youth of uncommon resolution; although a minor, he took control of the business from the time of his father's death, with the blessing of his guardians, his mother and maternal uncle.[30] Justinien's poem recounts Burnicard's story and testifies to his admiration for his friend's initiative, admiration perhaps tinged with envy as Justinien chafed at the restrictions imposed by his own mother:

[26] G. de Valous, 'Les familles consulaires de Lyon aux XVIe et XVIIe siècles', *Bulletin Philologique et Historique* (1962), pp. 453–73.

[27] *La Rodomontade de Pierre Baillony*... (anon. pamphlet, Lyons: Jean Pillehotte, 1589), p. 24.

[28] Lyons, Archives Départementales, Fonds Frecon, dossiers rouge, vol. 11, s.v. 'Platel' (unpaginated); Gascon, *Grand commerce*, I, p. 450.

[29] Gascon, *Grand commerce*, II, p. 508. Pense and Burnicard both probably fell victim to the plague epidemic of 1564–5. The religious troubles of the 1560s and the roles played by Pense, Platel and Burnicard are discussed on pp. 467–91.

[30] Lyons, Archives Départementales, 3 E 573 (21 March 1571), a document formally granting the younger Burnicard his inheritance and the guardianship of that of his younger brother André, explains that since his father's death he had directed the family business 'comme faysoyt sond. feu pere de la personne'.

...prudent and gracious, like a little head
Of the family, today in good and prosperous peace,
You rule your house, to the great happiness
Of she who carried you nine months in her womb.[31]

Pense may have written some of the other texts which are not specifically labelled as his work, for example *Las ne viendra jamais* from the first book, which expresses the longing of a stranger in Antwerp for his native Lyons and the woman he has left there:

Alas, will the long-awaited hour never come
When I shall see again the happy abode
Of my noble Lyons, and being home again,
I embrace as I wish my sweet Cytherée.
I curse a thousand times this miserable Antwerp,
Which keeps me here, and night and day I do nothing
But pine for the time when I made love
Kissing and kissing again that sugared mouth.
Everything here displeases me, except when sometimes
Cupid leads me to places where I see
The girls of Antwerp vaunted as the most beautiful,
  Not that my mind be smitten with them at all,
But it brings me great pleasure to contemplate in them
Some feature of the beauty of she who has captivated me.[32]

It is tempting to speculate that Pense was sent to Antwerp after the Orlandine affair; this would place him in the city at the time the partbooks were commissioned and copied, and this sonnet could have been inspired by his separation from his beloved.

If indeed by Pense, *Las ne viendra jamais* is one of his happier efforts; not so the ode *Ce dieu lascif*, with its halting rhythm, stale imagery and rather curious metamorphosis from love poem to expression of gratitude to God for salvation from the traps of love (perhaps another reflection of the Orlandine adventure?). The form of the poem (sestets rhyming ABBACC, similar to the Pense–Pournas

---

31   '...prudent et accort, ainsi qu'ung petit pere / De famille aujourdhuy en paix bonne et prospere, / Tu regis ta maison, au grand contentement / De celle qui porté t'ha neuf mois dans ses flancqs.' F-Pn f.fr. 25536, fol. 53ᵛ.

32   'Las ne viendra jamais l'heure tant desirée / Que je puisse revoir le bienheureux sejour / De mon gentil Lyon, et qu'estant de retour / J'embrasse à mon souhait ma doulce Cytherée. / Je maudis mille fois cest Anvers malheurée / Qui me retient icy, ne faisant nuict et jour / Que regretter le temps ou je faisois l'amour, / Baisant et rebaisant ceste bouche sucrée. / Tout icy me deplaist, sinon quand quelquefois / Cupidon me conduit aux endroits ou je voy / Les fillettes d'Anvers, qu'on vante les plus belles/ Non qu'en rien mon esprit pour elles soit espris, / Mais ce m'est grand plaisir de contempler en elles / Quelque trait des beautés ce celle qui m'ha pris.' F-Pn f.fr. 25536, fols. 6ᵛ–7.

cycle, which has sestets ABABCC) and its subject matter make Pense seem the likely author. This hypothesis is supported by the later publication history. In a 1592 print Castro substituted the first twelve sections of *Ce dieu lascif* for the final twelve of the Pense–Pournas cycle, combining the two pieces into one (see Table 1 (p. 138); publication history is discussed in detail below).

Ce dieu lascif is noteworthy for its concentration on an element which is prominent in much of Pense's work, a naïve and moralising brand of piety which probably stemmed from the religious climate in Lyons and the role his family played in contemporary religious controversy. Lyons was in the 1560s a city deeply divided on religious grounds. Its location as a border town close to the Calvinist stronghold of Geneva, its active printing establishment and the immense financial resources of its bankers and merchants made it a focal point of the strategies of both Protestants and Catholics. Despite the diplomatic policies of the Consulate, aimed at maintaining a stable environment for trade, clashes between the two sides were frequent and in April 1562 Protestant forces occupied the city. Justinien's father Gerardin, a Catholic and member of the Consulate, was obliged to flee Lyons and waited out the Protestant occupation in Montluel in his family's native Piedmont.[33] During his absence his wife's brother Leonard Pournas was elected as a member of the new Protestant Consulate.[34]

The Protestants lost control of Lyons in May 1563 but religious unrest continued through the remainder of the decade, culminating in the Lyonnais St Bartholomew massacre (28 August–2 September 1572) closely following that of Paris. In between were the plague epidemic of 1564–5, the worst of the century, and the disastrous flood of 1570. These catastrophes at home combined with the religious troubles in the Low Countries contributed to the creation of a highly volatile market and rapidly escalating prices. Both Protestants and Catholics interpreted the natural and economic disasters as signs of God's displeasure, and the climate was ideal for the propagation of religious rhetoric and the encouragement of lay piety as a remedy for the multiple ills afflicting the city.

It was in this environment that Justinien Pense wrote the poetry set to music in the Pense partbooks, so it is hardly surprising to find

---

[33] Gascon, 'Lyon, marché de l'industrie', p. 514.
[34] Gascon, *Grand commerce*, II, p. 481.

in his work a concentration on themes familiar from the *chanson spirituelle* and characteristic of popular literature emanating from both sides of the religious controversy. These themes include that of the contrast of worldly trouble with God's ageless serenity and of the fragility of earthly things opposed to the eternal life promised to the faithful. For example, in Justinien's poem to his sister Leonore he reminds her to think of the state of her soul, as physical beauty is only transitory:

> While, my sister Leonore,
> You are still young in age
> And while beauty still ornaments
> The springtime of your life,
> Beauty which like that of the rose
> Soon fades and is lost,
> Shun laziness and do not expose
> Your soul to the sins of luxury.[35]

Another frequently found theme is that of the dissemination of the news of God's grace, perhaps a reflection of the increased emphasis on preaching concomitant with the Reform. Justinien thus often situates his private concerns – family ties, friendship, romantic love – within a broader context of reform and self-correction which reflects some of the major concerns of the society to which he belonged.

Only a few of the texts of the partbooks are certainly not by Pense. *Je suis banny de joye et de lyesse* and *Gardes vous bien du gouffre perilleux* are settings of anonymous poems which frequently appeared in poetic anthologies starting in 1538.[36] The motet *Laudate dominum* has Psalm 150 as its text. A few other poems probably did not come from Pense's pen, although their attribution is uncertain. These include *Pour blasmer le baiser*, an uncharacteristically frank sonnet whose neatness of construction and attractive rhythm are reminiscent of the Ronsard of the mid-1550s; *Phebus oyant un jour*, an

---

[35] 'Pendant ma soeur Leonore / Qu'encor tu es jeune d'ans / Et qu'une beauté decore / De ton age le printans, / Beauté quy comme la rose / Bien tost se perd et se flestrit / Fuis la paresse et n'expose / Aux delices ton esprit.' F-Pn f.fr. 25536, fol. 55ᵛ.

[36] Both texts (in substantially different forms from those preserved in the manuscript) appear in the *Petit Traicté, contenant en soy la fleur de toutes joyeusetez...* (Paris: Bonnemere, 1538). For later appearances, see F. Lachèvre, *Bibliographie des recueils collectifs de poésies du XVIe siècle* (Paris, 1922), pp. 374 and 402.

epigramme set by both Philippe de Monte and Severin Cornet;[37] and *Bien scay que tu n'as pas*, discussed below.

A few texts in the Pense partbooks offer some clues about what the manuscripts may have been used for. According to Pense's poem *Je ne veux pas, mon precepteur*, Norry was an accomplished lutenist; it is probably not coincidence that in both partbooks the large historiated initial beginning the chanson devoted to Norry features a lute. Pense credits Ferraris with encouraging him in his own musical endeavours in the poem dedicated to his friend. But he did not write the poem which tells us the most of his musical activities, *Bien scay que tu n'as pas*, a set of interlocking quatrains addressed to him and containing his motto (the same tooled on the manuscript's binding). The poet is a musician offering his works to Pense, so it seems likely that Castro himself was the author:

> Well I know that you have no need of gold or silver,
> You have enough; and furthermore you
> Have no care or desire to amass worldly goods,
> Seeking only the treasure that resides in virtue.
>
> Thus, since your nature is to cherish
> Rhetoric, to you, with a gentle salute,
> O Pense humble and gracious, these little verses I offer,
> Newly woven of the sinews of my lute.
>
> Knowing also that you find great solace in singing,
> And that, as well as in Rhetoric, in playing instruments
> You exercise your mind, and that you are never tired
> Of listening to or singing music,
>
> And that even to practitioners of this so learned art,
> Attendance and pleasure you give: I offer you as well,
> To give you comfort, a fine harmonious song,
> Noble heart, virtue more prized than gold.[38]

---

[37] Cornet in *La fleur de chansons à troys parties*..., ed. Castro (Louvain and Antwerp: Phalèse and Bellère, 1574) for three voices, and Monte in *Sonetz de P. de Ronsard*... (Paris: Le Roy & Ballard, 1575) for five voices.

[38] 'Bien scay que tu n'as pas d'or ny d'argent besoing' / Asses en a chez toy; puis aussy ta personne / N'ha pour biens terriens amasser cure et soing, / Cercant le seul thresor qui en vertu foisonne. / Or que ton naturel à caresser s'adonne / La Retorique, à toy avec ung doux salut, / O Pense humble et courtois, ces petits vers je donne, / Recentement ourdis sur les nerfz de mon luth. / Davantage sachant qu'au chant prens grand soulas, / Et qu'aux instruments oultre la Retorique, / Ton esprit exerçant, et que jamais n'es las / Ou soit à escouter ou chanter la musique, / Voire et qu'aux professeurs de si docte pratique, / Assistence et plaisir tu fais; je t'offre encor, / Pour te donner soulas, un beau chant harmonique, / Noble coeur, la vertu plus estimé que l'or.' F-Pn f.fr. 25536, fols. 42ᵛ–43.

Although the implication is that the partbooks were prepared for the sort of amateur music-making described in the texts, particularly singing with perhaps lute accompaniment, the manuscripts themselves show few of the customary signs of use: no corrections in hands other than Pollet's, and particularly in the superius, no marks for page turns, or indeed any wear at all. The bassus shows some discoloration which could have resulted from page turns, but overall both manuscripts are in extraordinarily fine condition. The illuminations offer no clues as to how instrumental or vocal performance of the pieces in the partbooks could have been realised.

Soon after the copying of the Pense partbooks, Castro began to publish pieces from the collection; they continued to appear in print at fairly regular intervals for most of the rest of his career (see Table 1). Their inclusion in the manuscripts proves a *terminus ante quem* essential to establishing a chronology for Castro's works, since many of these chansons were not printed until more than twenty years after they were copied into the manuscripts. Furthermore, although only the superius and bassus of the Pense partbooks have so far come to light, comparison of these extant voices with later prints yields in many cases evidence of substantial revision, and shows how Castro's thinking on issues such as modal propriety and text setting may have developed in the intervening years.

In the same year the manuscripts were copied, Castro included the eight-voice psalm *Laudate dominum* in a motet collection printed by Phalèse and Bellère.[39] A few years later, he edited two anthologies for Phalèse, *La fleur de chansons à troys parties...* (Louvain and Antwerp: Phalèse and Bellère, 1574) and the *Livre de meslanges ... à quatre parties choisy des plus excellens auteurs de nostre temps par Jean Castro musicien...* (Louvain and Antwerp: Phalèse and Bellère, 1575). For the 1574 volume, he excerpted three-voice sections from two longer pieces in the manuscripts in which the number of voices varied from section to section: *Ah quantefois au son* and *Ne permets plus* were extracted from the twenty-section ode *Ce dieu lascif*, and *Qui est celluy qui ne caresse* was excerpted from the six-section *L'estoille allors*. The text of the latter chanson was by Pense, dedicated to his sister

---

[39] *Sacrorum cantionum quinque et octo vocum...* (Louvain, 1571); modern edition by H. Kammerling, Denkmäler Rheinischer Musik 17 (Düsseldorf, 1974).

Marie, but although the extracted section features the name of Marie's husband Cacherano and discusses their marriage the print has no rubric explaining the background of the piece. None of the excerpted sections bears any indication that it is a section of a longer work.

The 1575 *Meslanges* contains only complete chansons: *Je suis à toy*, *Je suis banny de joye et de lyesse*, *Je ne veux pas mon precepteur* and *Las ne viendra jamais*. Since the *Meslanges* were published in Antwerp, Castro must have thought it politic to soften somewhat the image of the city presented in the latter text; the reference to 'cest Anvers malheurée' is accordingly changed to 'cest Anvers fortunée'. *Je ne veux pas mon precepteur* has a text by Pense, dedicated to Miles de Norry, but again the print has no explanatory comment.

Two chansons from the Pense partbooks appeared in Castro's 1586 *Livre de chansons à cinq parties...* (Antwerp: Phalèse and Bellère). The composer's practice of altering texts to suit the circumstances is once more in evidence in *Phebus oyant ung jour*, which in the Pense partbooks (as well as in the Cornet and Monte settings of the same poem) has a text describing the talents of a woman named Marthe. In the print the song bears a dedication to 'vertueuse jeune damoyselle Isabeau le Fort', no doubt a young relation of the François le Fort to whom Castro dedicated his *Chansons, odes et sonetz de Pierre Ronsard* of 1576. Each time the name 'Marthe' appeared in the text it was changed to 'Isabeau' (despite the disastrous effect on the poem's scansion) and the rhythm of the chanson was adjusted in each case to accommodate the extra syllable.

In 1592 Castro started in earnest to publish pieces with texts by Justinien Pense and directly related to the Pense family, beginning with two-thirds of the Pense–Pournas cycle plus the first twelve sections of *Ce dieu lascif* under the title *Trois odes contenant chascune d'elles douze parties...* (Douai: Bogard, 1592). None of the rubrics was retained for the print, and in the preface, signed from Cologne, Castro makes no reference to the authors of the texts. The substitution of *Ce dieu lascif* for Pournas's second set of chansons means that the cycle ends with an extension of Justien's response to his mother. The title page of the print furnishes a synopsis of the new cycle: 'In the first part, the mother complains of her disobedient son; in the second, the son comes to recognise the wrong he has done his mother, asking her pardon and forgiveness; in the third he detests and abhors improper love, and gives thanks to the Almighty for delivering him from amorous folly.'[40]

Finally, in 1594, Castro published a collection almost entirely composed of pieces from the manuscripts, the *Quintines, sextines, sonets*. Printed in Cologne by Grevenbruch, the volume is rather misleadingly labelled; according to the title page the works it contains were 'novellement composées'. All of the chansons drawn from the manuscripts feature texts by Pense, dedicated to his sisters Marie and Leonore, his brother-in-law Cacherano and his friend Burnicard. None of the texts was explained in the print, and virtually all of the proper names were left unchanged. The music-buying public of the north in the 1590s was hardly likely to be aware of the family connections in Lyonnais merchant circles of the 1570s, so perhaps Castro saw nothing strange in publishing works based on such intimate texts since few people would know to whom they applied. Or perhaps since Pense was no longer one of Castro's patrons, the composer felt free to use the music to his own best profit. In any case it is evident that the Pense partbooks represent a repertory from which Castro drew pieces as he needed for virtually all of his publishing career, even though this meant divorcing the texts of the chansons from the social context in which they were conceived.

Castro seems to have been pleased enough with the eight-voice *Laudate dominum*, the single piece printed in 1571, to allow it to be published without any changes. Except for a few differences in orthography the superius I and II parts of f.fr. 25536 and the bassus I and II of n.a.f. 1818 exactly match the printed version of the motet. By the mid-1570s, however, he was evidently dissatisfied with certain aspects of the music contained in the Pense partbooks; whether because he felt the music needed to be 'improved' or because he wished to take account of the tastes of the northern music-buyer in order to increase sales of the printed music is not clear. The chansons included in the two Phalèse anthologies of 1574 and 1575 vary from those of the manuscripts not only in expected ways, such as occasional missing or added accidentals or

[40] 'En la premiere [partie], la mere se complainct de son fils à elle desobeissant: en la seconde, le fils vient à recognoistre sa faute commise envers sa mere, luy demandant grace et pardon: en la troisiesme, il deteste & abhorre l'amour impudique, rendant graces au Tout-puissant de l'avoir delivré de la rage amoureuse.'

slight differences in orthography or rhythm, but also in some significant respects, indicating that Castro made thorough revisions before publishing. As the title pages and dedications of the anthologies make it very clear that Castro was the editor, the differences between the Pense partbooks and the prints almost certainly originated from the composer and not from the publisher Phalèse. The most striking of these differences is that virtually all of the cadences at the ends of sections of multi-section pieces and at the finals were completely rewritten.

For *La fleur des chansons* comparison of the print with the manuscript is made somewhat difficult by the lack of a manuscript bassus part (n.a.f. 1818 is tacet for all of the three-voice pieces included in *La fleur*, indicating that the lowest voice was probably included in the now missing tenor of the Pense partbooks). Comparison of the superius of f.fr. 25536 with the music of the print can still show, however, some of the changes Castro effected. For example, the final cadence of *Qui est celluy* was rewritten to a perfect cadence on F. In the manuscript the superius ends on G, which given the overall tonality of the cycle from which the piece was drawn, ♭F, indicates that the original cadence pitch was probably C (Example 1). An intermediary cadence on C was perfectly normal for a longer piece, but Castro seems to have thought the cadence on the fifth inappropriate for the excerpted section on its own and so rewrote it to end on the modal final. It is difficult to determine the motive for the recomposition of the final cadence of *Ah quantefois au son* without the missing voices of the manuscript (the superius ends on G in f.fr.

Example 1. *Qui est celui*, bars 45–7

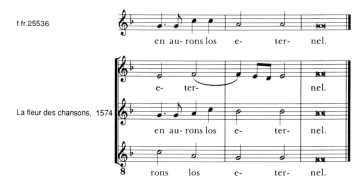

117

25536 and B natural, harmonising a perfect G cadence in the lower voices, in the print), but it is possible that it was changed for similar reasons. The final cadence of *Ne permets plus* was reworked in order to omit a four-bar cadential extension.

Castro made even more extensive changes in the cadences of the pieces printed in the 1575 *Meslanges*. Each case is slightly different, but the alterations were made along clear lines (see Table 2). Cadences in inner sections of multi-section pieces were moved away from the modal *finalis* in *Je suis à toy* (in which the cadence of the *première partie* was changed from the *finalis* G to the dominant D), *Je ne veux pas mon precepteur* and *Las ne viendra jamais* (in which the cadences of the *secondes parties* were similarly moved from G to D)[41] (Examples 2a–c). Cadential extensions (most often plagal) which originally ended off the modal *finalis* were dropped or reworked in *Je suis à toy*, *Las ne viendra jamais* and *Je ne veux pas mon precepteur* (Exam-

Example 2a. *Je suis à toy*, bars 72–5 (end of *première partie*)

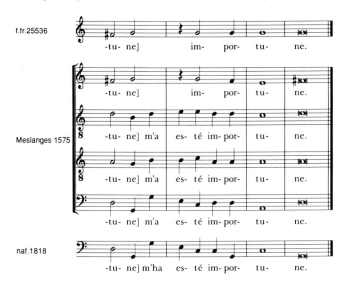

Example 2b. *Je ne veux pas mon precepteur*, bars 96–100 (end of *seconde partie*)

Example 2c. *Las ne viendra jamais*, bars 101–5 (end of *seconde partie*)

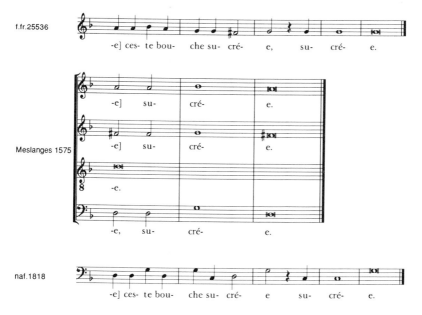

ples 3a–c). The closing bars of *Je suis banny* were completely rewritten and a lengthy section cut at the end, even though the final cadence appears to have remained unchanged. The results of the revisions are that (1) all final cadences are on the modal *finalis*, usually with the final and a dissonant suspension in the superius, (2) in the single piece of two sections the intermediary cadence is on

Example 3a. *Je suis à toy*, bars 141–50 (final cadence)

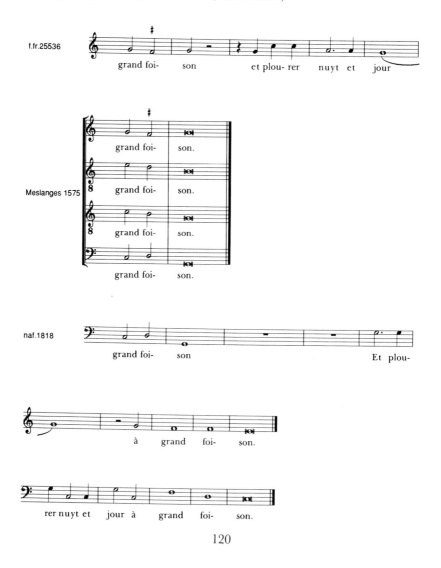

Example 3b. *Las ne viendra jamais*, bars 176–80 (final cadence)

Example 3c. *Je ne veux pas mon precepteur*, bars 155–65 (final cadence)

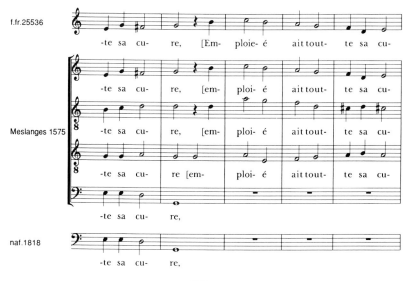

Example 3c – *cont.*

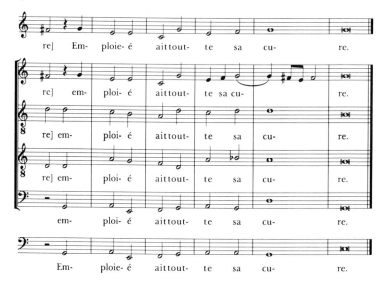

the dominant of the prevailing tonal type and (3) in pieces of three sections the cadences alternate final, dominant, final.[42]

Castro continued to adopt the same approach for later prints, and each time pieces from the Pense partbooks were published they appeared with many of the major cadences reworked. Of the two pieces printed in the 1586 *Livre de chansons à cinq*, one, *Pour blasmer le baiser*, appeared with a new closing, a perfect cadence on the modal final C replacing the older plagal extension. It is again difficult to know exactly what changes Castro made to the pieces comprising the *Trois odes* of 1594, since the only extant voice of the print is an incomplete bassus partbook preserved in Leipzig. It is evident from comparison of this partbook with n.a.f. 1818 that the majority of the changes Castro made were again concerned with cadences (see Table 3). Of the five voices of the 1594 print *Quintines, sextines, sonets*, three – the superius, tenor and bassus – are available for comparison with the Pense superius and bassus (Table 4). As in the *Trois odes*, cadences were substantially reworked; virtually all of the plagal extensions were omitted, and the final cadence pitch often

---

[42] The exception is the three-section *Je suis banny*, a piece in a tonality, E, which posed particular problems at cadence points; the original cadence pattern D, E, E was, however, altered to A, E, E.

changed, particularly in pieces in the tonal type ♮–c1–G in which many of the terminal C cadences were shifted to E or D.

Both *La fleur* and the *Meslanges* advertise on their title pages that their contents are 'put in convenient order according to their Modes'.[43] Concepts of mode and tonal structure, at least as a method of organisation, were evidently on Castro's mind in the mid-1570s. The revisions to the cadences of pieces from the Pense partbooks (which are not in any discernible modal order or grouping but which follow a poetic order possibly determined by Pense) suggest that theories of the cadential hierarchy within modal groups and the function of cadences in the determination of tonal structure were by 1574 a concern as well. The revisions almost always result in patterns in which cadential excursions away from the modal *finalis* are balanced by returns. For example, in *Si au premier apvril*, a high-cleffed piece in the flat system with F as tonal centre, the original cadence pattern for the five sections was F, C, C, C, C (the C cadences frequently following a strong F cadence just before); the revised cadences are F, C, F, C, F. In *Pendant ma soeur Leonore* (♮–G–c1) the original pattern G, C, G, C, C, G was revised to G, D, G, G, C, G. The results are cadences which function as poles for the definition of an overall tonal plan; the replacement of plagal extensions with more powerful perfect cadences ensures that these poles function audibly as well as structurally.

---

[43] '... mis en ordre convenable suivant leurs Tons.' For Castro, 'modal order' seems to have meant arranging the pieces in tonal groups rather than following an eight- or twelve-mode system in numerical order as it is now generally understood. The *Meslanges* contains nineteen pieces by Castro and fifty-two songs by other composers; the order is: 1 (a twelve-section cycle) b–c1–F; 2–7 ♮–g2–C; 8–10 ♮–c1–G; 11–13 b–g2–G; 14 b–g2–F; 15–19 (ending Castro's section) ♮–c1–A; 20–6 b–c1–F; 27–31 b–c1–G; 32–44 b–g2–G; 45 b–g2–F; 47–53 ♮–c1–A; 54–5 ♮–c1–E; 56–9 ♮–c1–G; 60–3 ♮–g2–C; 64–9 ♮–g2–D; 70–3 ♮–c1–D. Courtney Adams has observed that *La fleur* is organised by final and clef combination. 'The Early Chanson Anthologies Published by Pierre Attaingnant (1528–1530)', *Journal of Musicology*, 5 (1987), p. 530n. Castro's 1576 *Chansons, odes et sonets de Pierre Ronsard* is organised by tonal group in the same way as the *Meslanges*, although this fact is not included in the title page as it was in the earlier collection. Rudolf Rasch has suggested that Phalèse's 1576 print of the popular *Septiesme livre des chansons* was also edited by Castro, since for the first time the title page bears the label 'Toutes mises en ordre convenable suivants leurs tons' and the contents are reorganised in tonal groups according to system, final and cleffing. *Atti del XIV Congresso della Società internazionale di musicologia*, Bologna, 27 August–1 September 1987 (Torino: Edizioni di Torino, 1990), 1, pp. 310–13. See also Henry Vanhulst, 'Un succès de l'édition musicale: le *Septiesme livre des chansons à quatre parties* (1560–1661/2)', *Revue Belge de Musicologie*, 32–3 (1979), pp. 97–120.

Another important aspect of the cadential revisions is the new relationship between modal *finalis* and secondary tonal goals. In the original chansons the most important secondary goal was not always a fifth away from the *finalis* (the 'dominant' in the modern functional sense). Instead, the modal dominant of traditional eight-mode theory or another modally important pitch was emphasised. In the revised chansons, however, the fifth, and to some extent the third, above the final receive considerably more cadential stress. The changes bring Castro's music into new alignment with Zarlino's recommendations about cadence pitch and tonal structure. His discussion of the proper cadence pitches in each mode in *Le istitutione harmoniche* represents a radical departure from the treatment afforded by his predecessors, who generally based their choice of cadence pitches around the characteristic rise from the final to the reciting tone in each mode. Unlike earlier theorists, Zarlino permitted principal cadences only on the first, third and fifth degrees of each of the modal scales.[44] Strict adherence to this rule would produce music in which some of the idiosyncrasies of each tonal structure were ironed out, and was a step towards the tonic–dominant polarity which would characterise later music. Although Castro did not completely eliminate principal cadences on degrees other than the *finalis* and the fifth, he certainly reduced their number, and his revisions may have been inspired by a new familiarity with the theories of Zarlino or of one of his followers.

The other sort of significant revision Castro effected in later prints of the Pense partbook music concerns alterations in rhythm. In several of the pieces, sections of printed chansons differ in rhythm and text underlay – although not in pitch – from the version preserved in the partbooks. The voice reflecting these changes is most often the superius, although in a few pieces the bassus rhythm underwent substantial alteration as well. These differences are too great to be accounted for by vagaries of printing, and in each case the revision results in substantially better text setting. One especially clear example of this practice is found in bars 11–14 of the superius of *Ah quantefois au son*, in which the rhythmic emphasis on the unimportant word 'son' is shifted to the

---

[44] A comparison of cadence pitches advocated by Zarlino with those permitted by Aron is provided in the preface to Gioseffo Zarlino, *On the Modes* (bk 4 of *Le istitutione harmoniche*), trans. and ed. V. Cohen (New Haven, CT, 1983), p. xiv.

Example 4. *Ah quantefois au son*, bars 11–14

Example 5. *Las ne viendra jamais*, bars 81–7

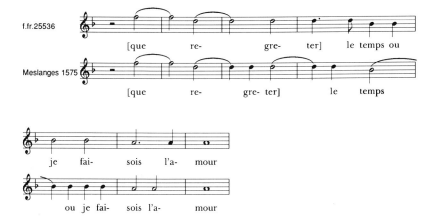

noun 'huys' (Example 4). Another is in bars 81–7 of *Las ne viendra jamais* where emphasis is shifted away from the unaccented syllable of 'regreter' and more stress is placed on 'temps', less on 'je fai-', just as it would be if the text were spoken (Example 5). Similar changes were made in bars 112–16 of *Je suis à toy*, bars 76–9 of *Je suis banny de joye*, bars 32–4 of *Ah quantefois au son* and bars 145–9 of *Las ne viendra jamais*.

Castro's revisions show him to have been aware of some of the most discussed musical issues of the 1570s. Recent articles by Harold Powers, Howard Mayer Brown and James Haar as well as the work of Bernhard Meier have shown how modal theory grew in importance throughout the sixteenth century and how it affected practice.[45] Another important trend in the chanson of the 1560s and

[45] H. Powers, 'Tonal Types and Modal Categories in Renaissance Polyphony', *Journal of the American Musicological Society*, 34 (1981), pp. 428–70; 'Modal Representation in Polyphonic Offertories', *Early Music History*, 2 (1982), pp. 43–86; H. M. Brown, 'Theory

1570s was that of textually determined musical rhythm. Its most extreme manifestation was to be found in Baïf's Académie de Poésie et de Musique (awarded its royal charter in November 1570 at about the same time as the copying of the Pense partbooks), which had as one of its major goals the development of a musical style rhythmically dependent on quantitative poetic metre.[46] But Baïf's academy represents only one facet of a general interest in rhythms directed by accurate reflection of textual stress, an interest shared by many other late sixteenth-century chanson composers. The Italian Fabrice Marin Caietain tells us in the preface to his *Airs mis en musique à quatre parties* (Paris: Le Roy & Ballard, 1576) that he has asked Lambert de Beaulieu and Thibault de Courville to correct his settings of French poetry, since as a foreigner Caietain might not have accurately reflected textual stress in his music. In the preface to *Les Amours de P. de Ronsard, mises en musique à quatre parties* (Paris: Le Roy & Ballard, 1576),[47] Anthoine de Bertrand apologises for any errors in text setting, saying that he had not been as careful in text declamation in these early works as he later became. Claude Le Jeune in at least one instance made substantial revisions between printings in a chanson for reasons of text declamation.[48]

A detailed study of Castro's revisions to the music of the Pense partbooks as well as a more complete picture of how these revisions illustrate contemporary thinking must wait until more of his works are edited. The Pense partbooks are evidently of primary import-

and Practice in the Sixteenth Century: Some Preliminary Notes on Attaingnant's Modally Ordered Chansonniers', *Essays in Musicology: A Tribute to Alvin Johnson*, ed. E. Roesner and L. Lockwood (Philadelphia, PA, 1990; I would like to thank Professor Brown for allowing me to read his article in typescript); J. Haar, 'The *Capriccio* of Giachet Berchem: A Study in Modal Organization', *Musica Disciplina*, 42 (1988), pp. 129–56; and B. Meier, *Die Tonarten in der klassichen Vokalpolyphonie* (Utrecht, 1974), rev. edn trans. E. Beebe as *The Modes of Classical Vocal Polyphony* (New York, 1988).

[46] The most substantial study of Baïf's academy remains F. Yates, *The French Academies of the Sixteenth Century* (London, 1974; reprint with foreword by J. B. Trapp, London, 1988). See also D. P. Walker, 'The Aims of Baïf's Académie de poésie et de musique', *Journal of Renaissance and Baroque Music*, 1 (1946–7), pp. 91–100; and 'Musical Humanism in the Sixteenth and Early Seventeenth Centuries', *Music Review*, 2 (1941), pp. 1–13, 111–21, 220–7 and 288–308.

[47] Bertrand's collection, including the preface, is edited in H. Expert, Monuments de la Musique Française au Temps de la Renaissance 4 (Paris, 1927). The modern edition is based on the 1578 reprint edition of the volume.

[48] The revisions made to *Rossignol mon mignon* (text by Ronsard) are discussed in detail in I. His, 'Les *Meslanges* de Claude Le Jeune (Anvers: Plantin, 1585): Transcription et étude critique' (Ph.D. dissertation, University of Tours, 1990), pp. 260–322.

ance in the editing process, not only as the earliest known source for all of the music they contain but as an important tool for understanding Castro's compositional technique and a rare example of evidence for systematic revision in music of the late Renaissance. Furthermore, the partbooks and subsequent prints offer material for the study of interaction, through the same music, between the composer and two audiences: a private patron who seems to have had some musical skill and who participated in the works' genesis, and an anonymous public of northern music-buyers.

After the signing of the preface to the Pense partbooks in March 1571, Castro seems to have remained in contact with the copyist Pollet until at least 1574, when a motet in memory of Pollet's wife (*Uxor Joannes Pollet Sara*) was printed in Castro's *Triciniorum sacrorum*[49] (see Appendix 2 for the later history of the partbooks themselves). The Pense family liquidated their Antwerp assets in 1572,[50] but Justinien probably continued to support Castro, at least initially; the composer's *Livre de chansons nouvellement composé à troys parties...* of 1575 is dedicated to Pense. The preface of this volume refers to Pense's collection of Castro's works: 'Aware, Monsieur Pense, of the good will and particular affection you bring to this noble art of music ... and with what careful diligence you have had my works collected...'[51] The first chanson of the collection, labelled 'A noble & vertueux Seigneur, Monsieur Justinien Pense Lyonnais', is Castro's setting of a poem – perhaps also by the composer – praising Pense for his patronage of music:

> Pense not only claims to love
> Sweet harmony and melodious sounds,
> But by his deeds shows that protector
> He is of music and of her offspring.[52]

---

[49] *Joannis a Castro musici celeberrimi Triciniorum sacrorum...* (Louvain: Phalèse/Bellère, 1574), fol. 45. I would like to thank Professor Henri Vanhulst for bringing this motet to my attention.

[50] Lyons, Archives Départementales, 3 E 574 (16 May 1572), cited by Gascon, 'Lyon, marché de l'industrie', p. 516.

[51] 'Cognoissant (Monsieur Pense) le bon vouloir & curieuse affection que portez à ce noble art de musique ... & qu'avec si soigneuse diligence vous faictes faire recueil de mes oeuvres' (Paris: Le Roy & Ballard). The preface appears only in the bassus part, fol. 1ᵛ; it is reproduced and the music of the volume edited in Bernstein, *Jean de Castro*.

[52] 'Pense non seulement se dit estre' amateur / De la douce armonie et melodieux sons: / Mais encor' par effect fair voir que protecteur / Il est de la musique et de ses nourriçons.' In the *Meslanges* of the same year (see above) Castro included the same piece, the only

Castro continued to maintain ties with the French business community in Antwerp through the 1570s,[53] and when religious troubles forced him to leave the Low Countries he fled to Lyons, perhaps hoping for some support from his old patron Pense. If this was the case he was probably disappointed; his collection *Second Livre de chansons, madrigalz et motetz à troys parties...*, signed from Lyons on 1 January 1580 and containing a preface explaining his reasons for coming to the city, bears a dedication not to Pense but to the consul François de La Porte.[54] The Pense family business was in deep economic trouble, and later in 1580 went bankrupt.[55] Justinien moved to Paris, where he became attached to the court of Henri III and was one of the founding members of two of the king's penitential confraternities, the Congrégation de l'Oratoire de Nôtre Dame de Vie Saine and the Confrérie de la Mort et Passion de Notre Seigneur Jésus Christ, both of which shared members with intellectual groups such as the Palace Academy.[56] Evidently the ideas of self-reform that permeate Pense's poetry of *c.* 1570 were still an important facet of his life ten years later. Pense may have been afforded an entry into Parisian academic circles by his old friend and teacher Norry, who enjoyed such connections from the mid-1570s. There Pense would rub shoulders with some of the most influential music patrons of the period, including the Count and Countess of Retz and several members of the powerful Guise family.[57]

Richard Gascon has pointed to Justinien Pense as an example of a social type he considers characteristic of sixteenth-century Lyon-

difference being that the name 'Pense' was replaced by the name 'Goovarts'. Castro apparently originally wrote the piece for an Antwerp patron and then adapted it for the Pense collection or vice versa.

53 His *Chansons, odes et sonetz de Pierre Ronsard...* (Louvain and Antwerp: Phalèse and Bellère, 1576) was dedicated to François le Fort, a merchant from Vitré established in Antwerp from 1559. Coornaert, *Les Français et le commerce*, p. 304.

54 Paris: Le Roy & Ballard, 1580; modern edition in Bernstein, *Jean de Castro*. Pense may have helped Castro make this connection, however, since his mother-in-law was Emeraude de La Porte, no doubt a relative of the consul. See the Bullioud genealogy in F-Pn MS f.fr. 27040 (pièces originales, vol. 586).

55 Lyons, Archives Départementales, 3 E 556 (19 November 1580).

56 Yates, *French Academies*, p. 327, and J. Boucher, *La cour de Henri III* (Paris, 1986), p. 197. I would like to thank Isabelle His for bringing Pense's Parisian connections to my attention.

57 On the Retz, see my article 'The Countess of Retz and the *Air de cour* of the 1570's', *Le concert dex voix et des instruments à la Renaissance: Actes du XXXIVe Colloque International*, ed. J.-M. Vaccaro (Paris, forthcoming).

nais merchant families. For a member of the third generation engaged in trade in Lyons, immigration and the early struggle to establish the business were a distant memory. Gerardin, Justinien's father, was a solid businessman: his profits were reinvested in trade, and his style of living was comfortable but by no means ostentatious. The inventory of his possessions made after his death includes plates of pewter rather than silver, woollen clothing rather than silk or velvet and furniture of no great luxury.[58] Everything about his career suggests prudence, moderation and keen business sense. Justinien was in contrast typical of the generation which looked to trade as a means of attaining 'higher' things. Once in control of the family business he used its profits to buy land; one of his purchases was the Seigneurie de Ste-Croix, and he was soon styling himself 'noble Justinien Pense, gentilhomme ordinaire de la maison du roi et seigneur de Sainte-Croix'. He had constructed at Ste-Croix a 'grand portail de pierre de taille à la rustique' which, as Gascon observes, is quite different from the simple country home owned by his father Gerardin; the elder Pense used his country residence mainly to grow fruit and vegetables and raise livestock for the family's use.

Justinien's admiration for art and learning are manifest in the poems he wrote for Castro's settings, as well as a scorn for worldly goods characteristic of one who has never had to live without them. His texts are explicit about what he considered admirable; the poem dedicated to François Platel praises Platel's horsemanship and his graceful speech (and specifically his ability to charm women with his discourse), the poems to Miles de Norry and Jean-Jacques de Ferraris laud their musical skill and the verses to Palemon Cacherano speak highly of his diplomacy, political acumen and civic responsibility. All of these attributes and pursuits were advocated in numerous sixteenth-century books of manners aimed at rehabilitating the nobility, and would have been considered appropriate to the social class to which Justinien aspired.

[58] Lyons, Archives Départementales, 3 E, unclassed inventory, 1565, cited by Gascon, 'Lyon, marché de l'industrie', p. 515. The differences in the characters and goals of Justinien and Gerardin Pense are discussed on pp. 515–17. Gascon's reference to the inventory does not correspond to any current classification in the Archives Départementales, and he did not furnish the name of the notary by whom it was copied. Repeated searches in the Archives have failed to uncover it. According to Gascon's description, the inventory contains no mention of a library; he does not specify whether Gerardin owned any music books or musical instruments.

In the second half of the century, boundaries between the aristocracy and the commoners or *roturiers* were fluid as they had seldom been before, and the relative mobility of French society would permit Pense to acquire a social status to which he had not been born.[59] He may have been encouraged in this endeavour by his mother Pournas, who contributed poetry to the Pense partbooks and who seems to have been a powerful influence in the lives of all of her children. Justinien's cultivation of music in general and specifically the commission of the Pense partbooks thus seem characteristic of a desire to leave trade behind and to use the family fortune as a lever for entry into the class of the nobility. Commissioning the partbooks was an act of self-defining and representation in the same way that naming himself 'noble Justinien Pense' would be. Despite his aspirations, however, the direction his patronage took was influenced by his background in trade; Pense imported his music from Antwerp just as his family had imported fabric.

The Pense partbooks are less revealing about Castro, whose music furnished no information on the order of that supplied by Pense's texts, but they fit nevertheless into a perceivable work pattern and mentality. The dedications of Castro's printed collections show that he spent a good part of his career catering to the tastes of the merchant class and of the bourgeoisie. The list of his patrons includes not only Pense but the Lyonnais merchant François de La Porte, François le Fort of Antwerp, several members of the Hooftman family of Antwerp and numerous city officials (one print is dedicated collectively to the burghers of Cologne). Like the pieces of the Pense partbooks, much of his music seems designed for domestic consumption; Castro was one of the most important composers of the last third of the century to write a large number of two- and three-voice chansons, forms notable for their use by amateurs at home.[60] Like Pense's poems, the texts of many

---

[59] D. Bitton, *The French Nobility in Crisis 1560–1640* (Stanford, CA, 1969), is a study of the problems besetting the nobility and the solutions proffered by contemporary writers; see especially chapter 6, 'The Ambiguity of Noble Status', for discussion of *anoblissement* and the encroachment of commoners into areas previously reserved for the aristocracy.

[60] On the three-part chanson and Castro's contribution to the genre, see C. Adams, 'The Three-Part Chanson During the Sixteenth Century: Changes in its Style and Importance' (Ph.D. dissertation, University of Pennsylvania, 1974). Castro's dedication to Marguerite and Beatrice Hooftman in the *Chansons, Stanses, Sonets et epigrammes à deux parties* (Antwerp: Phalèse and Bellère, 1592) clearly specifies that the music is for the two young women to sing, accompanying themselves with the lute or spinet.

of Castro's pieces commemorate momentous events in the lives of
people whom history has otherwise passed by, as for example the
songs in his *Livre de chansons à cinq parties* (Antwerp: Phalèse and
Bellère, 1586) labelled 'Sur le mariage de Seigneur David Scolier'
and 'Sur le mariage du Seigneur Verreyken'. The Pense partbooks
are an early manifestation of a pattern that Castro would follow
throughout his composing career.

Establishing a context for the Pense partbooks is somewhat difficult, as they are in some respects unique. Manuscript sources
which can be firmly connected to Lyons are scarce. The number of
extant printed sources from late sixteenth-century Lyons is considerably greater, and here we are on much firmer ground in trying
to fit the Pense partbooks into a history of Lyonnais patronage and
musical culture.[61] Most of the individuals to whom secular music
prints published in Lyons were dedicated owed their fortunes to
commerce. Most came from families which, like the Pense, had
their origins outside France, and many supported foreign or
recently immigrant musicians. The banker Nicolas Baillivi, to
whom Didier Lupi's *Psalmes trente du royal prophet David* (Lyons:
Beringen, 1549) was dedicated, was a Lyonnais of Florentine
heritage; the merchant, banker and noted Protestant George
Obrecht, sponsor of two prints of the music of Philibert Jambe-de-
fer, came to Lyons from Strasbourg. The prints which have the
closest rapport to the Pense partbooks were both dedicated to
members of the Buonvisi family, bankers originally from Lucca.
These publications, which appeared in the same decade that the
Pense partbooks were copied, were Regolo Vecoli's *Primo libro di
madrigali à cinque voci...* (Lyons: Clément Baudin, 1577), dedicated
to Lorenzo Buonvisi, and the *Opera nuova chimata la Fama...* of
Gasparino Fiorino (Lyons: the author, 1577), a volume of the texts
only of sixty-one *canzonelle* [*sic*] *alla napolitana* dedicated to Lucretia
Buonvisi. The Fiorino volume is particularly interesting because
each of the *canzonelle* bears a dedication to a prominent lady of
Lyons; among the dedicatees are 'madamiscella di Monsieur
Giustinian Pansa', 'Madame Isabella Cionacci di Monsi. Cesare
Pansa' (Cesar Pense's wife Isabeau Cionacci, whom he married in

---

[61] For most of the following information on Lyonnais music prints I am deeply indebted to
Laurent Guillo. All of the editions mentioned here are discussed in detail in his recent
study, *Les éditions musicales de la Renaissance lyonnaise* (Paris, 1991).

1576) and 'Madamiscella sorella del Signor Cesare Pansa' (Cesar's only sister, Charlotte Pense). A survey of sixteenth-century music prints associated with Lyons also yields evidence for a Pense family precedent in music patronage. *Le troysieme livre contenant plusieurs duos et trios...* (Paris: Granjon and Fezendat, 1551), intabulated for guitar by Simon Gorlier of Lyons, bears a dedication to François Pournas, Marguerite's father and Justinien Pense's grandfather.

Thus the newly rediscovered Pense partbooks contribute to our understanding of the special character of Lyonnais musical culture. The result of collaboration between a Lyonnais poet/patron and a Flemish musician (not to mention the northern copyist and unknown binder and illuminator), they are as international as the trade fairs of Lyons itself. The biographical information they furnish about Pollet and Castro helps to fill some gaps in our knowledge of these two important Renaissance musical personalities; and the evidence they supply as the first version of music that would later undergo substantial revision offers a rare glimpse of Castro's working methods and compositional process. The later publication history of the music contained in the manuscripts seems to provide a fruitful avenue for further exploration of the dissemination, reception and consumption of music in France and the Low Countries in the latter part of the century. Finally, the unique insight the partbooks afford into Pense's life and aspirations are especially valuable for what they tell us of the cultural and social forces shaping the patronage of a sixteenth-century merchant and the working environment of the musicians he employed.

University of Southampton

APPENDIX 1

Description of F-Pn f.fr. 25536 (superius)
and n.a.f. 1818 (bassus)*

A. Make-up of the MS

1. Number of leaves: superius, 71; bassus 69 (fols. 14 and 71 missing).

2. Foliation: superius, 1–71; bassus, 1–70; top right recto; hand of Pollet. In the superius, two consecutive leaves foliated 32, no fol. 33.

* Description applies to both MSS unless otherwise specified.

3. Materials: vellum leaves.

4. Leaf dimensions: 305 mm × 220 mm (oblong format).

5. Dimensions of written block: 230 mm × 150 mm.

6. Staves: six five-line staves.

7. Gathering structure: bassus, I⁴ flyleaf–3; II⁴ 4–7; III⁴ 8–11; IV³ 12–15 (fol. 14 missing); V⁴ 16–19; VI⁴ 20–3; VII⁴ 24–7; VIII⁴ 28–31; IX⁴ 32–5; X⁴ 36–9; XI⁴ 40–3; XII⁴ 44–7; XIII⁴ 48–51; XIV⁴ 52–5; XV⁴ 56–9; XVI⁴ 60–3; XVII⁴ 64–7; XVIII³ 68–70 (stub at fol. 71). Superius binding too tight to examine gathering structure; possibly restitched in eighteenth century? No catchwords or quire signatures in either MS; both have inconsistent pattern of flesh and hair sides.

8. Annotations: superius, inner cover: label 'FR. 25,536' [present collocation]; flyleaf: 'No 3536' (ink, ?eighteenth century) [number in La Vallière sale catalogue], 'Lavall No 120' (pencil) [number in the La Vallière collection in the Bibliothèque Nationale]; fol. 2, 'suppl' (ink) overwritten 'Lavall 120' (ink); bassus, inner cover: label 'fr. nouv. acq. 1818' [present collocation], bookplate of Nicolas Yemeniz with number 659 (pencil) [number in Yemeniz's catalogue], 'R. C. 6033' (ink) [Bibliothèque Nationale acquisition number]; '2654' (pencil).

B. Handwriting and notation

1. Script: humanist cursive, Jean Pollet throughout.

2. Rubrics: see Table 1.

3. Changes of scribe: none.

4. Contemporary marginalia: none.

5. Notation: white mensural.

C. Decoration

1. Superius: (*a*): Large historiated initials (3): 100 mm sq. Fol. 4ᵛ: Virgin, seated, with Jesus and John the Baptist; fol. 27ᵛ: lute, background of pansies and leaves; fol. 49ᵛ: female saint with crown and martyr's palm. (*b*): Small historiated initials (120): 50 mm × 45 mm. Beginning of each section of each piece; fruit, flowers, birds, insects, small dogs, rabbits, deer, abstract designs, all unrelated to text. (*c*): Miniatures: two oval portraits, fol. 2; two coats of arms, fol. 2ᵛ. Right portrait, ?Jean de Castro; left portrait, ?Justinien Pense. Right coat of arms, Bullioud family (per bend argent and azure with three hurts and three plates in orle, countercharged); left coat of arms, Pense family (bendy argent and azure, chief or and the second, with three mullets of the first; crest, a demi-unicorn argent with motto 'humble et courtoys'; mantling azure lined argent).

2. Bassus: (*a*): Large historiated initials (3): 100 mm sq. Fol. 4ᵛ: two books, olive branch, banner 'humble et courtoys'; fol. 27ᵛ: lute standing

vertically, background of flowers and leaves; fol. 49^v: carnations with butterfly, ladybird and snail. (*b*): Small historiated initials (118): 50 mm×45 mm. Most on same themes as in superius, but at least sixteen initials directly related to text. (*c*): Miniatures: two oval portraits, fol. 2; two coats of arms, fol. 2^v. Portraits of same subjects as in superius, posed in same way but clothed in different colours. Right coat of arms, Pense impaled with Bullioud; left coat of arms, Pense.

D. Binding

1. Date and origin: 1571, ?Lyons.
2. Technique: leather over pulp boards; superius, tan; bassus, red.
3. Decoration: blind stamped front and back with Pense coat of arms (see C, 3 above) and labels 'superius' and 'bassus'. Superius gilded (possibly later addition). Ornamental metalwork missing on superius (small nail holes remain at centre top and bottom and on open side); bassus features four metal lion heads (two each, open side front and back; centre top and bottom are missing but nail holes remain to indicate position). Superius has later addition glued to spine, brown leather stamped and gilded 'CHANSONS / PAR JEAN / DE CASTRO // M^{ss} S. VELIN / AVEC / MIGNATUR' ('manuscript – or manuscripts? – on vellum with miniatures') with four sprigs of acorns.

E. Provenance

1. Recipient: Justinien Pense.
2. Later owners: superius, Louis César de la Beaume Le Blanc, duc de La Vallière (1708–80); Paris, Bibliothèque Nationale (acquired early 1784); bassus, Nicolas Yemeniz (1783–1871), acquired between 1804 and 1865; Paris, Bibliothèque Nationale (acquired 15 July 1867).

F. Title pages and preface

1. Title pages (fols. 1, 26, 48 in both MSS; in imitation of contemporary prints; orthography and line distribution from superius):

LE PREMIER LIVRE / DES CHANSONS A QUATRE / Parties, composées et mises en musique / par M. Jean de Castro // Cantus [Bassus] // Escriptes en Anvers par Jean Pollet Lillois demourant / audict Anvers anno 1571.

LE SECOND LIVRE / DES CHANSONS A QUATRE ET / cincq parties, composées & mises en musique / par M. Jean de Castro // Cantus [Bassus] // Escript en Anvers par Jean Pollet Lillois demourant / audict Anvers anno 1571.

LE TIERS LIVRE DES / CHANSONS A CINCQ PARTIES / composées et mises en Musique par / M. Jean de Castro // Cantus [Bassus] // Escript en Anvers par Jean Pollet Lillois demourant / audict Anvers anno 1571.

2. Preface (fol. 1^v in both MSS; orthography from superius): Au

vertueux, et discret seigneur Justinien Pense Lyonnais salut. Il nya à mon advis aucune personne de bon esprit quy ne sache que la Musique a des anciens esté non seullement honorée, mais aussi tenue en grand pris & estime, car estants les semences d'ung art tant excellent divinement plantées es coeurs des creatures humaines (tellement qu'Aristoxenus afferme hardiment l'ame estre & consister d'une Musicalle harmonie) ce n'est de merveille si les hommes du premier aage et enfance du monde estant poussés d'un instinct naturel, la trouverent incontinent apres la creation d'icelluy. Car la saincte Bible nous tesmoigne que Jubal fut le pere et maistre de ceus quy sonnent de la harpe et des orgues. Or les saincts peres recognoissans d'ung coeur non ingrat ung tel et si grand don de Dieu, en ont usé à celebrer les louanges et magnifier les oeuvres de ce grand donneur de touttes choses tresbonnes et tresparfaictes, à ce que le chant joint à la parolle de Dieu eust plus d'efficace à esmouvoir les coeurs des hommes à devotion. En oultre Socrates, Plato, et Pythagoras les plus sages quy fussent entre les Grecz eurent le soing et tindrent la main à ce que les enfans & jeunes adolescents fussent abreuvés de ceste discipline. Je pourroy encores icy mettre en avant plusieurs exemples et tesmoignages de ce quy ont cheri et honnoré cest art tant excellent pour responde à ceux quy entreprendroient le vituperer comme chose non assez digne qu'on emploie quelque travail pour parvenir à la cognoissance d'icelle, mais ce que j'en ay touché suffira quand à present. Maintenant est il temps que je declare ce quy m'a faict mettre ce petit discours en avant. C'est Monsieur qu'ayant à vostre aveu composé et mis par ordre trois livres de Musique, le premier et le second à quatre parties, et le tiers à cincq, j'ay bien voulu les vous dedier et presenter comme à celluy auquel je suis du tout affectioné, & ce principalement pourtant que je vous cognoy sur tous aultres que je sache grandement amateur de touttes vertus singulierement de la Musique tant Theoricalle et Praticalle comme instrumentale de diverses manieres. Ce sont les causes pour lesquelles je vous ay bien voulu dedier ces livres de Musique fruits de mon labeur et industrie; vous priant les recevoir avec autant d'affection comme de bonne coeur je vous les offre et presente: me reputant heureux si j'ay en cecy faict chose qui vous soit aggreable, en Anvers ce .14. jour de Mars, 1571.

Vostre affectioné serviteur Jean de Castro.

Jeanice Brooks

APPENDIX 2

Provenance of the Pense partbooks

One of the most immediate questions surrounding the manuscripts is why they have eluded the notice of scholars for so long. Nothing is known of what happened to the entire set of partbooks after they were copied for Justinien Pense in 1571; presumably they were kept by the family for some time before the set was split up and the partbooks sold individually. No trace of the missing altus, tenor and quintus parts has yet been uncovered. Information regarding the superius and bassus discussed in this paper allows us to trace their history only back to the end of the eighteenth century.

Although the superius is not entirely unknown it has been almost completely unstudied, largely because of the way it appears in the various catalogues of the Bibliothèque Nationale. It belongs to the *fonds* La Vallière, which entered the library in the eighteenth century, and it was never catalogued or described with the other music holdings.[1] After La Vallière's death in 1780, the manuscript was catalogued for a sale to be held in December 1783.[2] Two hundred and fifty-five books, including f.fr. 25536, were taken out of this part of the collection by the royal library in payment of taxes and entered the library in 1784.[3] Edmund vander Straeten was aware of its existence and included a reference to f.fr. 25536 under its present collocation in his article on Jean de Castro in *Grove*, 5th edn.[4] Lawrence Bernstein, in his *New Grove* article on Castro, transmitted the reference without, however, including the shelf number.[5]

Somewhat more complex is the history of the bassus partbook, which was acquired by the Greek collector Nicolas Yemeniz in Lyons some time between 1804 and 1865.[6] Yemeniz apparently thought he had purchased

[1]   On the famous bibliophile the duc de La Vallière and his collection, see A.-J.-V. Le Roux de Lincy, *Recherches sur Jean Grolier, sur sa vie et sa bibliothèque* (Paris, 1866), I, pp. 146–7.
[2]   G. Buré, *Catalogue des livres de la bibliothèque de feu M. le duc de La Vallière* (Paris, 1783), II, pp. 481–2.
[3]   L. de Lisle, *Le cabinet des manuscrits de la Bibliothèque impériale* (Paris, 1868), I, p. 550.
[4]   *Grove's Dictionary of Music and Musicians*, 5th edn, ed. E. Blom, 9 vols. (London, 1954 and suppl.), II, pp. 117–18.
[5]   *The New Grove Dictionary of Music and Musicians*, ed. S. Sadie, 20 vols. (London, 1980), III, pp. 877–8. I would like to thank M. Pierre Vidal of the music department and the staff of the manuscript division of the Bibliothèque Nationale for their aid in locating f.fr. 25536.
[6]   According to Le Roux de Lincy, Yemeniz moved to Lyons in 1799 and began collecting books about 1804; N. Yemeniz, *Catalogue de la bibliothèque de M. N. Yemeniz*, with preface by Le Roux de Lincy (Paris, 1867), p. xiv. See also J. Guignard, *Nouvel armorial du bibliophile* (Paris, 1890), II, pp. 476–8. A description of the manuscript was included in Yemeniz's privately printed catalogue of 1865. N. Yemeniz, *Catalogue de mes livres* (Lyons, 1865), I, p. 137.

the manuscript described in the printed catalogue made for the sale of the collection of the duc de La Vallière, not realising that the description applied to the superius partbook which had already been acquired by the Bibliothèque Nationale.[7] When cataloguing his books he thus erroneously referred to the catalogue La Vallière for the description. The Bibliothèque Nationale purchased the bassus through the bookseller Potier at the Yemeniz sale of 15 July 1867; the purchase is noted in Acquisitions Register C of the library, no. 6033. The book was assigned the shelf number nouvelles acquisitions françaises 1818 and catalogued with a reference to the catalogues of Yemeniz and La Vallière. The result was that the two partbooks were separated into two completely different *fonds* and catalogued with references back to the same description (which applied to only one manuscript). As neither book was ever included in the catalogue of the music division, it is hardly surprising that the connection between them was never made and that they have never been the subject of serious study.

---

[7] Buré, *Catalogue*, ii, pp. 481–2. La Vallière seems to have possessed only one partbook, although the catalogue does not specify for which voice. A manuscript notation in the copy of the Buré catalogue in the Salle des Manuscrits of the Bibliothèque Nationale and the notes on the inside cover and flyleaf of the superius (including the sale catalogue number) clearly show, however, that it is the partbook in question.

Table 1 *Contents of the Pense partbooks*

Folio	Title	Rubric	Later publication
1	[title page, *premier livre*]		
1ᵛ	[preface]		
2	[two oval portraits]		
2ᵛ	[two oval arms]		
3	[table, *premier livre*]		
3ᵛ–4	[blank]		
4ᵛ	(1) Gentil Platel nourisson des charités	J.P. à François Platel Lyonnais	
5	S'il est besoing		
5ᵛ	Quand à picquer [bass tacet]		
6	Puis s'il te plaist		
6ᵛ	(2) Las ne viendra jamais		*Livre de meslanges ... choisy ... par Jean Castro* (Louvain and Antwerp: Phalèse and Bellère, 1575)
7	Tout icy me deplaist		
7ᵛ	(3) Bons dieux et qu'est-ce cy	Margarite Pourvas à son filz	First two sections (fols. 7ᵛ–19) in *Trois odes, contenant chascune d'elles douze parties* (Douai: Bogard, 1592)
8	Je sens toutte mon ame		
8ᵛ	Quel envieux Daymon		
9	Las et comment veux tu		
9ᵛ	Tes esgarés esprits		
10	Si la Cicogne		
10ᵛ	Es tu doncq bien mon filz		
11	Je m'esbahy de toy		
11ᵛ	Suffit il pas		
12	Certes on dict bien vray		
12ᵛ	O Dieu qui as le soing		
13	Sinon o Roy des cieux		
13ᵛ	De laisser mes esbatz	Justinien Pense à sa mere	
14ᵃ	Mon ame ainsy qu'on voit		

Folio	Contents		
14v	Las Orlandine las		
15	Ores presque me voy estre		
15v	Que seray je povret		
16	Ah Fortune tu m'es par trop		
16v	Je confesse et cognoy		
17	Puis doncques que les Dieux		
17v	Courage donques mon ame		
18	Ma mere mon secours		
18v	Si le prodigue		
19	Prens je te pry esgard	Margarite Pourvas à son filz	
19v	Tous les malheurs		
20	Et principalement		
20v	Si que je resemblois		
21	Mes parens et amis		
21v	Mais là c'estoit en vain		
22	En par fin qu'en j'eux fait		
22v	Or maintenant ainsy		
23	Dont croy moy j'en reçoys		
23v	Si grand est le plaisir		
24	Aussi raison le veult		
24v	Fais mon filz		
25	Or puis que Dieu		

SECOND LIVRE (four and five voices):

Folio	Contents		
25v	[blank]		
26	[title page, *second livre*]		
26v	[table, *second livre*]		
27	[blank]		
27v	(1) Je ne veux pas mon precepteur	J.P. à maistre Milles de Norry	*Livre de meslanges*, 1575 (see *premier livre*, 2)
28	Ainçois je veux mon cher Norry		
28v	Oultre encor' ta perfection au luth		

Table 1 continued

Folio	Title	Rubric	Later publication
29	(2) Je suis banny de joye		Livre de meslanges, 1575 (see premier livre, 2)
29ᵛ	Or puis qu'ainsy		
30	Nuict je ne dors		
30ᵛ	(3) Je suis à toy		Livre de meslanges, 1575 (see premier livre, 2)
31	N'ay je pas donc		
31ᵛ–32	(4) Giamay nel mar		
32ᵛ	(5) Ce dieu lascif		First (?) twelve sections (fols. 32ᵛ–38) in Trois odes, 1592 (see premier livre, 3); sections marked with an asterisk were printed separately in La fleur de chansons à trois parties, edited by Castro (Louvain and Antwerp: Phalèse and Bellère, 1574)
33ᵇ	Pour quelque temps		
33ᵛ	Si tost qu'elle m'eut		
34	Plus en aultruy		
34ᵛ	Ah quantefois au son* [3 vv; bass tacet]		
35	J'estois ja faict		
35ᵛ	Comme au milieu		
36	Ny plus ny moins		
36ᵛ	Quand ce grand Dieu		
37	Lors j'apperceu		
37ᵛ	Je vy encor la beaulté [bass tacet]		
38	Bref j'en de tout		
38ᵛ	Comme ung captif		
39	Ainsy apres que j'ay esté		
39ᵛ	Je gouste et preuve	Icy commencent les Chansons à Cincq	
40	Donc O mon Dieu		
40ᵛ	Puis qu'il t'ha pleu		
41	Ne permets plus* (3 vv; bass tacet]		
41ᵛ	Fay moy ce bien		
42	Lors dans mon coeur		

Folio	Incipit	Dedication	Source
42ᵛ	(6) Bien scay que tu n'as pas		
43	Davantage sachant		
43ᵛ	(7) Ainsy qu'un jour seulet		
44	O Jouvenceau		
44ᵛ	Seulle tu es [bass tacet]		
45	Ce neantmoins		
45ᵛ	La nuyt n'est pas		
46	(8) Sachant ma Muse		
46ᵛ	C'est luy quy d'une amour		
47	Sus donc ma Muse	J.P. à Jean Jacques de Ferraris Mantuan	
47ᵛ	TIERS LIVRE (five voices): [blank]		
48	[title page, *tiers livre*]		
48ᵛ	[table, *tiers livre*]		
49	[blank]		
49ᵛ	(1) Bien qu'ung homme	J.P. au seigneur Palemon Cacherano	*Quintines, sextines, sonets . . . à cinq parties* (Cologne: Grevenbruch, 1594) without 'Et pourtant'
50	Duquel bien que l'edifice		
50ᵛ	Sinon l'effort		
51	Mais icelluy quy honore [bass tacet]		
51ᵛ	Et pourtant comme j'estime		
52	Je ne metz cy par escript		
52ᵛ	(2) L'estoile allors	J.P. à sa soeur Marie Pense	*Quintines, sextines*, 1594 (see *tiers livre*, 1); section marked with asterisk published separately in *La fleur*, 1574 (see *second livre*, 5)
53	Palemon en quy		
53ᵛ	Quy est celluy* [3 vv; bass tacet]		
54	Chacun scait quelle experience [superius tacet]		
54ᵛ	Oultre ce qu'il est		
55	Et toy sur toutte autre Marie		
55ᵛ	(3) Pendant ma soeur Leonore	J.P. à sa soeur Leonore Pense	*Quintines, sextines*, 1594 (see *tiers livre*, 1)
56	D'accueillir ne t'appareille		

141

Table 1 *continued*

Folio	Title	Rubric	Later publication
56ᵛ	Et si tu as		
57	Vertu quy de gloire		
57ᵛ	Car aux hommes		
58	Quy est ung bien		
58ᵛ	(4) De tous les biens de Nature	J.P. à Cesar Pense Lyonnois	
59	Elle chasse le martire		
59ᵛ	O mon cousin quelle joie		
60	Donques la chaine amoureuse		
60ᵛ	Puisse icelle l'ame tienne		
61	(5) Si au premier Apvril	J.P. à Jacques Bornicard Lyonnois	*Quintines, sextines,* 1594 (see *tiers livre,* 1)
61ᵛ	Voiant dy je reluyre		
62	Et qu'ainsy soit		
62ᵛ	Dont prudent et accort		
63	Vy donc amy heureux		
63ᵛ	(6) Tu scais que ceste humaine	J.P. à Balthazar Pecoul Lyonnois	
64	Mais vaincre il convient		
64ᵛ	Car quand on est		
65	Par quoy la personne		
65ᵛ	Si comme en tesmoigne		
66	Beny soit l'heur		
66ᵛ	(7) Gardes vous bien du gouffre		
67	Donc si desir aves		
67ᵛ	(8) Pour blasmer le baiser		*Livre de chansons à cinq parties* ... (Antwerp: Phalèse and Bellère, 1586)
68	Le baiser se doibt prendre		*Livre de chansons,* 1586 (see *tiers livre,* 8)
68ᵛ–69	(9) Phebus oyant un jour		*Sacrorum cantionum quinque et octo vocum*
69ᵛ–70	(10) Laudate dominum [8 vv; superius I and II, bassus I and II]		... (Louvain: Phalèse and Bellère,

1571)

70ᵛ	(11) Ingredere et votis
71	[superius ruled for music but left blank; bassus has no folio 71]

ᵃFolio 14 is missing in the bassus part (n.a.f. 1818).
ᵇThis folio is incorrectly numbered 32 in the superius (f.fr. 25536); the following folio is labelled 34 to correct the error.

Table 2 *Revisions to final cadences of the Pense partbooks in 1574, 1575 and 1586*[a]

Title	Tonal type[b]	Original cadence	Revised cadence
1574			
Quy est celluy [3 vv; bass tacet]	b–c1–F	?C [g in superius]	F
Ah quantefois au son [3 vv; bass tacet]	b–g2–G	?G [g in superius]	G, b in superius
Ne permets plus [3 vv; bass tacet]	b–c1–G	G [g–♮–g in superius]	G, four bars cut, dissonant suspension added in superius
1575			
Je ne veux pas mon precepteur [4 vv]	♮–c1–G	(1) G	(1) no change
(2) Ainçois je veux		(2) G	(2) D
(3) Oultre encor		(3) G in bar 156, final cadence on C	(3) G
Las ne viendra jamais [4 vv]	b–g2–G	(1) plagal A [with fermata but no break]	(1) G
[(2) Ne faisant nuict et jour]		(2) G with extension	(2) D with extension
(3) Tout icy me desplaist		(3) G in bar 175 with extension to plagal D	(3) G

Je suis banny de joye [4 vv]	♮–c1–E	(1) D	(1) A
(2) Or puis qu'ainsy		(2) E	(2) no change
(3) Nuict je ne dors		(3) E	(3) E, but bars 182–6 rewritten and bars 186–94 [end] cut
Je suis à toy [4 vv]	♮–c1–G	(1) G in bar 73 with extension to plagal G in bar 75	(1) D
(2) N'ay je pas doncq		(2) G in bar 142, extension to C in bar 150	(2) G, bars 142–50 cut
1586			
Phebus oyant ung jour [5 vv]	♮–c1–G	G	no change
Pour blasmer le baiser [5 vv]	♮–g2–C	(1) plagal G	(1) no change
(2) Le baiser se doibt prendre		(2) C in bar 134, extension to plagal C in bar 137	(2) C, bars 133–5 rewritten, one bar added

a Comparison of f.fr. 25536 and n.a.f. 1818 with full transcriptions of later prints.
b Tonal type is indicated by system, cleffing of the highest voice and final (here, the final of the entire piece rather than of its component sections). For an explanation of this method, see H. Powers, 'Tonal Types and Modal Categories in Renaissance Polyphony', *Journal of the American Musicological Society*, 34 (1981), pp. 428–70.

145

Table 3 *Final cadences of* Trois odes *(1592) and* n.a.f. 1818[a]

Title	Tonal type	Original cadence	Revised cadence
Bons dieu	♮–c1–G	G	no change
(2) Je sens toutte		B♭	E
(3) Quel envieux		G, with four-bar plagal extension	G, extension omitted
(4) Las et comment		C	no change
(5) Tes esgarez espritz		C	D
(6) Si la Cicogne		G	no change
(7) Es tu bien		C	E
(8) Je m'esbahy de toy		D	no change
(9) Suffit il pas		G, with two-bar plagal extension	G, extension omitted
(10) Certes on dict		D	no change
(11) O Dieu qui as		C	E
(12) Sinon o Roy		G, with four-bar plagal extension	G, extension omitted
De laisser mes esbatz	b–g2–G	G	no change
[(2) Mon ame]		missing in n.a.f. 1818 (see Table 1)	G
[(3) Las Orlandine]		missing in n.a.f. 1818 (see Table 1)	D
(4) Ores presque me voy		D	no change
(5) Que feray je		F	B♭
(6) Ah Fortune		G	no change
(7) Je confesse et cognoy		D	no change
(8) Puis donques		A	A, final pitch 8ve higher
(9) Courage doncq mon ame		G	no change

Title	Range	Cadence	Alteration (Leipzig/printed bassus)
(10) Ma mere mon secours		G[c]	no change
(11) Si le prodigue		D	no change
(12) Prens je te pry	b–G–g2	G, with two-bar plagal extension	G, extension omitted [on page 24, missing in Leipzig partbook]
Ce dieu lascif			
(2) Pour quelque temps		D	[on page 25, missing in Leipzig partbook]
(3) Si tost qu'il m'eut		D	no change
(4) Plus en aultruy		G	no change
(5) Ah quantefois [see also Table 2, 1574]		[bass tacet]	[bass tacet]
(6) J'etois ja faict		D, with three-bar plagal extension	G, substantially rewritten; eight final bars, incl. extension, omitted
(7) Comme au milieu	♮–A–g2	A	no change
(8) Ny plus ny moins		D	no change
(9) Quand ce grand dieu		A	no change

[a] Evidence for alteration of final cadences is drawn from comparison of the bassus partbook of the *Trois odes* preserved in the Leipzig Staatsbibliothek and the manuscript bassus of n.a.f. 1818. The final section of the Leipzig bassus, from p. 33 to the end, is missing. These pages presumably contained the three following sections of *Ce dieu lascif* ('Lors j'apperceu', 'Je vy encor' and 'Bref j'en de tout') but as the table of contents is also missing this is impossible to determine with certainty.

[b] The closing words of this text are 'amertume le fiel'; text painting thus accounts for this rather unusual cadence.

[c] Text painting on the final words of this poem seems to have involved voice crossing. Although the final pitch of both the manuscript and printed bassus is D, the manuscript superius in f.fr. 25536 (g''–f♯''–g'') indicates that the cadential degree was actually G and that another voice, probably the tenor, sounded the lowest pitch in the final sonority.

Table 4 *Final cadences in the* Quintines, sextines, sonets *(1594)*[a]

Title	Tonal type	Original cadence	Revised cadence
Bien qu'ung homme	b–g2–G	A	G; only final pitch rewritten in bassus, but superius rewritten bars 38–40 and 56–9
(2) Duquel bien que l'edifice		G	no change
(3) Sinon l'effort		D	D; change in approach to cadence, bars 33–4
(4) Mais icelluy qui honore		bass tacet; f♯ in superius	bass tacet; a in superius
(5) Pourtant que j'estime		D	entire section omitted
(6) Je ne metz ci par escript		G	no change
L'estoille allors[b]	b–c1–F	F, with two-bar plagal extension	F, extension omitted
(2) Palemon en qui		C	no change
(3) Qui est celluy[c]		bass tacet; g in superius	bass tacet; e in superius [i.e. quinta of MS]
(4) Chascun scait		C	no change
(5) Oultre ce qu'il est		C	no change
(6) Et toy sur toutte autre		C	F

Pendant ma soeur Leonore	♮–c1–G	G	no change
(2) D'acueillir ne t'appareille		C	D
(3) Et si tu as		G	no change
(4) Vertu qui as		C	G; three bars added to original cadence
(5) Car aux hommes		C	no change
(6) Quy est ung bien		G	no change
Si au premier apvril	b–g2–F	F	no change
(2) Voyant dy-je reluyre		C	no change
(3) Et qu'ainsy soit		C	F
(4) Dont prudent et accort		C	no change
(5) Vy donc amy heureux		C	F

[a] Evidence is based on comparison of the manuscript superius and bassus of the Pense partbooks with the superius, tenor and bassus of the print.

[b] The superius and either the quinta or contra seem to have been switched for the print of this piece, so that the manuscript superius and the print superius do not preserve the same part. Comparison in this case is drawn between the manuscript and print bassus parts.

[c] See Table 2 above. Castro seems to have changed the original C cadence to an F cadence for the print of 1574 but to have left it unchanged for the 1594 print.

Early Music History (1992) Volume 11

PETER JEFFERY

THE LOST CHANT TRADITION OF EARLY CHRISTIAN JERUSALEM: SOME POSSIBLE MELODIC SURVIVALS IN THE BYZANTINE AND LATIN CHANT REPERTORIES*

In memoriam Niels Krogh Rasmussen, OP, 1935–1987

The medieval chant traditions of the Eastern and Western churches can generally be traced back to about the tenth century, when the earliest surviving notated manuscripts were created. In these earliest sources, the various traditions are already distinct from each other and fully formed, each with thousands of chants that are assigned to at least eight modes and belong to dozens of melody types or families, carefully distributed across the daily, weekly and annual cycles of a complicated liturgical calendar. Yet we have hardly any information at all as to how these traditions evolved into the highly complex state in which we first find them. Where did they come from and when did they originate? How and when did they achieve the relatively fixed form in which we know them? Questions such as these have been important in chant research during the last thirty years, ever since Willi Apel outlined what he called 'the "central" problem of the chant, that is, the question concerning its origin and development'.[1] But attempts to

---

* Early forms of this article were read at the 17th International Byzantine Congress in Washington, DC (August 1986), the Annual Meeting of the American Musicological Society in Cleveland, Ohio (November 1986), the Annual Meeting of the North American Academy of Liturgy in Tarrytown, New York (January 1987), and the Yale Institute of Sacred Music (October 1989). I am grateful to the many people who offered advice and suggestions.
[1] W. Apel, *Gregorian Chant* (Bloomington, IN, 1958), p. 507. See also Apel, 'The Central Problem of Gregorian Chant', *Journal of the American Musicological Society*, 9 (1956), pp. 118–27.

investigate these questions have often been conceived too narrowly, overlooking as much evidence as they include or more. For instance, many scholars have written about 'the central problem' as if it belonged mainly to Gregorian chant and its close relative, the Old Roman or special Urban repertory, when in fact the origins and early history of almost every tradition of Eastern and Western chant are equally obscure. Comparative studies dealing with all or many of the medieval Eastern and Western repertories could do much to help us define the central problem better and to propose imaginative yet plausible solutions to it. Because the state of the surviving evidence is different for each tradition, aspects of the problem that seem intractable in some chant traditions are sometimes relatively well documented in others, so that they can help us acquire a clearer picture of what the real issues are and what kinds of imaginative leaps can be justified in attempting to solve these issues.

In addition, many recent investigations have limited themselves further by considering only or mainly the strictly musical evidence, such as the origin and semiology of the earliest (Gregorian) notations, or the possibility that particular (Gregorian and Old Roman) melodic characteristics may be clues to the interaction of various means of oral and written transmission during the formative period(s) of these two traditions. While these issues are extremely important, indeed essential, many other kinds of evidence are no less crucial, including the evidence of the texts and the evidence of the liturgical contexts and structures. Music historians are sometimes sceptical of these kinds of evidence because of the simplistic and credulous ways they have sometimes been used in the past, particularly by those who lacked the necessary linguistic and theological training or experience. But critical evaluation of the non-musical evidence remains essential, for it can tell us much that purely musical evidence cannot.

In fact a comparative approach to the central problem, and one that would give equal weight to musical and non-musical evidence, would not focus in the first instance on Gregorian and Old Roman chant but rather on an Eastern chant tradition that is far better documented in its earliest stages. Though its melodies are much more poorly preserved than those of Gregorian chant, its surviving textual and liturgical sources are far richer, so that its entire history can be traced, from the formation and expansion of the repertory in the fourth to eighth centuries to its demise in the twelfth. Indeed, it may have been the first Christian chant repertory anywhere to have been committed to writing, and throughout its history it exercised considerable influence on the other Eastern and Western traditions, including the familiar Gregorian, Old Roman, Ambrosian and Byzantine repertories whose melodies are best preserved. This early, well-documented and highly influential chant tradition is the one native to Jerusalem. Because it developed in the historic centre and holy city of the Christian religion,[2] and in Greek, the central language of early Christianity,[3] it was the leader in the historical development of the chant, and even the source of many of the forces that shaped all the repertories of early Christian chant. Because Jerusalem chant was constantly heard and admired by pilgrims from all over the ancient world, it was able to exert considerable influence on most of the other Eastern and Western traditions of liturgical chant, which borrowed from it and imitated it unashamedly.[4] It is precisely because Jerusalem chant was so influential that it is so much better documented than any other medieval chant repertory: relatively little evidence survives in sources from the city itself, but quite a bit from places that wholly or partly adopted the Jerusalem liturgy. In almost every way, in other words, this was 'the central tradition in early Christian

---

[2] See, for instance, F. E. Peters, *Jerusalem: The Holy City in the Eyes of Chroniclers, Visitors, Pilgrims, and Prophets from the Days of Abraham to the Beginning of Modern Times* (Princeton, NJ, 1985); J. D. Purvis, *Jerusalem, the Holy City: A Bibliography* (Metuchen, NJ, 1988).

[3] On the languages of early Christianity see: C. Mohrmann, *Études sur le latin des chrétiens*, 4 vols., Storia e Letteratura 65, 87, 103, 143 (Rome, 1958–77); J. Quasten, *Patrology*, I: *The Beginnings of Patristic Literature* (Utrecht, Antwerp and Westminster, MD, 1962), pp. 20–2; A. Quacquarelli, ed., *Complementi interdisciplinari di patrologia* (Rome, 1989); W. Jaeger, *Early Christianity and Greek Paideia* (Cambridge, MA, 1961); W. den Boer *et al.*, eds., *Romanitas et christianitas: Studia Iano Henrico Waszink A.D. VI Kal. Nov. A. MCMLXXIII XIII lustra complenti oblata* (Amsterdam and London, 1973); B. M. Metzger, *The Early Versions of the New Testament: Their Origin, Transmission, and Limitations* (Oxford, 1977); T. Klauser, *A Short History of the Western Liturgy: An Account and Some Reflections*, trans. J. Halliburton, 2nd edn (Oxford, 1979), pp. 18–24; C. Vogel, *Medieval Liturgy: An Introduction to the Sources*, trans. and rev. W. G. Storey and N. K. Rasmussen, NPM Studies in Church Music and Liturgy (Washington, DC, 1986), pp. 293–7, 368–72; G. Sanders and M. Van Uytfanghe, *Bibliographie signalétique du latin des chrétiens*, Corpus Christianorum: Lingua Patrum 1 (Turnhout, 1989).

[4] See my article, 'The Sunday Office of Seventh-Century Jerusalem in the Georgian Chantbook (Iadgari): A Preliminary Report', *Studia Liturgica*, 21 (1991), pp. 52–75. Much information will be published in my book *Liturgy and Chant in Early Christian Jerusalem (Fourth–Twelfth Centuries)*.

music'[5] – an obvious starting-point for investigating the central problem of medieval chant.

There are probably two reasons why Jerusalem chant has been overlooked so completely in the past. First, very few of the sources survive in the original Greek. Most are known only in medieval Armenian and Georgian translations, made when the churches of these lands decided to import the liturgy and chant of Jerusalem to celebrate them as their own. Only very recently have these Armenian and Georgian texts been published, and many have yet to be translated into any international scholarly language. Nevertheless, they have already attained their rightful place in liturgical studies, recognised as among the most important sources of information about the early history of the liturgy. There is therefore a rapidly growing scholarly literature about them that promises to be of great help to chant research.[6]

The second reason musicologists have paid so little attention is that, while we have all the texts of Jerusalem chant in a number of manuscripts, few of these sources are notated, so that most of the Jerusalem melodies do not survive. On the other hand, we can determine the modes of most of these lost melodies, because sources dating from the seventh century onwards give the modal number before almost every text, using the medieval Byzantine system of numbering.[7] Yet a significant number of Jerusalem chant texts

[5] O. Strunk, *Essays on Music in the Byzantine World* (New York, 1977), p. 39. Strunk actually intended to describe Byzantine chant, lumping together all the Greek chant repertories indiscriminately. It is in fact more accurate to recognise that the city of Byzantium or Constantinople was only one of many centres of liturgical chant in Greek, just as Rome was only one of many centres that cultivated liturgical chant in Latin. Of all the Greek centres, neither Byzantium nor Greece proper nor southern Italy exerted as much international influence during the earliest period as Jerusalem and the towns and monasteries surrounding it.

[6] See, for instance: A. Nocent, *The Liturgical Year*, 4 vols., trans. M.J. O'Connell (Collegeville, MN, 1977); J.D. Wilkinson, *Egeria's Travels to the Holy Land*, rev. edn (Jerusalem and Warminster, 1981); P. Bradshaw, *Daily Prayer in the Early Church* (London, 1981); R.M. Payne, 'Christian Worship in Jerusalem in the Fourth and Fifth Centuries: The Development of the Lectionary, Calendar and Liturgy' (Ph.D. dissertation, Southern Baptist Theological Seminary, Louisville, KY, 1981); R. Taft, *The Liturgy of the Hours in East and West: The Origins of the Divine Office and its Meaning for Today* (Collegeville, MN, 1986); T.J. Talley, *The Origins of the Liturgical Year* (New York, 1986); J. Baldovin, *The Urban Character of Christian Worship: The Origins, Development, and Meaning of Stational Liturgy*, Orientalia Christiana Analecta 228 (Rome, 1987); K. Stevenson, *Jerusalem Revisited: The Liturgical Meaning of Holy Week* (Washington, DC, 1988); Baldovin, *Liturgy in Ancient Jerusalem*, Alcuin/GROW Liturgical Study 9 (Bramcote, Nottingham, 1989).

[7] That is, the four authentic modes (modes 1, 3, 5 and 7 in the familiar Latin numbering) are numbered 1, 2, 3, 4. The plagal modes (Latin 2, 4, 6, 8) are numbered 1 plagal, 2 plagal, 3 plagal, 4 plagal.

were also used in the Gregorian and other known chant traditions, and at least sometimes this seems likely to be due to direct borrowing from Jerusalem. In such cases the borrowed texts often seem to have brought their melodies with them, at least partially. By comparing the Gregorian and other melodies that survive for each text in the various medieval chant repertories, it is possible to recognise certain common features that appear to be vestiges of the original melodic tradition of Jerusalem. It is also possible to distinguish these apparent survivals from features that arose locally and more recently in each of the chant traditions into which the Jerusalem original was incorporated. This in turn gives an especially interesting glimpse of the way some of the most prominent and well-known medieval chant melodies were transmitted in the centuries before our first notated manuscripts.

I. THE SOURCES OF JERUSALEM CHANT

As in the other Eastern and Western chant traditions,[8] the earliest witnesses are not actual chant manuscripts but indirect sources that happen to preserve information about the chant repertory, even though they were created primarily for some other purpose. Most important among these are the sermons delivered by Jerusalem bishops and clergy between the fourth and seventh centuries, beginning with St Cyril, who was bishop from about 351 until his death in 387. The purpose of these sermons was to explain to the people the liturgical ceremonies, the feasts of the liturgical year and the readings and psalms associated with these feasts; as a result they frequently tell us which psalms were sung on which liturgical occasions, and sometimes give us further valuable information about how they were performed and even which verse was selected to be used as the refrain.[9]

---

[8] See my forthcoming articles: 'Rome and Jerusalem: From Oral Tradition to Written Repertory in Two Ancient Liturgical Centers', *From Rome to the Passing of the Gothic: Festschrift in Honor of David Hughes*, ed. G. Boone (Cambridge, MA, forthcoming); 'Jerusalem and Rome (and Constantinople): The Musical Heritage of Two Great Cities in the Formation of the Medieval Chant Traditions', *Cantus Planus: Papers Read at the Fourth Meeting, Pécs, Hungary, 3–8 September 1990*, ed. L. Dobszay *et al.* (Budapest, 1992), pp. 163–74.

[9] The more important sermons of Jerusalem origin can conveniently be listed according to the number assigned them in *Clavis Patrum Graecorum* (hereafter *CPG*), ed. M. Geerard, 5 vols. (Turnhout, 1974–87): (1) Cyril of Jerusalem (bishop *c.* AD 351–87), *Catecheses* (*CPG*, 3585), *Mystagogiae* (*CPG*, 3586, 3622); (2) Hesychius of Jerusalem (d. after 450), *Homiliae*

Much valuable information is also preserved in the accounts left by pilgrims to the city, which describe the impressive buildings and the no less impressive services that took place within and around them. By far the most informative of these pilgrim authors was Egeria, a French or Spanish woman who visited the city from 381 to 384 and described the entire liturgical year celebrated in 383.[10] Many of these pilgrims returned home, bringing with them memories of Jerusalem's churches, liturgies and chant – but others chose to remain, becoming monks or nuns in one of the numerous monasteries that surrounded the city and near-by Bethlehem. Of those whose writings survive, three of the most important were Westerners: Jerome (*c.* 347–419/20), the famed translator of the Latin Vulgate who spent the last half of his life in Bethlehem,[11] John Cassian (*c.* 365–*c.* 433), whose writings on monasticism give us much information about the psalmody of the Office in Palestine, Egypt and southern Gaul,[12] and the Roman woman Melania the

(*CPG*, 6565–81), see also his Commentaries on the psalms and odes (*CPG*, 6552–5); (3) Chrysippus of Jerusalem (fifth century; *CPG*, 6705–8); (4) Theognius of Jerusalem (*c.* 460), *Homilia in Ramos Palmarum* (*CPG*, 7378); (5) Peter of Jerusalem (bishop 524–52; *CPG*, 7017–18), see also M. van Esbroeck, 'L'homélie de Pierre de Jérusalem et la fin de l'Origénisme palestinien en 551', *Orientalia Christiana Periodica*, 51 (1985), pp. 33–59; (6) Timotheus of Jerusalem (sixth century; *CPG*, 7405–10); (7) Sophronius of Jerusalem (bishop 634–9; *CPG*, 7637–43); (8) John Damascene (*c.* 675–*c.* 749; *CPG*, 8057–68). For other sermons, many of them anonymous, see *CPG*, 1685, 1698–1701, 4740, 6515, 6712, 6715, 6917–18, 7021, 7815, 7825. Extensive discussion of the value of sermon evidence for reconstructing the early history of liturgical chant will be found in my forthcoming book *Prophecy Mixed with Melody: From Early Christian Psalmody to Gregorian Chant*.

voyage (itinéraire), Sources Chrétiennes (hereafter SC) 296 (Paris, 1982). The best English translation with commentary is J. Wilkinson, *Egeria's Travels to the Holy Land*, rev. edn (Jerusalem, 1981). The generally accepted date of 381–4 is defended in P. Devos, 'La date du voyage d'Égérie', *Analecta Bollandiana*, 85 (1967), pp. 165–94. For more recent discussion of her identity and date, see: U. Domínguez del Val, *Estudios sobre literatura latina hispano-cristiana*, I: *1955–1971* (Madrid, 1986), pp. 102–15; V. Väänänen, *Le journal-épître d'Égérie (Itinerarium Egeriae): Étude linguistique*, Annales Academiae Scientiarum Fennicae, ser. B, tom. 230 (Helsinki, 1987), and the review of this book by B. Löfstedt in *Romance Philology*, 43 (1990), pp. 448–52; H. Sivan, 'Who was Egeria? Piety and Pilgrimage in the Age of Gratian', *Harvard Theological Review*, 81 (1988), pp. 39–72; C. Webber, 'Egeria's Norman Homeland', *Harvard Studies in Classical Philology*, 92 (1989), pp. 437–56. For writings by other early pilgrims, see *Itineraria et alia geographica*, Corpus Christianorum Series Latina (hereafter CCL), 175–6 (Turnhout, 1965); J. Wilkinson, *Jerusalem Pilgrims Before the Crusades* (Jerusalem, 1977).

[11] Jerome's works are listed in E. Dekkers, ed., *Clavis Patrum Latinorum*, 2nd edn (Steenbrugge, 1961), 580–642 (hereafter *CPL*). For his activity in Palestine, see Y. M. Duval, ed., *Jérôme entre l'Occident et l'Orient: 16ᵉ centenaire du départ de Jérôme de Rome et son installation à Bethléem: Actes du Colloque de Chantilly (septembre 1986)* (Turnhout, 1988).

[12] For his writings, see *CPL*, 512–14. The most important one has been edited more recently by J.-C. Guy, *Jean Cassien, Institutions cénobitiques*, SC 109 (Paris, 1965). For the

Younger (*c.* 383–439), who founded monasteries on the Mount of Olives just outside Jerusalem, and drew up an order for the Office they were to celebrate, as recorded by her associate Gerontius in his account of her saintly life.[13]

A second stage in the history of the Jerusalem liturgy begins with the first liturgical book. A complete annual cycle of biblical readings, responsorial psalms (comparable to the graduals of Gregorian chant) and alleluias for the masses of the liturgical year may already have existed by the late fourth century, when the pilgrim Egeria observed and wrote about the liturgy. By the early fifth century, all these texts had been collected and written down in a liturgical book, of the kind known as a lectionary. Though the original Greek text is lost, its contents are known from an Armenian translation made when the Church of Armenia adopted the Jerusalem rite as the basis of its own; the oldest surviving manuscripts of the Armenian lectionary, though dating from about the tenth century, preserve a liturgy very close to the one described by Egeria. The presence of a feast for Bishop John of Jerusalem shows that the lectionary must date from after 417, the year of his death. But rubrics elsewhere in the book seem to indicate that the churches built by the Empress Eudokia, beginning with her visit about 438/9, had not yet been built. Thus the Greek Vorlage of the Armenian lectionary is believed to date from between AD 417 and 438–9.[14]

A much later and more developed state of the Jerusalem lectionary, dating from about the eighth century, is preserved in Georgian translation – for the Church of Georgia, like that of neighbouring Armenia at an earlier time, adopted the liturgy of Jerusalem as its own. These Georgian lectionaries preserve not only the texts of the graduals and alleluias, but also the incipits of many troparia, poetic stanzas for the Mass and certain parts of the Office, comparable to

significance of his liturgical information, see Taft, *Liturgy of the Hours*, p. 407; Bradshaw, *Daily Prayer*, p. 186.

[13] *CPL*, 2211. A newer edition of this work is *Vita S. Melaniae Junioris*, ed. D. Gorce, SC 90 (Paris, 1962). An English translation was published by E. A. Clark, ed., *The Life of Melania the Younger*, Studies in Women and Religion 14 (New York, 1984).

[14] A. Renoux, ed., *Le codex arménien Jérusalem 121*, 2 vols., Patrologia Orientalis (hereafter PO) 35/1 and 36/2 (Turnhout, 1969, 1971) (with French translation). On the date and the manuscripts, see especially vol. 35/1, pp. 169–81, and vol. 36/2, pp. 170–2; P. Devos, 'L'année de la dédicace de Saint-Étienne à Jérusalem: 439', *Analecta Bollandiana*, 101 (1983), pp. 43–70.

the Byzantine troparia, or (more roughly) to the antiphons of Western rhymed offices.[15] Though there is no music notation to tell us the melodies of these troparion texts, the majority of texts are preceded by the number of the mode to which the lost melody belonged.[16]

At some point the hymnodic troparia texts came to be collected in a book of their own, a tropologion or chant book separate from the lectionary. This, too, was adopted by the medieval Church of Georgia, and thus survives only in a Georgian translation. It may have been the first liturgical book from any Christian tradition exclusively devoted to chant texts, and it is certainly the oldest surviving book in which chant texts are classified by a system of eight modes.[17] The extant manuscripts seem to preserve two recensions: an earlier one made from a lost Greek text of the sixth or seventh century,[18] and a later one, still unedited, that may date from the eighth century or later.[19]

With the manuscripts of the heirmologion, a few of which contain neumes, we begin to see a shift in liturgical leadership from the city of Jerusalem to the nearby monastery of St Sabas, and from

[15] See the following articles by A. Hughes, 'Modal Order and Disorder in the Rhymed Office', *Musica Disciplina*, 37 (1983), pp. 29–51; 'Late Medieval Rhymed Offices', *Journal of the Plainsong & Medieval Music Society*, 8 (1985), pp. 33–49; 'Rhymed Offices', *Dictionary of the Middle Ages*, ed. J. R. Strayer *et al.*, x (New York, 1988), pp. 366–77.

[16] M. Tarchnischvili, ed., *Le grand lectionnaire de l'église de Jérusalem (V^e–VIIIe siècles)*, 2 vols. in 4, Corpus Scriptorum Christianorum Orientalium (hereafter CSCO) 188–9, 204–5 (Louvain, 1956–60) (with Latin translation). On more recent research, see B. Outtier, 'K. Kekelidzé et le lectionnaire géorgien', *Bedi Kartlisa*, 38 (1980), pp. 23–112.

[17] See Jeffery, 'The Sunday Office', my forthcoming article, 'The Earliest Book of the Eight Modes: The Rediscovered Georgian Oktoechos', and Jeffery, *Re-Envisioning Past Musical Cultures: Ethnomusicology in the Study of Gregorian Chant* (Chicago, 1992), pp. 000–00.

[18] There are two modern editions: (1) A. Šanije, A. Marṭirosov and A. Jišiašvili, eds., *Čiletraṭis Iadgari* [The Papyrus-Parchment Iadgari], Jveli Kartuli Enis Jeglebi 15 (Tbilisi, 1977); (2) El. Meṭreveli, C. Čankieva and L. Xevsuriani, eds., *Ujvelesi Iadgari* [The Oldest Iadgari], Jveli Kartuli Mcerlobis Jeglebi 2 (Tbilisi, 1980). All references in this article are to the 1980 edition. Throughout this article, all Georgian transliterations follow H. I. Aronson, *Georgian: A Reading Grammar* (Columbus, OH, 1982), pp. 15–27. The three editors of the 1980 edition briefly explain their work in 'Le plus ancien tropologion géorgien', *Bedi Kartlisa*, 39 (1981), pp. 54–62; see also the review by A. Wade, 'The Oldest *Iadgari*: The Jerusalem Tropologion, V–VIII c.', *Orientalia Christiana Periodica*, 50 (1984), pp. 451–6.

[19] See H. Métréveli, 'Les manuscrits liturgiques géorgiens des IXe–Xe siècles et leur importance pour l'étude de l'hymnographie byzantine', *Bedi Kartlisa*, 36 (1978), pp. 43–8. MSS of both the earlier and later types are described in the catalogue of Georgian manuscripts on Mount Sinai, reviewed by M. van Esbroeck in *Bedi Kartlisa*, 39 (1981), pp. 316–17.

there to the Studion monastery in Constantinople.[20] The last and best-known witness to the Jerusalem chant tradition is the Greek typikon for Holy Week and Easter Week, the only liturgical book from the city proper that survives in the original language. It was copied in 1122, ironically after the Jerusalem rite had already been supplanted by the new Byzantine liturgy, fusing material that originated in the city of Constantinople with material from St Sabas and other Palestinian monasteries.[21]

II. SOME MELODIC GROUPS OF APPARENT JERUSALEM ORIGIN

Many of the texts that occur in Jerusalem sources were also in use elsewhere, whether through direct or indirect borrowing or through a common exegetical interpretation linking particular psalms to particular feasts. The present article discusses a few such texts, chosen because they share several interesting features. These texts are mostly refrains sung with responsorial psalms, equivalent to the graduals of the Roman Mass or the prokeimena of the Byzantine Divine Liturgy. The refrains chosen for discussion here can be shown to have been in use continuously throughout the history of the Jerusalem rite. In most cases they are first attested either by Egeria or in the Armenian lectionary of the early fifth century, and they continue to be mentioned in the Georgian sources of the seventh and eighth centuries, if not also in the Greek typikon of 1122 (should they fall during the two-week period of the liturgical year that this source preserves). In addition, the texts that have been selected are significantly represented in the medieval Byzantine and Western chant traditions, in which they are transmitted with melodies. Most significantly, the texts discussed here have been chosen because, unlike many of the texts shared by Jerusalem

---

[20] The early Georgian heirmologia are studied in El. Meṭreveli, ed., *Jlispirni da Ǧmrtism-šoblisani ori jveli redakcia X–XI ss. xelnaçerebis mixedvit* [Heirmoi and Theotokia: Two Ancient Redactions after MSS of the 10th–11th Centuries] (Tbilisi, 1971). A Greek manuscript from St Sabas, dating from the same period, is published in facsimile in J. Raasted, ed., *Hirmologium Sabbaiticum: Codex Monasterii S. Sabbae 83 phototypice depictus*, Monumenta Musicae Byzantinae 8, 2 vols. in 3 (Copenhagen, 1968–70).

[21] Τυπικὸν τῆς ἐν Ἱεροσολύμοις Ἐκκλησίας, in A. Παπαδόπουλος-Κεραμεύς, ed., Ἀνάλεκτα Ἱεροσολυμιτικῆς Σταχυολογίας, ιι (St Petersburg, 1894; Brussels, 1963), pp. 1–254.

with other traditions, their extant melodies exhibit certain similarities which suggest that they are somehow related to each other historically. Because these similarities are consistent with the modal assignments of the lost Jerusalem melodies, which are preserved in the Georgian and Greek sources, the most plausible explanation seems to be that, despite the many differences among these Byzantine, Gregorian, Old Roman, Ambrosian and Mozarabic melodies, all have been derived in some way from one form or another of the lost Jerusalem melody. Though each melody has undergone much reworking and development within the tradition that absorbed it, the remaining similarities to melodies in other traditions appear to preserve the last vestiges of the melody or melodic tradition with which the text was customarily sung at Jerusalem.[22] Though we do not have nearly enough information to attempt to reconstruct these lost Jerusalem melodies, the musical vestiges we can identify appear to fall naturally into three groups, each group perhaps representing an ancient melodic or modal type of some sort.

(a) Two responsorial psalm refrains for Palm Sunday and Epiphany/Christmas in the authentic G mode, and some antiphons derived from them. The first melodic group is transmitted with responsorial Psalm 117 [118], sung with the refrain *Benedictus qui venit*, 'Blessed is the one who comes in the name of the Lord' from verse 26.[23] It was originally associated with processions on Palm Sunday and in the Christmas/Epiphany season, though it later become the gradual of the Mass on these days. This is the only chanted psalm text that the pilgrim Egeria actually quoted in her description of the Jerusalem liturgy; she heard it sung on two occasions during the year 383 that she spent in Jerusalem. One of

---

[22] A much broader variety of texts from the Jerusalem sources, with their counterparts from other medieval chant traditions, will be discussed in my forthcoming book *Liturgy and Chant in Early Christian Jerusalem (Fourth–Twelfth Centuries)*.

[23] In ancient times there were three ways of numbering the psalms: (1) the Hebrew numbering, followed in most modern English Bibles, (2) the Greek numbering, also used in the Latin Bible and in translations made from the Latin, (3) the Syriac numbering. Within each psalm, there are two ways of numbering the verses: (1) the English system used in the Authorised or King James Version and in most subsequent English translations, (2) the system used in the Hebrew, Greek, Latin, Syriac and most other versions. In the present article, psalms and psalm verses are cited according to the Greek–Latin numbering, while the English numberings (as used, for instance, in the New Revised Standard Version) are given in brackets.

these was the procession on Palm Sunday, recalling the triumphal entry Jesus had once made into the city, riding on a donkey and greeted by a crowd waving palm branches. In Egeria's time, the people of Jerusalem gathered outside the city on the Mount of Olives, where they spent the afternoon singing and listening to readings.

At five o'clock the passage is read from the Gospel about the children who met the Lord with palm branches, saying, 'Blessed is he that cometh in the name of the Lord' [i.e. Matt. 21: 1–17].

At this the bishop and all the people rise from their places, and start off on foot down from the summit of the Mount of Olives. All the people go before him with psalms and antiphons, all the time repeating, 'Blessed is he that cometh in the name of the Lord'. The babies and the ones too young to walk are carried on their parents' shoulders. Everyone is carrying branches, either palm or olive, and they accompany the bishop in the very way the people did when once they went down with the Lord. They go on foot all down the Mount to the city, and all through the city to the Anastasis, but they have to go pretty gently on account of the older women and men among them who might get tired. So it is already late when they reach the Anastasis [i.e. the building now known as the Church of the Holy Sepulchre]...[24]

Egeria also heard this text sung on the evening before Epiphany, 6 January, as the people returned to Jerusalem from Bethlehem, where they had celebrated Jesus's birth.[25] Though most of her description is lost owing to a lacuna in the manuscript, the extant text begins again with the quotation of this verse as the crowd approaches Jerusalem.

'Blessed is he that cometh in the name of the Lord', and so on. They have to go slowly for the sake of the monazontes [i.e. monks] who are on foot, so they arrive in Jerusalem almost at daybreak, but just before it is light, at the moment when people can first recognize each other.[26]

Later Jerusalem sources confirm that this psalm continued to be sung on Epiphany and Palm Sunday. Its melody or melodies were

[24] Maraval, *Égérie*, pp. 274–5; Wilkinson, *Egeria's Travels*, p. 133.

[25] It was not until the sixth century that the church of Jerusalem accepted the custom of celebrating Jesus's birth on 25 December, and reinterpreted 6 January as the feast of Jesus's baptism (as at Constantinople). See Jeffery, 'The Sunday Office', p. 57; P. Raffin, 'La fête de Noël, fête de l'événement ou fête d'idée?', *Le Christ dans la liturgie: Conférences Saint-Serge, XXVIIe Semaine d'Études Liturgiques, Paris, 24–28 juin 1980*, ed. A. M. Triacca and A. Pistoia, Bibliotheca 'Ephemerides Liturgicae' Subsidia 20 (Rome, 1981), pp. 169–78.

[26] Maraval, *Égérie*, pp. 250–1; Wilkinson, *Egeria's Travels*, pp. 126–7.

usually assigned to the authentic G mode.[27] The processions and
other special ceremonies in Jerusalem were attended by many foreign pilgrims like Egeria, and it was doubtless through such people
that the Palm Sunday celebration and the other distinctive
ceremonies of the Holy City were spread almost everywhere, and
came to be imitated in many of the medieval liturgical traditions.[28]
Thus Psalm 117 [118]: 26 found its way into the Western chant
traditions, where it survived in both the Palm Sunday celebration
and the season of Christmas, the feast of Christ's birth that corresponds to the original meaning of Epiphany at Jerusalem.[29] Comparison of the extant melodies for this text shows that almost all of
them share certain similar traits, particularly at the beginning,
which may perhaps be regarded as survivals of a common ancestral
melody from which they are all somehow descended.

In Example 1, the Byzantine prokeimenon or gradual (melody 1)
may be the closest relative to that of Jerusalem; at least it is the
same text sung in the same language, assigned to the same liturgical days of Palm Sunday and Epiphany, and it is also in the same

[27]   In the Armenian lectionary it is sung at the Palm Sunday processions, but not mentioned
at Epiphany; see Renoux, *Le codex*, II (=PO 36), pp. 258–9. Its continuing use in the
Palm Sunday procession is confirmed by an anonymous sermon published in M.
Aubineau, ed., *Les homélies festales d'Hésychius de Jérusalem*, 2 vols., Subsidia Hagiographica
59 (Brussels, 1978–80), II, pp. 748–77. One manuscript of the later Georgian lectionary
assigns this text to the plagal E mode, another to the authentic G mode as the gradual of
the Mass of the day; see Tarchnischvili, *Le grand lectionnaire*, 1/2 (=CSCO 189), pp. 81n,
83. In the Greek typikon of 1122 it occurs as the gradual of the Palm Sunday Mass,
assigned to the authentic G mode; see Παπαδόπουλος-Κεραμεύς, ed., Ἀνάλεκτα, II, p.
24. In the Georgian Iadgari or chant book, it does not occur on Palm Sunday but does
occur as the gradual of the Mass on Epiphany (with verse 27 as the refrain rather than
verse 26), assigned to the plagal G mode; see Metreveli, *Ujvelesi*, p. 56.

[28]   For the Palm Sunday procession in particular, much of the classic research stems from
the period of the Roman Catholic reform of Holy Week during the 1950s, and thus
antedates the recent burst of new research on Jerusalem. See: G. Mesnard, 'Vers la
restauration du dimanche des rameaux', *Études Grégoriennes*, 1 (1954), pp. 69–81; A.
Bugnini and C. Braga, *Ordo Hebdomadae Sanctae instauratus: Commentarium ad S.R.C.
Decretum 'Maximae Redemptionis Nostrae Mysteria' diei 16 Novembris 1955 et ad 'Ordinem Hebdomadae Sanctae Instauratum'*, Bibliotheca 'Ephemerides Liturgicae', Sectio Historica 25
(Rome, 1956), pp. 28–39; H. A. P. Schmidt *et al.*, *Hebdomada Sancta*, 2 vols. (Rome, 1956–
7), I, pp. 271–2, II, pp. 694–705, 968–9; H. J. Gräf, *Palmenweihe und Palmenprozession in der
lateinischen Liturgie*, Veröffentlichungen des Missionspriesterseminar St Augustin, Sieg-
burg 5 (Kaldenkirchen, 1959). For more recent discussion, see: A. Nocent, *The Liturgical
Year*, II: *Lent*, trans. M. J. O'Connell (Collegeville, MN, 1977), pp. 184–201; I. H.
Dalmais, P. Jounel and A. G. Martimort, *The Church at Prayer: An Introduction to the Liturgy*,
IV: *The Liturgy and Time*, new edn, ed. A. G. Martimort, trans. M. J. O'Connell (Collegeville, MN, 1986), pp. 70–1, 75; Talley, *Origins*, pp. 176–89.

[29]   Anton Baumstark, *Comparative Liturgy*, rev. B. Botte, ed. F. L. Cross (Westminster, MD,
1957), p. 156.

Example 1

mode: G authentic.[30] Its three most prominent melodic features, which also occur in other Byzantine prokeimena in this mode, are the upward leap of a fifth *G–d* at the beginning, the tendency to continue reciting on and around the pitch *d*, and the ending on *G*, the final of the mode. The Latin chants, less closely related to Jerusalem in both language and modality, all preserve these three features to some degree, though all appear to have been modified in ways that bring them stylistically closer to the local Latin repertories. For instance, all the Latin melodies tend to recite on *c*, a tone lower than the Byzantine *d*, though some hold to this pitch more tenaciously than others. This reflects the general Western preference for *c* as a reciting tone, evident (for example) in the Gregorian psalm tones and in many other Western chant melodies. Of the Latin melodies in Example 1, all except the Ambrosian melody 4 approach this *c* recitation with some variant of the fifth leap. In melodies 3 and 6, the opening fifth has become a 'major triad' of two successive thirds, beginning in each case on the final (*F* in melody 3, *c* in melody 6). In the case of melody 3, the shift of the final from *G* to *F* reflects the strong predilection among the Gregorian graduals for melodies in the authentic F mode. On the other hand, in the Ambrosian melody 5, which preserves the *G* final, the opening leap has been shortened to a fourth, *G–c*. In the Old Roman melody 2, which like the Gregorian melody 3 has an *F* final, the opening on *G* survives, though the leap up to the fourth has been filled in stepwise, reflecting a common Old Roman tendency to fill in skips. Ambrosian melody 4, which has the least in common with the others, exhibits the formulas of the familiar *Justus ut palma* group of graduals (see below). It either has no historic relationship to the old Jerusalem melody, or else it has undergone the most extensive remodelling to fit the local conventions of the Ambrosian chant tradition.

Example 2 illustrates another gradual text with essentially the same liturgical assignments: Palm Sunday and Epiphany in

---

[30] Because the modes were numbered differently in East and West, the use of modal numbers is avoided here. Instead, modes are referred to by their final (D, E, F or G) and range (authentic or plagal). Individual pitches are referred to using the letter notation of the medieval Western gamut: capital letters *A–G* for the lowest octave, lower-case letters *a–g* for the next octave, with *c* as middle C, and double letters *aa–ee* for the upper fifth. See Example III-2 in R. H. Hoppin, *Medieval Music* (New York, 1978), p. 63. The melodies in the music examples and their sources are fully identified below, pp. 187–90.

Example 2

Jerusalem,[31] Christmas (the Western counterpart to Epiphany) in the West. This is Psalm 97 [98] with the refrain *Viderunt omnes* from verse 3, 'All the ends of the earth have seen the salvation of our God'. The practice of singing this psalm on Epiphany had spread to the West by the sixth century, for it is indicated in a fragmentary Gallican lectionary of that date, as well as in an anonymous Latin sermon.[32] Its Jerusalem melody was also in the authentic G mode,[33] and the surviving melodies, all Western, have two of the same traits as the Western melodies of *Benedictus qui venit*, namely the 'major triad' opening (partially filled in in the Old Roman melody 3) and the recitation on *c*.

How do we know that these similarities are not merely coincidental? It might be objected, for instance, that the Western melodies that begin with *F–a–c* and then recite on *c* look like elaborations of the Gregorian fifth psalm tone – is this not a more appropriate comparison than one with a hypothetical Jerusalem melody that does not even survive, or a Byzantine melody in a different mode? The truth, however, is that the refrains of the Gregorian graduals *Beneductus* and *Viderunt* are melodic mavericks within the Gregorian repertory. Willi Apel was unable to fit either into his scheme of centonisation formulas for the fifth mode, and remarked that *Viderunt omnes* is 'among the very few responds that are entirely idiomelic'.[34] Surely this means that the origin and history of these melodies was somehow different from that of the 'rest' of the group, and this inevitably draws our attention to the fact that these are the very two whose texts appear to have come, like the feast of Palm

---

[31]   In the Armenian lectionary this psalm is sung during the octave of Epiphany, with its second verse serving as refrain; on Hypapante or Presentation (2 February) with its third verse serving as refrain, and on Palm Sunday, with the eighth and ninth verses serving as the refrain; see Renoux, *Le codex*, II (=PO 36), pp. 222–3, 228–9, 256–7.

[32]   The lectionary is published in A. Dold, ed., *Das älteste Liturgiebuch der lateinischen Kirche: Ein altgallikanisches Lektionar des 5./6. Jhs aus dem Wolfenbüttler Palimpsest-Codex Weissenburgensis 76*, Texte und Arbeiten 26–8 (Beuron, 1936), p. 38, where our psalm, with the first verse indicated as the refrain, is assigned to Epiphany. The sermon, of uncertain authorship and date, is published in *Patrologia Latina, Supplementum* (hereafter *PLS*), II, col. 1057.

[33]   In the Georgian lectionary, this psalm is assigned to Epiphany week with the third verse (*Viderunt omnes*) as refrain, to Hypapante (the Presentation or Purification feast on 2 February) with the same refrain and assigned to the authentic G mode, and to Palm Sunday, with the refrain from the eighth verse and assigned to the authentic D mode. See Tarchnischvili, *Le grand lectionnaire*, I/2 (=CSCO 189), pp. 26–7, 34–5, 82–3. The provisions of the Iadgari are the same, except that there is no modal assignment on Palm Sunday, see Meṭreveli, *Ujvelesi*, pp. 67, 98, 175.

[34]   *Gregorian Chant* (Bloomington, IN, 1958), pp. 347, 350.

Sunday itself, from Jerusalem. In other instances, too, one finds that, when a Western chant text was also in use at Jerusalem, it is transmitted with a melody that is somehow distinctive or different from other Western melodies of the same type or mode – further examples will be given below. The best explanation for these coincidences may be that they are not coincidences at all. If a melody that seems to be somewhat anomalous within its 'home' repertory is attached to a text that is likely to have been imported from another tradition, then perhaps the melody developed from one that originated in the same place as the text, or at least one that was being transmitted with the text at the time that the newer repertory imported and incorporated both of them.

The opening fifth leap, in its various forms, occurs also in another genre that is especially identified with Palm Sunday: the processional troparion or antiphon. Melodies 5 and 6 of Example 1 are taken from such chants, but there are many other instances. Example 3 compares five processional chants from Palm Sunday that begin with the word 'Hosanna',[35] taken from the same psalm (Psalm 117 [118]: 25) as the 'Benedictus qui venit...' text (Psalm 117 [118]: 26).[36] Again, the opening fifth $G–d$ is evident in melodies 1–3.[37] Mozarabic melodies 4 and 5 also seem to have leaped

[35] The meaning of this word has been the subject of much debate, both in the Middle Ages and in the present. See: E. Werner, '"Hosanna" in the Gospels', *Journal of Biblical Literature*, 65 (1946), pp. 72–122; C.C. Richardson, 'Blessed is He that Cometh in the Name of the Lord', *Anglican Theological Review*, 29 (1947), pp. 96–8; J. Spencer Kennard, '"Hosanna" and the Purpose of Jesus', *Journal of Biblical Literature*, 67 (1948), pp. 171–6; H.J. Lehmann, 'Hosanna: A Philological Discussion in the Old Church', *Armeniaca: Mélange d'études arméniennes publiés à l'occasion du 250ᵉ anniversaire de l'entrée des pères Mekhitaristes dans l'île de Saint-Lazare (1717–1967)* [ed. Mesrob Gianascian] (San Lazzaro, Venice, 1969), pp. 165–74; W. F. Albright and C. S. Mann, eds., *Matthew*, The Anchor Bible (Garden City, NY, 1971), p. 252; E. Lohse, 'ὡσαννά', *Theological Dictionary of the New Testament*, ed. G. Friedrich, trans. and ed. G. W. Bromiley, 9 (Grand Rapids, MI, 1974), pp. 682–4; G. C., 'Hosanna au Fils de David (Mt 21,9)', *Esprit et Vie*, 80 (1980), pp. 65–6.

[36] Melodies 3 and 4 are transmitted with texts that are related to the Greek troparion Εἰσερχομένου σου, which occurs in the Typikon of 1122 in the authentic E mode; see Παπαδόπουλος-Κεραμεύς, ed., Ἀνάλεκτα, II, p. 31. For other Western texts derived from this troparion, see M. Huglo, 'Source hagiopolite d'une antienne hispanique pour le dimanche des rameaux', *Hispania Sacra*, 5 (1952), pp. 367–74.

[37] Melody 1 has had some notoriety in the musicological literature, since it has often been said to be adapted from a drinking-song preserved in an ancient Greek epitaph, the 'Skolion of Seikilos'. The claim seems to have been made first in A. Möhler, *Die griechische, griechisch-römische und altchristliche Musik: Ein Beitrag zur Geschichte des gregorianischen Chorals*, Römische Quartalschrift für christliche Alterthumskunde und für Kirchengeschichte, Supplementheft 9 (Rome, 1898), pp. 55–7, although P. Spitta laid some of the groundwork by asserting that the melody of the skolion could be considered

Example 3

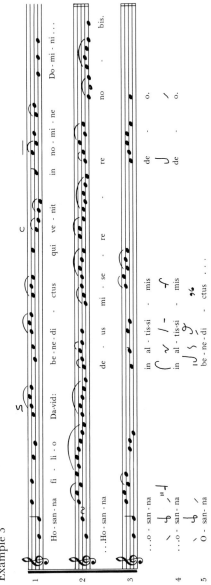

upward on the second syllable of 'Osanna', which in each case bears a large *pes* neume – but the exact pitches can no longer be determined.

The processional chants in Example 4 combine the two texts, 'Hosanna...' and 'Benedictus...'. The text of the first one, though in Latin, is identical with a Greek processional troparion in the Jerusalem typikon of 1122, where it is assigned to the plagal G

Example 4

169

Peter Jeffery

mode.[38] Melodies 2 and 3 are set to texts that closely resemble another chant in the 1122 typikon: a troparion sung after the Gospel of the Palm Sunday Mass.[39] The first three melodies preserve some of the characteristics of this mode, namely the use of the pitch *G* as both reciting tone and modal final. All three also preserve the 'major triad' opening, though this has been transposed to *C–E–G* in melody 1, *F–a–c* in melodies 2 and 3. Melody 4, an Aquitanian trope, introduces the Palm Sunday introit with the word 'hosana', set to a melody that approximates to the 'major triad' opening on *F*.

Many of the Western melodies discussed so far have been said to exhibit a certain amount of remodelling or adaptation, altering the supposed Jerusalem original in the direction of local preferences. Further examples of how this remodelling process might have operated can be seen in Example 5, where melodies 1 and 2 are two different settings of the same text.[40] Melody 1, like melodies 2 and 3

Mixolydian; see 'Eine neugefundene altgriechische Melodie', *Vierteljahrsschrift für Musik-wissenschaft*, 10 (1894), pp. 103–10, see p. 110. This apparent example of a Gregorian chant based on an ancient Greek song has been repeated by many subsequent writers, notably C. Vivell in 'Direkte Entwicklung des römischen Kirchengesangs aus der vor-christlichen Musik', *Kirchenmusikalisches Jahrbuch*, 24 (1911), pp. 21–54, and A. Gastoué in *Les origines du chant romain: L'antiphonaire grégorien*, Bibliothèque Musicologique 1 (Paris, 1907), pp. 40–1, until it finally found a place in such influential handbooks as: G. Reese, *Music in the Middle Ages with an Introduction on the Music of Ancient Times* (New York, 1940), pp. 49, 115; E. Werner, *The Sacred Bridge: The Interdependence of Liturgy and Music in Synagogue and Church during the First Millennium* (New York, 1959; repr. New York, 1979), pp. 338, 354.
   Yet the alleged similarities between the chant melody and the skolion melody are mostly illusory, as was demonstrated by A. W. J. Holleman in 'The Oxyrhynchus Papyrus 1786, and the Relationship Between Ancient Greek and Early Christian Music', *Vigiliae Christianae*, 26 (1972), pp. 1–17, see pp. 16–17. More accurate transcriptions and discussions of the skolion melody will be found in: E. Pöhlmann, *Denkmäler altgriechischer Musik: Sammlung, Übertragung und Erläuterung aller Fragmente und Fälschungen*, Erlanger Beiträge zur Sprach- und Kunstwissenschaft 31 (Nürnberg, 1970), pp. 54–7, and I. Henderson and D. Wulstan, 'Introduction: Ancient Greece', *A History of Western Music*, ed. F. W. Sternfeld, I: *Music from the Middle Ages to the Renaissance* (London, 1973), pp. 27–58, see pp. 49–51.

38 Ὡσαννὰ ἐν τοῖς ὑψίστοις, in Παπαδόπουλος-Κεραμεύς, ed., Ἀνάλεκτα, ΙΙ, p. 17. A processional troparion with almost the identical text is given in the Iadgari; see Metreveli *et al.*, *Ujvelesi*, p. 175. This and the other troparia mentioned in this article are among the chants that will be treated in my book *Liturgy and Chant in Early Christian Jerusalem*.
39 Πρὸ ἓξ ἡμερῶν, in Παπαδόπουλος-Κεραμεύς, ed., Ἀνάλεκτα, ΙΙ, p. 25, assigned to the plagal E mode. The text of *Ante sex dies* (melody 3) occurs in one of the earliest Western sources of Palm Sunday processional ordines, the Romano-Germanic pontifical of the tenth century; see C. Vogel and R. Elze, *Le Pontifical romano-germanique du dixième siècle*, ΙΙ, Studi e Testi 227 (Vatican City, 1963), pp. 46, 54.
40 Originally sung during the Office of Palm Sunday, these two antiphons were introduced

170

Example 5

of Example 4, shows the 'major triad' motif on the word 'Hosanna', and the final on *G*. Melody 2, on the other hand, seems to owe more to a Western model than to one from Jerusalem, for the music of the word 'Benedictus' in the second staff resembles the opening of melody 3, a Gregorian chant for Ember Saturdays. In this case,

into the Palm Sunday procession with the reform of Holy Week in the 1950s, and thus appear in editions of *The Liber Usualis with Introduction and Rubrics in English* (Paris, Tournai and Rome) and other liturgical books published after 1955. The melodies were edited from unidentified 'manuscrits anglais', according to J. Claire, 'Les nouvelles pièces de chant de la semaine sainte', *Revue Grégorienne*, 39 (1960), pp. 138–49, see pp. 140–2. However, melody 1 can be found in the Worcester antiphoner, published in Paléographie Musicale, 1st ser., 12 [ed. L. McLachlan] (Solesmes, 1922, repr. Bern, 1971), p. 113; melody 2 can be found in W. H. Frere, ed., *Antiphonale Sarisburiense: A Reproduction in Facsimile from Early Manuscripts* (London, 1901–24, repr. Farnborough, 1966), p. 207. The text also occurs in the tenth-century Romano-Germanic pontifical; see Vogel and Elze, *Le Pontifical*, II, p. 48.

perhaps, there were two melodic models or traditions from which a melody for this text could be developed: one represented by the Gregorian melody 3, the other one originating ultimately in Jerusalem.

Again, one may object that, even if the similarities in all these Palm Sunday melodies reflect a common source, this source need not have been Jerusalem. Would it not be more conservative, for example, to trace the characteristics to the Byzantine melody that actually survives (melody 1 in Example 1), rather than to Jerusalem melodies that do not? In fact it is difficult to argue that the Latin chants could derive from Byzantium, for the Palm Sunday procession was of limited importance in the liturgy of Constantinople, and eventually disappeared from the Byzantine rite altogether. The rite of the imperial city seems originally to have used a different psalm for chanting during the procession.[41] Medieval liturgical sources from Constantinople show that the Palm Sunday procession was a relatively minor observance there: only one processional chant is given, a troparion that probably originated in Jerusalem,[42] just as the Byzantine prokeimenon probably did. In short, the incorporation of these texts into the Byzantine rite, which permitted the survival of notated melodies for them, is due to the liturgical and musical influence of Jerusalem on Constantinople, which is known to have been considerable.[43]

(b) Three responsorial psalm refrains sharing an ambiguous plagal G or E modality. In each locality, melodies that were shared with, or borrowed from, Jerusalem inevitably came into

---

[41] In a sermon that may have been delivered while he was patriarch of Constantinople, John Chrysostom seems to say that Psalm 145 [146] was sung there rather than Psalm 117 [118], see *Patrologia graeca* (hereafter *PG*), LV, p. 520. For discussion, see Talley, *Origins*, pp. 186–7.

[42] Τὴν κοινὴν ἀνάστασιν. J. Mateos, ed., *Le typicon de la grande église: Ms. Saint-Croix nᵒ 40, Xᵉ siècle*, II: *Le cycle des fêtes mobiles*, Orientalia Christiana Analecta 166 (Rome: Pontificium Institutum Orientalium Studiorum, 1963), pp. 62–3, 66–7. This troparion serves as the introit of the Palm Sunday Mass in the seventh-century chant book and in the Georgian lectionary; see Metreveli *et al.*, *Ujvelesi*, p. 175; Tarchnischvili, *Le grand lectionnaire*, I/2 (=CSCO 189), p. 83. The Roman and Byzantine Palm Sunday rites are compared in: A. Baumstark, 'La solennité des palmes dans l'ancienne et la nouvelle Rome', *Irénikon*, 13 (1936), pp. 3–24.

[43] See Jeffery, 'The Sunday Office'; Taft, *The Liturgy of the Hours*, pp. 273–91. The most detailed study of this influence is: G. Bertonière, *The Historical Development of the Easter Vigil and Related Services in the Greek Church*, Orientalia Christiana Analecta 193 (Rome, 1972).

contact with the developing local melodic tradition, and with the passage of time they were gradually adapted to the dominant musical conventions of the area. Some of the processes by which elements from Jerusalem were assimilated locally can be seen in the next group of three chants, all of which were assigned in the Jerusalem sources to the modes on *G* and *E*. The lack of consensus on mode seems to reflect an earlier period in the development of medieval Christian chant, when these two modal areas were not yet fully distinct from each other.[44] The uncertainty continued as these melodies were brought to the West, when they were not quite fully absorbed into the so-called *Justus ut palma* group of graduals. This group of chants has frequently intrigued both medieval and modern scholars, for of all the families of gradual melodies within the Gregorian tradition it is simultaneously the most stereotyped formulaically and the most ambiguous modally – yet too little attention has been paid to its counterpart melodic groups in the Old Roman and Ambrosian chant repertories.[45]

[44] Kenneth Levy once observed that many early Eastern and Western melodies for the Ordinary of the Mass occupied a 'broad pre-Oktoechic modal area that combines aspects of the modes on *E* and *G*. ... Its central scale is a series of white notes from *E* up to *c*; *F* is of minor importance; ... its pattern of melodic nodes and attractions may be projected in a scheme of interlocking fourths (*E–a*; *G–c*) and conjunct thirds (*E–G–b*) ...' See 'The Byzantine Sanctus and its Modal Tradition in East and West', *Annales Musicologiques*, 6 (1958–63), pp. 7–67, especially pp. 56–7. Many other melodies belonging to this 'pre-Oktoechic modal area' will be discussed in my book *Liturgy and Chant in Early Christian Jerusalem*.

[45] On the so-called *Justus ut palma* group of graduals see: [A. Mocquereau,] 'De l'influence de l'accent tonique latin et du cursus sur la structure mélodique et rythmique de la phrase grégorien', *Le répons-graduel Justus et palma: deuxième partie*, Paléographie Musicale, 1st ser., 3 (Solesmes, 1892, repr. Bern, 1974), pp. 1–77, especially pp. 31–52; J. Pothier, 'Graduel "Haec dies," du jour de Pâques', *Revue du Chant Grégorien*, 4 (1895–6), pp. 113–20; M. Daras, 'Le psaume de Pâques', *Les Questions Liturgiques et Paroissiales*, 4 (1913–14), pp. 337–49; Peter Wagner, *Einführung in die gregorianischen Melodien: Ein Handbuch der Choralwissenschaft*, III: *Gregorianische Formenlehre: Ein choralische Stilkunde* (Leipzig, 1921, repr. Hildesheim and Wiesbaden, 1962), pp. 7–16, 370–6; L. David, 'Le répons et l'antienne "Haec dies" du jour de Pâques', *Revue du Chant Grégorien*, 29 (1925), pp. 33–8; David, 'Le graduel des défunts et celui de Pâques', *Revue du Chant Grégorien*, 43 (1939), pp. 97–105; D. Johner, *Wort und Ton im Choral: Ein Beitrag zur Aesthetik des gregorianischen Gesanges* (Leipzig, 1940; 2nd edn 1953), pp. 314–19; Apel, *Gregorian Chant*, pp. 357–63; B. Stäblein, 'Graduale (Gesang)', *Die Musik in Geschichte und Gegenwart*, ed. F. Blume, 14 vols. (Kassel and Basle, 1949–68 and suppls.), v, cols. 631–59, see cols. 640–2 and Beispiel 1; H. Hucke, 'Die gregorianische Gradualeweise des 2. Tons und ihre ambrosianischen Parallelen: Ein Beitrag zur Erforschung des ambrosianischen Gesanges', *Archiv für Musikwissenschaft*, 13 (1956), pp. 285–314; E. Gerson-Kiwi, ' "Justus ut Palma": Stufen hebräischer Psalmodien in mundlicher Überlieferung', *Festschrift Bruno Stäblein zum 70. Geburtstag*, ed. M. Ruhnke (Kassel, 1967), pp. 64–73; S. Kojima, 'Die Ostergradualien "Haec Dies" und ihr Verältnis zu den Tractus des II. und VIII. Tons', *Colloquium Amicorum: Joseph Schmidt-Görg zum 70. Geburtstag*, ed. S. Koss and H.

Example 6

Example 6 – *cont.*

Peter Jeffery

Example 6 illustrates one of the most widely used chant texts of all, Psalm 117 [118] with the refrain from verse 24, *Haec dies*, 'This is the day the Lord has made'. Some two dozen sermons and other sources state that, as early as the fourth century, this psalm was already being sung on Easter in many places.[46] At Jerusalem it was assigned to the plagal G mode.[47] Melodies 2 and 3, from Byzantium and Milan, betray a similar melodic contour: from *G* down to *D* and back on 'Haec dies', up to *c* on 'quam fecit' and the tendency to remain there until the end of the line.[48] The Mozarabic melody 1, in unheightened neumes, could also be interpreted as reflecting a melody similar to the Byzantine one: the *punctum* and *pes* on the syllables 'Haec' and 'quam' corresponding to the Byzantine step-wise ascents *G–a–b* and *E–F–G*, the three *pes* neumes on 'di-' corresponding to the Byzantine ascent from *D* to *G*. The Gregorian and Old Roman melodies, 4 and 5, resemble melodies 2 and 3 on the words 'quam fecit', but are rather different everywhere else,

---

Schmidt (Bonn, 1967), pp. 146–78; F. Haberl, *Der responsoriale Gesang des gregorianischen Graduale* (Rome, 1979), pp. 43–71. A detailed reconstruction of the history of this melodic group will be published in my book *Prophecy Mixed with Melody*.

[46] Fourth-century sources in which it is asserted that this psalm was sung on Easter include: Zeno of Verona (CCL 22, pp. 63, 85), Gregory of Nyssa (*Gregorii Nysseni Opera*, ix: *Sermones*, 1, ed. G. Heil *et al.* [Leiden, 1967], pp. 249, 279, 310), Amphilochius of Iconium (Corpus Christianorum, Series Graeca (hereafter CCG) 3, p. 157). Sources of the late fourth and early fifth centuries include sermons by: John Chrysostom (*PG*, lv, pp. 328–38), Chromatius of Aquilea (CCL 9A, p. 78), Maximus of Turin (CCL 23, pp. 214–16), Jerome (CCL 78, pp. 545–7 and 548–51) and especially Augustine of Hippo (*Patrologia Latina* (hereafter *PL*), xxxviii, cols. 1098, 1099, 1103–4; SC 116, pp. 344–50; *PLS*, ii, cols. 556–8, 585). Sixth-century sources include Caesarius of Arles (CCL 104, p. 819), and Leontius of Constantinople (SC 187, pp. 368–85, 431–41), and verse 24 is marked as a refrain in the St Germain psalter of the same century; see M. Huglo, 'Le répons-graduel de la Messe: Évolution de la forme, permanence de la fonction', *Schweizer Jahrbuch für Musikwissenschaft*, neue Folge, 2 (1982), pp. 53–77, especially p. 60. In addition, the singing of this psalm and refrain on Easter is also cited in many anonymous sermons: *PG*, l, cols. 821–4; CCL 87, pp. 56–9; *PLS*, i, col. 737; *PLS*, ii, cols. 1199, 1250, 1254, 1289–90; CCL 101, p. 213.

[47] In the Armenian lectionary this psalm and refrain are sung at the Easter Vigil, while in the Georgian lectionary and the Greek typikon of 1122 it has moved to the Mass of Easter day and is assigned to the plagal G mode. See Renoux, *Le codex*, ii (=PO 36), pp. 298–9; Tarchnischvili, *Le grand lectionnaire*, i/2 (=CSCO 189), p. 114; Παπαδόπουλος-Κεραμεύς, ed., Ἀνάλεκτα, ii, pp. 201, 253–4. The text is also cited in an anonymous Easter sermon from Jerusalem, published in SC 187, pp. 318–25; *CPG*, 4740. In the Iadgari it is the gradual of the Mass, both on Easter and on the Sunday following, but in the first location there is no modal assignment – only in the second location is it assigned to the plagal G mode; see Metreveli, *Ujvelesi*, pp. 217, 225.

[48] See also the remarks in K. Levy, 'Byzantine Rite, Music of the', *The New Grove Dictionary of Music and Musicians*, ed. S. Sadie, 20 vols. (London, 1980), iii, pp. 553–6, especially p. 556.

where they correspond to the melodic stereotypes of the so-called *Justus ut palma* group of graduals.[49] Perhaps this means that melodies 2 and 3 (if not also melody 1) retain more of the melodic shape of the lost Jerusalem melody, while melodies 4 and 5 retain much less, and have been largely, but not completely, assimilated to the Gregorian and Old Roman forms of the *Justus ut palma* melody type. For the sake of comparison, the Ambrosian form of this melody type is illustrated in melody 6 (the same as melody 4 of Example 1).

Examples 7 and 8 offer further instances of Gregorian and Old Roman graduals that tend to resemble their Byzantine counterparts near the beginning, in precisely the place where they depart from the conventions of the *Justus ut palma* melodic group. Example 7 illustrates a popular psalm for feasts of the apostles, Psalm 18 [19] with the refrain from verse 5 [4], *In omnem terram*, 'Into all the earth their sound has gone out'.[50] Staff 4 shows the Gregorian *Justus ut palma* formula that we would expect to find over the syllables 'exivit so-' in Gregorian melody 3. Instead, the melody that actually does occur there (marked with square brackets) seems to have more in common with the Byzantine melody, particularly in the descending leap to *a* on '-vit'. Example 8 shows Psalm 68 [69], often sung in Lent or Passiontide, with its refrain from verse 18 [17], *Ne avertas*, 'Do not turn your face away from your servant'.[51]

---

[49] See the convenient centonisation table in Apel, *Gregorian Chant*, pp. 360–1.

[50] The Armenian lectionary repeatedly assigns this text to feasts of apostles; the Georgian lectionary and Iadgari continue this tradition, assigning the melody to the authentic E mode. In the Greek typikon, the text is assigned to Easter Monday and the melody to the plagal G mode. See Renoux, *Le codex*, II (=PO 36), pp. 356–7, 362–3, 364–5, 370–1; Tarchnischvili, *Le grand lectionnaire*, I/2 (=CSCO 189), pp. 16, 37, 61, 73, 120, and II/2 (=CSCO 205), pp. 10, 12, 14, 30, 41, 44, 46, 48, 57, 62; Meṭreveli, *Uǰvelesi*, pp. 29, 130, 226, 232, 260; Παπαδόπουλος-Κεραμεύς, ed., Ἀνάλεκτα, II, p. 211. After Ambrose (*PL*, XVI, col. 1020 [1063]) in the fourth century, Western sources include sermons of Augustine (*PL*, XXXVIII, col. 1367; *PLS*, II, cols. 600–1, 604) and some anonymous sermons (*PLS*, II, col. 1162; *CCL* 101, p. 377).

[51] The Armenian lectionary assigns this psalm to Good Friday with verse 22 [21] as refrain; see Renoux, *Le codex*, II (=PO 36), pp. 288–9. A Syriac lectionary dating from about a century later places it on Good Friday, with verse 21 [20] serving as refrain; see F. C. Burkitt, 'The Early Syriac Lectionary System', *Proceedings of the British Academy* (1921–3), pp. 301–38, especially p. 309. The Georgian lectionary indicates it a number of times during Lent and Holy Week, with various refrains and in various modes; on Good Friday, however, the refrain verse 22 [21] and the mode is G authentic; see Tarchnischvili, *Le grand lectionnaire*, I/2 (=CSCO 189), pp. 47, 62, 95, 102, and II/2 (=CSCO 205), p. 113. On Good Friday in the 1122 typikon, however, the mode has shifted to plagal E; see Παπαδόπουλος-Κεραμεύς, ed., Ἀνάλεκτα, II, p. 152. The Georgian Iadgari assigns the psalm to Lent with refrains from verses 17–18 or 18, in the second case with a

Example 7

The standard *Justus ut palma* opening is given in staff 7. The rather different opening of the Gregorian melody 6 could be seen as a mere variant of this, were it not for the *a–E–a* opening of Old Roman melody 5, which somewhat resembles the *G–a–D–D–F–a* opening of the four Byzantine melodies. Here, as in Example 1, the beginning of the Old Roman melody seems to stand midway between the openings of the Byzantine and Gregorian melodies, suggesting that,

modal assignment to plagal G; see Meṭreveli, *Ujvelesi*, pp. 130, 523. The Palestinian supplement to the typikon of Constantinople places the psalm on Sunday Vespers, with verse 18 [17] as the refrain, in the plagal G mode; see Mateos, *Le typicon*, II, p. 179. In the West, the sixth-century St Germain psalter also gives verse 18 [17] as the refrain *Ne avertas*; see Huglo, 'Le répons-graduel', p. 60. Another sixth-century Western document, the *Tituli psalmorum series I* of the same century, states that the psalm is to be 'read' during Passiontide; see P. Salmon, *Les 'Tituli Psalmorum' des manuscrits latins*, Collectanea Biblica Latina 12 (Rome, 1959), p. 65.

Example 8

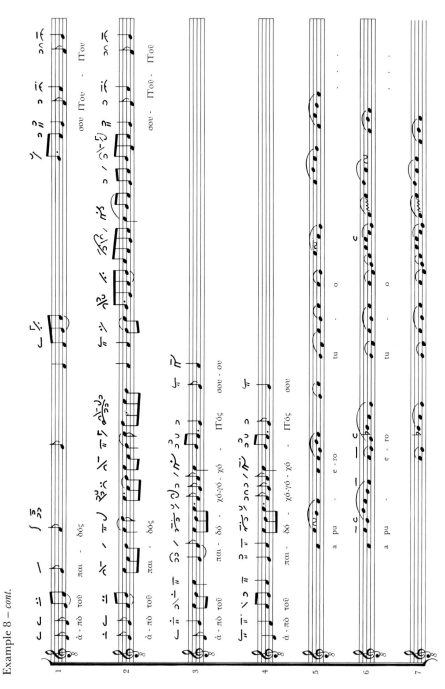

Example 8 – *cont.*

in this respect at least, the Old Roman tradition has preserved more of the original Jerusalem melody than the Gregorian.

(c) Two responsorial psalm refrains in D modes. The next two examples may illustrate particularly interesting cases, in which melodic elements from Jerusalem proved more difficult than usual to assimilate into the Western chant dialects. These texts have no modal assignments in the Georgian chant book, suggesting that they were difficult to classify in the early days of the eight-mode system. The somewhat later Georgian lectionary and the Greek typikon tend to vacillate among D authentic, D plagal and G authentic, though in some cases differing psalm verses have been selected for use as refrains. Few melodies survive for either of the two texts.

The text illustrated in Example 9 is Psalm 40 [41] with the refrain *Ego dixi* from verse 5 [4], 'I said, "Lord, have mercy on me..."'. Though it was in use fairly widely, it was less firmly attached to a specific liturgical day than the other texts we have seen so far.[52] Some Jerusalem sources assigned the melody to the plagal D mode, and there is no extant Byzantine melody. The Ambrosian melody still fits more or less into the plagal D ambitus,

---

[52] The Armenian lectionary places the psalm on Friday of the first week of Lent (refrain: verse 5 [4]), Wednesday in Holy Week (same refrain) and on Good Friday, with verse 7 [6] as refrain; see Renoux, *Le codex*, II (=PO 36), pp. 240–1, 264–5, 270–1, 284–5, while the early Syriac lectionary assigns the psalm to Wednesday in Holy Week, with the same refrain; see Burkitt, 'The Early Syriac Lectionary', p. 308. The Georgian lectionary assigns this psalm to Wednesday in Holy Week (refrain from verses 7–8 [6–7], plagal F mode), Holy Thursday (refrain from verse 9 [8], plagal D mode) and Good Friday (refrain from verse 7 [6], no mode specified); see Tarchnischvili, *Le grand lectionnaire*, I/2 (=CSCO 189), pp. 88–9, 93, 99, and II/2 (=CSCO 205), pp. 99, 102, 111. The 1122 Greek typikon gives the refrain as verse 7 [6], and the mode as G authentic; see Παπαδόπουλος-Κεραμεύς, ed., Ἀνάλεκτα, II, p. 148. In the Georgian Iadgari, however, Psalm 40 [41] with a refrain from 5 [4] is placed at Cheese Week (the week before Lent), but without a modal assignment; see Metreveli, *Ujvelesi*, p. 107.

Early Western sermons that witness to the singing of this psalm do not clearly specify the occasion: Augustine *Sermo Mai 17* (CCL 41, pp. 231–4, 374; Peter Chrysologus (CCL 24, pp. 88–92); Pseudo-Augustine (*PLS*, II, cols. 1123–4). The *Tituli psalmorum series I* says the psalm is to be read with Isaiah in Passiontide; see Salmon, *Les 'Tituli Psalmorum'*, p. 60; the St Germain psalter marks verses 2 and 5 as refrains; see Huglo, 'Le répons-graduel', p. 59. An Egyptian papyrus of about the same period, a fragment of a lectionary, assigns this psalm to Saturday before the First Sunday in Lent, with verse 5 [4] as refrain; see H. J. M. Milne, 'Early Psalms and Lections for Lent', *Journal of Egyptian Archaeology*, 10 (1924), pp. 278–82, especially p. 280. At Constantinople this psalm was sung on Thursday in the second week of Lent, with the refrain from verse 5 [4] and in the G authentic mode, as part of a series of psalms in numerical order throughout Lent; see Mateos, *Le typicon*, II, pp. 28, 74.

Example 9

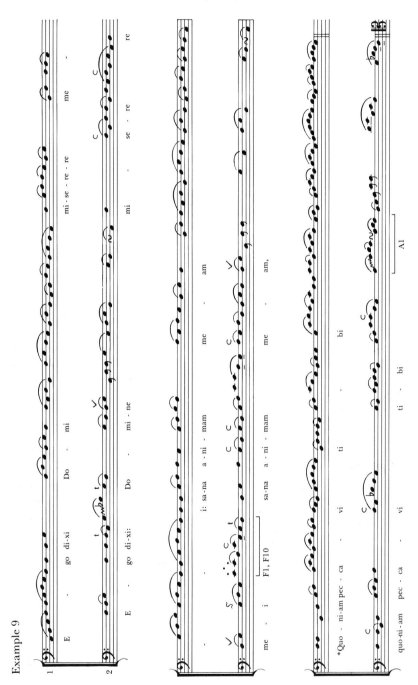

Example 9 – *cont.*

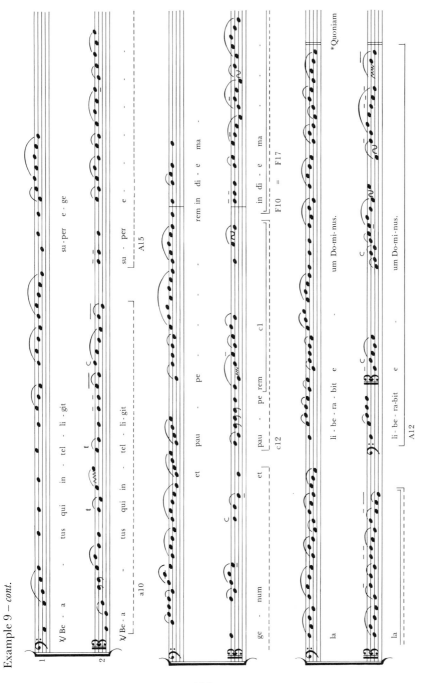

with its tendency to recite on F and a. The Gregorian melody, however, has developed incompletely in two different directions, with a tendency to alternate sections rooted on F with sections rooted on c. In some places it corresponds to melodic formulas of the *Justus ut palma* type (marked with solid brackets beneath the staff), in other places to formulas common to the graduals of the authentic F mode (marked in broken brackets).[53] It is as though, at the time the Gregorian repertory was fixed in writing, neither melody type had completely won out. In the Old Roman tradition, on the other hand, the process was carried to its logical conclusion, for the text is set to a pure *Justus ut palma* melody.[54] Thus in this case, it is the Old Roman that appears to have developed farther away from the Jerusalem original than the Gregorian, while the Ambrosian may have remained the closest.

As in the other cases we have seen, it is towards the beginning that the melodies in Example 9 are both the least formulaic and the most similar to each other, notably in the descent from F to C at the end of the word 'Domine' and the leap back to F at the beginning of 'miserere'. The second half of the Gregorian melody, on the other hand, is entirely composed of native Gregorian melodic formulas. This suggests that the processes of melodic transmission worked in such a way that the melodies were least likely to change at the beginning – though the rest of the melody would become more fully assimilated to the local style, the opening phrase retained more of the Jerusalem original, so that it is at this point that the widely scattered descendants most resemble their common ancestor.

Example 10 may show what happened to melodies that were not remodelled successfully. In ancient times it was one of the most common chant texts for feasts of martyrs, Psalm 115 [116] with the refrain from verse 6 [15], *Pretiosa in conspectu Domini*, 'Precious in the sight of the Lord is the death of his saints'.[55] Yet it disappeared

[53] The letters and numbers beneath the brackets (e.g. 'F1, F10', 'a10', 'A15') refer to the centonisation tables published in Apel, *Gregorian Chant*, pp. 360–1 (the *Justus ut palma* type), 348–9 (the F authentic types).

[54] B. Stäblein and M. Landwehr-Melnicki, eds., *Die Gesänge des altrömischen Graduale, Vat. lat. 5319*, Monumenta Monodica Medii Aevi 2 (Kassel, 1970), p. 91.

[55] This psalm and refrain occur repeatedly in the Armenian lectionary; see Renoux, *Le codex*, II (=PO 36), pp. 173, 224–5, 226–7, 230–1, 346–7, 350–1, 352–3, 358–9). The Georgian lectionary assigns the authentic G mode on the feast of St Stephen, and the authentic D mode in the common of martyrs, while the Iadgari has no modal assignment; see Tarchnischvili, *Le grand lectionnaire*, I/2 (=CSCO 189), p. 31; II/2 (=CSCO

Example 10

from most of the medieval chant traditions, so that only an Old Roman and a Byzantine melody survive.[56] At Jerusalem the text was sung in the authentic D mode, but this lost melody may have had a relationship with the ancestor of the melodies in Example 9, for the melodies in both Examples 9 and 10 include a long descent of a fourth from F to C (c–G on the last syllable of 'Pretiosa' in the

205), pp. 64–5), and Metreveli, *Ujvelesi*, p. 114, in both of which the editors have confused the Hebrew and Greek verse numberings. The singing of this psalm is also cited in a sermon of Hesychius of Jerusalem; see Aubineau, *Les homélies*, I, pp. 546, 554.

Outside Jerusalem, the liturgical reading or singing of this psalm is explicitly mentioned in the early Syriac lectionary (Burkitt, 'The Early Syriac Lectionary', pp. 311, 313, where the refrain is also from verse 6 [15]), and in sermons by Ambrose (*Corpus Scriptorum Ecclesiasticorum Latinorum* (hereafter *CSEL*), LXII, p. 84; Augustine (SC 116, pp. 338–42; *PL*, XXXVIII, cols. 1400–5; *PLS*, II, cols. 587–8, 781–5); Caesarius of Arles (CCL 104, p. 868), and many anonymous sermons, published in *PLS*, II, cols. 1011–12, 1083; CCL 87, pp. 81, 83, 86. See also: J. Leclercq, 'Les inédits africains de l'homiliaire de Fleury', *Revue Bénédictine*, 58 (1948), pp. 53–72, see pp. 68–9; C. Lambot, 'Les sermons de saint Augustin pour les fêtes de martyrs', *Analecta Bollandiana*, 67 (1949), pp. 249–66, reprinted in *Revue Bénédictine*, 79 (1969), pp. 82–97; V. Saxer, *Morts, martyrs, reliques en Afrique chrétienne aux premiers siècles*, Théologie Historique 55 (Paris, 1980), p. 317. On the peculiar structure and verse numbering of this psalm, see: M. L. Barré, 'Psalm 116: Its Structure and Its Enigmas', *Journal of Biblical Literature*, 109 (1990), pp. 61–78.

56 The final stage in this process can be observed in some of the earliest manuscripts of the Gregorian chant tradition, where the text still survives with a minor place in the repertory, but it is no longer provided with a notated melody. In the famous cantatorium St Gall 359, for instance, the text scribe did not even bother to leave spaces for the melismas, recognising that for this text no neumes would be added. See *Paléographie Musicale*, 2nd ser., II: *Cantatorium de Saint-Gall* (Solesmes, 1924, repr. 1968, 1988), p. 131.

Old Roman melody) followed by a sudden return to F (or c). If this is not mere coincidence, it may mean that, in this case, the Old Roman tradition has remained closer to that of Jerusalem than either the Gregorian or the Ambrosian, which lack this text altogether. The disappearance of a text that was once so popular, both in Jerusalem and in the West, may have been related to the possibility that the original melody, like the ancestor of the melodies in Example 9, did not assimilate well into the melodic conventions of Western chant. The apparent tendency to treat F and c indifferently as the central pitch may have been part of the problem, leading to confusion that became less acceptable as the modal system and the gamut became more secure.

This briefest of presentations illustrates three basic points that could have been demonstrated more fully at much greater length. First, chant texts in use at Jerusalem from the fourth and fifth centuries onward were also imported into or shared with other Eastern and Western chant traditions, where medieval melodies for them survive. Secondly, the medieval melodies associated with each text exhibit many melodic and modal similarities, despite the wide chronological and geographic dispersal of the chant traditions that preserve them, and despite the many other ways in which these melodies differ from one another. These similarities are best seen as survivals of the lost Jerusalem melody, particularly as they are consistent with the mode(s) indicated in Jerusalem textual sources. Thirdly, the Jerusalem elements in each melody were acted on differently in each tradition that imported them, in accordance with the modal and formulaic preferences operative in the local chant tradition.

For the psalmodic graduals, at least, that is the closest we can come to recovering the melodies of Christianity's holiest city, the home of its most influential and earliest fully attested chant repertory – melodies which from the fourth century on were heard, remembered and carried back home by pilgrims from all over the Christian world.

University of Delaware/Harvard University

SOURCES OF THE MUSICAL EXAMPLES

Example 1: 'Blessed is the one who comes in the name of the Lord...', Psalm 117 [118]: 26.

(1) BYZANTINE: prokeimenon for Epiphany and Palm Sunday, G. Hintze, *Das byzantinische Prokeimena-Repertoire: Untersuchungen und kritische Edition*, Hamburger Beiträge zur Musikwissenschaft 9 (Hamburg, 1973), p. 109.

(2) OLD ROMAN: gradual for the second Mass of Christmas, B. Stäblein and M. Landwehr-Melnicki, eds., *Die Gesänge des altrömischen Graduale, Vat. lat. 5319*, Monumenta Monodica Medii Aevi 2 (Kassel, 1970), pp. 147–8.

(3) GREGORIAN: gradual for the second Mass of Christmas, *Graduel neumé*, ed. E. Cardine (Solesmes, [1967]), p. 31; cf. *Graduale triplex seu Graduale Romanum Pauli Pp. VI Cura Recognitum & Rhythmicis Signis a Solesmensibus Monachis Ornatum, Neumis Laudunensibus (Cod. 239) et Sangallensibus (Codicum San Gallensis 359 et Einsiedlensis 121) nunc Auctum*, ed. M.-C. Billecocq and R. Fischer (Solesmes, 1979), p. 45.

(4) AMBROSIAN: psalmellus for Sunday after Christmas, *Paléographie musicale*, VI: *Antiphonarium Ambrosianum du Musée Britannique (XIIᵉ siècle) Codex Additional 34209: Transcription* [ed. P. Cagin and C. Mégret] (Solesmes, 1900; repr. Bern, 1972), p. 103.

(5) AMBROSIAN: from the processional psallendum *Pueri clamabant* for Palm Sunday, *Paléographie musicale*, VI, p. 266.

(6) AMBROSIAN: from the processional psallendum *Inclinasti caelos* for Palm Sunday, *Paléographie musicale*, VI, p. 267.

Example 2: 'All the ends of the earth have seen the salvation of our God, jubilate to God all the earth', Psalm 97 [98]: 3–4.

(1) AMBROSIAN: psalmellus for Christmas week, *Paléographie musicale*, VI, p. 98.

(2) GREGORIAN: gradual for the third Mass of Christmas, *Graduel neumé*, pp. 33–4; cf. *Graduale triplex*, pp. 48–9.

(3) OLD ROMAN: gradual for the third Mass of Christmas, Stäblein and Landwehr-Melnicki, *Die Gesänge*, pp. 150–1.

Example 3: 'Hosanna...', Psalm 117 [118]: 25.

(1) GREGORIAN: processional antiphon for Palm Sunday, *Graduel neumé*, p. 155; cf. *Graduale triplex*, p. 137.

(2) AMBROSIAN: processional psallendum for Palm Sunday, *Cum ramis olivarum*, *Paléographie musicale*, VI, pp. 267–8.

(3) GREGORIAN: from the processional antiphon *Introeunte te* for Palm

Sunday, *Paléographie musicale*, XIII: *Le codex 903 de la Bibliothèque nationale de Paris (XIᵉ siècle): Graduel de Saint-Yrieix* (Tournai, 1925), p. 120 (fol. 60ᵛ).

(4) MOZARABIC: from the praelegendum *Quum introires* for Palm Sunday, *Antifonario visigótico mozárabe de la catedral de León: Edición facsímil*, Monumenta Hispaniae Sacra 5/2 (Madrid and Barcelona, 1953), fols. 153ᵛ–154ʳ.

(5) MOZARABIC: praelegendum *Osanna benedictus* for Palm Sunday, *Antifonario visigótico*, fol. 154ʳ.

Example 4: 'Hosanna in the highest, blessed is the one who comes in the name of the Lord...', Psalm 117 [118]: 25–6.

(1) AMBROSIAN: processional psallendum for Palm Sunday, *Paléographie musicale*, VI, p. 268.

(2) AMBROSIAN: from the processional psallendum *Venite omnes adoremus* for Palm Sunday, *Paléographie musicale*, VI, p. 268.

(3) GREGORIAN: from the processional antiphon *Ante sex dies* for Palm Sunday, *Graduel neumé*, p. 162.

(4) AQUITANIAN: from the introit trope *Hodie namque* for Palm Sunday, G. Weiss, ed., *Introitus-Tropen*, I: *Das Repertoire der südfranzösischen Tropare des 10. und 11. Jahrhunderts*, Monumenta Monodica Medii Aevi 3 (Kassel, 1970), p. 331.

Example 5: 'They all praise your name together and say: "Blessed is the one who comes in the name of the Lord, Hosanna in the highest."'

(1) GREGORIAN: antiphon for Palm Sunday, *Ordo Hebdomadae Sanctae iuxta ritum monasticum*, ed. monks of Solesmes (Tournai, 1957), p. 35.

(2) GREGORIAN: antiphon for Palm Sunday, *Ordo Hebdomadae Sanctae*, p. 36.

(3) GREGORIAN: canticle for Ember Saturday, *Graduel neumé*, pp. 16–19; cf. *Graduale triplex*, pp. 372–5.

Example 6: 'This is the day that the Lord has made, ...', Psalm 117 [118]: 24.

(1) MOZARABIC: psalmo for Easter, from Toledo, Biblioteca Capitular, ms. 35.5, fol. 187ʳ; cf. José Janini, ed., *Liber misticus de cuaresma y pascua (Cod. Toledo, Bibl. Capit. 35.5)* (Toledo, 1980), p. 113.

(2) BYZANTINE: prokeimenon for Easter, Hintze, *Das byzantinische Prokeimena-Repertoire*, pp. 121–2.

(3) AMBROSIAN: psalmellus for Easter, *Antiphonale Missarum juxta ritum sanctae ecclesiae Mediolanensis* [ed. Gregorio Sunyol] (Rome, 1935), p. 208.

(4) GREGORIAN: gradual for Easter, *Graduel neumé*, p. 221; cf. *Graduale triplex*, pp. 196–7.

(5) OLD ROMAN: gradual for Easter, Stäblein and Landwehr-Melnickï, *Die Gesänge*, p. 95.

(6) AMBROSIAN: psalmellus for Sunday after Christmas, *Paléographie musicale*, VI, p. 103.

Example 7: 'In all the earth their sound has gone out, . . .', Psalm 18 [19]: 5 [4].

(1) BYZANTINE: prokeimenon for feasts of apostles, Hintze, *Das byzantinische Prokeimena-Repertoire*, pp. 120–1.

(2) OLD ROMAN: gradual for vigils and octaves of the feasts of apostles, Stäblein and Landwehr-Melnicki, *Die Gesänge*, pp. 88–9.

(3) GREGORIAN: gradual for the vigil of the feast of St Peter, *Graduel neumé*, pp. 494–5; cf. *Graduale triplex*, p. 427.

(4) GREGORIAN: typical melodic formula of the *Justus ut palma* group of gradual melodies, W. Apel, *Gregorian Chant* (Bloomington, IN, 1958), p. 360, formula A₁.

Example 8: 'Do not turn your face away from your servant . . .', Psalm 68 [69]: 18 [17].

(1) BYZANTINE (Psaltikon): great prokeimenon for Meat and Cheese Weeks, soloist version, Hintze, *Das byzantinische Prokeimena-Repertoire*, pp. 158–9.

(2) ITALO-BYZANTINE (Psaltikon): great prokeimenon for Meat and Cheese Weeks, soloist version, Hintze, *Das byzantinische Prokeimena-Repertoire*, pp. 158–9.

(3) ITALO-BYZANTINE (Asmatikon): great prokeimenon for Meat and Cheese Weeks, choir version, Hintze, *Das byzantinische Prokeimena-Repertoire*, p. 160.

(4) BYZANTINE (Asmatikon): great prokeimenon for Meat and Cheese Weeks, choir version, Hintze, *Das byzantinische Prokeimena-Repertoire*, p. 160.

(5) OLD ROMAN: gradual for Wednesday in Holy Week, Stäblein and Landwehr-Melnicki, *Die Gesänge*, pp. 99–100.

(6) GREGORIAN: gradual for Wednesday in Holy Week, *Graduel neumé*, pp. 178–9; cf. *Graduale triplex*, pp. 155–6.

(7) GREGORIAN: typical opening melodic formula of the *Justus ut palma* group of gradual melodies, Apel, *Gregorian Chant*, p. 360, formula A₁.

Example 9: 'I said, "Lord, have mercy on me, cleanse my soul, for I have sinned against you" ' ℣ 'Blessed is the one who is understanding toward the needy and the poor, in the day of trouble the Lord will deliver him', Psalm 40 [41]: 5 [4], 2 [1].

(1) AMBROSIAN: psalmellus for the third Sunday in Lent, *Paléographie musicale*, VI, p. 229.

(2) GREGORIAN: gradual for the first Sunday after Pentecost, *Graduel neumé*, p. 291; cf. *Graduale triplex*, pp. 279–80. The solid brackets beneath the staff identify the melodic formulas of the *Justus ut palma* group, and the dotted brackets identify the melodic formulas of the graduals in the authentic F mode, as identified and labelled in Apel, *Gregorian Chant*, pp. 360–1, 348–9.

Example 10: 'Precious in the sight of the Lord . . .', Psalm 115 [116]: 6 [15].

(1) OLD ROMAN: gradual for the feast of St Sebastian, Stäblein and Landwehr-Melnicki, *Die Gesänge*, pp. 122–3.

(2) BYZANTINE: prokeimenon for saints' days, Hintze, *Das byzantinische Prokeimena-Repertoire*, p. 118.

ANDREW KIRKMAN

THE STYLE OF WALTER FRYE AND AN ANONYMOUS MASS IN BRUSSELS, KONINKLIJKE BIBLIOTHEEK, MANUSCRIPT 5557*

The Brussels manuscript 5557 is one of the most important sources of the later fifteenth century. Not only is it the one northern manuscript from the period to have survived largely intact, but it was apparently compiled for the chapel of no less a magnate than Charles the Bold, Duke of Burgundy.[1] Presiding over one of the most opulent courts of Europe, Charles was more than just a great patron of the arts: he was an active composer himself. The sophisticated taste of his establishment is reflected in the extraordinary quality of the music in the Brussels manuscript: great masses by Dufay and Regis rub shoulders with most of the surviving motets of Charles's great employee, Antoine Busnoys, while the original nucleus of the manuscript boasts a clutch of English masses rivalled only by that in Trent 93/90.[2]

The source is also unusual in the proportion – nearly three-quarters – of its works which carry attributions. Were it not for the pruning suffered by the pages of the manuscript, still more might have come down to us. Even the few anonymous works are mostly found with ascriptions elsewhere. Indeed, but for a few small addi-

* Grateful thanks are due to David Fallows and Rob Wegman for reading earlier drafts of this study and offering valuable suggestions.

[1] See R. C. Wegman, 'New Data Concerning the Origins and Chronology of Brussels, Koninklijke Bibliotheek, Manuscript 5557', *Tijdschrift van de Vereniging voor Nederlandse Muziekgeschiedenis*, 36 (1986), pp. 5–21.

[2] Trent, Museo Diocesano, MS BL (Trent 93) and Trent, Castello del Buonconsiglio, MS 90. For a detailed inventory of the Brussels manuscript, see G. R. K. Curtis, 'The English Masses of Brussels MS. 5557' (Ph.D. dissertation, University of Manchester, 1979), pp. 6–7. For a more cursory inventory and details of manuscript structure, see Wegman, 'New Data', p. 20.

tions, only two pieces remain of unknown authorship: a Magnificat, and a three-voice mass *Sine nomine* on folios 90ᵛ–99ʳ.

In such a major source amid such elevated company, any anonymous mass cycle seems to beg attention: what is the nature of its style? How does it relate to other works in the repertory? How might it expand our perception of musical taste at the Burgundian court? And most thornily, where and by whom might it have been composed? On closer acquaintance with the piece, such questions become all the more urgent, for the mass turns out to be a work of great interest. A large network of features leads overwhelmingly to the conclusion that this, like the five masses which open the manuscript, was the work of an English composer. With deepening familiarity, however, a far more detailed picture emerges. In both style and structure, the mass relates closely to the works of none other than the greatest English mass composer of the mid-fifteenth century, Walter Frye.

The fragmentary and largely anonymous survival of music from the fifteenth century might seem to render unrealistic attempts to demonstrate the authorship of individual works. None the less, this largely patchy scenario also encompasses a few more felicitous accidents of survival whose value in illuminating stylistic contours deserves to be fully exploited. Stylistic similarities between the anonymous cycle and the three complete masses attributed to Frye are already suggestive, though it would be unrealistic to attempt a demonstration of common authorship on their basis alone. However, Reinhard Strohm's discovery in 1963 of the Lucca choirbook brought to light the fragmentary Kyrie from a fourth mass by Frye. The more specific similarities between the Brussels anonymous mass and this work are such that the authorship of Frye, or at the very least of someone working closely in his orbit, seems highly likely.

I propose to assess the style of the mass in a number of stages: first, the assertion that it is English will be considered. From there, I will examine the style of Frye's three complete cycles, and proceed to compare them with the anonymous mass and with other contemporary cycles. Against this background of an enhanced understanding of the mass's style, I will then examine its structural and musical links with the fragmentary mass and with Frye's motet *Sospitati dedit*.[3]

[3] Similarities between this work and the anonymous mass have led Rob Wegman and

ENGLISH ORIGINS

It has become increasingly apparent in recent years that many of the features once supposed to be 'hallmarks' of English idiom are in fact more widespread than was once thought. In consequence, the identification of 'English' works among the anonymous repertory in Continental sources now appears a far more hazardous exercise than hitherto. English works were, of course, widely copied, and their influence was such that it is sometimes difficult, particularly in the earlier Continental mass repertory, to distinguish between English models and Continental emulations. On the other hand, to jettison the idea of English style in the mid-fifteenth century altogether would surely be to go too far in the other direction. Many Continentals undoubtedly saw something highly distinctive about English music, and frequently responded, either by emulating it themselves, or, in the case of scribes, by modifying English works to suit local preferences. However far some English idioms may have travelled, it is still true that many of them predominate in demonstrably English pieces, a fact that can be illustrated with reference to the many works for which there is external evidence of English authorship.

Among continentally transmitted anonymous pieces, there can be few which combine such a persuasive body of predominantly English characteristics as the anonymous Brussels mass. Although the feature most often cited as English, the prosula Kyrie, is absent here, the structure of the short Kyrie, which apparently calls for alternatim performance, relates it closely to the fragmentary cycle by Frye in Lucca. I will come back to this significant relationship later. Moreover, the mass belongs to a larger family of small-scale cycles, including works by Bedyngham and Standly, many of which were clearly intended for votive, most commonly Marian, observance.

In common with most English masses, and some Continental ones, the cycle has a basic groundplan in which the same mensural scheme and a similar succession of major cadences is followed in each movement. As in most such cycles, the pattern is varied somewhat in the final two movements to allow for the standard

Gareth Curtis to speculate independently that the mass may be by Frye. See, most recently, Wegman's review of Curtis's edition, *The Brussels Masses*, Early English Church Music 34 (London, 1989) in *Early Music*, 17 (1989), pp. 584–7.

Table 1 *Missa sine nomine*

Kyrie

bar(s)		15	32		47–58
mensuration	O	C			O
voices	3	3	2		3
final	D	D	D		D

Gloria

bar(s)	19	27	30	48	63	68	79	89	95–108
mensuration	O			C					O
voices	3	2	2	3	3	2	3	2	3 3
final	D	G	A	D	C		F	C	C D

Credo

bar(s)	27	35	44	54	63	67	87	100	109–21
mensuration	O			C					O
voices	3	2	2	3	3	2	3	2	3 3
final	D	G	D	D	F	G	D	A	F D

Sanctus

bar(s)	35	44	53	69	91	102	111		132–48
mensuration	O			C					O
voices	3	2	2	2	3	2	2	2	3
final	D	C	A	D	D	G	A	D	D

Agnus

bar(s)	8	10	34	45	58	65	74		100–12
mensuration	O							C	O
voices	3	2	3	2	2	2	2	3	3
final	D	D	D	A	D	C	D	C	D

positionings of extra duos (see Table 1). Following standard English procedure, these duos, which frequently alternate in scoring from phrase to phrase of the text setting, are divided by double bars or simultaneous rests.[4]

The Agnus Dei follows the typical pattern of shifting to *tempus imperfectum* at the third invocation and back to *tempus perfectum* for

---

[4] These occur in the usual positions as follows: Sanctus: 'Pleni sunt celi || et terra || gloria tua' ||, 'Benedictus [rests] qui venit || in nomine domini' ||; Agnus II: 'Agnus dei [rests] qui tollis peccata mundi || miserere nobis' ||. Though this practice is not unheard of outside English masses, its occurrence elsewhere is restricted to early Continental cycles showing clear English influence as, for instance, Domarto's *Missa Spiritus almus*, Simon de Insula's *Missa O admirabile commercium* (Trent, Castello del Buonconsiglio, MS 88 (hereafter Trent 88), fols. 304ᵛ–311ʳ) and Ockeghem's *Missa Caput*. Even in these works, however, its use is not as consistent and regular as in most English cycles.

'dona nobis pacem'.[5] Texting is very specific in the tenor and contratenor as well as in the discantus,[6] and the presence of only two 'sanctus' invocations[7] and underlay in the Agnus beginning at 'qui tollis'[8] betray the original intention to precede the polyphony in these two movements with plainsong incipits in the standard English manner. In short, as a number of scholars have already noted, many aspects of this setting suggest English origin, and none offer distinctive reasons to doubt it.[9]

FRYE'S STYLE

It is now more than a quarter of a century since Sylvia Kenney wrote her pioneering study of Walter Frye. Though somewhat marred by an overemphasis on discant, a concept so broadly conceived that it lost much of its meaning, Kenney's stylistic analysis none the less drew attention to some of the most characterful aspects of Frye's art. However, she largely refrained from digging more deeply into the fascinating tissue of compositional decisions that weave together his highly sophisticated style. The subtlety and

---

[5] This practice, though sometimes without the final return to *tempus perfectum*, is almost ubiquitous in English Agnus settings. Occasionally, as in the anonymous *Missa Quem malignus spiritus* and in Bedyngham's *Missa Deul angouisseux*, the first mensural change occurs at the second setting of 'miserere', a procedure also followed in a few Continental cycles as, for instance, in the masses *O admirabile commercium* and *Grüne Linden* (Trent 88, fols. 375ᵛ–383ᵛ). However, the usual Continental practice of changing mensuration at Agnus II is almost unheard of in English settings.

[6] While full texting in lower voices, except in apparently faithful copies of English works, is rare in Continental manuscripts, English practice generally favours texting of contratenors and fluid tenor lines. This tendency has been noted by Alejandro Planchart, 'Fifteenth-Century Masses: Notes on Performance and Chronology', *Studi Musicali*, 10 (1981), p. 29, and Curtis, *The Brussels Masses*, p. xiv.

[7] This can be seen in most insular copies of English Sanctus settings, and in Continental ones which give reason to suspect closeness to English models. Many English copies, and some Continental ones, supply an incipit, though this is usually omitted in Continental copies, and the extra invocation is more often than not underlaid to the polyphony. A clear illustration of this type of discrepancy can be seen in the various copies of the Sanctus from the *Missa sine nomine* ascribed to Bedyngham: while the readings in Trent 93 and Trent 90 carry three invocations of the opening word, that in Oxford, Additional MS C87 (hereafter Add. C87) has only two invocations and a plainsong incipit.

[8] The same situation obtains here as in the case of English Sanctus settings: most insular copies, and Continental readings which seem close to English antecedents, begin the polyphonic setting at 'qui tollis', while most Continental copies incorporate the opening words into the polyphony.

[9] See, for instance, S. W. Kenney, *Walter Frye and the Contenance Angloise* (New Haven, CT, and London, 1964), p. 54; R. C. Wegman, 'Concerning Tempo in the English Polyphonic Mass, c. 1420–70', *Acta Musicologica*, 61 (1989), p. 64, and Wegman's review cited above, note 3.

imagination of Frye's musical idiom remain little recognised to this day; yet here is a musician of exceptional ability and apparently limitless imagination. Like many fine artists, Frye achieves a sense of freedom and invention while working within a stylistic framework which is in fact highly consistent. Admiration at the constant interplay of ideas and rhythms and subtle sense of timing in Frye's music only deepens with increasing acquaintance.

In sketching out the style of Frye's masses, it seems sensible to begin with the smallest building-blocks, and from there to proceed to illustrate the different ways in which they are laid out and combined.[10] Phrases are usually quite short, and are broken up by frequent minim rests on the beat. When the voice re-enters on the following half-beat, it is often with one of three patterns which are very common components of Frye's melodic idiom. The first consists of a minim followed by a note of longer value, often a semibreve, but frequently a longer note (see Examples 5 and 7). The second is the division, common in music of the period, of an upward-leaping fourth into a second followed by a third (see Example 5). The third, which, as Kenney observed,[11] is a virtual cliché in Frye's work, occurs when the voice has sunk to the bottom of its range, and comprises an octave leap broken by the minim rest. Another common idiom found particularly often in Frye, the dotted semibreve beginning on an off-beat, is also frequently introduced after a minim rest. There is even an instance, in the Agnus Dei of *Summe trinitati*, where Frye begins a complete breve on the half-beat (see Example 2).

Kenney has commented on the restricted nature of the melodic style, which she sees as arising from the constraints imposed by discant.[12] A melodic idea can often be repeated, sometimes exactly (see, for instance, *Summe trinitati*, Sanctus, discantus bar 27). On occasion, the same figure is repeated in duos by both parts in close imitation, creating a brief ostinato effect (see Example 4). However, exact repetitions are far outnumbered by repeats which are varied, often in a rather superficial way. At bars 36–9 of the Agnus Dei of *Summe trinitati*, for example, the same phrase is heard

[10] All musical references are to Gareth Curtis's recent edition, *The Brussels Masses*, Early English Church Music 34 (London, 1989). The masses are also published in S. W. Kenney, ed., *Walter Frye: Collected Works*, Corpus Mensurabilis Musicae 19 (n.p., 1960).
[11] Kenney, *Walter Frye and the Contenance Angloise*, p. 135.
[12] *Ibid.*, p. 130.

Example 1. *Flos regalis*, Sanctus, bars 60–2, discantus and bassus

three times, with the first beginning slightly differently from the other two.[13] In bars 60–2 of the Sanctus of *Flos regalis*, greater rhythmic variety is introduced when a simple rising third figure in both parts is rhythmically varied at each occurrence (Example 1). Similar examples could be cited across the three masses. Since the composer has set up the expectation of an exact repeat, the introduction of a subtle change immediately attracts the ear.

On other occasions, repetition in one part is disguised by varied activity in the others. Kenney noted an instance of this in bars 121–5 of the Gloria of *Nobilis et pulchra*, where an almost exactly repeated figure in the contratenor is set against a figure in the tenor which is stated in three subtly different ways.[14] Bars 40–3 of the Agnus of *Summe trinitati* provide another typical example, in which attention is distracted from a simple repeated figure in the discantus by a rhythmically tortuous contratenor line (Example 2).

Diluted still further, the principle of melodic repetition emerges in the more general practice of returning repeatedly to a single note, or to both the upper and lower extremes of a small range (see Example 7). In its most basic form this creates an obsessive, ostinato effect, which often lends extra impetus to the following melodic idea. A wholesale use of such repetition occurs in *Summe*

Example 2. *Summe trinitati*, Agnus Dei, bars 40–3, discantus and contratenor

---

13 Quoted in *ibid.*, p. 134. Kenney's barring is 71f.
14 *Ibid.*, p. 131. Kenney's barring is 153f.

Example 3. *Flos regalis*, Credo, bars 84–5, 88–9, 92–4, discantus and contratenor

trinitati, in which the many repeated *d'*s of the cantus firmus become an aural 'tag' which recurs at regular intervals throughout each movement.[15] A related, but more concentrated effect involves a repeated alternation of the same notes between two parts in duos. This effect can be repeated at intervals, giving structural cohesion to a duet passage, as in Example 3, from the Credo of *Flos regalis*.[16]

Imitation, at least in the later manner of articulating new phrase settings, is not significant to Frye's style. When parts do share motifs after rests, it is almost always in duo passages in which the effect is often more of the exchange of an idea or of a short echo than of thoroughgoing motivic structuring. Imitation in Frye's masses is typically much more subtle, involving the exchange of brief motifs within phrases. This approach imbues the music with a sense of cohesion without the straitjacketing of the pervasive imitation of later times (see, for instance, *Summe trinitati*, Gloria, bars 46–7). When Frye does indulge in imitation, much of the interest is typically rhythmic, with close imitation setting up cross-rhythms (Example 4). A subtle instance of rhythmic imitation helps to articulate the contrast between brief duos of low and high voices in the Gloria of *Flos regalis*. At bar 54 the discantus enters, albeit at a different point in the perfection, with the same rhythmic pattern with which, some three bars earlier, the bass had begun the previous duo, but moving in the opposite direction.

---

[15] The same idea also occurs in the contratenor, for instance in the Agnus, bar 3. Curtis's view that Frye's 'interest in the c.f. was not primarily connected with any distinctive melodic character it may have had in its normal form' should perhaps be questioned in the light of such structural exploitation of the contour of a borrowed melody. (See 'The English Masses', p. 71.) Closely similar figures occur elsewhere in Frye's work: see, for instance, *Sospitati dedit*, bars 26–8 and 49–50, and *Nobilis et pulchra*, Credo, bars 43–4 (see Example 21).

[16] Bars 43–6 of the Credo of *Nobilis et pulchra* (see Example 21) provide a similar example. This passage was cited in the same connection by Kenney, *Walter Frye and the Contenance Angloise*, p. 134.

Example 4. *Summe trinitate*, Credo, bars 49–50, discantus and contratenor

Indeed, while melodic repetition is common in Frye's work, the repetition of rhythmic cells is far more integral to his style. Surely one of the most musically satisfying examples of this is the wonderful climax of the first part of the Gloria of *Flos regalis*, where repeated rhythmic passages in three of the four parts are woven together with a freely ranging contratenor altus (see Example 5). Kenney also commented on the powerful effect of this passage,

Example 5. *Flos regalis*, Gloria, bars 59–68

noting that 'the setting of all voices against one another in conflicting rhythmic schemes ... intensifies the effect'.[17] Repeated rhythmic ideas often leap out of the texture, especially when, as here,
they contradict the predominant metre. Such tactics can lend the
melodic line enormous momentum, as in the duple divisions of the
tempus perfectum bars 42–3 of the Credo of *Flos regalis*, which propel
the discantus into one of its most rhythmically ornate passages
(Example 6).

Example 6. *Flos regalis*, Credo, bars 42–7, discantus

Brief rhythmic ideas are often very cleverly used to give cohesion
to a particular passage in which they are repeated at intervals,
sometimes in one voice alone, but more usually across the voice
parts. A typical example may be seen in bars 12–20 of the motet
Salve virgo mater, which in all likelihood is a contrafact of the original
Kyrie of *Summe trinitati*.[18] During these nine bars, the same figure,

[17] *Ibid.*, p. 134. The passage is quoted on p. 133.

[18] A possibility first broached by B. L. Trowell ('Frye, Walter', *The New Grove Dictionary of
Music and Musicians*, ed. S. Sadie, 20 vols. (London, 1980), VI, p. 877). The length of the
work presupposes the original setting of a prosula Kyrie. Trowell suggested the prosula
Conditor Kyrie, the text prescribed by the Sarum use for Trinity Sunday, the feast from
which the cantus firmus of the mass is taken. The issue was explored in greater depth by
Curtis, 'The English Masses', I, pp. 96–106. Curtis also attempted a reconstruction using
the prosula *Omnipotens pater* (*ibid.*, II, pp. 26–9).

More recently (*The Brussels Masses*, pp. 188–9), Curtis adopted a more cautious line,
noting that while the poor relation between text and music may suggest that the work as
it now stands is a contrafact, this need not necessarily imply that it was originally a
Kyrie. As he observes, the motets in some so-called mass-motet cycles survive in different
sources with distinct texts. Still, it is difficult to see how a mass-motet cycle would fit into
the English mass tradition, especially since, as Reinhard Strohm has pointed out, all the
other cases are largely confined to the related, Germanic, Trent and Strahov (Prague,
Strahov Monastery, MS DG. IV. 47) manuscripts ('Messzyklen über deutsche Lieder in
den Trienter Codices', *Liedstudien: Wolfgang Osthoff zum 60. Geburtstag*, ed. M. Just and R.
Wiesend (Tutzing, 1989), pp. 88–9).

Strohm's view of two separate traditions involving, on the one hand, five-movement
cycles including contrafact Kyries and, on the other, *bona fide* six-movement mass-motet
cycles, seems to make best sense of the surviving repertory, but even this is not without
its problems. The most significant of these centres on the still little-understood role of the
prosula Kyrie outside England: if, as Strohm suggests, the masses on *Meditatio cordis* and
Hilf und gib rat share with the *Missa Summe trinitati* the status of decapitated masses with
contrafact Kyries, it is difficult to explain the lengths of these movements otherwise than
as erstwhile prosula settings.

involving an upward leap to a dotted minim followed by descending crotchets, occurs three times, twice in the discantus and once in the contratenor. The figure is heard on three further occasions later in the motet (bars 49–50, 54 and 63–4), though only on the last occurrence in precisely the same form, in a contrapuntal context strikingly similar to its first statement at bar 11. On other occasions such rhythmic figures are used to relate similar passages separated by other material.[19] The immediate aural impact of rhythmic repetition is often exploited to provide structural articulation, as at bars 56–9 of the Credo of *Flos regalis*, where it is combined with sequence. Here, the tactic forces attention on the short duo passage, which becomes a focal point, breaking up two fully scored blocks. Sequence, as in the work of other composers of the period, is infrequent, and, as in this instance, usually proceeds in a downward direction.[20]

Rhythmic repetitions are also often introduced to provide a sense of cohesion at climactic points, as at the conclusion of the Gloria of *Flos regalis*, where five statements of the same simple rhythmic idea (semibreve rest–semibreve–breve) considerably tighten up the texture (see bars 138–44). Two such repetitions help to give a resounding conclusion to part one of the Credo of the same mass. The first is a two-voice idea in which the melodic shape of the discantus line is inverted on its repetition three bars later, while the second, which is less prominent, involves the similar inversion in the contratenor of a figure first heard in the bass (Example 7).

In fact, mastery of structure is perhaps the most impressive and sophisticated aspect of Frye's art. Melodic and rhythmic ideas which are often extremely simple give a sense of cohesion and structural poise lacking in the work of many of his contemporaries. A classic example is provided by the Credo of the *Missa Summe trinitati*. A short–long repeated-note motif first heard in the tenor in the second bar is immediately repeated in the discantus and thereafter pervades the whole movement. Far from becoming tedious, this simple motif is treated with the utmost taste and restraint, by turn saturating the texture, occurring in isolation and disappearing

---

[19] As in the Credo of *Summe trinitati*, see below.
[20] See also, for instance, *Nobilis et pulchra*, Kyrie, bars 44–7 (two parts). Upward-moving sequences do occur occasionally, as at bars 47–52 of the contratenor in the Credo of *Nobilis et pulchra*.

Example 7. *Flos regalis*, Credo, bars 70–4

altogether. With the exceptions of the lengthy duos which open the two sections, this movement is almost entirely fully scored. There are only two other, very brief, duo passages, and here again Frye shows his grasp of internal balance. In both cases, a tenor line which revolves around repeating *d'*s from the cantus firmus is paired with a discantus line which rises from *d'* to *a'* and back again.[21] Kenney noted similar, more extensive, structural repetition in the discantus line in the duos of *Flos regalis*.[22] The absence of the cantus firmus lends such reworking of material in duos a particular cohesive force.

This type of musical articulation of structural junctures provided by changes in texture occurs quite frequently, and is emphasised by a variety of means. The second part of the same movement provides another fine example at bar 58, where the tenor entry finally fills out the texture after a duo introduction of no fewer than eighteen bars. The *g* on which the tenor enters provides the cadence note of the duo passage, yet this in turn is a springboard to a further cadence on c at the end of the same bar, emphatically stated via contrary motion in the discantus and contratenor (bar 58). As if to emphasise the sense of arrival still further, the same motion is immediately repeated by both parts (see Example 8).

One of the most obvious effects of reduced scoring is to lend

---

[21] See bars 31–2 and 80–1.
[22] *Walter Frye and the Contenance Angloise*, p. 144.

Example 8. *Summe trinitate*, Credo, bars 57–9

emphasis to the fully scored passages which follow. That Frye was acutely aware of this is clear from the various ways in which he exploits its structural potential, as in the above instance. He is especially inventive in this regard in *Flos regalis*, where the four-voice texture allows for greater contrast than is possible in the other, three-voice, masses.[23] A particularly successful example can be seen in part two of the Gloria, where full scoring is finally introduced after no fewer than forty bars of duos for varying combinations. Only two bars into the full scoring (bar 112), the discantus hits *e''*, the top note of its range, for the first time in the whole section. The climactic effect is particularly emphasised by the fact that the final duo combination had involved the top two voices, with the discantus venturing up to *d''*, but no higher. Its placing on the first beat of the bar underlines still more forcefully the sense of arrival. In fact, *e''* is used sufficiently rarely in this mass for its introduction to provide a focal point elsewhere also. Another instance where this potential is exploited is at bar 155 of the Credo, where the *e''* at the beginning of the bar provides a strong sense of arrival only four bars before the end of the movement.

Frye typically draws on a whole network of features to create a powerful sense of arrival at a fully scored section, and his subtle sense of pace and climax could be illustrated by almost any instance. It is particularly impressive, however, in the four-voice *Flos regalis*, of which the example just discussed in the Gloria is typical. An acceleration of motion towards the end of the preceding

---

[23]   As Kenney points out, the potential for reduced trio sections is almost never exploited (*ibid.*, p. 145). However, this, as David Fallows pointed out to me, was standard practice in the mid–late fifteenth century.

duo, coupled with syncopation and close imitation, creates a strong drive to the full scoring at bar 110. But as soon as this point is reached, the music broadens impressively to a majestic pace: besides the rise to e'' already discussed, the sense of arrival is underlined by longer note values in regular, unsyncopated rhythms. The repeated b's in the discantus also serve a broader structural function, relating this entry to almost every other discantus entry in the Gloria. Repeated bs signify the entry of the discantus at the beginnings of other fully scored sections (bars 21 and 35), and underpin other important moments (as, for instance, at bars 127–8).

The extraordinary integration of Frye's style should by now be clear. It is a hallmark through which he stands out as a master with full control over his musical resources. Deepening familiarity with these masses only adds to one's admiration at their endless fund of subtlety and sophistication. Though clearly recognisable as products of the same mind, however, Frye's masses display differing emphases of his characteristic idioms. Such distinctions may help to give some idea of the relative chronology of the three pieces. The compilation of the nucleus of the Brussels manuscript for the marriage of Charles the Bold and Margaret of York in 1468, as demonstrated by Rob Wegman,[24] provides at least a *terminus ante quem* from which to work. Perhaps surprisingly, in view of the disposition of scoring across the three masses, the most striking stylistic distinction between them separates *Nobilis et pulchra* from the other two. The stylistic consistency and elegance of *Summe trinitati* and *Flos regalis* are to a large degree missing in *Nobilis et pulchra*, which by comparison sounds like the work of a composer who has not yet truly found his feet. The impression of this as a somewhat earlier work is supported by the style of the contratenor: this is a genuine contratenor *altus et bassus*, continually crossing and recrossing the tenor and sometimes, as in bars 13–14 of the Agnus, where it lurches through no less than an octave and a fourth, covering a lot of ground over a very short period. A date in the 1450s, and probably rather earlier than later, would seem appropriate, placing it chronologically alongside such other English works of the period as the masses by Bedyngham.

---

[24] See note 1.

By comparison, the contratenor of *Summe trinitati* keeps for the most part below the tenor, to which it gives harmonic support. Although such contrasts of contratenor behaviour are crude features on their own by which to propose chronological distinctions, they are symptomatic of quite different approaches to texture and motivic style. Moreover, their value in drawing such contrasts increases when one is dealing with works from the same pen which show other suggestive distinctions. This is a very advanced work for its time, the more so since the presence in TrentC 88 of the related motet *Salve virgo mater*, probably, as outlined above, a contrafact of the Kyrie of the mass, would seem to presuppose a date prior to 1462.[25]

Flos regalis belongs with a very small group of English masses scored for four voices. Indeed, the anonymous masses *Caput* and *Veterem hominem* are almost its only indisputable companions to have survived intact.[26] This coincidence of scoring has led some writers to draw close comparisons between the works.[27] However, beyond their shared scoring and similar use of stock English practices, it is difficult to see any great similarity between *Flos regalis* and the other

---

[25] See S. E. Saunders, 'The Dating of the Trent Codices from their Watermarks, with a Study of the Local Liturgy of Trent in the Fifteenth Century' (Ph.D. dissertation, University of London, King's College, 1985), pp. 87–8. Saunders notes, however, that the motet was added to the source by a hand not present elsewhere in the manuscript. This view is supported by Rebecca Gerber, who adds, though, that Johannes Wiser, the main scribe of the source, added the clefs on the recto of the opening which contains the copy ('The Manuscript Trent, Castello del Buonconsiglio, 88: A Study of Fifteenth-Century Manuscript Transmission and Repertory' (Ph.D. dissertation, University of California at Santa Barbara, 1984), pp. 19, 23, 25). She infers from this that Wiser must have been close at hand when the motet was copied, though it seems more likely that his small additions came about through *post facto* editing due to negligence on the part of the main scribe of the piece. Whether this means that the work was copied significantly later than the main body of the manuscript, however, remains open to question.

[26] The other indisputably English example to have survived complete is the anonymous *Missa Salve sancta parens* in Trent 93/90, though Margaret Bent has proposed that one of the voices in this mass may in fact be a later addition to a three-voice work (*Four Anonymous Masses*, Early English Church Music 22 (London, 1979), p. 181). Possible further candidates among the anonymous repertory include the cycle on folios 65ᵛ–75ʳ of Rome, Cappella Sistina 14 (with a fragmentary concordance on fol. 30bis of Lucca, Archivio di Stato, Biblioteca Manoscritti MS 238 (the Lucca Choirbook) and the *Missa Meditatio cordis*, a 'mass-motet cycle' whose motet, like that of *Summe trinitati*, may also be a contrafact prosula Kyrie (Strahov, fols. 85ᵛ–92ʳ; motet in Trent 88, fols. 284ᵛ–286ʳ).

The various fragmentary cycles include Plummer's *Missa Nesciens mater*, partly preserved in London, British Library Add. MS 54324, the *Missa Requiem aeternam* in Add. C 87, and a *Missa Alma redemptoris mater* of which parts survive in London, British Library Add. MS 54324 (Add. 54324) and in the Lucca Choirbook.

[27] See Wegman's review of Curtis, *The Brussels Masses*, p. 587.

four-voice cycles. Though the *Caput* mass is undoubtedly a major achievement, by comparison with *Flos regalis* its style appears rather antiquated. The consistency, pacing, structure and more integrated texture of the Frye mass surely belong to a later time, and it is difficult to imagine that the two masses can be separated by much less than fifteen, or even twenty, years. It seems likely that *Flos regalis* was a fairly recent work when it was copied for the celebrations of 1468.

THE BRUSSELS ANONYMOUS MASS

On assessing the anonymous mass, it must be acknowledged from the outset that there is one fundamental structural feature which separates it decisively from the masses ascribed to Frye: while the latter are, of course, all based on borrowed melodies, the anonymous work appears to be freely composed. This distinction is all the more marked since Frye sticks to his borrowed melodies very faithfully, and, at least in the two three-voice masses, keeps to a closely similar rhythmic format for each statement. That said, however, the tenors of these masses owe nothing to the monolithic, long-note format of many early cyclic mass tenors; indeed, the rhythms of the borrowed lines commonly conform almost as closely to the character of the accompanying parts as does the tenor of the anonymous mass. And while the unascribed work may lack the backbone of a *cantus prius factus*, it has, like the three ascribed masses, a structural groundplan in which at least the three central movements follow a fairly consistent pattern.[28] As is typical in English masses of this period, parallels are particularly strong between Gloria and Credo, and motivic links between corresponding points across the movements are by no means unusual, as can be seen, for example, in a comparison between the openings of fully scored sections in the Gloria (bar 30) and Credo (44) (Example 9).

Presence or absence of a cantus firmus clearly has a great deal to do with the function of the mass concerned, and it is certainly true that a large-scale, festive mass with a prosula Kyrie is far more likely to be based on a borrowed melody than a modest, ferial or votive, work. This important distinction notwithstanding, however,

---

[28] See Table 1. For outlines of the structures of Frye's masses, see Curtis, 'The English Masses', pp. 66–95.

Example 9. *Sine nomine*
(a) Gloria, bars 30–1

(b) Credo, bars 44–5

on turning directly from the masses ascribed to Frye to the
anonymous work, one immediately feels on familiar ground: the
surface contours are recognisable at once, and if an impression of a
less ambitious work none the less comes through, this is surely
because the original function of the work never demanded that it be
anything else.

Similarities in the melodic and rhythmic style are everywhere
evident. As in the masses ascribed to Frye (see p. 196), phrases are
generally short, and are divided up by minim rests on the beat. The
line frequently resumes after such breaks with one of the patterns
familiar from similar junctures in the Frye masses: a minim followed by a longer note, an upward-moving fourth divided into a
second and a third (both illustrated by Example 10), or, when the
voice has moved to the lowest part of its range, an octave leap (see
Example 14). The restricted melodic style and rhythmic integra-

Example 10. *Sine nomine*, Kyrie, bars 49–51, discantus

tion of the three parts of this mass are even more noticeable than in the masses ascribed to Frye. Yet although he is operating on a more modest scale, the composer of the anonymous mass frequently makes his sense of architecture keenly felt. As in the ascribed works, melodic and rhythmic ideas often seem calculated to make a structural point, either drawing attention to a climactic moment or giving a section cohesion through judicious repetition.

Exact repetition of melodic ideas is not especially frequent, though it does occur, sometimes within the prevailing metre (see Example 14), but on other occasions, more interestingly, against it (Example 11). As in the ascribed masses, the effect of repetition in one part is sometimes cleverly masked by subtle variation in another, as at bars 13–15 of the Credo, when a repeated figure in the contratenor is set against rhythmic imitation between tenor and discantus, which hovers around the interval from a' to f' (Example 12). This type of obsessive concentration on a single note or inter-val is a hallmark which is similarly scattered through all four masses. A similar instance in Agnus II, involving obsessively repetitious figures in both discantus and tenor, creates a dynamic effect that drives the music forward to the conclusion of the section (Example 13). As in the Frye masses, this sort of pattern, hovering around the same note or interval, is far more usual than clear repetition.

As in the ascribed masses, repetitions which are varied, often in a minor way, are much more common than exact repeats, and make an intriguing aural impact. Exact repetition is often carefully pla-

Example 11. *Sine nomine*, Gloria, bars 59–61, discantus

Example 12. *Sine nomine*, Credo, bars 13–15

Example 13. *Sine nomine*, Agnus Dei, bars 65–73, discantus and tenor

ced to attract the ear and, having succeeded, is liquidated and diffused through the other parts, lending a passage great cohesion. Example 14 shows a highly effective instance of this from Agnus

Example 14. *Sine nomine*, Agnus Dei, bars 21–34

Dei I: a trochaic falling figure which is exactly repeated only once instigates a series of descending stepwise figures to which the other two parts also latch on. The result is to give the concluding cadence which follows a powerful sense of arrival.[29]

As in the Frye masses, imitation is often only part of a more thoroughgoing motivic unity which can lend a passage considerable structural backbone. A particularly effective instance occurs towards the end of part two of the Gloria, where a short motif, anticipated in the discantus, is repeated and fragmented in the tenor before spreading into the other two parts, driving the section towards its conclusion (Example 15). Clear imitation is no more prominent in this work than in the three masses ascribed to Frye, and instances involving – as here – all three parts are rare. Again, when it does appear, it is usually within phrases in duos, where it serves to bind the two parts together motivically. The cohesive effect is particularly strong when the interval between entries is close. Such close imitation creates a powerful drive towards the end of the first section of the Sanctus, where the sense of unity is enhanced by descending sequence in curious five-minim units (see Example 16). Imitative exchange between all three parts is very rare, though not unknown (as, for instance, in the Credo, bars 17–18).

A glance at the examples already cited is sufficient to confirm that much of the interest in the motivic interconnections of this mass is, as in those ascribed to Frye, rhythmic. Indeed, rhythmic repetition in general is surely the most fundamental cohesive force in all four works. In the anonymous mass, as in the three ascribed ones, this is frequently syncopated, and often demands attention, as in the previous example, by jolting the rhythmic pulse away from the basic metre. Instances of rhythmic imitation far outnumber those in which there is a clear melodic correspondence, and the Credo provides a fine example at bars 35–40, where the two parts are woven together by short rhythmic cells. As so often here and in

---

[29] Examples of such use of repetition to create a sense of arrival could be multiplied many times. The conclusion of Agnus III, before the final 'Dona nobis pacem' is similarly climactic: here both discantus and tenor play with repeated ideas, in one case involving imitation between them (see, for example, Agnus Dei, bars 83–99). This passage gives a further indication of the subtle range of possibilities available within the basic principle of repetition: by turn, it can be exact or varied, immediate or separated by other material.

Example 15. *Sine nomine*, Gloria, bars 71–88

Example 16. *Sine nomine*, Sanctus, bars 58–63

the ascribed masses, this passage seems calculated to make a structural impact, in this case highlighting the following fully scored setting of 'Et incarnatus est', which crowns and concludes this section of the movement. In a more specific case, a curious syncopated passage of dotted semibreves in the contratenor in the Sanctus of the *Missa Nobilis et pulchra* is mirrored by a similar case in the tenor in the same movement of the anonymous mass (Example 17).[30]

Example 17
(a) *Nobilis et pulchra*, Sanctus, bars 55–7, contratenor

(b) *Sine nomine*, Sanctus, bars 27–9, tenor

The anonymous composer, in common with Frye, can imbue a section of his mass with unity by means of the simplest of musical devices. Like the Credo of the *Missa Summe trinitati*, in which Frye weaves the musical fabric together beautifully with a simple short–long repeated note figure, the anonymous Credo gains a similar, if less eloquent, cohesion by means of repeated notes. These are mostly on a', when they are always followed by descending motion to f' or e'. Such repeated-note figures usually instigate a passage of obsessive return to the note in question, as at bars 67–74 (Example 18). In two cases, at 'Et resurrexit' (bar 67) and 'Et iterum' (bar 87), the figure takes the same form, though on other occasions, as at 'Et incarnatus' and 'et in unum' it is subtly varied. It may sometimes be tempting to read too much into text underlay, though

Example 18. *Sine nomine*, Credo, bars 67–74, discantus

---

[30] A similar passage occurs in close imitation between discantus and contratenor in bars 11–12 of the Credo of *Summe trinitati*.

it is worth noting that in all these cases (and in the case of 'et vitam') the phrase set begins with the word 'et'. The underlay in the source is, moreover, generally highly specific. In fact, the repeated use in the Credo of falling figures beginning on a' turns out to form only part of the more thoroughgoing motivic unity which, as in the Frye masses, is such a striking feature of this work as a whole: similar motifs are prominent in the Gloria, and to a lesser degree pepper the whole mass.

COMPARISON WITH OTHER MASSES

The broad extent of stylistic relationships between the masses by Frye and their anonymous companion in the Brussels manuscript should by now be beyond doubt. Yet such comparisons, however persuasive, are of limited usefulness in isolation. Any suggestions of related or common authorship need to be checked against a range of contemporary works, a concern which might perhaps be viewed as especially urgent here in view of Tinctoris's disparaging judgement on what he saw as the monotonously uniform state of English music in the mid-fifteenth century.[31]

One of the most obvious areas in which to look for masses related to the Brussels anonymous might initially appear to be the output of John Bedyngham; his, after all, is the name most frequently mentioned along with Frye's as one of the two dominant English figures of mid-century. Yet Bedyngham's two masses bear little resemblance to those of Frye or to the Brussels anonymous mass: their texture is altogether denser, with little motivic interconnection between parts, lower voices which are frequently slower-moving than the discantus and many prominent internal cadences. Such differences are scarcely surprising in view of the much earlier copying dates for the Bedyngham masses in Trent 93 and 90,[32] and it seems likely that between ten and twenty years separated their composition from that of the anonymous mass and *Summe trinitati*.

In fact, chronology presents the most serious problem to any

---

[31] Albert Seay, ed., *Johannis Tinctoris: Opera theoretica*, IIa: *Proportionale musices*, Corpus Scriptorum de Musica 22 (n.p., 1978), p. 10.

[32] Saunders gives paper dates of 1450–2 for the earliest copies of movements from the *Missa sine nomine* in Trent 93, and 1454–8 for the earliest copies of movements from *Deul angouisseux* in Trent 93 (see 'The Dating of Trent 93 and Trent 90', *I codici musicali trentini*, ed. N. Pirrotta and D. Curti (Trent, 1985), pp. 70, 73).

attempt to find a context for the masses in the Brussels manuscript: very few demonstrably English masses from the 1460s survive with which to compare them. One possible candidate outside the manuscript itself is the *Missa sine nomine* in the Strahov manuscript by Standly.[33] However, this extremely modest work is also a very different animal from the Frye or anonymous masses, whose textural interest and rhythmic and motivic ingenuity it entirely lacks.

The two cycles in the Brussels manuscript by Richard Cox and John Plummer are, sadly, almost the only contemporary English masses to have survived complete, but neither of these has much in common, either, with the works by Frye or the anonymous composer. The Cox mass pits a comparatively melodious upper voice against a duo texture which seems largely to consist of a series of elaborated repeats of the same progression.[34] It is an appealing work with a surprising emphasis on sonorous, homophonic textures, though it cannot approach its more sophisticated companions in motivic and structural ingenuity. The *Sine nomine* mass by Plummer, on the other hand, belongs, if not to a later date, then at least to a later phase of development: its elaborate filigree surface is a harbinger of things to come in the Eton Choirbook, while it makes extensive and sophisticated use of the imitative texture for which Plummer is noted.

Apparently rather closer in style to the masses under scrutiny is what remains of Plummer's *Missa Nesciens mater*, parts of which survive in the fragmentary source London, British Library Add. MS 54324.[35] However, although there is at least a suggestion here of the rhythmic integration between voices so familiar from the Frye and anonymous masses, the similarity is at best superficial. Moreover, the cantus firmus-bearing tenor often moves in comparatively long note values, a relatively infrequent feature of the Frye masses, and there is little suggestion of an attempt at motivic unity.

The only surviving northern manuscript from the same period as

---

[33] Strahov, fols. 53ʳ–53ᵛ, 164ᵛ–165ʳ, 167ᵛ–171ʳ.

[34] For an examination of the structure of this mass, see Curtis, 'The English Masses', pp. 110–15.

[35] Rob Wegman, who has made a study of the paper which comprises this source, informs me that the closest paper he has been able to trace to that on which the Plummer mass is copied can be dated 1456–8. See G. Piccard, *Die Ochsenkopf-Wasserzeichen* (Stuttgart, 1966), nos. 385 and 391, pp. 427–8.

Brussels is, of course, the fragmentary Lucca Choirbook. Indeed, the earliest stage of this source, consisting largely of English masses, was apparently copied between *c.* 1467 and 1469, and is thus exactly contemporary with the English nucleus of Brussels.[36] Though some of these masses, such as *Caput* and *Quem malignus spiritus*, are clearly much earlier than the source itself, others could well have been quite new at the time they were copied. One work in particular bears comparison with the Frye and anonymous masses under scrutiny: a *Missa Alma redemptoris mater* of which parts of the Credo, Sanctus and Agnus have survived in Lucca.[37] The free paraphrase of the cantus firmus, highly unusual in a four-voice English mass from this period, helps to give the surface of this work some similarity with that of the *Missa Flos regalis*, whose cantus firmus presentation varies rhythmically from statement to statement. The frequently syncopated rhythmic style is also reminiscent of Frye, though, in contrast to Frye, repetition and sequential ideas, as Reinhard Strohm has noted, are absent. The rather nervous gyrations of the melodic lines, to some degree reminiscent of the Plummer mass, lack the purpose and integration which bind Frye's textures together so distinctively.

THE FRAGMENTARY MASS IN LUCCA

There is, however, another mass in the Lucca Choirbook which bears far more than a passing resemblance to the Frye and Brussels anonymous masses: this, not surprisingly, is the fragmentary work by Frye mentioned at the beginning of this article. Only the discantus line of the Kyrie survives, though its profile is entirely consistent with those of the four masses already discussed: the same constantly shifting and heavily syncopated rhythm is again hitched to a restricted range with familiar-sounding passages involving constant returns to the same note.

Although the rest of the original texture is lost, Brian Trowell cleverly spotted that the discantus line fits perfectly against the

---

[36] For a discussion and dating of Lucca, see R. Strohm, *Music in Late Medieval Bruges* (Oxford, 1985), pp. 120–36.

[37] Parts of the Kyrie are found in Add. 54324 (see note 26). Strohm, p. 127, contains a description of the mass and (pp. 220–5) a transcription of the Sanctus up to the end of Osanna I. I am grateful to Professor Strohm for drawing my attention to the stylistic similarities between this mass and those under discussion.

tenor of Frye's or Bedyngham's song *So ys emprentid*. Having also realised that the two-voice fabric could be completed by lightly paraphrasing the song's contratenor, Trowell was able to arrive at a highly convincing reconstruction of the entire Kyrie.[38] The resulting piece is thus a curiously unique paraphrase of the entire song.

But there are aspects of this work which link it much more closely to the Brussels anonymous mass. The most immediately striking of these is its structure: both this Kyrie and the one in the Brussels mass have two settings of the Christe, in a format apparently calling for alternatim performance in which alternate invocations, beginning with the first, would have been sung in plainsong. This feature relates these pieces to the large number of sectionally constructed independent ninefold Kyries in the earlier Trent Codices and elsewhere, though its application in cycles – and the Lucca fragment must surely have been part of one – is most unusual.[39]

This feature alone gives at least a *prima facie* reason to suspect some sort of relationship between the two works, though on closer inspection their similarities come much more sharply into focus. The head-motif of the two works (see Example 19) is closely similar, and although its opening figure has, of course, one of the commonest opening profiles in fifteenth-century music in general, it is also true, as the example shows, that not only the first section but each of the four sections begins very similarly in each case. This is particularly clear in the case of the second Christe, in which the Brussels setting follows a contour similar to that of Lucca throughout most of its length. Other movements of the Brussels anonymous mass, which uses a consistent head-motif, show further similarities with the profile of the Lucca discantus, and in some cases these are even closer than those of the Kyrie. A case in point is the setting of the first Agnus invocation in Brussels, which is compared with Lucca in Example 20. Similar resemblances come and go in the course of the other movements.

The question remains, of course, how did such similarities come

---

[38] See 'Frye, Walter', p. 877. See also Strohm, pp. 125, 173.

[39] I know of only one cycle, which is otherwise totally unrelated to the two under discussion, with a Kyrie containing two distinct invocations of the Christe. This is the *Missa Regina celi* on folios 25ʳ–33ʳ of Trent, Castello del Buonconsiglio, MS 91. Two other cycles include ninefold sectional Kyries: Dufay's *Missa Ave regina celorum*, and the mass by Pullois, both of whose structures involve internal repetition.

Example 19

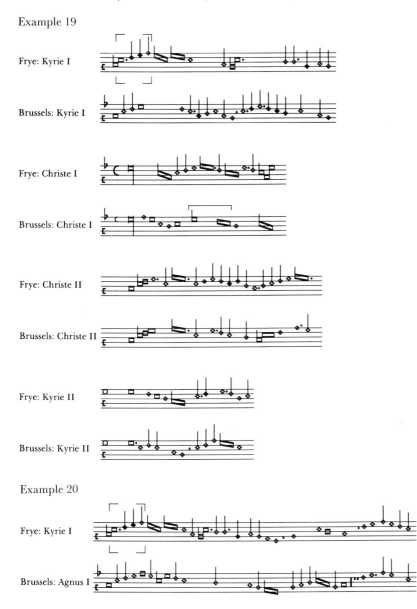

Frye: Kyrie I

Brussels: Kyrie I

Frye: Christe I

Brussels: Christe I

Frye: Christe II

Brussels: Christe II

Frye: Kyrie II

Brussels: Kyrie II

Example 20

Frye: Kyrie I

Brussels: Agnus I

about? It is difficult to imagine that they can have arisen fortuitously in different minds, although it is not impossible that one was used as a model for the other by a different composer. If this possibility were allowed, the emulator would surely have to be the composer of the Brussels mass, given the reliance of the Frye discantus on *So ys emprentid*. But in view of the quality of the Brussels mass and its manifest similarities to its companions by Frye in the same source, this scenario seems unlikely.

If we go one stage further and accept that the two works are by the same composer, is it possible to envisage that one was composed without regard to the other? This seems unlikely, though it is not of course impossible that a composer, writing two modest mass cycles closely together, could have unconsciously re-used musical ideas which were floating around in his mind at the time. A definitive answer to this question is perhaps not possible, though the important point here is that it is more than likely that these works are by the same composer, and that that composer was Walter Frye.

SOSPITATI DEDIT

Yet two significant pieces in the jigsaw puzzle remain missing: first, while the Brussels anonymous mass is apparently freely composed, the masses ascribed to Frye are, as I commented earlier, all based systematically on borrowed material. And secondly, the disposition of the voices in the Brussels anonymous differs from that in any of Frye's other masses. A context for both of these problems can be seen in another work by Frye: his motet *Sospitati dedit*.[40]

This work also, of course, draws on borrowed material: the Prose for the Feast of St Nicholas,[41] which, linking into a long English tradition of migrant cantus firmus settings, passes freely between voices. Not only is the chant allowed to wander from part to part, but it is sometimes so heavily diluted that, as Sparks showed, it is difficult to demonstrate that it is actually present at all.[42] At the other extreme, we have, in the case of the Kyrie on *So ys emprentid*, a paraphrase of a complete pre-existent song which, as Reinhard Strohm pointed out, is unique in the surviving repertory of the mid-fifteenth century.[43]

---

[40] For editions, see Kenney, ed., *Walter Frye: Collected Works*, pp. 17–19, and S. R. Charles, ed., *The Music of the Pepys MS 1236*, Corpus Mensurabilis Musicae 40 (n.p., 1960), pp. 131–3.

[41] It may be worth noting in view of the cantus firmus of this one surviving motet by Frye that the composer was himself a member of the Confraternity of St Nicholas in London (see Curtis, *The Brussels Masses*, p. ix).

[42] For an analysis of the cantus firmus treatment, see E. H. Sparks, *Cantus Firmus in Mass and Motet* (Berkeley and Los Angeles, 1963), pp. 75–9.

[43] Strohm, *Music in Late Medieval Bruges*, p. 125.

Frye was plainly capable of a range of approaches to the reworking of borrowed material that extended far beyond the basic principle of the tenor cantus firmus, and it is quite possible that the Brussels anonymous mass, with its widespread repetition and reworking of ideas, may also be hiding pre-existent music. But perhaps more significant is the observation that Frye was clearly a musical architect who was well capable of creating a large-scale and coherent musical structure, with or without the support of pre-existent material.

The distinct, rarely overlapping ranges of the voices of the Brussels mass, with the tenor as the lowest part in the texture, separate this work from all the masses ascribed to Frye. The closest of the ascribed works in terms of textural disposition is the *Missa Summe trinitati*, but although the voices of this mass are generally differentiated in range, it is the contratenor which, following the standard disposition of three-voice texture in the later fifteenth century, is the lowest part. The Plummer mass in Brussels follows the practice of the anonymous mass in placing the tenor at the bottom of the texture, though this mass is in other respects a very different, far more elaborate, work. By contrast, the anonymous mass appears, from its simple rhythmically integrated style and disposition in the almost entirely distinct ranges of tenor, mean and treble, to draw on the tradition of simple discant settings stretching back to the single movements in score in the Old Hall Manuscript. This again links the mass closely to *Sospitati dedit*, which, furthermore, survives in the Pepys Manuscript, a source noted for its preoccupation with works in the same simple, layered texture. The extremely rare clef combination of cl c3 c5 shared by the mass and *Sospitati dedit* is also found in a small group of *Alleluia* settings in Pepys.[44] Indeed, in terms of its melodic and textural contours, *Sospitati dedit* shows an even closer kinship to the anonymous mass than the three ascribed Frye masses.

The two works are also related in their closely aligned text setting in each part, and in a number of harmonic details: neither, like many similarly modest works, fights shy of parallel fifths, and the avoidance of part-crossing results in both in cadences which invariably follow the vii6–I type progression.[45]

---

[44] Nos. 30, 33, 34 and 43 in Charles, *The Music of the Pepys MS 1236*. Two further works, nos. 66 and 101, have the analogous combination c2 c4 f4.

[45] My thanks to Rob Wegman for this observation.

Turning finally to the melodic style, the most immediately
noticeable feature is the common head-motif formula that is also
used in the Brussels anonymous and fragmentary Lucca masses.
But beyond this, the general rhythmic and melodic profile is, after
examining the ascribed and anonymous masses, instantly familiar:
the constantly changing, highly syncopated lines with typical
rhythmic repetitions combine with frequent passages in which the
line returns repeatedly to a single note within a short space of time.
On a more detailed level, the obsessive, ostinato revolutions around
a single note of the type illstrated in Example 21 recall at once
similar figures in the masses.

Example 21

Sospitati dedit, bars 26–8.

Sospitati dedit, bars 49–50

Nobilis et pulchra, bars 43–6

In conclusion, then, it seems highly likely that the Brussels
anonymous mass is part of a related complex of works by Walter
Frye. Yet given its position in the Brussels manuscript, this need
scarcely surprise us: here we have a source compiled for a magnate
with a strong personal interest in music, with a large nucleus of
English masses in which Frye figures prominently, associated with

the ceremonies to celebrate his marriage to an English princess. Furthermore, although the manuscript was assembled piecemeal, the anonymous mass is copied on paper which is clearly related to that of the original nucleus from the same paper mill,[46] and was clearly used by the same court. The original nucleus of the manuscript gives as clear an illustration as could be hoped for of the chapel's appreciation of Frye's art, an appreciation which, it would appear, it was to maintain.

University of Manchester

[46] See Wegman, 'New Data', p. 13.

Early Music History (1992) Volume 11

PAMELA F. STARR

ROME AS THE CENTRE OF THE UNIVERSE: PAPAL GRACE AND MUSIC PATRONAGE*

In 1450 Giovanni Rucellai, a Florentine visitor to Rome, counted 1022 inns 'with signboards', and a quantity of other hostelries.[1] For centuries, Rome had been a magnet that drew the faithful by the tens of thousands to its venerable walls. The reason, of course, was that it was the ancestral home of the Holy See – the centre of the Holy, Catholic and Apostolic Church. Although *urbs Roma* could not boast of this honour throughout the entire Middle Ages, by the middle of the fifteenth century, with the reign of Nicholas V, the Holy See was securely re-established at Rome, never to depart again.

The flood of religious pilgrims to the Holy City, during Jubilee years and at other times, certainly accounted for a large part of the crowds of visitors to Rome. It is not, however, the Rome of the pilgrim that will concern us here, but the city that housed the papal Curia, the vast bureaucracy established to assist the pontiff with the temporal and spiritual responsibilities of his office. Thousands

* A shorter version of this article was delivered at the National Meeting of the American Musicological Society, Baltimore, 1988. A fellowship from the American Academy in Rome (1983–4) and summer research fellowships from the National Endowment for the Humanities (1988) and the Research Council of the University of Nebraska (1989) enabled me to carry out research in the Vatican Archives and in other collections in Rome. In addition to those mentioned in specific contexts below, I should like to thank the following friends and colleagues for their help and advice: Quentin Faulkner, Raymond Haggh, Paula Higgins, Herbert Kellman, Leeman Perkins, Alejandro Planchart, Pamela Potter, Christopher Reynolds and Anne Walters Robertson

This article uses the following abbreviations: ASV, Archivio Segreto Vaticano; ASR, Archivio di Stato di Roma; RS, *Registra Supplicationum*; RV, *Registra Vaticana*; RL, *Registra Lateranensia*; A, *Annatae*; SP, *Sacra Penitentiaria*; IE, *Introitus et Exitus*; l.p.t., *libra parvorum turonensis* (small pound of Tours); fl., papal florin.

[1] C. L. Stinger, *The Renaissance in Rome* (Bloomington, IN, 1985), p. 37.

of petitioners came to Rome not to seek plenary indulgence but to secure for themselves a particular and specific papal Grace. The Grace, *gratia*, was a free-will concession made by the pope, in response to a petition from an individual suppliant. When the petition touched on matters of private conscience – the *forum internum* – it was expedited by the office of the Apostolic Penitentiary, under the direct supervision of the Cardinal Penitentiary. When the request dealt with matters concerning church administration and relations of both laity and clergy with the church – the *forum externum* – it was routinely handled by the Signatura Apostolica (from the 1470s, reorganised and re-named the Signatura Gratiae). In both cases, the petitioner presented a formal request, or supplication. When a petition was sanctioned and signed, either by the Cardinal Penitentiary or his delegate or by the pope or his delegate, the requested Grace was conceded in the form of a papal bull, or *littera apostolica*. During these transactions, money changed hands only in the form of fees paid for the production of the letter.[2]

It was as suppliants for papal Grace that musicians or their representatives thronged the corridors of the Curia. And it was because of their particular prerogative that the popes of the fifteenth century increasingly came to play a major role in the support and development of polyphonic music in the secular chapels, cathedrals and collegiate churches of Europe. There were three principal areas in which the pope exercised the privilege and responsibility of the Grace on behalf of musicians and of music institutions. First, he provided ecclesiastical benefices to supplement the monthly stipends of professional musicians. Secondly, he authorised cathedrals and collegiate churches to convert the revenues of canonical prebends or parish churches into funds for the support of an enhanced choir able to perform polyphony. Thirdly, he granted dispensations and absolution to musicians guilty of canonical lapses or more serious crimes.

The evidence for such patronage of music and musicians on the part of the mid-fifteenth-century papacy comes directly from the

---

[2]   For the *gratia* see W. O'Neill, *Papal Rescripts of Favor* (Washington, DC, 1930); J. D'Amico, *Renaissance Humanism in Papal Rome*, Johns Hopkins University Studies in Historical and Political Science, 101st ser., 1 (Baltimore, 1983), pp. 21ff; R. Naz, 'Rescrit', *Dictionnaire de droit canonique* (Paris, 1935–42), vii, pp. 607–35; B. Katterbach, *Referendarii utriusque signaturiae a Martino V ad Clementem IX*, Studi e Testi 55 (Vatican City, 1931), pp. xi–xiv; and additional references presented below.

massive collection of documents emanating from the papal Curia and now housed principally in the Vatican Archives.[3] I have recently completed a systematic examination of the more than 300,000 documents preserved from the pontificates of Nicholas V, Calixtus III, Pius II and Paul II, whose reigns covered the years 1447–71. This examination yielded more than 1200 documents directly related to music institutions or musicians.[4] The present article examines each of the three aspects of the papal Grace as they bear on the support of music during the fifteenth century. To illustrate vividly the power and efficacy of papal patronage of music, I analyse several examples of concessions granted by these popes to composers and music institutions of historical importance.

'ARS ET PRAXIS BENEFICIORUM'

To music historians, the provision of ecclesiastical benefices is undoubtedly the most familiar of the three types of papal patronage of music.[5] It was also the most sought-after of papal Graces, by

---

[3] For the history and description of the various *fondi* of the Vatican Archives, particularly as they relate to the period of this article, see L. Boyle, *A Survey of the Vatican Archives and of its Medieval Holdings* (Toronto, 1972). Boyle also surveys the comparatively smaller number of fifteenth-century papal documents currently housed in the Archivio di Stato in Rome (p. 48). A fuller discussion of these documents is presented in E. Lodolini, *L'Archivio di stato di Roma* (Rome, 1960), pp. 65–84.

[4] All of the information gleaned from these documents will, in due course, be stored in REN*ARCH, the Renaissance archival database for music, currently housed at Columbia University under the direction of Professor Leeman Perkins.

[5] Franz Haberl set the stage with two monographs, one on the career of the quondam papal musician Guillaume Du Fay and another that attempted to investigate the means by which the Renaissance popes supported their own *cappella pontificia* – both works depending heavily on documents from the Vatican Archives. See his *Bausteine für Musik-geschichte*, I: *Wilhelm Du Fay* (Leipzig, 1885) and III: *Die römische 'Schola Cantorum' und die päpstlichen Kapellsänger bis zur Mitte des 16. Jahrhunderts* (Leipzig, 1888), both volumes reprinted together (Hildesheim, 1971). Although many studies in this century have utilised information about benefices to good effect in documenting the life of Renaissance musicians (see C. Reynolds, 'Musical Careers, Ecclesiastical Benefices, and the Example of Johannes Brunet', *Journal of the American Musicological Society* (hereafter *JAMS*), 37 (1984), pp. 49–97, n. 3, for a substantial list of such studies), there are comparatively fewer recent works that attempt to deal systematically with the beneficial system as an element of music patronage. These include J. Noble, 'New Light on Josquin's Benefices', *Josquin des Prez: Proceedings of the International Josquin Festival-Conference Held at the Juilliard School at Lincoln Center in New York City, 21–25 June 1971*, ed. E. E. Lowinsky and B. J. Blackburn (London, 1976), pp. 76–102; R. Sherr, 'The Papal Chapel ca. 1492–1513 and its Polyphonic Sources' (Ph.D. dissertation, Princeton University, 1975); L. Lockwood, 'Strategies of Music Patronage in the Fifteenth Century: The Cappella of Ercole I d'Este', *Music in Medieval and Early Modern Europe: Patronage, Sources and Texts*, ed. I. Fenlon (Cambridge, 1981), pp. 227–48; idem, *Music in Renaissance Ferrara, 1400–1505*

musicians no less than by other members of the clergy. Until now, studies of patronage through the use of benefices have confined themselves either to a single musician or to a specific group, such as the members of a secular chapel. But only when one systematically confronts all the petitions presented to the papacy during a given period does the sheer volume of such requests actually register: more than a thousand supplications in a thirty-year period, from musicians and their patrons in every European kingdom, in princely secular chapels, in collegiate churches and in cathedrals. Few musical figures, important or minor, are absent from the roster of those who requested benefices of the pope.

The reasons why the clergy determinedly (one might even say, in some cases, relentlessly) pursued benefices – and pursued them in Rome – are fairly well known to students of church history.[6] An ecclesiastical benefice has been defined as 'a juridical entity . . . consisting of a sacred office, with the right of collecting the revenues from the endowment attached to the office'.[7] Originally, the spiritual and temporal components of a benefice – the duties and the income – were considered to be inseparable. They were the responsibility and the prerogative of a single incumbent. As the Middle Ages progressed, it became steadily easier and more desirable for a clergyman to accumulate benefices – or rather, to collect the incomes from several benefices, while retaining deputies to take on the spiritual responsibilities of the offices. During the same period, the power of conferring benefices fell increasingly into the hands of the papacy. By the fifteenth century, both pluralism and papal provision of benefices were common facts of life within the

(Oxford, 1984), pp. 173–95; Reynolds, 'Musical Careers'; L. Perkins, 'Musical Patronage at the Royal Court of France under Charles VII and Louis XI (1422–83)', *JAMS*, 37 (1984), pp. 507–66; P. Starr, 'Music and Music Patronage at the Papal Court, 1447–1464' (Ph.D. dissertation, Yale University, 1987); and A. Planchart, 'Guillaume Du Fay's Benefices and his Relationship to the Court of Burgundy', *Early Music History*, 8 (1988), pp. 117–71.

6   Studies useful for the evolution of the papal provision of benefices include: D. Heintschel, *The Medieval Concept of an Ecclesiastical Office*, Catholic University of America Canon Law Studies 363 (Washington, DC, 1956); G. Mollat, 'Bénéfices ecclésiastiques', *Dictionnaire de droit canonique*, II (Paris, 1935–42), pp. 407ff; idem, *La collation des bénéfices ecclésiastiques sous les papes d'Avignon*, Bibliothèque de l'Institut de Droit Canonique, Université de Strasbourg 1 (Paris, 1921); and G. Barraclough, *Papal Provisions: Aspects of Church History, Constitutional, Legal and Administrative, in the Later Middle Ages* (Oxford, 1935). See also Starr, 'Music and Music Patronage', pp. 15–31, and Reynolds, 'Musical Careers', pp. 52–3.

7   *Codex iuris canonici* (Rome, 1918), can. 1409.

church. At this time, too, politics had a profound influence on the beneficial system. The popes, like their temporal colleagues, perpetually in search of political allies, used the provision of benefices to reward faithful allies and the servants of these allies. Thus, a secular ruler in good odour with the papal court could surround himself with courtiers and familiars whose fidelity was ensured with lucrative benefices procured from Rome, and procured with automatic dispensations for prolonged absence from the seat of the benefice. We shall see below an excellent example of the way this arrangement worked on behalf of prince and pope alike.

The special conditions of the professional musician's career made the acquisition of benefices a distinct necessity.[8] Three of these conditions that seem especially pertinent are itinerancy, competitive recruitment, and the effects of ageing. The itinerant musician required the stability and permanence of an income from benefices, particularly those held *in absentia*.[9] Secondly, benefices played a prominent role in the cut-throat competition among princes to attract the best musicians to their chapels.[10] Finally, benefices could be relied upon to provide financial security when age and failing musical powers took their inevitable toll on a musician's ability to perform his professional duties.[11] In sum, the pos-

---

[8] I have discussed these conditions at some length in the paper 'From Cradle to Grave: New Light on the Careers of Renaissance Musicians', presented at the annual spring meeting of the American Musicological Society Midwest Chapter, Milwaukee, 5–6 April 1991.

[9] Christopher Reynolds discusses the phenomenon of musicians' itinerancy in great detail in a chapter of his forthcoming book on fifteenth-century music and musicians at St Peter's in Rome (I thank Professor Reynolds for kindly supplying me with a draft of this chapter). See also *idem*, 'Southern Pull or Northern Push?: Motives for Migration in the Renaissance', *Atti del XIV Congresso della Società internazionale di musicologia*, Bologna, 27 August–1 September (Bologna, 1990), pp. 155–61; D. Fallows, 'The Contenance angloise: English Influence on Continental Composers of the Fifteenth Century', *Renaissance Studies*, 1 (1987), pp. 189–208; and B. Haggh, 'Itinerancy to Residency: Professional Careers and Performance Practices in 15th-Century Sacred Music', *Early Music*, 17 (1989), pp. 358–66.

[10] See especially Lockwood, 'Strategies of Music Patronage'; *idem*, *Music in Renaissance Ferrara*, pp. 185–95; Reynolds, 'Musical Careers'; and P. Starr, 'The Ferrara Connection: A Case Study of Musical Recruitment in the Renaissance', *Studi Musicali*, 18 (1989), pp. 3–17.

[11] It was but part of the 'good lordship' of Renaissance princes to provide a comfortable retirement for the members of their household chapel, either with benefices within their collation (as, for example, the dukes of Burgundy, who were richly endowed with ecclesiastical patronage with which to reward members of their household), or with help in acquiring benefices from Rome. For the patronage by the dukes of Burgundy, see C. Wright, *Music at the Court of Burgundy, 1364–1419*, Musicological Studies 28 (Henryville, PA, Ottawa and Binningen, 1979), pp. 67–70; J. Marix, *Histoire de la musique et des*

session of a clutch of benefices was essential to the musician in particular; benefices functioned like particularly luxurious medieval retirement plans.

Some musicians were more fortunate than others in acquiring benefices. One might suppose that such success depended on the status of a musician within his profession. The evidence indicates instead that remunerative benefices fell most often to those who were skilled in the *ars beneficiorum* – the 'art of securing benefices' – and blessed, as well, with influential patrons.[12]

This conclusion can be illustrated with the examples of two composers, considered pre-eminent in their own time as well as today: Johannes Okeghem and Guillaume Du Fay. Both musicians petitioned the pope for the provision of one or more benefices in the mid-fifteenth century. Okeghem addressed his supplication to Paul II in 1466; Du Fay requested a benefice from Nicholas V in 1453. One of these illustrious petitioners was successful in his quest for a benefice, and one was not. The reasons for this had very little to do with their respective standing within the profession.

Let us first consider the case of Okeghem. In May 1466 the distinguished *protocapellanus* of the French royal chapel requested the provostship, with canonry and prebendal income of 100 gold florins, at the church of St Martin in Candes-St-Martin in the archdiocese of Tours.[13] Although already lavishly beneficed, the composer chose to apply for two additional benefices at this time: the provostship at the collegiate church in Candes-St-Martin and a

  musiciens de la cour de Bourgogne sous le règne de Philippe le Bon (1420–1467) (Strasbourg, 1939; repr. Geneva, 1972), 157–202; R. Strohm, *Music in Late Medieval Bruges* (Oxford, 1985), pp. 11–41; and Planchart, 'Guillaume Du Fay's Benefices', pp. 134–8. The Vatican records for the years 1447–71 show that members of the Burgundian chapel fared exceptionally well with benefices acquired through Rome.

12 For example, in my study of the papal chapel that covers the years 1447 to 1464 ('Music and Music Patronage', pp. 114–98) I document the beneficial histories of each of its musicians. Although each singer possessed the same advantages, resident at the papal Curia and employed by the pope – the ultimate source of patronage through benefices – they had widely diverging degrees of success in the pursuit of benefices. And the most fortunate in this respect were by no means always the most senior or the most illustrious. The inevitable conclusion is that here, as with musicians outside the papal sphere, much depended upon the canniness of the individual seeker after benefices.

13 Candes-St-Martin is a small village in Touraine, near the confluence of the Loire and Vienne rivers, and the site of a medieval church of note dedicated to St Martin. I thank Professor Leeman Perkins for having helped clarify the location of this benefice of Okeghem.

canonry at Notre Dame in Paris.[14] The Vatican Archives preserve indisputable evidence that Okeghem not only received the papal concession of this benefice but that he had taken uncontested possession of it by April 1467. On 24 October 1466 Johannes Puyllois pledged, on Okeghem's behalf, to remit to the Apostolic treasury annates of 50 papal florins. This sum was to be paid within six months of the time that Okeghem had been received by the collegiate chapter in Candes-St-Martin. (See documents 1A and 1B in Appendix 1 for transcriptions and translations of these documents.)

We have known since 1907 that the papal singer Puyllois had served as procurator for Okeghem.[15] With the help of this information, I was able to assemble the complete collection of documents from the papal Curia that relate to the acquisition of Okeghem's benefice.[16] The documents testify both to the arduous tasks confronting Puyllois as procurator and to the knowledge and skills that made him an ideal person to assist Okeghem to a new benefice.

The process of wresting a benefice from the papal bureaucracy was so difficult to master that potential suppliants to the papal court were well advised to secure for themselves a procurator.[17] He could expedite the supplication of a petitioner present in Rome, or

---

[14] Okeghem is known to have held these benefices: the Dignity of Treasurer, collegiate church of St Martin in Tours; the Dignity of Provost, with canonry, at St Martin in Candes-St-Martin; a canonry at the cathedral of Notre Dame in Paris; Chaplaincy of the altar of St Louis, collegiate church of St Benoît, Paris; and a canonry at the cathedral of Chartres.

For the relevant documents, see ASV *RS* 595, fols. 148ᵛ–149ʳ and *RL* 629, fol. 80ᵛ (Notre Dame, Paris); *RS* 717, fols. 210ᵛ–211ʳ and a document contributed by Jeremy Noble to the REN*ARCH database (Chartres); and the documents cited in note 16 below (Candes-St-Martin). For recent literature on the benefices of Okeghem see Perkins, 'Musical Patronage at the Royal Court of France', pp. 523–7; *idem*, 'Ockeghem, Johannes', *The New Grove Dictionary of Music and Musicians*, ed. S. Sadie, 20 vols. (London, 1980), XIII, pp. 489–90; F. Lesure, 'Ockeghem à Notre-Dame de Paris (1463–1470)', *Essays in Musicology in Honor of Dragan Plamenac on his 70th Birthday*, ed. G. Reese and R. Snow (Pittsburgh, PA, 1969), pp. 147–54; and C. Wright, *Music and Ceremony at Notre Dame of Paris, 500–1550* (Cambridge, 1989), pp. 303–5.

[15] The fact was reported by E. R. Vaucelle in 'Les Annates du diocèse de Tours, 1421–1521', *Bulletin Trimestriel de la Société Archéologique de Touraine*, 16 (1907–8), p. 116. Recent articles that make use of this information include Reynolds, 'Musical Careers', p. 62, n. 40, and Perkins, 'Musical Patronage at the Royal Court of France', pp. 532–4.

[16] The documents are, in chronological order (in the ASV): *RV* 513, fols. 14 and 17ᵛ–19ʳ; *RS* 595, fol. 148; *RL* 629, fols. 81ᵛ–83ʳ; *A* 17, fol. 183ᵛ; *IE* 467, fol. 32ʳ; ASR *MC* 841, fol. 157ᵛ; and ASV *RS* 647, fol. 232.

[17] So advises the anonymous author of a late fifteenth-century handbook on the acquisition of benefices, *Practica cancellariae apostolicae saeculi XV. exeuntis*, ed. L. Schmitz-Kallenberg (Münster, 1904), pp. 41–2.

could serve as deputy for one *in partibus*. The papal court of the fifteenth century abounded in procurators.[18] They had put themselves through a rigorous theoretical and practical course, first by studying such books of protocol for the expedition of papal supplications as the *Practica cancellariae*, and then by carrying through the process of petitioning many times over. Such a man was Johannes Puyllois, who, in his more than twenty years as a member of the papal chapel, lodged forty-four petitions with four popes.[19] Among the papal singers he was unquestionably the most successful beneficiary of papal provisions. The income from a lifetime spent accumulating benefices might have been as much as 3000 florins, or five times that of Binchois at his death, and six times that of Du Fay.[20] Puyllois appears to have served in this capacity for a fellow musician only once.[21] The tale of his labours on behalf of Okeghem and the benefice in Tours is protracted and complicated. I shall abbreviate it somewhat here, while retaining the essentials and important implications.[22]

The first step was to prepare the papal petition. Under Puyllois's capable supervision, the supplication (presented as document 2 in

[18] On the role and duties of the procurator at the papal court, see E. F. Jacob, 'To and From the Court of Rome in the Early Fifteenth Century', *Essays in Later Medieval History* (Manchester, 1968), pp. 58–78; J. Kirsch, 'Andreas Sapiti, englische Prokurator an der Kurie im 14. Jahrhundert', *Historisches Jahrbuch*, 14 (1893), pp. 582–603; A. Clergeac, *La Curie et les bénéficiers consistoriaux: Étude sur les communs et menus services, 1300–1600* (Paris, 1911), pp. 56–77; R. Heckel, 'Das Aufkommen der ständigen Prokuratoren an der päpstlichen Kurie', *Miscellanea Francesco Ehrle*, ii, Studi e Testi 38 (Vatican City, 1924), pp. 290–321; and G. Barraclough, 'Praxis Beneficiorum', *Zeitschrift der Savigny-Stiftung für Rechtsgeschichte*, Kanonische Abt. 27 (1938), pp. 94ff.

[19] A calendar of the benefices sought in Rome by Puyllois can be seen in Starr, 'Music and Music Patronage', pp. 287–8.

[20] Figures for Du Fay and Binchois come from Fallows, *Dufay*, p. 216.

[21] His name is associated only with the supplication for the benefice at St Martin in Candes-St-Martin, but Puyllois probably lodged another supplication for Okeghem at the same time, for a canonry at Notre Dame in Paris. Both supplications bear the same date, and appear consecutively in the papal register.

We know of only two other instances when musicians at the papal court served as procurators for colleagues. The veteran papal singer Johannes Hurtault assisted Johannes Regis to his *scholastria* at St Vincent in Soignies (1464); and Nicholas Rembert, sometime singer at San Pietro and an official in the apostolic Chancery, represented Tinctoris in his quest for a canonry at the cathedral of Liège (1476). (For Hurtault, see ASV *A* 15, fol. 39ᵛ; Rembert's role is discussed in Noble, 'New Light on Josquin's Benefices', pp. 81–4 and Reynolds, 'Musical Careers', p. 62).

[22] For the more protracted and detailed discussion of the process of acquisition of Okeghem's benefice, see Starr, 'Music and Music Patronage', pp. 31–62. The narrative relies heavily on the primary source *Practica cancellariae*, as well as secondary literature cited below. A more condensed description of the process of acquiring a benefice can also be found in Sherr, 'Papal Chapel', pp. 10–12.

Appendix 1) was drawn up and then fair-copied by one of the many professional notaries resident in Rome, or even conceivably by Puyllois himself.[23] It presented, clearly, concisely and persuasively, the information furnished to Puyllois by Okeghem. Puyllois first made sure that all facts about Okeghem and his desired benefice were accurately expressed in impeccable *stylus cancellariae*. An inaccuracy or a mistake in diction might have rendered the supplication suspect – or worse, invalid.[24] This is one of many reasons why the registers of supplications are so useful to music historians. The biographical data about musicians presented therein, including the very orthography of their names, is as accurate as we can hope for. So, for example, we are virtually assured in this supplication of the correct spelling of Okeghem's surname. Puyllois, a former colleague of Okeghem's at the principal collegiate church in Antwerp, would doubtless have known how to spell the composer's name.[25] As an efficient procurator, he would have taken stringent precautions that it be correctly copied into the papal documents, where it receives the uniform orthography used in this study.[26]

Okeghem's procurator, a shrewd tactician, took care to mention

[23] For public notaries, see G. Barraclough, *Public Notaries and the Papal Curia* (London, 1934). There is a formidable quantity of literature on the papal supplication. The oldest and newest treatments are the most useful: the *Practica cancellariae*, pp. 1–15, and Thomas Frenz's exhaustive study, *Die Kanzlei der Päpste der Hochrenaissance (1471–1527)*, Bibliothek des Deutschen Historischen Instituts in Rom 63 (Tübingen, 1986). Other useful studies include B. Katterbach, *Specimina supplicationum ex registris vaticana* (Rome, 1927); *Calendar of Scottish Supplications to Rome, 1418–1422*, ed. E. R. Lindsay and A. I. Cameron, Publications of the Scottish History Society, 3rd ser., 23 (Edinburgh, 1934); U. Berlière, *Suppliques de Clément VI (1342–1352)*, Analecta Vaticano-Belgica 1 (Rome, 1906), pp. i–xxii; P. Rabiskauskas, *Diplomatica pontificia*, 3rd edn (Rome, 1972), pp. 45–140; and E. Pitz, *Supplikensignatur und Briefexpedition an der Römischen Kurie im Pontifikat Papst Calixtus III*, Bibliothek des Deutschen Historischen Instituts in Rom 42 (Tübingen, 1972).

[24] See *Practica cancellariae*, p. 2. Errors in style might cause the Curial bureaucracy to reject the supplication out of hand. Errors in fact, including incorrect orthography, might ultimately cause the papal provision to be invalid in law. In the Registers of Supplications at the Vatican one sees countless examples of the *reformatio*, a document presented expressly to correct factual error in the original supplication.

[25] See J. Van den Nieuwenhuizen, 'De koralen, de zangers en de zangmeesters van de Antwerpse O.-L.-Vrouwekerk tijdens de 15e. eeuw', *Antwerps Katedraalkoor*, ed. P. Schrooten (Antwerp, 1978), pp. 40 and 47–8. See also Starr, 'Music and Music Patronage', pp. 162–3 and 168–9.

[26] David Fallows ('The Life of Johannes Regis, 1425 to 1496', *Revue Belge de Musicologie*, 43 (1989), p. 157, n. 86), also endorses this version of the name as one that is used by 'all sources with any claim to a connection with the composer'.

On the authority of the version of musicians' names found in Vatican documents, see Starr, 'Music and Music Patronage', pp. 43–4 and 54–5. Hence the version of Johannes Puyllois's name used in the present article – the version that appears in all supplications and papal bulls that bear this composer's name.

early in the document the fact that Okeghem had received a grant of an expectative benefice from Pope Paul's immediate predecessor, Pius II, at the request of Louis XI of France.[27] While no cleric was ever assured of succeeding to a benefice granted *in expectativis*, receiving such a provision laid the groundwork for a secure legal claim to the benefice when it did become vacant.[28] Prominent mention of King Louis of France was not accidental, either. Relations between the Holy See and the 'Most Christian King' had achieved a tenuous cordiality during the 1460s, in part achieved through Louis's abrogation of the Pragmatic Sanction of Bourges in 1461. During this period, the popes were inclined to favour petitions emanating from the French court.[29]

The correct and canny formulation of the supplication was but the first step in a labyrinthine progress through the various and comparatively far-flung offices of the Curia, from which Puyllois would emerge with the signed and sealed letters mandating provision of Okeghem's benefice. Puyllois undoubtedly used his influence as a papal familiar to ensure prompt signature of the supplication, in this case by the Referendarius Petrus Ferriz, Bishop of Tarrazona. This official was empowered to sign some supplications on behalf of the pope.[30] Once signed, the supplication

27 ASV *RV* 513, fols. 14 and 17ᵛ–19ʳ, dated 4 January 1464. This is the papal response to a supplication from Louis IX, dated 17 April 1463, submitted on behalf of various nominees, courtiers, familiars and many members of his chapel. The letter confirms the provision of expectative graces, and also bestows the requisite dispensations for clerics who held two or more 'incompatible' benefices. For a discussion of this document see Perkins, 'Musical Patronage at the Royal Court of France', p. 533, n. 68.

28 On the uses (and frequent abuses) of expectatives, see especially Mollat, *Collation*, pp. 69–75 and *idem*, 'Expectatives', *Dictionnaire de droit canonique*, v, pp. 678–90; C. Tihon, 'Les expectatives *in forma pauperum*', *Bulletin de l'Institut Historique Belge de Rome*, 5 (1925), pp. 51–118; and F. Baix, 'De la valeur historique des actes pontificaux de collation des bénéfices', *Hommage à Dom Ursmer Berlière* (Brussels, 1931), pp. 57–66.

29 Classic studies of the effects of the Pragmatic Sanction of Bourges and its abrogation on relations between France and the Holy See are N. Valois, *Histoire de la Pragmatique Sanction de Bourges sous Charles VII*, Archives de l'Histoire Religieuse de la France 4 (Paris, 1906); P. Bourdon, 'L'abrogation de la Pragmatique et les règles de la chancellerie de Pie II', *Mélanges d'Archeologie et d'Histoire*, 28 (1908), pp. 207–24; J. Salvini, 'L'application de la Pragmatique Sanction sous Charles VII et Louis XI au chapitre cathédral de Paris', *Revue d'Histoire de l'Eglise de France*, 3 (1912), *passim*. See especially Bourdon, 'L'abrogation', pp. 214–18, on the correspondence between Pius II and Louis XI about privileges to be granted to the royal crown for the presentation of benefices in France.

30 The typical signature of the Referendarius read 'concessum ut petitur in praesentia dom. nostri papae'. Supplications actually signed by the pope bore a version of the phrase 'fiat ut petitur'. For the Referendarius, see B. Katterbach, *Referendarii utriusque signaturiae a Martino V ad Clementem IX*, Studi e Testi 55 (Vatican City, 1931); *idem*, *Specimina*, pp. i–xvii; and Frenz, *Kanzlei*, pp. 91–7.

would be sent on to the office of the Datarius, for the imposition of the all-important official date: in this case, 24 May 1466. The date was crucial to Okeghem's *ius*, his legal right to the benefice, especially if it should be contested by other applicants. Priority of dating conferred an inestimable legal advantage in the litigation that inevitably arose over benefices with multiple claimants.[31] The next stop for the signed and dated supplication was the Registry of Supplications, where the document was eventually copied into the capacious folio-size volumes that are preserved in the Vatican Archives as the *Registri Supplicationum*.[32]

Only then was the original document released to Puyllois for the second stage of the process, the preparation of the various drafts of the papal bull of provision: the minute, the fair copy and the registered copy.[33] When the fair copy of the papal bull had been sealed with the heavy leaden *bulla* (hence the designation of this most formal of papal rescripts), a Chancery official presented the final bill to Puyllois. The registered copy of the bull tells us that the Chancery fee for the expedition of Okeghem's bull was 27 *carlini*, or nearly 3 papal florins.[34]

The last stage of the protracted process took Puyllois to still another group of offices in the Apostolic Camera. Here long-standing regulations required him to furnish proof of Okeghem's worthiness to hold the benefice – proof in the form of a notarised

---

[31] See L. Célier, *Les dataires du xve siècle et les origines de la Daterie apostolique*, Bibliothèque des Écoles Françaises d'Athènes et de Rome 103 (Paris, 1910), pp. 71ff; and Frenz, *Kanzlei*, pp. 97–100.

[32] On the Registry of Supplications see especially Katterbach, *Specimina*, pp. i–xviii; *Calendar of Scottish Supplications*, pp. i–xx; Pitz, *Supplikensignatur*, pp. 1–50; and Frenz, *Kanzlei*, pp. 100–4.

The *Practica cancellarie* (p. 20) alerts the procurator to the possibility of long delays between the dating and the registering of a supplication. Puyllois would undoubtedly have contrived, either by personal influence or through monetary incentives, to see that his supplication was processed within the statutory three days.

[33] Three recent studies treat exhaustively the offices of the Apostolic Chancery and its expedition of the papal bull of provision: Pitz, *Supplikensignatur*; Frenz, *Kanzlei*; and B. Schwarz, *Die Organisation kurialer Schreiberkollegien von ihrer Entstehung bis zur Mitte des 15. Jahrhunderts*, Bibliothek des Deutschen Historischen Instituts in Rom 37 (Tübingen, 1972).

[34] ASV *RL* 629, fol. 83. The date of registration of the bull, 9 October 1466, appears at the end of the document. Following the date is the name Antonio de Piscia, one of two *regentes cancellariae*, who were charged with the final proof-reading of the registry copy; and, finally, the amount of the total fee assessed for the letter. (See Frenz, *Kanzlei*, pp. 128–31.) Note that the process of expedition of this papal bull took nearly six months, from the official dating of the supplication (24 May 1466) to its final copying into the papal registers.

statement that Okeghem had passed an examination in grammar, writing and singing. (Presumably this would have given Okeghem little difficulty, although one reads of clergy who had some trouble with the music portion of the test.)[35] At last Puyllois could set down his pledge to produce the annates on the benefice. And these annates were duly paid on 9 April 1467.[36]

Puyllois's efforts on behalf of the benefice for Okeghem were, manifestly, crowned with success. To achieve this success, Puyllois was obliged to advance a considerable sum. (When one counts in the inevitable 'tips' to help oil the wheels of a recalcitrant bureaucracy, the amount might well have approached the 8 florins that Puyllois earned monthly as a papal singer.) More costly, even, was the time and knowledge lavished on this single quest for a benefice. Five extant papal documents, the supplication, the papal bull, the pledge to pay annates and the receipts for annates paid, testify to the care and expertise exercised on Okeghem's behalf by the papal singer and procurator *par excellence*, Johannes Puyllois.[37]

Guillaume Du Fay, on the other hand, was not so fortunate in his petition to Pope Nicholas V. The petition did not result in the provision of a benefice; consequently, we lack the impressive array of documents that has survived for Okeghem's benefice. Only one document has survived, and that, unfortunately, not the petition itself. But the papal bull that did survive would have been closely based on the information contained in the missing supplication. It is a previously unknown letter from the pope to Du Fay, dated 19 January 1454 (new style).[38]

---

[35] See Starr, 'Music and Music Patronage', pp. 57–8.

[36] ASV *A* 17, fol. 183[v], note added to the right-hand margin of the original pledge to pay the annates (See Appendix 1, document 1B). This payment is corroborated in ASV *I.E.* 467, fol. 32[r], and ASR *MC* 841, fol. 157[v].

[37] Procurators customarily charged a handsome fee for their services, one that included reimbursement for the numerous fees and tips involved in the procurement of a papal provision (see, for example, Jacob, 'To and From the Court of Rome'). We have no way of knowing whether money changed hands between Okeghem and Puyllois – over and above, of course, the probable reimbursement for the fees advanced by Puyllois. One would prefer to imagine that Okeghem might have rewarded his former musical colleague in a more appropriate currency, that of new sacred polyphony apt for performance by the members of the papal chapel. But this must remain only conjecture. At the least, we may infer in this act of procuration an instance of written communication between the two musicians.

[38] ASV *RL* 483 fol. 295[r]–295[v]. At the time of my discovery of this document, in May 1984, Du Fay scholars were unaware of its existence. Shortly after the announcement of its discovery and discussion of its significance in my paper to the AMS National Meeting in

The letter confirms much that is already known or surmised about Du Fay's position and whereabouts in the 1450s, and suggests even more. It supplies reinforcement for the supposition that Du Fay held an official and important position in the ducal chapel of Savoy: the letter refers to a petition to the pope from Louis of Savoy for the 'councillor, master and first chaplain of his chapel'. Although David Fallows has suggested that Du Fay's position might have been merely titular,[39] the Vatican document confirms for 1454 (and probably earlier) his official status and rank within the duke's chapel.[40] Du Fay's successor as *primus capellanus*, as described in payment records dating from 1458, was Bartholomeus Chuet, who had been for many years a singer in the duke's chapel.[41] So it is likely that Du Fay's responsibilities at the Savoyard court were more than merely honorary. Further, the document, whose salutation reads: 'Nicolaus etc., dilecto filio Guillermo Du Fay canonico cameracensis, bacallario in decretis . . .', provides the most forthright and official corroboration we have of Du Fay's attainment of the bachelor's degree in canon law.[42] Finally, the

---

Baltimore, 1988, Professor Alejandro Planchart also discussed the document in his article 'Guillaume Du Fay's Benefices' (p. 139). The letter is published for the first time as document 3 in Appendix 1 below.

[39] Fallows, *Dufay*, p. 69. Fallows bases this conclusion on the fact that Du Fay's name does not appear in the virtually complete payment records of the ducal chapel for the years 1451–8.

[40] I am obliged, however, to register a small *caveat* here. The wording of the document is as follows: '. . . pro quo dilectus filius nobilis vir Ludovicus Dux Sabaudiae asserens te dilectum consiliarium suum et magistrum ac primum capellanum capellae suae *fore*' (italics mine). The connotation of the word 'fore' is probably to be understood from the perspective of the author of the letter to Du Fay, Pope Nicholas, as referring to the legal status of the composer when he actually petitioned for a specific benefice in Savoy (a status that would confer priority in the collation to certain benefices in Savoy). So even if the letter does not absolutely confirm the fact of Du Fay's status as the *magister cappellae* of the duke's chapel in January 1454, it certainly demonstrates the intention of both Du Fay and the duke that the composer would be ensconced in that position when he submitted a petition for the benefice alluded to in this letter. Although the letter by no means rules out the possibility that Du Fay was already installed in 1454, it is possible that the duke's petition to the pope had been drawn up in hopeful anticipation of that fact – as, indeed, an aggressive tool of recruitment.

I thank Katherine Gill for her helpful suggestions with respect to the interpretation of the language in the papal letter to Du Fay.

[41] M. Bouquet, 'La cappella musicale dei duchi di Savoia dal 1450 al 1500', *Rivista Italiana di Musicologia*, 3 (1968), pp. 244–5.

[42] See Planchart, 'Guillaume Du Fay's Benefices', p. 132, for a discussion of Du Fay's degree and a list of the five documents that mention the degree, which was most probably conferred between 1436 and 1439. The papal bull is the only official Vatican document that contains this information, and, as I shall maintain below, its inclusion in this particular document was quite deliberate.

letter reinforces the validity of the version of Du Fay's name common to all papal documents concerning the composer, and thus likely to be the one used by Du Fay.[43]

The implications of the document are even more interesting. In the first place, it suggests that Du Fay in 1454 had every intention of remaining at the court of Savoy for a protracted period – even, possibly, for the remainder of his life. The letter grants to Du Fay papal permission to obtain and to secure the necessary dispensations to hold a non-conventual priorate within the duchy of Savoy. Nowhere is a particular benefice specified, and rightly so. This document was intended merely to lay the legal groundwork for a subsequent request for a specific benefice, much as the *rotullus* presented by Louis XI for his chaplains prepared the way for Okeghem's petition for the provostship at St Martin.

The Duke of Savoy – or rather his procurator – must have lavished as much care and expense upon this petition on behalf of Du Fay as did Puyllois upon Okeghem's supplication.[44] It would have made emphatic use of the name and rank of Du Fay's patron, Louis of Savoy. Relations between the Holy See and Savoy in the early 1450s were quite similar to those with France a decade later. The abdication of the antipope Felix V, and the consequent termination of the last papal Schism in 1449, produced an atmosphere of conciliation in which Nicholas V strove to win adherents in Savoy through decrees reinstituting ducal privileges over benefices.[45] A petition from the duke on behalf of an important official of his court would undoubtedly receive prompt and favourable action. Du Fay's educational attainment, the baccalaureate in canon law, was also prominently displayed, and this was the only surviving papal document about Du Fay to do this.[46] It was usually *de rigueur*

---

[43] See Planchart, 'Guillaume Du Fay's Benefices', pp. 169–71, for a corroborative view. Professor Planchart has examined many papal documents that bear the composer's name, and he has confirmed that the version used here is common to all of them.

[44] Thanks to the oft-cited letter from Du Fay to Piero and Giovanni de' Medici, dated 22 February either 1454 or 1456, we can guess that Du Fay's procurator in this matter was the Florentine ambassador to Savoy, Francesco Sachetti, who had recently assisted Du Fay 'when I was in need of something from the court of Rome'. See F. D'Accone, 'The Singers of San Giovanni in Florence', *JAMS*, 14 (1961), pp. 318–19; also C. Wright, 'Dufay at Cambrai', *JAMS*, 28 (1975), p. 190; and Fallows, *Dufay*, p. 71.

[45] Pastor, *History of the Popes*, II, pp. 41–2; E. Delaruelle, E. R. Labande and P. Orliac, *L'église au temps du Grand Schisme et de crise conciliaire (1378–1449)*, I (Paris, 1962), p. 313.

[46] Planchart, 'Guillaume Du Fay's Benefices', pp. 132–3. The fact that Du Fay failed to include this information even in his all-important papal supplication of 1436 for the

for university graduates to include mention of the highest academic degree attained, but in this case its inclusion was also a matter of expediency. In Savoy most dignities and prebends were hedged with restrictions, requiring of incumbents a patent of nobility or a university degree. Du Fay himself encountered this problem in the 1430s, when he aspired to a canonry at the cathedral of Geneva.[47] The dukes had a persistent problem securing important benefices for the members of their chapel, in part because of these restrictions.[48] The document indicates that considerable capital was invested in this supplication for benefices in Savoy: at least 46 *carlini*, or nearly 5 papal florins. In short, nothing was spared to prepare the way for Du Fay to begin to acquire substantial benefices in the duchy of Savoy.

The second interesting implication of the document – like the dog barking in the night – is what did not happen thereafter. The next step would have been for Du Fay to lodge a petition for a specific benefice, one carefully chosen to fulfil the terms of the first papal concession, and one that would prove comparatively easy of collation – something of the order of, for example, Okeghem's provostship at the collegiate church in Candes-St-Martin. Had Du Fay made such a petition, there should be some shred of evidence for it in the papal records.[49] The complete lack of such evidence suggests to me, quite simply, that Du Fay never lodged the petition: that he chose not to exercise his 'option' on the non-conventual priorate in the territories of the Duke of Savoy.

canonry at Cambrai suggests to me that he had not obtained the degree by that time. The benefice was reserved as a *prebenda libera jurista*, and may have been provided to Du Fay in anticipation of his receiving the degree. (See Wright, 'Dufay at Cambrai', p. 186.)

[47] Planchart, 'Guillaume Du Fay's Benefices', p. 132.

[48] Two documents from the 1450s testify to this: ASV *RL* 505, fols. 82ʳ–83ᵛ, dated 20 April 1455, a renewal of the dispensation for Bartholomeus Chuet to retain his canonry in the cathedral of Geneva, which required either the status of nobility or a university degree more advanced than the B.dec. held by Chuet; and *RS* 461, fol. 114ʳ–114ᵛ, dated 22 July 1452, a request for a *creatio in nobilem*, the granting of a patent of nobility to Johannes Clisse and to other musicians in the duke's chapel so that they might qualify to hold prebends in the cathedrals of Lausanne and Geneva.

[49] The possible evidence from Du Fay's letter to the Medici should be mentioned here. If the later dating, preferred by Wright, is used, then the letter may allude to help furnished by Sachetti to Du Fay in a second petition to the papal court. If we accept the earlier dating, as suggested by D'Accone, then Du Fay must be referring to Sachetti's assistance in procurating the petition that yielded the papal bull of 1454. Although Wright's arguments are persuasive, I am inclined towards the earlier date of 1454, simply because there is absolutely no other evidence of a second supplication presented by Du Fay (see the references cited in note 44).

At some time between 1454 and 1458 Du Fay decided that he would not make a permanent home at the court of Savoy, that benefices in Savoy would therefore be of little further use to him, and that he would instead return north to cultivate the benefices he held in the diocese of Cambrai.[50] Alejandro Planchart explains Du Fay's decision to return as one based solely on the failure of Duke Louis to provide benefices for his *magister capellae*.[51] If that were so, we should expect to see some further sign of an attempt to secure a benefice in Savoy. David Fallows interprets Du Fay's letter to the Medici brothers as an oblique application for employment in Florence (see the discussion of this letter in note 44 above).[52] True, the letter does have an ingratiating air, but who can say that this was not the tone normally used by Du Fay in letters to important patrons? Moreover, if the motive for leaving Savoy did, in fact, primarily involve concern over benefices, then Florence would be an unlikely place for Du Fay to set his sights.[53] One might interpret the letter simply as Du Fay's attempt to solidify patronage in Italy before returning permanently to Cambrai. I believe that Du Fay decided to leave Savoy for reasons of his own, reasons that may have had more to do with a realisation of advancing years and the natural desire to finish his days in his birthplace, comfortably ensconced in the dignity and easy circumstances of a canon of Cambrai.

PRO AUGMENTO DIVINI CULTUS

'For the increase of divine worship' is a phrase that appears in many of the fifty-five documents dated between 1447 and 1471 that request the Grace of papal sanction: permission from the pope to alter the administrative and financial structure of cathedrals and collegiate churches. Some excellent recent studies of music in individual churches or particular cities of the Low Countries and northern France during the fifteenth century have discussed the

---

[50] For Du Fay's benefices, see F. Baix, 'La carrière "bénéficiale" de Guillaume Dufay', *Bulletin de l'Institut Historique Belge de Rome*, 8 (1928), pp. 265–72; Fallows, *Dufay, passim*; Wright, 'Dufay at Cambrai'; and Planchart, 'Guillaume Du Fay's Benefices'.
[51] Planchart, 'Guillaume Du Fay's Benefices', p. 139.
[52] Fallows, *Dufay*, p. 71.
[53] See Starr, 'Music and Music Patronage', pp. 208–19, for a discussion of the relative undesirability of benefices in Italy.

importance to the respective institutions of such restructuring.[54] But it is the array of papal supplications and bulls that most vividly conveys the extent of this movement. Petitions from cathedrals and collegiates from the dioceses of northern France and the Low Countries, central and southern France, Germany, Spain and England – in short, from nearly everywhere in Europe – arrived at the papal Curia in steadily increasing numbers from the mid-century onward.[55]

The petitions are unanimous in using the present disarray of the divine service as justification for change. None of the supplications expresses in any but the most oblique terms the reason at the heart of this disarray, the failure of the canons to discharge two of the principal responsibilities attached to their prebends. These were residence, and the participation in the divine services of their cathedrals and collegiate churches.[56] The proliferation of non-residency among the canons was an unpleasant side-effect of the increase in papal control of important benefices in the churches of Europe. Many canonries were granted *in absentia* to members of the papal Curia. Still others were awarded to the nominees of local magnates.[57] Churches were forced to fill the gaps in their choirs with vicars, normally unbeneficed clergy who were paid by the

---

[54] See, for example, R. Strohm, *Music in Late Medieval Bruges* (Oxford, 1985), pp. 10–41; K. Forney, 'Music, Ritual and Patronage at the Church of Our Lady, Antwerp', *Early Music History*, 7 (1987), pp. 1–57; B. Haggh, 'Music, Liturgy, and Ceremony in Brussels, 1350–1500' (Ph.D. dissertation, University of Illinois, 1988), pp. 97–226; *idem*, 'Itinerancy to Residency'; Wright, *Music and Ceremony at Notre Dame*, pp. 18–27 and 165–95; R. Wegman, 'Music and Musicians at the Guild of Our Lady in Bergen op Zoom, c. 1470–1510', *Early Music History*, 9 (1990), pp. 175–249; A. Walters Robertson, 'The Mass of Guillaume Machaut in the Cathedral of Reims', *Plainsong and Polyphony in the Later Middle Ages and Renaissance*, ed. T. Kelly (Cambridge, 1991), pp. 100–39; and E. Schreurs, 'Het muziekleven in de Onze-Lieve-Vrouwekerk van Tongeren (circa 1400–1797)' (Ph.D. dissertation, Katholieke Universiteit Leuven, 1990). (I thank Barbara Haggh for the last citation, and for her substantial notes on the dissertation, which was not available to me when writing this article.)

[55] See Appendix 2 for a list, arranged by geographical region and diocese, of the churches that submitted papal supplications.

[56] The petition from the collegiate church of Ste Croix in Cambrai [4] is the only one to state directly that the eight choral vicars to be appointed to permanent posts would fill in for eight permanently absent canons. (The number in brackets refers, in all cases, to the number of the document as listed in Appendix 2.)

[57] Consider, for example, Reinhard Strohm's succinct assessment of the problem: 'Because many singers of the [Burgundian] ducal chapel held their prebends *in absentia*, the collegiate church actually subsidized the music of the court' (*Music in Late Medieval Bruges*, p. 23). This 'subsidy', moreover, worked to the actual detriment of music at the collegiate church.

service to participate in the Mass and offices of the church.[58] The funds that paid the vicars came from a variety of sources, including church property not already encumbered to support prebends, augmented by fines, fees, taxes and special endowments.[59] Therein lies the second rationale for the petitions to the pope.

The chapters were not reticent in their complaints about the insufficiency of funds to pay chaplains or vicars, citing continually the depredations of 'pestilence, war, and mortality' upon the endowments and other funds earmarked for this purpose.[60] Without these funds, churches had increasing difficulty maintaining a stable, resident corps of choral vicars. Moreover, the chapters lacked the power to enforce on their vicars compliance with the requirements of residency, decorum and an adequate performance of their liturgical and musical duties. Lurking behind these is a third rationale, the 'éminence grise' of polyphony. No papal document of this period mentions polyphony,[61] but the studies alluded to above demonstrate that it was an established practice at many of the churches named in papal documents from this period. Private endowments and the fifteenth-century lay religious confraternities were the driving forces behind the inauguration of regular polyphony at these churches. The pressure thus exerted upon the chapters to provide for – and to maintain – a regular supply of musicians qualified to perform polyphony must have piled the last

[58] Anne Walters Robertson ('The Mass of Guillaume de Machaut') reports that as early as 1352 the chapter of the cathedral of Rheims sought papal approval for a restructuring of capitular funding to pay the salaries of choral vicars, as well as four *pueri choriales*, who were needed to remedy the dwindling number of canons present in choir for daily services. Unfortunately, the copy of the original papal supplication, one of the earliest of this type to be reported, has not been preserved in the Vatican Archives.

[59] Haggh, 'Music in Brussels', pp. 101–5.

[60] 'Guerras, mortalitates, et pestes', as the collegiate church of St Wolfram in Abbeville (Amiens diocese) puts it [1]. Apparently, no church in northern France or the Low Countries was immune from the sharp decline in the value of property from which prebendal income and endowments were principally derived during the fifteenth century. See H. Denifle, *La désolation des églises, monastères, et hospitaux en France pendant la guerre de cent ans* (Paris, 1897), especially II, pp. 761–4, for a general discussion relating to France; and Haggh, 'Music in Brussels', pp. 115–21 and 221–5, for the specific impact upon music in churches in the Low Countries.

[61] But see Forney, 'Music, Ritual and Patronage', p. 6, discussing the papal bulls of John XXIII (1414) and Martin V (1430), which provide twelve chaplaincies in Our Lady of Antwerp for musicians to sing services in discant. Strohm, *Music in Late Medieval Bruges*, p. 17, discusses an endowment of 1421 for a choral foundation that would establish a daily polyphonic mass.

straw upon the already burdened financial structure of cathedrals and collegiate churches.

The problems faced by these churches may have been essentially the same, but the proposed solutions varied with the specific conditions of each church. Fourteen petitions centre on finding ways either to support the existing corps of choral vicars or to increase their numbers. The number of vicars deemed appropriate ranged from four or five at more modest collegiate institutions in Mons [8], Thèux [14] and Nivelles [11–13] to eight or ten at collegiates in Abbeville [1] and the city of Cambrai [4]. The cathedral at Trier [37] could make do with only four vicars, but the chapter of the cathedral of Toul [29] saw the need to raise the number of vicars from ten to twelve. The collegiate church of St Ursinus in Bourges [18] admitted to employing no fewer than twenty-five adult vicars.

Other churches requested not enhancement of their choral forces but simply the means to pay them adequately, and to enforce residency and quality of performance.[62] The cathedral of Cambrai [2–3], whose complement of *petits vicaires* rested comfortably between thirteen and sixteen, merely hoped to put the musicians' stipends on a more secure financial footing. This, in turn, would ensure a supply of singers able to maintain the high standards of musical performance for which this cathedral was famous.[63] The collegiate church of St Gertrude in Nivelles [11–13] sought papal permission to replace absentee or 'irreverent' chaplains and vicars with ones who would be more likely to 'enhance the celebration of Masses'. The collegiate church of St Rumold in Malines [7] trumpeted its exalted reputation, 'inter alias collegiatas ecclesias illarum partum multum nobilis et famosa reputatur in cantu', to justify a request to transfer responsibility for the support of the choral vicars from the chapter to the municipality of Malines (presumably with the full consent and encouragement of the city council).

Twenty-five institutions sought means for the establishment,

---

[62] The requirement of residency appears in the wording of nearly all the petitions. Only the chapter of St Germain in Thèux [14] stipulated the hiring of non-resident singers.

[63] See Wright, 'Dufay at Cambrai', pp. 195–6, and see Appendix 1, document 4 below for a partial transcription and translation of a petition by the cathedral of Cambrai from 1453. It is possible that the canon Du Fay had a hand in the drawing-up of this document. He was serving as master of the *petits-vicaires* just before leaving for Savoy in 1452.

augmentation or improved sustenance of the choirboys who assisted in divine services.[64] Two of the supplicants, the cathedral of Notre Dame in Paris [26] and the collegiate church of Our Lady at Antwerp [5], could boast of venerable and flourishing choir schools; they merely wished to support an increase in the number of choirboys from six to eight and from ten to twelve, respectively. Other churches with well-established choir schools, such as the cathedrals of Tournai [15], Rennes [27], Limoges [24] and Carcassonne [19], and collegiates at Condé [6] and Soignies [9] in the diocese of Cambrai, petitioned the pope for financial remedy, in order to provide adequately for the present number of choirboys and their master(s). Nearly all the petitions issuing from dioceses in Spain [40–5], as well as from the French dioceses of Besançon [17], Tréguier [34], Tours [33], Saint Brieuc [28], Vannes [35], Rennes [27] and Chartres [20], refer to the establishment of a *psalleta*, the term used for the office containing a small number of choirboys and their masters 'in cantu et grammatica'. The name itself suggests a practical reason for their establishment: to enhance the music of the liturgy through the participation of trained choirboys. And that, in turn, suggests at least the occasional performance of polyphony by the members of the *psalleta*.[65]

Among the churches that sought other means to improve the music of the divine service, the cathedrals of Toledo [45] and Barcelona [38–9] stand out. The chapter at Toledo wished to be able to control the amount of stipend paid to the *succentor*, the official with principal responsibility for music in the services. The cathedral of Barcelona uniquely petitioned for means to support

[64] On the role of music training and performance in the *maîtrises* of this period, see O. Becker, 'The Maîtrise in Northern France and Burgundy during the Fifteenth Century' (Ph.D. dissertation, George Peabody College for Teachers, Nashville, TN, 1967). For a recent and thorough analysis of the workings of the *maîtrise* at the cathedral of Notre Dame in Paris, see Wright, *Music and Ceremony at Notre Dame*, pp. 165–95.

[65] Numerous recent studies demonstrate that choirboys took part in polyphony in churches throughout northern France and the Low Countries by the middle of the fifteenth century. See especially Haggh, 'Music in Brussels', pp. 154–68; Strohm, *Music in Late Medieval Bruges*, pp. 13, 22–3, and 36–8; Forney, 'Music, Ritual and Patronage', pp. 7–8 and 38; and P. Higgins, 'Tracing the Careers of Late Medieval Composers: The Case of Philippe Basiron of Bourges', *Acta Musicologica*, 62 (1990), pp. 1–28. Even at Notre Dame in Paris, where the performance of polyphony was ostensibly prohibited in the early fifteenth century, the choirboys were instructed in this art. And by the end of the century the choirboys took regular part in performance of polyphony at Notre Dame (Wright, *Music and Ceremony at Notre Dame*, pp. 166–9 and 173–4).

properly a 'bona organista' and to pay for the costs of repair for the instrument, 'quedam organa memorabilia et sumptuosa'.[66]

Although the means of procuring financial support for these reforms also varied with each institution, the basic strategies were two, easily summarised under the rubrics 'suppression, conversion, and merging' and 'sequestration'. What were to be suppressed or sequestered were benefices; the funds that had supported these benefices were to be diverted to the support of musicians. By far the most popular decision was to suppress a simple benefice, such as a perpetual chaplaincy. Once papal permission had been secured, *and when the chaplaincy had been vacated by its present incumbent*, the chapter would be free to void the benefice and to assign the funds that had supported it to the choral vicars and choirboys, or for other purposes related to music and worship. The drawback, of course, was the phrase in italics: many chapters had to wait years before the benefice was finally vacated and many had to endure legal complications and the expense of multiple petitions to the papal court before the benefice and its funds were available for conversion. Not every chapter was able to earmark one simple benefice with sufficient funds. In these cases, various creative solutions involved the merging of from two to seven benefices yielding comparatively small amounts.[67] The combined funds from the suppressed benefices (remember that the chapter would have to await the vacancy of all the benefices) would normally yield an annual income of between 25 and 50 *l.p.t.* to be used for the support of musicians. (A benefice with annual income of 24 *l.p.t.* was considered ample for the majority of clergy.)

When simple benefices were not available, chapters turned, more reluctantly, to the suppression and conversion of canonries with their prebends. Thus, the chapter of Notre Dame in Paris [26] paid for two additional choirboys by suppressing the next available canonry worth 20 *l.p.t.* and by adding that amount to the fund of 80 *l.p.t.* already being used to support the choirboys. Where there were thirty and forty-four prebends available, as in the cathedrals of

---

[66] The cathedral lodged two separate supplications. The first stipulated 24 *l.p.t.*; three years later, the figure was doubled. Both documents indicate that the organist himself would be responsible for carrying out repairs and tuning the instrument.

[67] Such merging is termed 'incorporation' by Barbara Haggh ('Music in Brussels', pp. 115–21), and could involve either chaplaincies controlled by the chapter or those administered under lay endowments.

Limoges [23] and Tournai [15], we must presume that the chapter would not miss one. Occasionally the prebends targeted for conversion were under the collation of a lay patron, as with the collegiates in Condé [6], Soignies [9] and Valenciennes [10] (the Duke of Burgundy), and in Blois [20] (the Duke of Orléans). In these cases, the supplication would come jointly from the chapter and the patron of the benefice in question.

Parish churches dependent on the chapters of cathedrals and collegiates, particularly ones with dwindling congregations or those dilapidated and in need of major repairs, were also fair game for suppression and conversion. Sometimes the incumbent rector of a parish church could be persuaded to co-operate in the suppression, as in the case of Jean Lohaer. He received a handsome pension upon resigning the parish church of Pedernet to the use of the chapter of the cathedral of Tréguier in Brittany [34].[68] The chapter at York Minster [46] had less luck with Thomas Passelewe, the incumbent of a rectorship in the parish church of Meterwalopp in the diocese of Windsor. Possibly the distance of this parish church from its 'mother church' in York had something to do with the rector's intransigence.

A different tack was taken by, among others, the cathedral of Tours [30–3]. In 1449 the chapter received papal permission to sequester an unspecified number of benefices, which were to be collated by the chapter only to those choral vicars well grounded 'in cantu et literatura'. The vicars not only had to demonstrate their qualifications to the chapter, but were bound by stringent requirements of residency, even if they simultaneously held benefices at nearby institutions, such as the collegiate church of St Martin. In 1453 the chapter adopted an even more unconventional measure: the reservation of four canonries to be granted to 'four honest men trained and erudite in the art and science of music, with voices sufficiently strong and loud (or high) and suitable to the psalmody of the church'.[69] These four musicians were required to attend all

---

[68] The funds from the suppression of this parish church, 130 *l.p.t.*, accrued to the newly established office of *psalleta*, whose master of the choirboys was Alanus Juvenis, a councillor of the Duke of Brittany. One suspects that pressure from the ducal court was applied to persuade Jean Lohaer to resign his parish church in favour of Juvenis and the *psalleta*.

[69] '... quatuor honestis viris cantoribus ... [in] scientia [et] arte musicae specialiter eruditis quisque vocem habeat sufficienter fortem et altum ac psalmodie ecclesie congruentem' [31].

day and night services and to be personally resident at the cathedral for at least nine months of the year. Permission to be absent was always to be obtained in writing from the chapter. Failure to meet this requirement would result in deprivation of the canonry. When one of the designated canonries became vacant, late in 1459, the chapter issued another petition that stipulated a further requirement, that the musicians were to be graduates and holders of advanced degrees in theology or law from a 'famosa universitas'.[70] The archbishop and chapter of the cathedral of Tours emphatically reiterated the strict requirements of residency. The chapter intended to have total and unprecedented control over the new canons: to establish qualifications, to choose and approve candidates, to supervise their performance and to remove them if their performance failed to satisfy.

When the popes affixed their 'fiat' to these fifty-five supplications from cathedrals and collegiate churches, they authorised a number of changes with consequences that were not necessarily desirable to all. The departed lay patrons who had endowed chaplaincies specifically for the salvation of their own souls may have had no redress from the grave when their endowments were diverted. But living parishioners deprived of the spiritual comfort of their local church and rector may well have registered protest. Secular magnates who lost the privilege of collation of certain important and lucrative benefices most assuredly complained, although many churches took pains to placate their most important secular patrons. The papacy itself suffered diminished control over the provision of important benefices in these churches. Thus a process of two centuries by which the papacy had steadily accrued to itself this prerogative was reversed. The popes ceded freely what many years' rigorous pressure from religious councils and secular monarchs could not accomplish: the transfer of rights of collation to local chapters in churches throughout Europe. Although it was not strictly in their best interests, nevertheless the fifteenth-century

---

[70] 'Quatuor probis viris literatis honeste vite morum et literatum scientia instructis in famosa universitate graduatis et specialiter qualificatis scilicet magistris, licentiatis aut baccalauris formatis in teologia vel adminus actu studentibus universitate et in proximis formandis seu licentiatis in altero iurium assegnarentur et conferrentur' [32].

I thank Katherine Gill for her kind assistance in examining the original of this document in the Vatican Archives, when my own copy proved defective. Dr Gill informs me that the phrase 'baccalaureus formatus' was used to refer to one of the four ranks of faculty at the University of Paris.

popes collaborated in a process of far-reaching importance to the history of music. They granted to churches the ability to develop and to support financially choirs trained and experienced in the performance of polyphony. Churches thus endowed would greatly enrich the cultural life of the cities in which they were situated. By the end of the fifteenth century many cathedrals and collegiate churches could take their place alongside secular music chapels as places where sacred polyphony and its composers flourished.

SACRA PENITENTIARIA

We come, finally, to the third and most intimate type of papal Grace, the provision of dispensation and absolution to the erring or sinning faithful. Such Graces were usually obtained through special application to the office of the Apostolic Penitentiary, which was deputed by the pope to deal with matters concerning the *forum internum*, or arena of personal conscience. These were originally the exclusive responsibility of the pope himself. As the volume of requests for dispensation and absolution increased to the point of unmanageability, the medieval popes appointed a body of theologians and canon lawyers to assist them.[71] By the early thirteenth century, this group had been replaced by a single official, the *penitentiarius maior*, or Cardinal Penitentiary. He had absolute authority over petitions concerning the *forum internum*. This authority is apparent in the way the Cardinal Penitentiary signed penitential supplications: he was uniquely authorised to use the papal 'fiat'.[72] A cadre of assistants, clerks and scribes was quickly recruited to help him deal with the flood of petitions. The procedures and paperwork involved in this type of papal Grace were much the same as that for the Graces of the *forum externum*, discussed above. A series of volumes, beginning in the early fifteenth century, preserves

[71] The standard work on the history of the Sacra Penitentiaria is E. Göller, *Die päpstliche Poenitentiarie von ihrem Ursprung bis zu ihrer Umgestaltung unter Pius V*, Bibliothek des Kgl. Preussischen Historischen Instituts in Rom 3–4 and 7–8 (Rome, 1907, 1911). Also useful are H. Lea, *A Formulary of the Papal Penitentiary of the Thirteenth Century* (Philadelphia, PA, 1892); *idem*, 'The Taxes of the Papal Penitentiary', *English Historical Review*, 8 (1893), pp. 424–33; and P. Chouet, 'Pénitencerie apostolique', *Dictionnaire de théologie catholique* (Paris, 1923), xii, 1, cols. 1138–68.

[72] F. Tamburini, 'Il primo registro di suppliche dell'Archivio della Sacra Penitenzieria Apostolica (1410–1411)', *Rivista di Storia della Chiesa in Italia*, 23 (1969), pp. 384–427 (esp. 420–5).

the supplications to the Cardinal Penitentiary; copies of the corresponding rescripts were preserved only from 1570.[73] Because of the stringent canonical requirements of secrecy, the so-called 'historical' archives of the Sacra Penitentiaria (those from the fifteenth and sixteenth centuries) were made generally available to scholars only in 1983; and even now one must obtain special permission to view them.[74]

A thirteenth-century formulary includes no fewer than ninety-three types of penitential supplication from both laity and clergy.[75] The majority of petitions from the laity required some form of marriage dispensation. Other frequently occurring supplications from lay persons concern dispensation or commutation of unfulfilled vows. The clergy, on the other hand, turned to the Holy See for dispensation and absolution from irregularities and crimes that affected their ability to function within the church hierarchy; that is, to celebrate the divine offices, to care for the souls of parishioners or to hold ecclesiastical benefices.

The volumes of the Sacra Penitentiaria are replete with requests for dispensation from the *defectus natalium*, the canonically disabling fact of illegitimacy. Clergymen born out of wedlock were required to secure dispensations in order to qualify to hold benefices.[76] Composers and performing musicians, some of the most celebrated of whom were offspring of clergy, were not exempt from this requirement.[77] During the years 1450–75, two papal musicians, Johannes

[73] On the archives of the Sacra Penitentiaria, see especially Tamburini, 'Il primo registro'; *idem*, 'Note diplomatiche intorno a suppliche e lettere di Penitenzieria (sec. xiv–xv)', *Archivum Historiae Pontificiae*, 11 (1973), pp. 195–8 and 475–7; *idem*, 'Un registro di bolle di Sisto IV nell'Archivio della Penitenzieria Apostolica', *Palaeographica, diplomatica, et archivistica: studi in onore di Giulio Battelli*, ii, Storia e Letteratura 140 (Rome, 1979), pp. 375–405; and K. Fink, 'Das Archiv des Sacra Poenitentiaria Apostolica', *Zeitschrift für Kirchengeschichte*, 83 (1972), pp. 88–92.

[74] Fink, 'Das Archiv', p. 92. Permission must now be obtained from the office of the Apostolic Penitentiary, located at the Palazzo della Cancelleria in Rome. I was extremely fortunate to be present in the Vatican Archives in 1983, when this *fondo* was, for a short period, made entirely available to the public without the need for obtaining special permission. Very few music historians have yet taken full advantage of this valuable resource.

[75] Göller, *Päpstliche Poeniteniarie*, iii, pp. 50–3.

[76] A sociological aside: petitioners were required to indicate the precise circumstances of their birth. The number of clergy in the fifteenth century born of illicit unions between members of the clergy (such as priests and nuns) is quite astonishing. Or perhaps not so, since a career in the church was probably the best means of advancement for an illegitimate child, especially one with patronage only among the clergy.

[77] See, for example, Alejandro Planchart's recent theory about the probable illegitimate

247

Postel and Johannes de Cruce (Monami), sought dispensation for the defect of illegitimate birth, as did Egidius Crispin of the ducal chapel in Savoy and Johannes Caron, *sommelier* of the Duke of Burgundy's chapel. Even Paris de Grassis, the illustrious master of ceremonies in the papal chapel of the early sixteenth century, turns out to have had less than ideal origins, being the son of a married man and a 'professed nun'.[78]

Several musicians were caught reneging on sworn undertakings. Without a dispensation from the Apostolic Penitentiary, the papal singer Johannes Saureux stood to lose the chaplaincy at the cathedral of Liège for which he had sworn 'perpetual residency'. Johannes de Fraxinis, a member of the ducal chapel in Savoy, suffered a sentence of excommunication for non-payment of long-standing debts to the Apostolic Camera. Papal absolution, plus, of course, the payment of his back debts, was required before he could resume his ecclesiastical duties in the duke's chapel.[79]

Crimes of violence by the clergy, and especially against other members of the clergy, always resulted in a sentence of excommunication and the concomitant disqualification of the guilty cleric from serving at Mass or offices.[80] Professional musicians who made their living serving in secular chapels or in the choirs of cathedrals and collegiate churches were especially vulnerable in such cases, yet that did not seem to discourage the occasional outbreak of violence among the musical clergy. One remarkable instance concerns a feud in the very confines of the papal Curia. No fewer than four papal musicians, Martinus Hanart, Johannes de Monstroeul, Jacobus Boni and Guillermus de Cault, were convicted of perpetrating violent acts against certain clergymen of the Curia.[81] Each musician had to submit his own petition for absolution and rehabilitation. From these petitions we can reconstruct a fight with

---

birth of Du Fay. Professor Planchart bases this conclusion on information gleaned from a papal document that suggests that the composer had failed to obtain the necessary dispensation for the *defectus natalium* before acquiring a particular benefice (Planchart, 'Guillaume Du Fay's Benefices', p. 118).

[78] ASV, *SP*, 4, fols. 11ᵛ and 13ʳ; *SP* 4, fol. 52ʳ; *SP* 17, fols. 99ᵛ and 191ʳ; *SP* 6, fol. 392ʳ; *SP* 31, fol. 196.

[79] ASV *SP* 3, fol. 203ᵛ; *SP* 10, fol. 170ʳ.

[80] Crimes of violence could also result in the loss of benefices. See Starr, 'Music and Music Patronage', pp. 184–6, for the story of Petrus Landrich, a papal musician who was forced to withdraw a petition for a benefice in the diocese of Utrecht because he had killed an assailant in self-defence.

[81] ASV *SP* 17, fol. 119ʳ; *SP* 18, fols. 133ᵛ, 181ʳ and 190ᵛ.

both fisticuffs and weapons, in which the other curialists appear to have come off the worse.[82]

Another petition presents an even more startling view of fifteenth-century mores among the members of the musical clergy. An entry for 28 February 1461 records the petition for absolution lodged by the *clericus* Anthonius de Busnes, incumbent of a perpetual chaplaincy in the cathedral of Tours, and more familiarly known as the composer Antoine Busnoys.[83] (See Figure 1.) Not only did he severely beat a priest within the cathedral close, but he confesses to having organised a group attack on the priest – not once but on five separate occasions. Furthermore, he had violated the restriction placed on him against celebrating Mass and Office until absolution had been procured. We will, alas, never know what provoked Busnoys to this crime of violent bloodshed: the chapter acts of the cathedral of Tours that could have amplified the story were destroyed during the French Revolution.[84]

The only document that remains to tell the tale is the supplication for absolution, with its protocol requiring the penitent to detail the precise nature and circumstances of his crime. This document, tantalisingly enigmatic as it may seem, tells us a number of useful things about the composer. It is, first of all, the earliest extant document relating to the composer. It corroborates and amplifies information presented by Paula Higgins that placed Busnoys in Tours, at the collegiate church of St Martin in 1465 at the latest.[85] It is unreasonable to suppose that there were two clergymen with this distinctive name both resident in Tours at the same time.[86] The

---

[82] The only musician alleged to have brandished a weapon was Guillermus de Cault, who again required absolution for another violent crime in 1476 (*SP* 24, fol. 102ʳ). The very act of bearing a weapon was a violation of canon law for a member of the clergy. One reads petitions from clergy in which the presence of a deadly weapon is euphemised as 'a knife for the paring of fruit'. (See, for example, ASV *RS* 655, fols. 205ᵛ–206ᵛ, a description of an altercation between two Benedictine monks of Poitiers.)

[83] ASV *SP* 9, fol. 134ʳ, published for the first time, as document 5 in Appendix 1.

[84] *Inventaire-sommaire des archives départementales antérieures à 1790: Indre-et-Loire*, ii, Archives Ecclésiastiques, ser. G, Clergé Séculier, ed. C. Grandmaison (Tours, 1882), pp. ii–iii and 12–76.

[85] Most recently discussed in 'Antoine Busnois and Musical Culture in Late Fifteenth-Century France and Burgundy' (Ph.D. dissertation, Princeton University, 1987), pp. 125–36; and '*In hydraulis* Revisited: New Light on the Career of Antoine Busnois', *JAMS*, 39 (1986), pp. 69–76 and 86.

[86] The version of his name in the document from St Martin is 'Antonius Bunoys', which is more than once associated in contemporary documents with the alternative version, 'de Busne' (see Higgins, '*In hydraulis* Revisited', pp. 83–4). As with the orthographies Du Fay, Okeghem and Puyllois discussed above, the use of the version 'Anthonius de Busne'

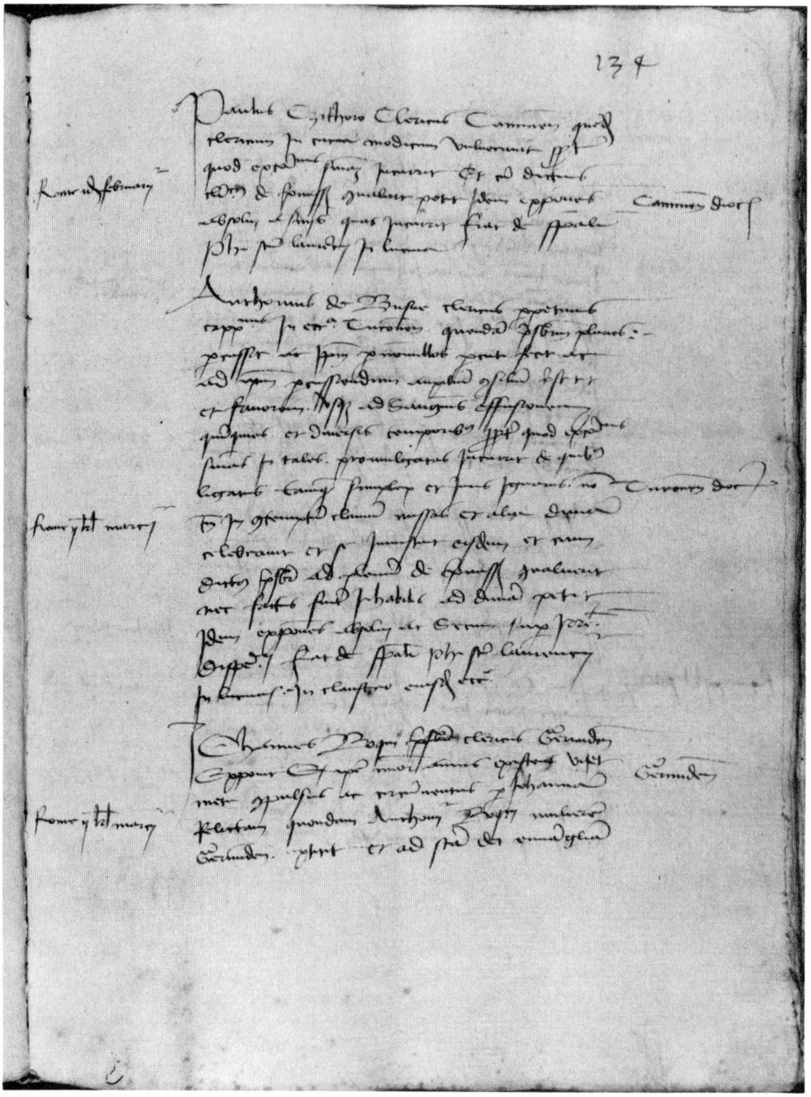

Figure 1   Archivio Segreto Vaticano, *Sacra Penitentiaria* 9, fol. 134[r]

papal document does not specify the precise identity of the
chaplaincy held by Busnoys in the cathedral, nor its duties.[87]

in a document emanating from the papal Curia confers upon that version a distinct air of
authority.

[87]   It is, nevertheless, the earliest allusion to a specific benefice held by Busnoys, and the

Busnoys might have held one of the four chaplaincies reserved by the cathedral of Tours for choral vicars (see the discussion above). If so, given the views of the chapter on compulsory residence of their choral vicars, he might have found it awkward to hold a simultaneous position at St Martin. (Yet we know that chaplains incurred the chapter's displeasure by attempting to do precisely this.) It is even possible that Busnoys was one of the four 'honest men trained and erudite in the art and science of music' to whom the chapter at Tours had proposed to offer canonries.[88]

We can now securely date Busnoys's presence in Tours from 1460 at the latest. This revised dating in turn opens several areas of speculation. For one thing, it helps us to come a bit closer to the still unresolved matter of the composer's birthdate. The fact that Busnoys held a chaplaincy from 1460 or earlier suggests that he was at least in his early maturity during the years he spent in Tours. Furthermore, although a sudden and unpremeditated attack on a senior clergyman might be the result of impetuous post-adolescence, for Busnoys to have organised five systematic assaults on the priest suggests to me that he was mature (at least in chrono-logical age) and not without influence in the cathedral chapter. If one postulates an age for Busnoys in 1461 of between twenty-two and twenty-five, then a birthdate for him might be set at between 1436 and 1439.[89]

We still do not know what drew this cleric, presumably from a village in Pas-de-Calais, to a city in the heart of France, rich with connections to the French court. But we do now have documen-tation for a substantial sojourn in Tours, one that covered at least the years of his early maturity as a musician.[90] We can therefore widen considerably the scope of opportunity for a fruitful pro-

only one not located in Burgundian territories. For benefices held by Busnoys, see Higgins, '*In hydraulis* Revisited', pp. 51–3; *idem*, 'Antoine Busnois', pp. 114–24; and B. Haggh, 'New Documents from the Low Countries', paper read at the Capitol Chapter meeting of the American Musicological Society, 20 January 1990. (I am grateful to Professor Haggh for providing me with a copy of this paper.)

[88] One might even be tempted to speculate whether one of these highly prized benefices was the cause of the quarrel between Busnoys and the priest. Perhaps the priest had balked the composer of this desirable appointment.

[89] Paula Higgins has informed me that she is in possession of new documents that similarly suggest that Busnoys 'was a composer of considerable stature already in 1465' (private communication to the author, 26 September 1990).

[90] For the possibility that Busnoys also received his education in Tours, perhaps at the *maîtrise* at St Martin, see Higgins, '*In hydraulis* Revisited', pp. 74–6.

fessional relationship between Busnoys and Johannes Okeghem. Such a relationship was first implied in the theoretical works of a contemporary of the composers, Johannes Tinctoris.[91] It has also been signalled repeatedly in recent literature. Paula Higgins has identified 'a web of intertextual relationships' among the chansons of the two composers. She has also made a very convincing case for a close – even emulatory – musical and textual relationship between the younger composer's motet *In hydraulis* and Okeghem's *Ut heremita solus*.[92] Leeman Perkins has called attention to a number of musical and procedural resemblances between the *L'homme armé* masses of the two composers, and to the evidence that they both drew material from the same polyphonic chansons, *Il sera pour vous/L'ome armé* and Okeghem's own *L'aultre d'antan*.[93] And Richard Taruskin has shown that both masses incorporate, at a crucial liturgical juncture, the 'Et incarnatus est', the same highly symbolic count of thirty-one *tactus*.[94]

Assuming that the two composers must at some time have worked in physical proximity, the most likely time for this was the period between about 1460 and 1465, when both men were resident in Tours. Okeghem was installed as Treasurer of St Martin in Tours by July 1459.[95] From the time of the accession of Louis XI in August 1461, the French court made extended stays in or near the royal city of Tours.[96] Busnoys, we now know, was a resident clergyman there as well from at least 1460. These must have been the

---

[91]   Both Leeman Perkins (*The Mellon Chansonnier*, ed. L. Perkins and H. Garey, i (New Haven, CT, 1979), p. 17) and Paula Higgins ('Antoine Busnois', pp. 247–50) have commented on the frequent pairing of the two composers in the pages of the theoretical works of Tinctoris, a pairing that suggests 'that he knew [these composers] better than by reputation alone' (*Mellon Chansonnier*, i, p. 17). Higgins has further suggested that the three men enjoyed a period of geographic proximity, a conclusion drawn from information provided by Ronald Woodley, which places Tinctoris at the University of Orléans during 1462–3 (and possibly from as early as 1457). (See his 'Johannes Tinctoris: A Review of the Documentary Biographical Evidence', *JAMS*, 34 (1981), pp. 225–8.) As Higgins points out, the city of Orléans is a mere seventy miles up-river from Tours.

[92]   Higgins, 'Antoine Busnois', pp. 138–46, 241–4; *idem*, '*In hydraulis* Revisited', pp. 76–83.

[93]   L. Perkins, 'The L'homme Armé Masses of Busnoys and Okeghem', *Journal of Musicology*, 3 (1984), pp. 363–91.

[94]   R. Taruskin, 'Antoine Busnois and the *L'homme armé* Tradition', *JAMS*, 39 (1986), p. 273.

[95]   Higgins, 'Antoine Busnois', p. 143. She notes also that Okeghem held, from 1458 at the latest, a provostship at St Martin.

[96]   B. Chevalier, *Tours, ville royale (1356–1520)*, Publications de la Sorbonne, MS Recherches 14 (Paris, 1975), pp. 243–7, as cited in Higgins, 'Antoine Busnois', p. 144. See also *idem*, 'Tracing the Careers of Late Medieval Composers', pp. 15–16; Perkins, 'Musical Patronage at the Royal Court of France', p. 539; P. Kendall, *Louis XI* (New York, 1971), pp. 116–18; and J. Tyrrell, *Louis XI* (Boston, MA, 1980), p. 63.

years that witnessed the fruitful musical relationship between the two composers noted above, and the foundation of a friendship proclaimed by Busnoys in his motet *In hydraulis*.[97]

Music history (especially of the early Renaissance, when contracts, personal letters and other solidly reliable written documentation are thin on the ground) frequently turns on inference – on the pinpointing of a time and place when a musical artefact might have been created, or a significant professional acquaintance formed. To the crux of the composers Okeghem and Busnoys in Tours in the early 1460s, we must add another potential point of contact, with Charles of Charolais, the future Duke of Burgundy. This prince spent nearly three weeks in Tours, from 22 November to 11 December 1461.[98] During these weeks Louis XI was resident in Tours as well, presumably along with the members of his domestic chapel.[99] At the same time the precincts of the cathedral might even still have been abuzz with the scandal of Busnoys's repeated attacks on a man of the cloth.[100] There is thus at least the possibility that the paths of these men crossed late in 1461 – that, perhaps through the offices of Okeghem, first chaplain of the king's chapel, the name of Busnoys might have come to the attention of the Count of Charolais. This is not, of course, to suggest that Busnoys was recruited to the service of Burgundy on the spot, but merely that a connection might have been established, one that would flower within six years into an informal association with the ducal chapel of Burgundy and, by 1471, into the most significant and longest-lasting post of Busnoys's career.[101] The forthright pug-

---

[97] For the full text and translation of *In hydraulis*, see Perkins, 'L'homme armé Masses', p. 364. See also Higgins, '*In hydraulis* Revisited', pp. 75–6, and *idem*, 'Antoine Busnois', pp. 148–58.

[98] H. Vander Linden, *Itinéraires de Philippe le Bon, duc de Bourgogne, 1419–1467, et de Charles, comte de Charolais, 1433–1467* (Brussels, 1940), pp. 435–6, as reported by Barbara Haggh in her communication to the editor of *JAMS*, 40 (1987), p. 143.

[99] Tyrrell, *Louis XI*, p. 51, and Kendall, *Louis XI*, pp. 114–18. The latter author discusses the efforts made by the new French king immediately after his coronation to recruit the friendship of the Count of Charolais. It is extremely likely, therefore, that Charles visited Tours as an honoured guest of Louis.

[100] We do not know the precise dates of the attacks planned by Busnoys. I would estimate, given the time required for the processing of a supplication at the papal court (between three and six months), that his actions probably took place in the autumn of 1460. The interval of a year would not, I think, be sufficient completely to stamp out gossip in the chapter about the imbroglio involving Busnoys.

[101] Paula Higgins ('*In hydraulis* Revisited, pp. 75) establishes the informal connection with the Burgundian court, implicit in the motet *In hydraulis*, as having occurred between 1465

nacity of Charles the Bold is well documented; he has even been considered an archetypal figure of the 'homme armé'.[102] Could this man of action, encountering the controversial figure of the composer Antoine Busnoys, perhaps have recognised a kindred spirit?

The words 'L'homme armé' have themselves achieved a certain notoriety in scholarly circles recently.[103] I would suggest that the historical crux mentioned above may also bear on the question of where and how at least one strand of the *L'homme armé* mass tradition began. To reiterate: both Okeghem and Busnoys were resident in the same city for substantial periods of the years between 1460 and 1465, and the future Duke of Burgundy spent several weeks in the same city during this time. The musical and ceremonial connections between the Burgundian Order of the Golden Fleece and the *Missa L'homme armé* (especially those versions by Busnoys, Okeghem and Du Fay, and the six anonymous settings in the Naples manuscript that have also been credited to Busnoys) have been ably and persuasively set forth by William Prizer and Richard Taruskin.[104] The remarkable affinities between the two versions by Busnoys and Okeghem were mentioned above. To the 'various floating facts and hypotheses of late'[105] touching on the origins of the *L'homme armé* mass tradition, I should like to propose yet another 'floating hypothesis' (one with the dubious claim of being undemonstrably right or wrong at present). It is that Charles of Burgundy's presence in Tours, at a time when Busnoys may have been – understandably – looking around for professional opport-

and 1467. In 'Tracing the Careers', p. 16, n. 70, she further narrows the period to early 1467.

[102] See, for example, L. Lockwood, 'Aspects of the "L'Homme armé" Tradition', *Proceedings of the Royal Music Association*, 100 (1973–4), p. 109; D. Fallows, *Dufay*, pp. 201–2; Haggh, 'Communication', and the response by Richard Taruskin immediately following. (But see Higgins, 'Antoine Busnois', p. 97, n. 170; and *idem*, review of R. Strohm's *Music in Late Medieval Bruges*, in *JAMS*, 42 (1989), pp. 155–6, n. 15, for a dissenting view.) The career and character of Charles of Burgundy is compellingly set forth in R. Vaughan, *Charles the Bold: The Last Valois Duke of Burgundy* (London, 1973).

[103] See especially the article by Richard Taruskin ('Antoine Busnois') and the various responses to that article, *JAMS*, 40 (1987), pp. 139–53 and 576–80.

[104] Taruskin, 'Antoine Busnois'; W. Prizer, 'The Order of the Golden Fleece and Music of the Fifteenth Century'. I am very grateful to Professor Prizer for kindly sending me a copy of this paper. (See also his 'Music and Ceremonial in the Low Countries: Philip the Fair and the Order of the Golden Fleece', *Early Music History*, 5 (1985), pp. 133–53, for observations on Burgundian ceremonial and music that also apply to the period under discussion.)

[105] To use Richard Taruskin's apt locution (Taruskin, 'Communication to the Editor', *JAMS*, 40 (1987), p. 149).

unities outside Tours, might conceivably have been a catalyst for the composition of a *Missa L'homme armé*.[106] Such a piece, both virtuosic and apropos, would admirably serve to follow up on a brief encounter between the count and Busnoys, and would demonstrate to the count the precise measure of Busnoys's skill as a composer. The composition and presentation to Charles of a work such as Busnoys's mass might, therefore, be the missing link in a chain comprising a meeting in 1461, the composer's self-designation, c. 1465–7, as 'illustris comitis de Chaulois indignum musicum', and Busnoys's appearance in 1471 as a fully-fledged (and fully paid) member of the ducal chapel of Burgundy.[107] It is even possible that work on this composition for Burgundy may have spurred the 'friendly emulation' evident in the versions of the *Missa L'homme armé* by Busnoys and Okeghem.

Should this scenario prove correct, then his original crime of bloodshed may well have turned out for Busnoys a most 'fortunate sin' indeed. Certainly he did not suffer any permanent consequences from it. Once absolution and rehabilitation had been obtained (through proper petition to the Apostolic Penitentiary and payment of the requisite fees), Busnoys was reinstated as a fully accredited member of the musical clergy, able to sing divine

---

[106] 'Catalyst' should not, however, be confused with specific commission. I entirely agree with William Prizer, who suggests that a direct commission from Charles in 1461 would have been not only unlikely but also inappropriate, since Charles was not then the official head of the Order of the Golden Fleece. (Prizer, 'Order of the Golden Fleece'). But the encounter might have provided at least a reason for Busnoys to cast about for a suitable project with which to impress a potential future employer.

[107] It is extremely difficult to pinpoint the precise time within the period 1461–5 at which Busnoys might have set to work on his *Missa L'homme armé*. I incline towards a later date, if only because the chanson 'Il sera pour vous / L'home armé', which so patently appears to have influenced the composition of the mass, has been dated convincingly to 1464. (See D. Fallows, 'Robert Morton's Songs: A Study of Styles in the Mid-Fifteenth Century' (Ph.D. dissertation, University of California at Berkeley, 1978), pp. 202–44.) I concur with Dr Fallows that the text of this chanson points conclusively to authorship by a colleague of Simon Le Breton's in the Burgundian chapel, and that Simon's retirement from the chapel in 1464 would have been the most obvious occasion for its performance (though its composition might have antedated the official occasion for its performance by some time). One is reminded that Okeghem made two visits to Cambrai, in 1462 and in 1464; that on both occasions he was the guest of Guillaume Du Fay, a close friend and neighbour of Simon Le Breton; and that Du Fay's residence was only a block from the suggestively named Maison de L'homme armé. (See Wright, 'Dufay at Cambrai', pp. 208–12.) The temptation is strong to wonder if Okeghem was the courier who brought the chanson to the attention of Busnoys in Tours in 1464 or even as early as 1462. For a hypothesis of the transmission of the 'L'Homme armé' tradition that in part supports my construction, see Lockwood, 'Aspects of the "L'Homme armé" Tradition', p. 110.

services, to hold positions of responsibility in the clerical hierarchy and to acquire benefices. And more, his crimes of violence may have brought him to the attention of an important music patron, one who would eventually offer to Busnoys all that a professional musician could ask: the chance to serve in one of the foremost music chapels of Europe, and the opportunity to create artful musical compositions.

To provide for security in old age through ecclesiastical benefices; to enhance the divine service with the performance of polyphony; to purge the soul from the consequences of sin: these were the motives that provoked Okeghem, Du Fay, the cathedral of Cambrai, Busnoys and countless other musicians to send their representatives to Rome and to the Holy See. For the Christian faithful of the fifteenth century, and most especially for members of the clergy, including virtually all professional musicians of the day, Rome was indeed the centre of the universe. And for those music historians who regard the records of the Holy See, preserved in the Vatican Archives, as the single most useful archival source for fifteenth-century music throughout Europe, Rome is still the centre of the universe.

University of Nebraska

APPENDIX 1

Documents[1]

Document 1A: Archivio Segreto Vaticano, *Annatae* 17, fol. 183ᵛ [24 October 1466]

Dicta die dominus Johannes Puyllois cantor capellae sanctissimi domini nostri papae procuratus ad infrascripta legittime constitutus ab domino Johannes de Okeghem Thesaurario ecclesiae beatissimi Martini Turonensis ut de ipsa procuratione plene constat instrumento publico acto in

---

[1]   I wish to thank the following people, who at various times helped to improve the transcriptions and translations of these documents: Brian Chaffin, Professors Neil Adkins, Thomas Bestul and Thomas Rinkevich of the University of Nebraska, Katherine Gill, and Monsignor Felippo Tamburini of the Biblioteca Apostolica Vaticana. If, despite the kind assistance of these scholars, errors remain, they are entirely the responsibility of this author.

vestibulo ecclesie Beatissimi Martini die quarta mensis septembris pro-
xime preteriti vigore dicti mandati in camera dimissi obligavit dictum
Johannem de Okeghem super annatis canonicatus et prebendae ac
praepositurae ecclesiae Sancti Martini Cadanten Turonensis diocesis
quorum fructus centum librorum Turonensis parvorum secundum
extimationem communem, vacantes per obitum quondam Guillermi
Bouchier olim dicte ecclesie canonici et praepositi extra romanam curiam
defuncti, et mandata provideri dicto Johanni de dictis beneficiis sub data
romae nono kalendas juni anno secundo.

On the aforesaid day, Johannes Puyllois, singer in the papal chapel, and
legitimately constituted procurator of Johannes de Okeghem, the
Treasurer of St Martin of Tours, his position having been fully established
by an instrument produced in the vestibule of St Martin on 4 September,
[Puyllois] obliged Okeghem to pay the annates of the canonry and provostship of the church of St Martin in Candes-St-Martin in the diocese of
Tours, the income of which is 100 *l.p.t.*, the benefices being vacated by the
death of the incumbent, Guillaume Bouchier, and having been ordered to
be provided to [Okeghem] under the date 'Rome, 24 May 1466'.

Document 1B: added to the right-hand margin of document 1A
Die 9 aprilis 1467 dictus Johannes solvit pro annatis florenos L. per manus
Societatis de Pazziis . . .

On 9 April 1467, the aforementioned Johannes paid the annates of 50 fl.
through the banking company of Pazzi.

Document 2: ASV, *Registra Supplicationum* 595, fol. 148
Beatissime pater dudum praepositura et canonicatus et praebenda
ecclesiae Sancti Martini Cadantensis Turonensis diocesis per obitum
quondam Guillermi Bouchier illorum ultimi possessoris extra romanam
curiam defuncti vacantes, devotus orator *Johannes de Okeghem*,
Thesaurarius ecclesiae Beatissimi Martini Turonensis vigore gratias
expectatives seu nominationes illustrissimi francorum Regis sibi per felicis
recordationis Pium papam secundum, vestrae sanctitatis predecessorem
concesse acceptavit . . . Supplicat igitur s.v. prefatus Johannes . . . spe-
cialem gratiam facientem de dicta praepositura qua in eadem ecclesia
dignitas non tamen principalis existit ac canonicatu et praebenda praedic-
tis quorum fructus centum librorum Turonensis parvorum secundum
communem extimationem valorem annuum non excedunt . . . Concessum
ut petitur in presentia domini nostri papae Petrus Tirasonensi. Datum
Romae apud Sanctum Marcum 9 kal. juni anno 2o

Most blessed father, the provostship and canonry of St Martin in Candes-St-Martin in the diocese of Tours being vacant by the death of Guillaume Bouchier, the latest incumbent, who died outside the Roman Curia, Johannes Okeghem, Treasurer of St Martin of Tours, having been granted expectative graces from the Most Christian King of France [Louis XI] through the concession of Pius II, of most blessed memory, Okeghem requests the grace of the provision of the provostship and canonry, whose annual income does not exceed 100 *l.p.t.* . . . Granted in the presence of the Pope. [signed] Petrus Tirasonensis [i.e. Petrus Ferriz, Bishop of Tarrazona, chief Referendarius to Paul II]. Dated Rome, at the basilica of San Marco, 24 May 1466.

Document 3: ASV, *Registra Lateranensia* 483, fol. 295
Nicolaus etc. dilecto filio Guillermo Du Fay canonico Cameracensis, bacallario in decretis salutem etc. litterarum scientia vite ac morum honestas aliaque laudabilia probitatis et virtutum merita super quibus apud nos fidedigno commendatis testimonio nos inducunt ut illa tibi favorabiliter concedamus que tuis commoditatibus fore conspicimus opportuna huiusmodi est quod nos volentes te pro quo dilectus filius nobilis vir Ludovicus Dux Sabaudiae asserens te dilectum consiliarium suum et magistrum ac primum capellanum capellae suae fore nobis super hoc humiliter supplicavit honorem intuitum favorem prosequens gratiose prefati ducis ac tuis in hac parte supplicationibus inclinati tecum ut statutum tuum eo decentius tenere valeas ut quemcumque prioratum non conventualem ordinis et valoris quorumcumque si tibi alias cancellaria conferatur seu commendetur recipere et unacum quibusvis beneficiis ecclesiasticis saecularibus etc. ex quibusvis apostolicis dispensationibus ad prius in titulum vel commendam obtines et impostere obtinebis . . . datum Romae apud Sanctum Petrum anno incarnationis domini 1453 14 kal. februariis.

Nicholas V to Guillaume Du Fay, canon of Cambrai, bachelor of decretes, greetings, etc. your knowledge of letters, the integrity of your life and habits and your honesty and various praiseworthy virtues, of which we have trustworthy evidence, persuade us to grant favourably what we perceive to be advantageous to your interests; such which our beloved noble son, Louis Duke of Savoy has humbly requested for you, declaring that you shall be his councillor and master and first chaplain of his chapel, we, desiring that you will pursue the honour, consideration and favour of this duke, who is attentive to your requests that you might be enabled more decently to maintain your condition, by obtaining whatever non-conventual priorate, of any order and value that is provided to you by the

Chancery and held with any secular ecclesiastical benefices under apostolic dispensations in title or *in commendam* . . .
[The letter proceeds with the chancery formulary used in all such conveyances, explaining in detail the legal rights to which Du Fay will be entitled upon the acquisition of the benefice.]
Dated Rome, at the basilica of S Pietro, 19 January 1454 (n.s.)

Document 4: ASV, *Registra Supplicationum* 461, fols. 29ᵛ–30ᵛ
Beatissime pater pro parte devotorum vestrorum decani et capituli ecclesiae Cameracensis v[estrae] s[anctitati] exponitur quod in ipsa ecclesia pro divini cultus augmento ac ipsius ecclesiae venustate et decore ultra numerum beneficiorum in ipsa ecclesia instituti fuerint quidam vicarii ad initum decani et capituli huiusmodi revocabiles qui pueri vicarii nuncupantur quique divinis officis diurnis et nocturnis interesse habent pro quorum sustentatione institutum est quoddam officium parvorum vicariorum nuncupatur super quo vicarii ipsi stipendia percipiunt cuiusquidam officii fructus etc. a deo temnes et exiles sunt ad ipsorum vicariorum parvorum sustentationem et onerum sibi supportationem minime suppetunt, et si parrochialis ecclesia de Herent Cameracensis diocesis que ad collationem provisionem privationem et omnimodis aliam dispensationem eorumdem decani et capituli pertinet hoc officio perpetuo uniatur annectatur et incorporetur vicarii ipsi sustentari et onera predicta supportare commodius possent. Quare pro parte decani et capituli ac vicariorum huiusmodi sanctitas vestra humiliter supplicatur quatenus in premissis opportune provideri ipso officio parvorum vicariorum eius fructus etc. verum valorem annuum habere dignitatem pro sufficienter expresse prefatam ecclesiam cuius fructus etc. centum librorum Turonensis parvorum secundum communem extimationem valorem annuum non excedunt perpetuo unire annectere et incorporare . . . Fiat ut petitur T[ommaso]. Datum Romae apud S Petrum kal. julii anno sexto.

Most blessed father, on behalf of the dean and chapter of the cathedral of Cambrai it is explained to Your Holiness that in this church, for the increase of divine worship and for the elegance and beauty of the church, an additional number of benefices were instituted by the dean and chapter, which revocable [beneficiaries] are called *petits vicaires*, and who must participate in the day and night services, for whose support was instituted a certain office, the revenues of which are meagre and slight, and which barely suffice for the support of the *petits vicaires*. But the parish church of Herent in the diocese of Cambrai, which remains at the collation, provision, privation, and otherwise at the complete disposal of the dean and chapter, may be perpetually united, annexed, and incorporated with the office, that the vicars may be more comfortably supported. Wherefore, on behalf of the dean and chapter and these vicars, it is humbly requested of Your Holiness that at the earliest convenience you provide for the office of *petits vicaires*, expressly that it might have sufficient funds, by perpetually uniting annexing and incorporating to it the aforesaid church, whose annual revenues, according to customary valuation, do not exceed 100 *l.p.t.* . . . [The remainder of this long document presents the chancery formulae for the legal incumbrancing of the benefice by the cathedral.] Let it be as requested, [signed] T [i.e. Tommaso Parentucelli, or Nicholas V]. Dated at St Peter, 1 July 1453

Document 5: ASV, *Sacra Penitentiaria* 9, fol. 134^r
[Rome, 28 February 1461]
Anthonius de Busnes clericus perpetuus cappellanus in ecclesia Turonensis quemdam presbyterem pluries in claustro eiusdem ecclesiae percussit ac ipsum per nonnullos percuti fecit ac ad ipsum percussiendum auxilium consilium prestitit et favorem, usque ad sanguinis effusionem quinquies et diversis temporibus propter quod excommunicationis sententias in tales promulgatas incurrit de quibus ligatus tamquam simplex et juris ignorans non tamen in contemptu clavium missas et alia divina celebravit et se immiscuit eisdem et cum dictus presbyter ad plenum de premissis convaluerit nec factus fuit inhabilis ad divinam petit idem exponens absolvi ac secum super irregularitate dispensando. Fiat de speciali Presbyter Sancti Laurentii in Lucina in claustro eiusdem ecclesiae.

Anthoine de Busnes, cleric and perpetual chaplain in the cathedral of Tours beat a certain priest in the cloister of the same church, and arranged to have him beaten by others, and encouraged these beatings, at five separate times, such that blood was shed; on account of which he incurred the sentence of excommunication under which, unaware of the law, and not in contempt of the Keys [of St Peter], he celebrated and took part in Mass and other divine offices. The said priest having fully recovered, nor having been rendered unfit for service, [Busnois] asks to be absolved [of the crime of bloodshed], and also asks dispensation for the irregularity [of having attended and celebrated Mass while excommunicated]. [Petition approved and signed by Cardinal Filippo Calandrini, Cardinal Penitentiary under Pius II]

APPENDIX 2

Supplications from cathedrals and collegiate churches[1]

I. Northern France and the Low Countries

(1) Amiens (diocese) coll. ch. St Wulfram, Abbeville, 14 April 1470. *RS* 655, fols. 61^r–62^v

(2) Cambrai, cathedral, 1 June 1452; 15 June 1455. *RS* 461 fols. 29^v–30^v; *RS* 491, fols. 182^r–183^v (see Appendix 1, document 4)

(3) Cambrai, cathedral, 21 Jan 1461. *Obligationes particulares* 4, fol. 19^v

(4) Cambrai (city) coll. ch. Ste Croix, 29 Aug 1452. *RS* 461, fols. 139^r–140^r; *RV* 422, fol. 48^v

(5) Cambrai (diocese) coll. ch. B. Maria, Antwerp, 28 Apr 1453. *RV* 400, fols. 243^r–244^r

(6) Cambrai (diocese) coll. ch. B. Maria, Condé, 7 Oct 1462. *RS* 555, fols. 272^v–273^v

(7) Cambrai (diocese) coll. ch. St Rumold, Malines, 4 Jan 1455. *RS* 477, fols. 71^v–72^r

(8) Cambrai (diocese) coll. ch. St Germain, Mons, 28 Aug 1451. *RV* 397, fol. 99

(9) Cambrai (diocese) coll. ch. St Vincent, Soignies, 9 Apr 1450. *RS* 443, fols. 61^r–62^r; *RV* 391, fols. 213^r–214^r

(10) Cambrai (diocese) coll. ch. B. Maria ad Aulari, Valenciennes, 5 Oct 1470. *A* 19, fol. 18

(11) Liège (diocese) coll. ch. St Gertrude, Nivelles, 4 Sept 1456. *RS* 493, fols. 37^v–38^r

(12) Liège (diocese) coll. ch. St Gertrude, Nivelles, 23 June 1470; 24 Nov 1470. *RS* 659, fols. 85^r–86^v; *RS* 661, fols. 55^v–56^v

(13) Liège (diocese) coll. ch. St Gertrude, Nivelles, 4 May 1470. *RS* 656, fol. 8^v–9^r

(14) Liège (diocese) coll. ch. St Germain, Thèux, 21 Nov 1452. *RS* 463, fol. 156^r

(15) Tournai, cathedral, 20 July 1451. *RV* 398, fol. 138

II. Central and southern France

(16) Besançon, cathedral, 16 Jan 1467. *RS* 605, fols. 290^r–291^r

(17) Besançon (diocese) coll. ch. St Maurice de Salvus, 19 Aug 1466. *RS* 599, fols. 128^r–129^r; *RL* 645, fols. 238^v–239^v

(18) Bourges (city) coll. ch. St Ursinus, 15 Dec 1468. *RS* 635, fols. 7^r–8^r

(19) Carcassonne, cathedral, 14 July 1467. *RS* 612, fols. 63^v–64^r

---

[1] Unless otherwise indicated, documents are located in the ASV.

(20) Chartres (diocese) coll. ch. St Sauveur, Blois, 13 May 1452. *RS* 459, fol. 194

(21) Chartres (diocese) coll. ch. Vendôme, 15 Dec 1466. *RS* 604, fol. 215

(22) Dignes, cathedral, 20 Feb 1470. *RS* 655, fols. 102^v–103^r

(23) Limoges, cathedral, 2 Oct 1459. *RS* 525, fol. 140

(24) Limoges (diocese) coll. ch., Le Dorat, 13 Oct 1450. *RL* 460, fols. 124^r–125^r

(25) Mâcon, cathedral, 4 Jan 1449. *RL* 446, fols. 11^r–12^r

(26) Paris, cathedral, 22 Apr 1467. *RS* 608, fols. 261^v–262^r

(27) Rennes, cathedral, 10 May 1471. *RS* 667, fols. 203^r–204^r

(28) St Brieuc, cathedral, 4 May 1455. *RS* 479, fols. 52^r–53

(29) Toul, cathedral, 1 Sept 1459. *RS* 522, fol. 109

(30) Tours, cathedral, 1 May 1449. *RV* 409, fols. 236^v–238^r

(31) Tours, cathedral, 24 Nov 1453. *RS* 469, fols. 253^r–254

(32) Tours, cathedral, 31 Dec 1459. *RS* 526, fols. 262^r–263^r

(33) Tours (diocese) coll. ch. B. Maria and St Florence, Amboise, 15 June 1470. *RS* 658, fols. 179^r–180^r

(34) Tréguier, cathedral, 4 Jan 1457; 20 Mar 1455. *RS* 496, fols. 155^v–156^r; *RS* 499, fols. 191^v–194^v; *RV* 457, fols. 17^v–19^r

(35) Vannes, cathedral, 15 Dec 1459. *RS* 526, fols. 63^r–64^v

III. Germany

(36) Halberstadt (diocese) coll. ch. Skt Nikolaus, Stendal, 13 June 1461. *RS* 461, fol. 105

(37) Trier, cathedral, 2 June 1459. *RS* 518, fol. 141

IV. Spain

(38) Barcelona, cathedral, 1 June 1468. *RS* 626, fols. 14^v–15^r

(39) Barcelona, cathedral, 22 June 1471. *RS* 668, fol. 236

(40) Burgos, cathedral, 29 July 1460. ASR, Cam. i. *Quittanze* 1123, fol. 189^v

(41) Calahorra, cathedral, 7 June 1464. *RS* 574, fol. 252

(42) Jaén (diocese) coll. ch. B. Maria, Baeza, 26 July 1468. *RS* 628, fols. 198^r–199^r

(43) Oviedo, cathedral, 1 Mar 1463. *RS* 561, fol. 92

(44) Palencia, cathedral, 30 July 1463. *RS* 565, fols. 231^r–232^r

(45) Toledo, cathedral, 11 June 1467. *RL* 654, fols. 20^v–21^v

V. England

(46) York, Minster, 11 July 1469. *RS* 647, fols. 1^r–2^r

Early Music History (1992) Volume 11

MARY E. WOLINSKI

THE COMPILATION OF THE MONTPELLIER CODEX*

The manuscript Montpellier, Bibliothèque Interuniversitaire, Section Médecine, H 196 (hereafter called Mo) has long claimed a place as one of the musical monuments of the thirteenth century. It is one of the most comprehensive sources of the early motet and is by far the largest anthology of French three-voice motets. It has long been thought that Mo was compiled in a number of stages that reflect gradual changes in musical notation and style during the second half of the thirteenth century. This assumption has been used to date repertory, theorists and composers.

It is well known that Mo is divided into eight fascicles. Each fascicle consists of a number of gatherings devoted to a particular repertory, and each is headed with large historiated initials and elaborate marginal scenes.[1] Fascicle 1 contains primarily liturgical polyphony. Fascicles 2–6 are segregated by language and number of voices into collections of four-voice French motets, three-voice motets with French tripla and Latin moteti, three-voice Latin motets, and three-voice and two-voice French motets, respectively. Fascicles 7 and 8 consist of a variety of three-voice motets. There are also 'supplements' of motets added to the ends of fascicles 3, 5 and 7 (see below Table 1).

* Earlier versions of this article were read at meetings of the New England Chapter of the American Musicological Society, May 1984, and the American Musicological Society, New Orleans, 1986. My warmest thanks to Jessie Ann Owens for her comments and suggestions and to Allan Adler for his help in organising the published version.

[1] A complete facsimile and transcription of Mo, together with commentary, appears in Y. Rokseth, *Polyphonies du XIIIe siècle: le manuscrit H 196 de la Faculté de Médecine de Montpellier*, 4 vols. (Paris, 1935–9). A more current edition and translation is *The Montpellier Codex*, parts 1–3, edited by H. Tischler; part 4, translated by S. Stakel and J. C. Relihan, Recent Researches in the Music of the Middle Ages & Early Renaissance, vols. 2–8 (Madison, WI, 1978–85).

It is widely believed that the motets of these fascicles developed gradually over the course of the entire thirteenth century. Friedrich Ludwig first posited that the repertory was written in three chronological stages: (1) the organa and motets of fascicles 1–6, dubbed the 'Old Corpus', dated from the late twelfth century to *c.* 1250; (2) the motets of fascicle 7 originated between *c.* 1250 and *c.* 1280; and (3) the motets of fascicle 8 were composed towards the end of the thirteenth century. Ludwig based his chronology on his understanding of the evolution of rhythmic style and on patterns of transmission of the motets in other sources.[2]

Based on her understanding of the evolution of the styles of the illuminators of Mo, Yvonne Rokseth postulated that the manuscript was compiled in three stages – (1) fascicles 1–6, *c.* 1280; (2) fascicle 7 at the end of the thirteenth century; and (3) fascicle 8 in the early fourteenth – each stage being well after the corresponding stylistic period defined by Ludwig.[3] Robert Branner has since revised Rokseth's dating of some of the styles of manuscript illumination and has reassessed the hands engaged in painting. He divided the fascicles into the following three groups of Parisian painters: (1) fascicles 2–6, Cholet and Henry VIII groups, active *c.* 1260–*c.* 1290; (2) fascicles 1 and 7, Late Royal Psalter group, active late thirteenth century; and (3) fascicle 8, from *c.* 1300.[4]

It is the purpose of this article to challenge the theory that Mo was copied in successive stages. The new hypothesis offered in this paper implies changes in the dating of the theorists, notational systems and motets that had been predicated on earlier assumptions about Mo's compilation. This study will begin with a re-evaluation of the production of Mo and a new identification of three distinct groups of artists and scribes. By showing that two of these

[2]   F. Ludwig, 'Studien über die Geschichte der mehrstimmigen Musik im Mittelalter II: Die 50 Beispiele Coussemakers aus der Handschrift von Montpellier', *Sammelbände der Internationalen Musikgesellschaft*, 5 (1903–4), pp. 200–3; *idem*, 'Die Quellen der Motetten ältesten Stils', *Archiv für Musikwissenschaft*, 5 (1923), pp. 194–207; and *idem*, *Repertorium organorum recentioris et motetorum vetustissimi stili*, 2nd, complete edn, ed. L. A. Dittmer, 2 vols. in 3 (Brooklyn, NY, 1964–78), I/2, pp. 345–408, 421–63, 547–66. Ludwig's theories were later articulated and developed by Heinrich Besseler, 'Studien zur Musik des Mittelalters, II: Die Motette von Franko von Köln bis Philipp von Vitry', *Archiv für Musikwissenshaft*, 8 (1926), pp. 137–87; and Ernest Sanders, 'The Medieval Motet', *Gattungen der Musik in Einzeldarstellungen: Gedenkschrift für Leo Schrade*, ed. W. Arlt *et al.* (Berne, 1973), pp. 530–8, 550–4.
[3]   Rokseth, *Polyphonies*, IV, pp. 28–30.
[4]   R. Branner, *Manuscript Painting in Paris during the Reign of Saint Louis: A Study of Styles* (Berkeley, CA, 1977), pp. 130–7, 237–9.

groups worked together, it will be demonstrated that fascicles 1–7 of Mo were compiled in a single collaborative effort. Evidence for dating the historiated initials then will be sifted and will provide the primary evidence for dating the first seven fascicles between the late 1260s and the 1280s. There will follow a discussion of the age and characteristics of fascicle 8 and an analysis of the foundations of the musical notations in Mo. Finally, I shall comment briefly on the consequences that these results have for our understanding of the development of the motet and its notation.

THE PRODUCTION OF MO: ARTISTS AND SCRIBES

Close physical inspection of the manuscript reveals that three types of parchment were used: a very delicate uterine vellum for fascicles 2–6; a heavier, stiffer, yet high-quality parchment for fascicles 1 and 7; and a somewhat thinner parchment for fascicle 8. The procedure for ruling and arranging voices on the page varies with each of the three types of parchment and their respective fascicles. In fascicles 2–6 the staves were drawn well in advance of the copying, for there are pages of blank staves left at the ends of the fascicles. The irregular lengths of the staff lines and the uneven spaces between them indicate that the lines were drawn one at a time. The staves of fascicle 8 were drawn with an 11-mm rastrum,[5] also well before the copying. In fascicles 1 and 7, however, the scribes often tailored the ruling to the proportions of each piece, or kind of piece. In fascicle 1 the opening three-voice conductus and four-voice hocket motets were ruled, respectively, with six and eight staves to a page, using an 11-mm rastrum, while the three-voice scores of the remaining pieces were arranged on six staves to a page with a 14-mm rastrum. The widths of the two columns of motet voices in fascicle 7 also vary in accordance with the proportion of triplum to motetus text.

There are eleven text hands, listed in Table 1 as numbers I–XI;[6]

---

[5] A 10-mm rastrum, however, was used on fols. 374 and 377, which form a bifolio.
[6] In his analysis of text hands, Gustav Jacobsthal ('Die Texte der Liederhandschrift von Montpellier H.196', *Zeitschrift für romanische Philologie*, 3 [1879], p. 534) did not realise that scribes I and III worked on both fascicles 1 and 7, and that scribe III texted the end of the supplement to fascicle 3. This accounts for the discrepancy between his fourteen text hands and the eleven proposed in this study.

ten identifiable music hands, numbered 1a–h, 2 and 3; and eleven
identifiable illuminators of the polychrome initials, numbered I, I',
IIa–h and III. Polychrome initials are painted in various colours
and decorated with abstract, floral and animal forms. By comparison, historiated initials, which will be discussed later in connection with dating, are larger, usually occur at the beginnings of
fascicles and depict human or divine figures.

These scribes and artists fall into three distinct groups that each
worked on one of the three types of parchment fascicles. The numbers I have used to designate music hands and illuminators indicate the groups to which they belong. Text scribes I–IV and the
corresponding music hands 1a–d copied fascicles 1 and 7 proper. In
addition, text scribes VI–X and music scribes 1e–h copied the
supplements at the ends of fascicles 3, 5 and 7. All these scribes
belong to what I call Group 1 by virtue of the distinctive system of
musical notation that they share and by the fact that illuminator I
painted all the polychrome initials of fascicles 1 and 7 and the
supplements (see Table 1). Group 2 consists of a single text and

Table 1   *Scribes and illuminators of Montpellier, Bibliothèque*
Interuniversitaire, Section Médecine, H 196

Fascicle	Text		Music		Illuminators of polychrome initials	
1	1^r–3^v:	I	1^r–4^r:	1a	1^v–22^r:	I
	4^v, 5^v–7^r:	II	4^v–5^r:	1b		
	5^r, 7^v–21^v:	III	5^v–21^v:	1c		
	22^r:	IV	22^r:	1d		
2	23^v–61^r:	V	23^v–61^r:	2	24^v–58^r:	IIa
3	63^v–83^r:	V	63^v–83^r:	2	66^v–68^v, 79^r–82^r:	IIb
	65^r,					
	sys. 5–6:	VII	65^r, 5–6:	1e	68^r–78^v:	IIa
	66^v, sys. 7–8:	VII	66^v, 7–8:	1e		
	81^r, sys. 7,					
	'lumen luminum':	VI				
Suppl.	83^v–85^r:	VI	83^v–86^v:	1f	83^v–85^r:	I
	85^r–86^r:	VIII				
	86^v:	III				
4	87^v–110^v:	V	87^v–110^v:	2	88^v–110^r:	IIa

Table 1 – *cont.*

Fascicle	Text		Music		Illuminators of polychrome initials	
5	111^r–227^r:	V	111^r–227^r:	2	112^v, 117^r–118^v:	I
					113^v–116^v, 127^r–142^v, 159^r–160^v, 162^v–163^v, 165^v–198^v:	IIb
					119^r–126^v, 151^v–158^v:	IIc
					143^r–149^r, 199^r–226^r:	IIa
					161^r, 164^r:	IId
Suppl.	227^v–228^r:	IX	227^v–228^r:	1g	227^v–228^r:	I
6	231^r–269^v:	V	231^r–269^v:	2	231^v–235^r, 236^v–237^v:	IIe
					235^v, 247^r–252^v, 254^r–261^v:	IIb
					238^r–238^v:	IIf
					239^r–245^v:	IIg
					246^v, 253^r–253^v:	IIh
					262^r–269^v:	IIa
7	270^r–331^v:^{a}	I	270^r–292^r:	1a	270^r–331^v:	I
			292^v–293^r:	1c		
			293^v–317^v:	1a		
			318^r–331^v:	1c		
Suppl. 1	331^v–343^v:	VII	331^v–343^v:	1e	331^v–343^v:	I'
Suppl. 2	344^r–346^r:	X	344^r–347^v:	1h	344^r–347^v:	III
	346^r–347^v:	III				
8	348^r–395^v:	XI	348^r–395^v:	3	348^r–395^v:	III

^{a}Uses the new pencil foliation, which omits the missing fols. 303 and 308. Thus, by fol. 308 the new foliation is two units lower than that of Tischler's edition.

music scribe (V/2) and illuminators IIa–h, all of whom copied and decorated the bulk of fascicles 2–6. Group 3 also consists of a single scribe (XI/3), who, together with illuminator III, produced fascicle 8. Illuminator III also painted the second supplement to fascicle 7.

It can be assumed that text scribes generally copied their own music, since Groups 2 and 3 each have a single text and music hand and because motet texts were copied first with some care taken that all voices should reach the same point in the music before the page-turn. Nevertheless, there are cases within Group 1 in which a single music scribe notated pieces copied by several text scribes, and vice versa. For example, on fols. 83^v–86^v music scribe 1f notated the texts copied by scribes VI, VIII and III. Because of the difficulty in distinguishing between the numerous music hands of Group 1, I can draw only tentative distinctions in fascicle 7 between music scribes 1a and 1c, who appear to have notated texts copied entirely by scribe I, and in fascicle 1 between music scribes 1a and 1b.

As indicated in Table 1, polychrome artists, who consistently painted the folios copied by scribes of a particular group, are assigned to that group and numbered accordingly. Thus, illuminators numbered I, II and III painted that which was copied by scribes of Groups 1, 2 and 3 respectively. There are only a few exceptions to this. Illuminator I of Group 1 filled in the outer bifolios of the first gathering of fascicle 5, which was otherwise copied and painted by members of Group 2. Illuminator III of Group 3 painted the initials of the second supplement to fascicle 7, which was in fact copied by scribes of Group 1.

While there are three distinct groups, there is substantial evidence that they collaborated at certain points in the production of Mo. First of all, despite the disparity in parchment type and ruling procedures among the three groups, the size of the writing area (averaging 77 × 127 mm) and its position on the page remain remarkably constant throughout the book, differing by no more than a few millimetres.[7] Thus, all the fascicles were intended to belong to this anthology.

Secondly, scribes of Group 1 aided the scribe of Group 2 in copying fascicles 2–6. Scribe VII/1e of Group 1, who copied the first supplement to fascicle 7, also copied short passages on fols. 65^r and 66^v of fascicle 3. These passages were not added or inserted later but were entered while the motets were first being copied. Figure 1, taken from motet no. 36 on fol. 65^r, begins with words and music copied by the main scribe V/2. Scribe VII/1e continued from the words 'inebrians animas' until the bottom line of the tenor, which was copied by scribe V/2. The passage by scribe VII/1e is neither cramped nor stretched out, as it might have been

<hr />

[7] This agrees with M. Everist, *Polyphonic Music in Thirteenth-Century France: Aspects of Sources and Distribution* (New York, 1989), pp. 110 and 132.

Figure 1   Mo, fol. 65ʳ. Copied by scribe V/2, except for text and music of
'inebrians animas . . . ad Mari-', copied by scribe VII/1e.

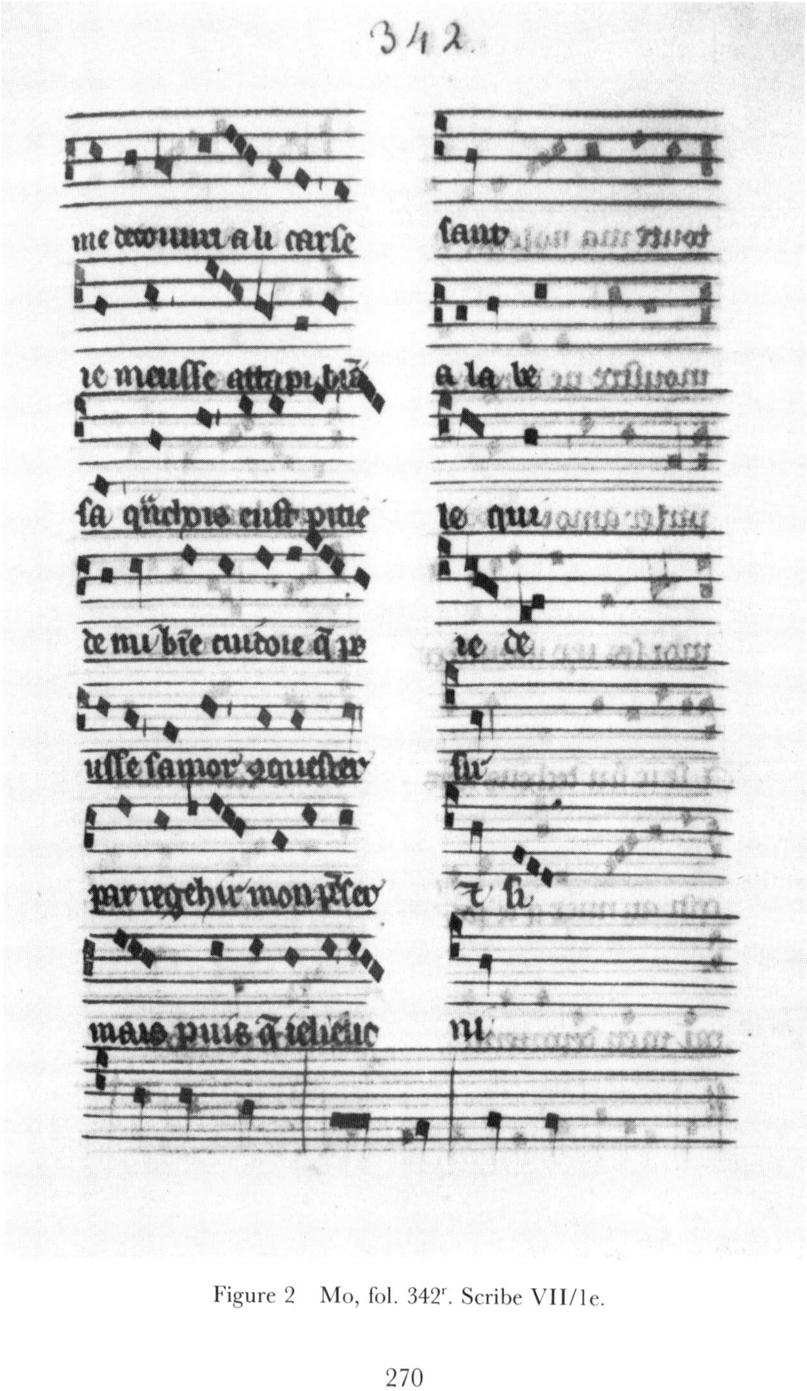

Figure 2 Mo, fol. 342^{r}. Scribe VII/1e.

had it been inserted later. Scribe V/2 continued the motetus from precisely where scribe VII/1e left off, beginning on fol. 66^r with the last syllable of 'Mariam'. The script of scribe VII, also visible in the supplement to fascicle 7 (cf. Figure 2), is distinguished from that of scribe V quite clearly by the round form of the final *s*, which slants markedly to the right. The C-clefs of scribe 1e are wider and squarer than those of scribe 2, and the two scribes write in different notational dialects. The longs in the tenor, ligated as ternariae by scribe 2, would have been written as single notes by scribe 1e (compare the tenors of Figures 1 and 2). The ligatures representing two semibreves and a breve over the words 'deseris' and 'ordibus' in Figure 1, written by scribe 1e with opposite propriety and without perfection, would have been written with perfection by scribe 2, according to that scribe's notational dialect (see p. 296 below).

Other scribes of Group 1 texted many of the tenors in fascicles 2–6, as indicated in the last column of Table 2. The main scribe V routinely copied first the texts of the upper voices and then the music of all the voices. Yet, for some inexplicable reason, he did not copy many of the tenor texts. In fascicle 2, in which all four voices are aligned in vertical columns across the page opening, it would have been a relatively simple matter to text the tenors at the same time as the upper voices. Nevertheless, scribe V only occasionally copied the tenor texts in fascicle 2, clearly before he entered the music.[8] In fascicles 3–6, where the tenor is allotted a continuous staff running along the bottom of an opening, scribe V seems to have added the tenor texts only after he had copied the music of entire gatherings or fascicles. He was assisted in texting the tenors by the Group 1 scribes VI, VIII and IX, who also copied the supplements at the ends of fascicles 3 and 5.[9] The main scribe V and the supplementary scribe IX entered their texts before the tenor initials were painted, evident from the paint and gold of the initials overlapping the written ink.[10] Scribes VI and VIII added

---

[8] See motets nos. 26, 28, 29, 30, 32 and 33, on fols. 41, 42, 45, 46, 50 and 52 respectively. Note also the awkward placement of the last syllable of 'Viderunt omnes' in the tenor on fol. 41^r, and the two beginning notes cramped to fit over the tenor word 'Fiat' on fol. 46^r.

[9] Jacobsthal ('Die Texte der Liederhandschrift', p. 534, n. 2) noted that many tenor texts were not written by the main scribe V, but perhaps by scribe VI – a possibility which he found difficult to accept.

[10] In addition, on fol. 52^r the illuminator partly rubbed off the tenor text 'Manere' of scribe V.

their texts well after the illumination took place, for their ink frequently overlaps the paint. Scribe VI also entered the words 'lumen luminum' just before the page-turn in the motetus of no. 45, a piece otherwise copied entirely by scribe V.

Dry-point guide words are visible in the margins beneath some of the tenors. Perhaps they were entered to assist the scribes in texting the tenors.[11] Scribe VI, working sometime after the manuscript had been illuminated, texted all tenors visibly supplied with guide words, except for the last two: 'Pro patribus' and 'Audi filia'. These were done by the main scribe V, who apparently also came back to the tenors of fascicles 3–6 well after he had copied the music.

It can be seen that certain Group 2 illuminators of polychrome initials consistently painted gatherings texted by certain tenor text scribes. The eight illuminators can be distinguished by the care they took in painting details, the colours they used and the distinctive faces of the dragons coiled within the initials.[12] Illuminators IIa and IIb painted most of the initials. Illuminator IIb, together with the lesser IIc, painted almost exclusively those gatherings whose tenors had been texted by scribes V and IX. (See Table 2, gatherings 11, 16–18, 20, 22–5 and 33.) These gatherings may have even passed directly from scribe to artist, since both scribes wrote

Table 2 *Illuminators and tenor text scribes of Mo*

Fascicle	Gathering	Illuminators of polychrome initials		Tenor text scribes	
1	1–3	1^v–22^r:	I		
2	4–5	24^v–58^r:	IIa	24^r–40^r:	VI
	6			41^r–46^r:	V
	7			47^r:	VI
				50^r–52^r:	V
	8			56^r–58^r:	VI

---

[11] Dry-point guide words still visible include: 'Johanne', fol. 25^r; 'Et gaudebit', fol. 64^r; 'Letabitur', fol. 69^r; 'Sustinere', fol. 74^v; 'Domino', fol. 90^r; 'Neuma', fol. 91^v; 'Alleluya', fol. 97^r; 'Dominus', fol. 105^r; 'Ave maria', fol. 106^r; 'Latus', fol. 232^v; 'T', fol. 233^v; 'F', fol. 234^r; 'Illuminare', fol. 237^r; 'Domino', fol. 239^r; 'Tu', fol. 242^v; 'Et g', fol. 243^r; 'Domino', fol. 244^v; 'Pro patribus', fol. 249^r; and 'Audi filia', fol. 255^v.

[12] See M. E. Wolinski, 'The Montpellier Codex: Its Compilation, Notation and Implications for the Chronology of the Thirteenth-Century Motet' (Ph.D. dissertation, Brandeis University, 1988), pp. 61–4.

Table 2 – *cont.*

Fascicle	Gathering	Illuminators of polychrome initials		Tenor text scribes	
3	9–10	66ᵛ–68ᵛ:	IIb	64ʳ–78ᵛ:	VI
		69ʳ–78ᵛ:	IIa		
	11	79ʳ–82ʳ:	IIb	81ʳ–82ʳ:	V
Suppl.		83ᵛ–85ʳ:	I		
4	12–14	88ᵛ–110ʳ:	IIa	89ʳ–109ᵛ:	VI
5	15	112ᵛ:	I	111ᵛ:	VI
		113ʳ–116ᵛ:	IIb	113ʳ–116ᵛ:	IX
		117ʳ–118ᵛ:	I	118ʳ:	VI
	16	119ʳ–126ᵛ:	IIc	119ʳ–141ᵛ:	V
	17–18	127ʳ–142ᵛ:	IIb		
	19	143ʳ–149ʳ:	IIa	143ʳ–147ᵛ:	VI
	20	151ᵛ–158ᵛ:	IIc	151ᵛ–160ᵛ:	V
	21	159ʳ–160ᵛ:	IIb		
		161ʳ:	IId		
		162ᵛ–163ᵛ:	IIb		
		164ʳ:	IId		
	22–5	165ᵛ–198ᵛ:	IIb	167ᵛ–198ᵛ:	V
	26	199ʳ–226ʳ:	IIa	199ʳ:	VI
	27–8			207ʳ–222ʳ:	VIII
Suppl.	29	227ᵛ–228ʳ:	I		
6	30	231ᵛ–235ʳ:	IIe	231ʳ–247ʳ:	VI
		235ᵛ:	IIb		
		236ᵛ–237ᵛ:	IIe		
		238ʳ–238ᵛ:	IIf		
	31	239ʳ–245ᵛ:	IIg		
	32	246ᵛ:	IIh		
		247ʳ–252ᵛ:	IIb	247ʳ–252ᵛ:	V
		253ʳ–253ᵛ:	IIh	253ᵛ:	VI
	33	254ʳ–261ᵛ:	IIb	254ʳ–261ᵛ:	V
	34	262ʳ–269ᵛ:	IIa	262ʳ–269ʳ:	VI
7	35–42	270ʳ–331ᵛ:	I		
Suppl. 1	43–4	331ᵛ–343ᵛ:	I′		
Suppl. 2		344ʳ–347ᵛ:	III		
8	45–50	348ʳ–395ᵛ:	III		

Mary E. Wolinski

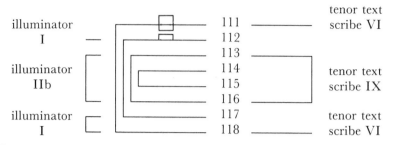

Figure 3   The structure of gathering 15, indicating illuminators of polychrome initials and tenor text scribes. (Boxes indicate historiated initials)

their texts before the penwork tenor initials and probably the poly-chrome initials of the upper voices had been entered. Illuminator IIa painted all of fascicles 2 and 4, as well as gatherings 10, 19, 26–9 and 34. Both his work and that of IIg wound up in the hands of the tenor text scribes VI and VIII, who entered their texts well after both the polychrome and tenor initials had been painted.[13]

Besides painting the supplements to fascicles 3 and 5, illuminator I of Group 1 painted the polychrome initials of the outer two bifolios of gathering 15 in fascicle 5 (see Figure 3). The outer bifolios had been removed to receive their historiated initials from the master painter. Once he had finished them, the outer bifolios were handed over to illuminator I and tenor text scribe VI. Mean-while, the inner two bifolios received their tenor texts from scribe IX and their polychrome initials from illuminator IIb.

Furthermore, the polychrome initials of the second supplement of fascicle 7 (copied by the Group 1 scribes X and III, see Table 1) were painted, strikingly enough, by illuminator III of fascicle 8. Illuminator III's initials can be distinguished from those of the preceding Group 1 artist by slight differences in colour and design. He uses a distinctive blue-violet paint, and draws trefoils tipped with gold dots and terminals that tend to point downwards.[14]

To sum up the codicological results, there is substantial evidence that the scribes and painters of Mo worked simultaneously. Throughout the manuscript the writing areas are virtually identical

---

[13]   A number of tenor texts in fascicle 2 were done by the main scribe V, but scribe V wrote them at the same time as the texts of the upper voices. Only in fascicles 3–6 did scribe V, like the other tenor text scribes, enter the tenor texts well after finishing the music.
[14]   See Wolinski, 'The Montpellier Codex', pp. 64–5.

in size and placement on the page. Scribes of Group 1 collaborated with the scribe of Group 2 both in copying passages of upper voices and in entering the tenor texts. Certain Group 2 illuminators consistently painted those folios and gatherings texted by certain Group 1 tenor text scribes. In one case, illuminator IIb painted his initials only after the Group 1 scribe IX had entered his texts. Illuminator I filled in some missing initials to help bring the manuscript to completion. The proof that members of Groups 1 and 2 worked together indicates that the first seven fascicles were copied at the same time. In addition, illuminator III of fascicle 8 painted the initials of the second supplement to fascicle 7. This, together with the similarity of its format, indicates that fascicle 8 was created to accompany the other fascicles.

THE HISTORIATED INITIALS OF FASCICLES 1–7

Dating the manuscript is difficult, but some evidence has been offered by studies of the illuminations. Robert Branner, as stated above, separated the historiated initials of Mo into three stylistic groups: the Cholet and contemporaneous Henry VIII group (fascicles 2–6)[15], the late Royal Psalter group (fascicles 1 and 7) and an unidentified artist dated *c.* 1300 (fascicle 8). The figures and drapery of paintings in the Cholet style of fascicles 2–6 tend to look two-dimensional or cartoon-like. Marginal decorations terminate in graceful cusped fiddle heads tipped with bud forms. Engaged in outdoor games or hunts, the figures in the lower margins move with angular, frantic or dance-like gestures. By comparison, the painter of fascicles 1 and 7, working in the Late Royal Psalter style, favours more modelled or three-dimensional garment folds, naturalistic leafy terminals on marginal decorations and figures that move with greater fluidity and grace. The illuminator of fascicle 8 increases the realism of his figures by lavishing even greater care on modelling faces, drapery and decorative details. It is striking that Branner's three style groups coincide with the three groups of parchments, scribes and polychrome artists postulated in the first

---

[15] An objection has been raised that the Henry VIII artist of fascicle 5 may be after all a member of the Cholet group; see Everist, I, pp. 128–9, citing M. Alison Stones.

part of this article. His stylistic distinctions agree with the divisions of labour I had deduced from physical and palaeographical evidence.

Other manuscripts painted by members of the Cholet group can be roughly dated on the basis of external or objective evidence anywhere from the 1260s to possibly 1290. Branner has localised this and other groups in Paris because of the opportunity the city afforded to numerous painters to collaborate on projects and because of the local ecclesiastical and courtly destinations of many of the books produced. The figures of Mo, fascicle 2, were painted by the artist of the St-Denis Missal (Paris, Bibliothèque Nationale, f. lat. 1107), which was copied after 1259 and before *c.* 1275 or 1286.[16] The miniatures of Mo, fascicles 3 and 6, were done by the painter of the Cholet missal (Padua, Bibliotheca Capitolare, D. 34), which was copied at some time after 1261, since the calendar caries the obit of Pope Alexander IV, and before the death of its owner Jean Cardinal Cholet in 1292 or 1293.[17] Peter Klein has identified aspects of the Cholet style in the English Apocalypse manuscript Oxford, Bodleian Library, Douce 180, which, on the basis of heraldry, appears to date from the late 1260s.[18]

While objective criteria allow a rather wide dating of the Cholet

[16] A. Walters ('The Reconstruction of the Abbey Church of St-Denis (1231–81): The Interplay of Music and Ceremony with Architecture and Politics', *Early Music History* 5 (1985), p. 194) notes that the St-Denis Missal includes the feast of SS. Sanctinus and Antonius, whose relics were granted to Matthieu de Vendôme, abbot of St-Denis in 1258–86. Walters dates the St-Denis Missal before *c.* 1275 on the basis of its liturgical format. At the very latest, it would have been copied before the death of Matthieu in 1286, since his obit is not in the calendar, while that of his predecessor Guillaume de Macouris (d. 4 March 1254) is cited.

[17] The statement of ownership names 'Johannis Cardinalis dicti Cholet' (quoted in A. Barzon, *Codici miniati, Biblioteca capitolare della Cattedrale di Padova* (Padua, 1950), p. 13). S. J. P. Van Dijk and J. H. Walker (*The Origins of the Modern Roman Liturgy* (Westminster, MD, and London, 1960), p. 404) assume that Cholet had the missal together with a matching epistolary (Padua, Biblioteca Capitolare, C. 47) and evangeliary (now lost) made for him while he was a papal legate in France, beginning 1283. Branner (p. 132) also supposes the books were made for Cholet, but not necessarily while he was cardinal.

[18] The arms of Crown Prince Edward and his wife, Eleanor of Castile-León, at the beginning of the French-texted apocalypse date from 1254 to 1272. The presence of the arms of Simon de Montfort and Gilbert de Clare in the battle scenes of the Latin-texted apocalypse further narrows it to some time after de Clare's opposition to the Crown in 1264–5. That Edward and Eleanor were out of the country between 1270 and 1274 makes it most likely that the book was created for them during the late 1260s. Klein, however, doubts the credibility of the heraldry in the Latin apocalypse and prefers to date the picture cycle of that part of the manuscript in the early 1270s on stylistic grounds; see P. Klein, *Endzeiterwartung und Ritterideologie: Die englischen Bilderapokalypsen der Frühgotik und MS Douce 180* (Graz, 1983), pp. 38–49, 61–3.

group, Branner believed that its stylistic closeness to the leading member of the Royal Psalter group, the St Louis Psalter (Paris, Bibliothèque Nationale, f. lat. 10525), places it before 1270, within the lifetime of St Louis.[19] Ellen Beer, on the other hand, considered fascicle 4 of Mo akin to and 'almost contemporary' with the intricate knotwork designs of certain Amiens manuscripts, dated in the 1280s, and the Psalter and Hours of Yolande de Soissons, dated soon after 1275.[20] Peter Klein preferred to date the Latin picture cycle of the Douce Apocalypse between 1270 and 1274 partly because he perceived similarities with the wall paintings and frescoes of Westminster Abbey and Palace, datable in the late 1260s and early 1270s, and with the illuminations of the Cholet group, which he considered a phenomenon of the 1270s.[21] Taken as a whole, these stylistic judgements place the Cholet artists between the 1260s and the 1280s.

The hand of the artist of fascicles 1 and 7 has not been detected in any other manuscript, although his work has been identified by Branner with a second major style – the late Royal Psalter group.[22] The artists of this group achieve greater delicacy and realism and devise new sorts of ornamental details, such as naturalistic leafy terminals on marginal decoration, painted gold on goldleaf backgrounds and gold four-pointed stars in the corners of scenes. This new manner is commonly called the *style Honoré*, named after the illuminator known to have been active in Paris between 1288 and 1300.[23]

Art historians have long recognised that this style existed well before Honoré's documented dates and that it was practised by various artists. Table 3 lists some manuscripts important for a chronology of the Honoré style and documents datings based on objective and stylistic criteria. One of the earliest sources is the Martyrology of St-Germain-des-Prés, which Gerhard Schmidt has

---

[19] Branner (p. 133) conjectures that the St Louis Psalter, made for the king, and the Isabella Psalter (Cambridge, Fitzwilliam Museum, MS 300), made either for the queen or for Louis's daughter Isabella, were both painted some time after Isabella's marriage to Thibaud of Navarre and Champagne in 1255.

[20] E. Beer, 'Pariser Buchmalerei in der Zeit Ludwigs des Heiligen und im letzten Viertel des 13. Jahrhunderts', *Zeitschrift für Kunstgeschichte*, 44 (1981), p. 84.

[21] Klein, pp. 44–6, 61–2.

[22] Branner, *Manuscript Painting*, pp. 136–7, 238–9.

[23] See E. Kosmer, 'Master Honoré: A Reconsideration of the Documents', *Gesta*, 14 (1975), pp. 63–8.

Table 3   *Manuscripts painted in the 'Style Honoré'*

Manuscript	Objective dating	Stylistic dating
Martyrology of St-Germain-des-Prés (Paris, Bibliothèque Nationale, f. lat. 12834)	between 1255 and 1278[a]	possibly before 1270[b]
London Evangeliary (London, British Library, Add. 17341)	after 1265–7[c]	c. 1275[d]
London Miscellany–Amiens? (London, British Library, Add. 11639)	datable entries between 1278 and 1286[e]	
Tours Decretals (Tours, Bibliothèque Municipale, MS 558)	sold by Honoré in 1288[f]	
Breviary of Philippe le Bel (Paris, Bibliothèque Nationale, f.lat. 1023)	main body of MS: between 1263–9 and 1288; calendar: 1288–97[h]	c. 1290[g]
Alphonso Psalter–English (London, British Library, Add. 24686)	1284[i]	
Olomouc Decretals (Olomouc, Statní archiv, MS C.D.39)		c. 1290[j]
Nuremberg Hours-breviary (Nuremberg, Stadtbibliothek, Cod. Solger 4, 4⁰)	1287–94[k]	
La Somme le Roy (London, British Library, Add. 54180 and Cambridge, Fitzwilliam Museum, MSS 192 and 368)		c. 1285[l] late 1290s[m]
Châlons-sur-Marne Missal-breviary (Paris, Bibliothèque de l'Arsenal, MS 595)	after 1247, before c. 1297[n]	end of the 13th, beginning of the 14th century[o]

Table 3 – *cont.*

[a]Based on the scribal entry of the decease of Abbot Thanus de Mauleon, d. 1255, and the later addition of that of Abbot Gerard de Moret, d. 1278; see Georg Graf Vitzthum, *Die Pariser Miniaturmalerei von der Zeit des hl. Ludwig bis zu Philipp von Valois und ihr Verhältnis zur Malerei in Nordwesteuropa* (Leipzig, 1907), p. 18.
[b]Beer, 'Pariser Buchmalerei', pp. 81–2.
[c]See this article pp. 279–80.
[d]Verdier *et al.*, *Art and the Courts*, I, pp. 51–2, 76–7.
[e]Narkiss, *Hebrew Illuminated Manuscripts*, p. 86, but see this article pp. 280–1.
[f]Kosmer, 'Master Honoré', p. 63.
[g]E. V. Kosmer, 'A Study of the Style and Iconography of a Thirteenth-Century *Somme le roi* (British Museum Ms. Add. 54180) with a Consideration of Other Illustrated *Somme* Manuscripts of the Thirteenth, Fourteenth and Fifteenth Centuries' (Ph.D dissertation, Yale University, 1973), p. 262.
[h]See this article p. 281.
[i]J. Alexander and P. Binski, eds., *Age of Chivalry: Art in Plantagenet England 1200–1400* (London, 1987), pp. 354–5.
[j]G. Schmidt, 'Materialien zur französischen Buchmalerei der Hochgotik I', *Wiener Jahrbuch für Kunstgeschichte*, 28 (1975), p. 164.
[k]D. H. Turner, 'The Development of Maître Honoré', *British Museum Quarterly*, 33 (summer 1968), pp. 58–9.
[l]Kosmer, 'A Study of the Style', p. 262.
[m]Schmidt, 'Materialen', pp. 163–4 and n. 24.
[n]See this article, p. 281–2.
[o]V. Leroquais, *Les sacramentaires et les missels manuscrits des bibliothèques publiques de France*, 3 vols. + plates (Paris, 1924), II, p. 189; and H. Martin and Ph. Lauer, *Les principaux manuscrits à peintures de la Bibliothèque de l'Arsenal à Paris* (Paris, 1929), p. 22, n. 1.

attributed to the young Honoré himself.[24] While it has been placed stylistically in the 1270s, necrological evidence allows a dating as early as the late 1250s and 1260s.

The first twelve folios of the London Evangeliary, which Branner placed alongside Mo 1 and 7 in the late Royal Psalter group, have also been considered an early manifestation of Honoré's work, *c.* 1275. Branner,[25] however, placed the London Evangeliary around 1290 because he thought that the Ste-Chapelle Evangeliary (Paris, Bibliothèque Nationale, f. lat. 17326), from which the London Evangeliary is believed to have been copied, was unbound for copying in the late thirteenth century. However, I do not believe this is necessarily the case. The inventory that lists the unbound cover of the Ste-Chapelle Evangeliary can be dated only some time after 1265 to 1267, when the inventoried relics of Mary Magdalene

[24] *Die Malerschule von St. Florian: Beiträge zur süddeutschen Malerei zu Ende des 13. und im 14. Jahrhundert* (Graz and Cologne, 1962), p. 115.
[25] *Manuscript Painting*, pp. 137 and 239.

were brought to the Ste-Chapelle by Louis IX.[26] Thus, the London Evangeliary could have been copied any time in the second half of the century after 1267.

The young Honoré has also been connected with illuminations in the London Miscellany, an extensive compilation of Hebrew texts.[27] Most of the datable entries fall in the second half of the manuscript and date from between 1278 and 1286. However, the manuscript is a miscellany with numerous scribes, it is not known when the full-page miniatures were entered into the book, and the Hebrew foliation may have been entered some time later.[28] Not only is it difficult to date with certainty, but the attribution to Honoré is far from secure. Broad, flat expanses of crudely painted, often runny pigment;[29] angular, etiloated figures[30] and unusual colours[31] place it well outside the orbit of the Parisian de luxe book,

[26] The inventory is preserved in a fifteenth-century copy (Paris, Bibliothèque Nationale, f. fr. 2833, fols. 139ᵛ–140ʳ), as well as in seventeenth- and eighteenth-century copies; printed in A. Vidier, 'Le trésor de la Sainte-Chapelle', *Mémoires de la Société de l'Histoire de Paris et de l'Ile-de-France*, 34 (1907), p. 202, and J. Petit, Gavrilovitch, Maury and Téodoru, *Essai de restitution des plus anciens mémoriaux de la Chambre des comptes de Paris*, preface by Ch.-V. Langlois, Université de Paris, Bibliothèque de la Faculté des Lettres 7 (Paris, 1899), pp. 163–4. Item 34 of the inventory lists two unbound evangeliary covers: 'Item custodes de évangiles, I. d'or à pierres precieuses et l'autre d'argent'. The golden cover with precious stones survives today as the cover of the Ste-Chapelle Evangeliary that was unbound to serve as the model of the London Evangeliary. The silver cover without gems is possibly that of an earlier evangeliary (Paris, Bibliothèque Nationale, f. lat. 8892) that consists of an old and new corpus and conceivably was unbound at the same time to receive the latter. The two covers are reproduced and described in P. Verdier, P. Brieger and M. F. Montpetit, *Art and the Courts: France and England from 1259 to 1328*, 2 vols. (Ottawa, 1972), I, pp. 123–6, and II, pls. 52–5.

[27] G. Sed-Rajna attributes those on fols. 516ᵛ–523ᵛ to Honoré in 'The Paintings of the London Miscellany, British Library Add. MS 11639', *Journal of Jewish Art*, 9 (1982), p. 30. She suggests (pp. 25–6) that these illustrations, together with those in the same manuscript attributed to the workshops of the Master of Aaron and the 'Roman de la Poire', were executed in the Amiens area where Honoré could have been active early in his career. Honoré is believed to have come to Paris from Amiens since he is listed in tax rolls of 1297 and 1299 as 'Honoré d'Amiens'. See F. Baron, 'Enlumineurs, peintres et sculpteurs parisiens des XIIIᵉ et XIVᵉ siècles d'après les rôles de la taille', *Bulletin Archéologique du Comité des Travaux Historiques et Scientifiques* (1969), p. 50.

[28] B. Narkiss, *Hebrew Illuminated Manuscripts*, foreword by C. Roth (New York, 1969), p. 86.

[29] As in the rendition of the skies, fol. 517ʳ, and in the background colouring of Solomon's judgement, fol. 518ʳ.

[30] The strongly modelled, muscular Adam and Eve of the London Miscellany, fol. 520ᵛ, resemble the Adam and Eve of the English manuscript Cambridge, St John's College, MS K.26 (reproduced in N. Morgan, *Early Gothic Manuscripts 1190–1285*, 2 vols. (London, 1982–8), II, pl. 381) far more than the gently curving, pliant bodies of the damned in the London Evangeliary, fol. 28ʳ (reproduced in Verdier *et al.*, *Art and the Courts*, I, p. 33).

[31] As, for instance, the use of magenta described by Narkiss, p. 86 and visible in pl. 23.

although its painters were undoubtedly influenced by the Parisian style.

The only manuscript that can be reasonably attributed to Honoré himself is the Tours Decretals, which was sold by him in 1288. Dating other manuscripts in this elegant style has rested to a great extent on historians' conjectures. The most meticulously and lavishly executed are thought to represent Honoré's late work, as, for example, the Breviary of Philippe le Bel. Its attribution to Honoré is a matter of controversy[32] and its dating is problematic. The last datable feast in the sanctorale is that of St Mary of Egypt, instituted for Parisian usage between 1263 and 1269. The Conception of the Blessed Virgin Mary, instituted in 1288, is not included.[33] The calendar, copied in a slightly different script from that of the main scribe, includes the Conception of the Virgin as an integral element, but lacks the feast of St Louis, instituted in 1297. The dating of this manuscript depends on whether we accept the calendar as original with the breviary proper, in which case the illumination could have been done between 1288 and 1297, or whether we consider the calendar a later addition to a book compiled at some time between the late 1260s and 1288. Noting stylistic similarities between the English Alphonso Psalter, dated 1284, and the Breviary lat. 1023, Sandler has suggested that elements of the Parisian style could have first appeared in England.[34] It is possible, however, that the style of the Breviary lat. 1023 did, in fact, precede and influence the painter of the Alphonso Psalter.

Other manuscripts attributed to Honoré and dated in the 1290s largely on the basis of style are the Olomouc Decretals, the Nuremberg Hours and the *Somme le Roy* (see Table 3). However, the Châlons-sur-Marne Missal-Breviary, which has been placed at the turn of the century, could have been copied somewhat earlier. The

[32] It is assumed that the breviary was made for Philippe le Bel for use in the Ste-Chapelle, but Kosmer ('Master Honoré', p. 65) has already pointed out that there is no necessary connection either between lat. 1023 and the payment listed in the Treasury Accounts of 25 August 1296 'pro uno breviario facto pro Rege' or between the breviary of 1296 and a payment made to Honoré, the illuminator, 'pro libris Regis illuminates' some time before Toussaint (1 Nov) 1296; listed in R. Fawtier, *Comptes du Trésor (1296, 1316, 1384, 1477)* (Paris, 1930), nos. 396, 407.

[33] For the dating of these feasts, see C. Wright, *Music and Ceremony at Notre-Dame of Paris, 500–1550* (Cambridge, 1989), pp. 73, 74, 76–8. My thanks to Professor Wright for sharing with me the proofs of his manuscript before publication.

[34] L. Freeman Sandler, *Gothic Manuscripts 1285–1385*, 2 vols. (London, 1986), I, p. 17.

latest datable feast copied by the main scribe in the calendar and sanctorale is the translation of St Alpinus, which took place at some time between 1237 and 1247 during the tenure of Bishop Geoffroy II de Grandpré.[35] Feasts instituted or saints canonised at the end of the thirteenth century or the beginning of the fourteenth, such as St Louis, St Thomas Aquinas, the Conception of the Virgin and Corpus Christi, were added later to the book. Thus, the Châlons Missal-Breviary can be dated objectively only some time in the second half of the thirteenth century. The figures of its historiated initials recall the realism of the figures of Mo, fascicles 1, 7 and 8. The elaborate tails of its penwork initials are also similar to those of Mo, fascicles 2–6, and the Breviary lat. 1023.

While the Honoré style has been dated in the last decade or so of the thirteenth century, there is evidence that manuscripts painted in that style existed as early as the 1260s and 1270s. Evidence for dating comes from the Martyrology, the London Evangeliary and even possibly the Breviary of Philippe le Bel and the Châlons-sur-Marne Missal-Breviary. This is quite compatible with the earliest period during which the Cholet artists were active, and, indeed, it is unlikely that they continued beyond 1290. For this reason, I am led to conclude that fascicles 1–7 of Mo, painted by Cholet and Honoré artists, were painted perhaps as early as between the late 1260s and the 1280s.

THE POSITION OF FASCICLE 8 IN THE COMPILATION OF MO

The historiated initial at the beginning of fascicle 8 shares some facial, head and body types with illuminations believed to date from the first third of the fourteenth century. The half-lidded eyes and prominent ears of the singers of Mo (see Figure 4) also appear in the figures of the Decretals of Gratian, Vatican, Biblioteca Apostolica Vaticana, Vat. lat. 1370 (see Figure 5).[36] The round cherubic head of the monk on the left in Mo much resembles that of the monk in the Vatican manuscript. The monk in the centre of

---

[35] See J.-P. Ravaux, 'La cathédrale gothique de Châlons-sur-Marne', *Mémories de la Société d'Agriculture, Commerce, Sciences et Arts du Département de la Marne*, 91 (1976), p. 173.

[36] My thanks to François Avril, who first drew my attention to the Papeleu Master and the painter of the Vatican Decretals.

Figure 4   Mo, fol. 348^r. Artist of fascicle 8.

Figure 5   Vatican, Biblioteca Apostolica Vaticana, Vat. lat. 1370, fol. 160ᵛ.

Mo, with his long nose, pointed chin and long forehead, resembles the bonneted layman of the Vatican source. However, there are differences. The drapery on the Vatican figures swirls and billows in graceful curls and the figures themselves have small heads and long bodies.

The Vatican manuscript, copied by one 'Petrus Picininus',[37] is difficult to date and to locate on the basis of external evidence. While the illumination is thought to be Parisian, the script is in the rounded Bolognese style, commonly used for juridical treatises. The manuscript may have passed between the two cities, or it could have been produced in one urban centre where both French painting and Italian script, or reasonable imitations, could be supplied on demand.[38] The division of the Vatican manuscript into three principal parts of 101 distinctions, thirty-six causes and a Tractatus *De consecratione* of five distinctions, together with the gloss of Bartholomew of Brescia, is typical of the ordering of the Decretals by the end of the thirteenth century.[39] Stylistically, the Vatican manuscript has been placed *c.* 1320 by Anthony Melnikas because of an affinity he perceived between the Vatican illuminator and the Parisian Papeleu Master.[40] Carl Nordenfalk, on the other hand, finds a greater resemblance between the figures of the Vatican illuminator and the elongated bodies of English painting *c.* 1330.[41]

---

[37]　See the explicit, fol. 320ᵛ.

[38]　For a description of this phenomenon in Decretals manuscripts, see C. Nordenfalk, review of Melnikas in *Zeitschrift für Kunstgeschichte*, 43 (1980), pp. 329–30.

[39]　The Decretals are believed to have been composed by Gratian shortly after the second Lateran council of 1139. Bartholomew of Brescia wrote his gloss some time after the Council of Lyons in 1245 and before his death in 1258; see G. Le Bras, Ch. Lefebvre, J. Rambaud, *L'âge classique 1140–1378: Sources et théorie du droit*, Histoire du Droit et des Institutions de l'Église en Occident 7 (Paris, 1965), pp. 57–8, 78, 310.

[40]　A. Melnikas, *The Corpus of the Miniatures in the Manuscripts of the Decretum Gratiani*, 3 vols., Studia Gratiana 16 (Rome, 1975), I, p. 57. The work identified with the Papeleu Master spans the period from 1289 (the date of the colophon of the *Summa copiosa*, Paris, Bibliothèque Ste-Geneviève, MS 329) to 1317 (the date of the colophon of the historiated bible, Paris, Bibliothèque de l'Arsenal, MS 5059, copied by Johannes de Papeleu). Udovitch prefers to place his activity somewhat later, discounting as a copying error the colophon of 1289, which had been crossed out in red ink. She considers the Papeleu Master to have flourished from 1295, the date of the colophon of the *Somme le Roy*, Paris, Bibliothèque Mazarine, MS 870, until well into the 1320s, which is where she places stylistically the historiated bible, Paris, Bibliothèque Nationale, f. fr. 157, and the Confraternity missal, Paris, Bibliothèque Nationale, f. lat. 861. She traces the roots of his style back to Honoré and the painter of the Châlons Missal-Breviary, Ars. 595. See J. Diamond Udovitch, 'The Papeleu Master: A Parisian Manuscript Illuminator of the Early Fourteenth Century' (Ph.D. dissertation, New York University, 1979), pp. 29, 94–107, 136–65.　　　　[41]　Nordenfalk, p. 329.

However, the figures of Mo, fascicle 8, have normal proportions and are not distorted in the manner of the Vatican Decretals or related English illuminations.

The singers of fascicle 8 do share the large ears, half-lidded eyes and normally proportioned bodies of the three monks of the *Cantate Domino* initial of the English Queen Mary Psalter.[42] The period 1310–20 has been suggested by other manuscripts stylistically similar to the Psalter, although none of the manuscripts illustrated by the artist of the Psalter has been dated exactly.[43] However, the dating of the English manuscripts seems far too late to be relevant to the age of fascicle 8. It is, on the contrary, quite possible that the artist of fascicle 8 provided the model that has long been lacking for the fourteenth-century style of English illumination.[44] The style of the fascicle 8 miniature is consistent with the ideals of the Honoré group and is the work of a most virtuosic and original painter. It is this very originality that places this painter outside any known thirteenth-century school. One can only hope that more work by this artist will be discovered.

The incomplete foliation of Mo has contributed to the mystery surrounding the age of fascicle 8. Both the medieval Roman numeral foliation and the table of contents[45] run only from folios 1 to 333 (new pencil foliation 331), and both stop short of fascicle 8 and the last two gatherings of fascicle 7. Although the foliator was not one of the motet scribes, the Roman foliation was entered while the tenor initials were being decorated,[46] that is, very close to the

---

[42] See the facsimile in G. Warner, *Queen Mary's Psalter: Miniatures and Drawings by an English Artist of the Fourteenth Century Reproduced from Royal MS. 2B.VII in the British Museum* (London, 1912), p. 225.

[43] See L. Freeman Sandler, *Gothic Manuscripts*, II, p. 66. A chronology of manuscripts associated with the Queen Mary workshop is suggested by L. Dennison, 'An Illuminator of the Queen Mary Psalter Group: The Ancient 6 Master', *The Antiquaries Journal*, 66 (1986), p. 305. Paul Binski noted similarities between Mo 8 and this English group, and directed my attention to the relevant bibliography.

[44] See Sandler, *Gothic Manuscripts*, I, pp. 18–19.

[45] The format of the table of contents differs considerably from that of the rest of the book. It consists of a ternio, the first two leaves of which have been cut away. (Jacobsthal had earlier described the remaining four leaves as a binio, in 'Die Texte' (1879), p. 528.) It is written on a thick, stiff parchment, yellow-brown and crude in appearance, by a scribe who copied neither motets nor foliation. The size of the writing area differs considerably from that of the body of the manuscript. The table includes the motets of the supplements to fascicles 3 and 5, the corrections made by a later hand to the numbering of fols. 226, 235 and 236, as well as the correction made by the main emendator of fascicles 2–6 to the beginning of the motetus of no. 246, *Hyer main touz seus*.

[46] Although the Roman foliation usually appears to swerve from the centre of the top

time of copying. The reason for the incompleteness of the foliation remains unknown. While it has been asserted that the motets beginning on fol. 333^v (new foliation 331^v) were later additions,[47] we cannot be certain of this. The last two unfoliated gatherings of fascicle 7 may have been still in the process of being copied or may have become separated from the rest of the manuscript while it was being foliated. Whether or not the last two gatherings were additions, it does not appear that they were added much later for the following reasons. The polychrome initials of fols. 331^v–343^v are still in the style of the Group 1 painters, although a grey-blue colour has replaced the bright ultramarine blue of their previous work. In addition, scribes VII and III, who worked on the previous fascicles, copied motets on fols. 331^v–343^v and 346^r–347^v, respectively (see Table 1).

Yvonne Rokseth assumed that fascicle 8 had originated as a separate manuscript in the fourteenth century in part because of its separate Arabic numeral foliation (numbered 1–48).[48] However, this assumption is unfounded. Far from originating in the fourteenth century, the Arabic numerals used (see Figure 6) are characteristic of fifteenth-century Italian and sixteenth-century manuscripts.[49] Short of pure speculation, there is no accounting for this separate foliation. We cannot assume that the actions of the sixteenth-century foliator had any connection with the circumstances surrounding Mo's compilation in the thirteenth century. Exactly when and by whom the Arabic foliation was entered also remains a mystery.[50] Written quite high up in the right-hand corner

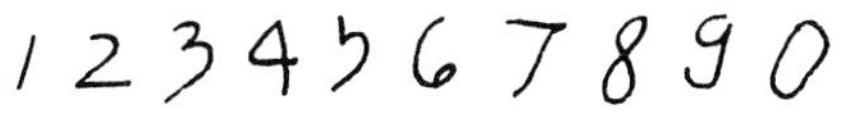

Figure 6   Arabic numerals of the foliation of Mo, fascicle 8.

margin to avoid running into the painted ornaments, on fol. 37^r the paint of the tenor initial filigree passes over the ink of the foliation, showing that at least in one case the numeral preceded the tenor illumination.

[47] Labelled 'Nachträge' by Ludwig, *Repertorium*, ɪ/2, pp. 455–63.

[48] Rokseth, *Polyphonies du XIIIe siècle*, ɪv, p. 26.

[49] See G. F. Hill, *The Development of Arabic Numerals in Europe Exhibited in Sixty-four Tables* (Oxford, 1915), pp. 46–7, table xɪɪ, nos. 6, 7, 8, 10, 14; pp. 50–1, table xv, nos. 5, 8; and, pp. 52–3, table xvɪ, nos. 1, 15, 20, 24. My thanks to Professor Anna Maria Busse Berger for confirming this information.

[50] The poet Estienne Tabourot bought the manuscript in 1587, as is testified to by the partially erased inscription on fol. 4^v: 'C'est à moy Tabourot / A tous accords / Achepté

of the page, this foliation was largely trimmed away, possibly at the time of the present binding, which dates at least from the seventeenth century.[51] There is no reason to doubt that fascicle 8 was intended to accompany the other fascicles. The initials of both fascicle 7, fols. 344[r]–347[v], and fascicle 8 were illuminated by the same painter. Also, the size of the writing area of fascicle 8 is similar to that of the other fascicles.

The style of fascicle 8's repertory, no less than its illumination and format, resembles in a number of ways that of the preceding fascicle. Both fascicles 7 and 8 are collections of three-voice motets in which French, Latin and bilingual pieces are mixed together without any perceptible organisation. Over a third of these motets feature a rhapsodic triplum weaving above and within a slower accompanimental motetus and tenor.[52] Motets actually having more than three semibreves to a tempus are relatively few, but those contained in fascicles 7 and 8 account for virtually all known Petronian motets.[53]

Fascicles 7 and 8 also share unusual types of motets. Nos. 275 and 300 of fascicle 7 and nos. 322, 339–41 and 343 of fascicle 8 feature melismatic passages, sometimes employing hocket and voice exchange. Ludwig, with some justification, has compared these to conductus with melismas.[54] There are also rhythmically

deux testons le i febvrier 1587'. In the upper left-hand corner, likewise erased, is the name 'P Durand', perhaps another owner, who remains unidentified. Wolinski, 'The Montpellier Codex', pp. 74–8.

[51] The parchment bifolio pasted to the front cover carries a descriptive title 'Livre de chansons ancienes et romant avec leurs nottes de musicque' that appears in both manuscript catalogues, dated before 1662, of Jean III Bouhier (1607–71). The catalogue entries are in Berlin, Deutsche Staatsbibliothek, Codices Phillippici Recentiores, 17. Phill. 1866, fol. 7, F33, and Troyes, Bibliothèque Municipale, MS 902, p. 34, E25. Wolinski, pp. 69–70, 80–1.

[52] In fascicle 7, of fifty motets, twenty-two feature this kind of triplum: nos. 253, 254, 255, 256, 258, 262, 263, 264, 269, 270, 272, 273, 274, 281, 289, 290, 293, 294, 297, 298, 299 and 302. In fascicle 8, of forty-three pieces, fourteen have an accompanied triplum: nos. 305, 306, 307, 309, 310, 311, 312, 314, 316, 317, 330, 332, 334 and 338.

[53] The two motet tripla attributed to Petus de Cruce are nos. 253 and 254 of fascicle 7. On the sources of their attribution, see E. H. Sanders, 'Petrus de Cruce', The New Grove Dictionary of Music and Musicians, ed. S. Sadie, 20 vols. (London, 1980), xiv, p. 598. Other motets having more than three semibreves to a tempus are nos. 264, 289, 299, 317, 332 and 338. Nos. 253, 254 and 264 are also transmitted in Turin, Biblioteca Reale, Varia 42. In addition, no. 40 of fascicle 3 features four semibreves to a tempus. A few additional motets in this style are documented in English sources by P. M. Lefferts, The Motet in England in the Fourteenth Century (Ann Arbor, MI, 1986), pp. 79–80.

[54] Ludwig, Repertorium, i/2, pp. 439, 554, 563. Mo, nos. 275 and 300 are discussed in T. Göllner, 'Zwei späte Ars-Antiqua-Motetten', Capella Antiqua München: Festschrift zum 25jährigen Bestehen, ed. T. Drescher (Tutzing, 1988), pp. 189–98.

unusual motets. In fascicle 8, no. 316 features imperfect third mode in the tenor. Nos. 323, 328 and 333 display rhythms in the manner of Odington's 'secondary modes' and his special case of third mode.[55] In fascicle 7, imperfect sixth mode is used in nos. 277 and 278.

Not only fascicle 7 but also fascicles 2–6 contain motets that betray textures and rhythmic features found in fascicle 8. The accompanied triplum texture is encountered in fascicles 2–6, and over half of the bilingual motets of fascicle 3 fall into this category.[56] In addition, there are two melismatic Latin motets[57] and one motet in imperfect sixth mode.[58]

It is not the intention here to use musical style as a means to date fascicle 8, or to show a closer connection between this fascicle and the preceding ones than the codicological evidence warrants. More objective criteria are required to date the fascicle more closely. Rather, I have tried to show that fascicle 8's repertory is consistent with that of the third quarter of the thirteenth century. This stylistic understanding can inform our perception of the tastes of the compiler should it become possible to pinpoint the period of copying. If fascicle 8 was produced in the 1270s, its motet style would be consistent with that of other thirteenth-century collections; if *c.* 1300, it would be a testament to the longevity of that style; if 1320 to 1330, not only would it show this style to be long-lived but it would reflect the conservative tastes of a compiler closer in spirit to Jacques de Liège than to the compiler of the new music of the *Roman de Fauvel*.

Fascicle 8 does differ from the preceding fascicles in the extent to which its repertory was disseminated. While the music of fascicles 1–7 generally was or became well known among the preserved sources, most of the music of fascicle 8 is unique. Of forty-three pieces, only four are transmitted complete in other sources.[59] Two more are found again in fascicles 2 and 7 of Mo itself.[60] Only certain

---

[55] Water Odington, *Summa de speculatione musicae*, ed. F. F. Hammond, Corpus Scriptorum de Musica [hereafter CSM] 14 (n.p., 1970), pp. 131, 139.

[56] Of eleven motets in fascicle 3 proper (not including the anomalous additions), six are in accompanimental style: nos. 36, 37, 38, 39, 40 and 44. This texture also appears in fascicle 4, nos. 52 and 53; and fascicle 5, nos. 77, 102, 103, 123, 124, 143, 144, and 164.

[57] Fascicle 4, nos. 62 and 70. No. 70 even features some slight voice exchange in bars 1–2.

[58] Fascicle 5, no. 164.

[59] Nos. 303, 318, 320 and 330.

[60] Nos. 345 and 338, respectively.

voices of nine additional motets exist in other manuscripts or in theorists' citations.[61] Similarly, all but one of the motets of the last two gatherings of fascicle 7 are unique to Mo,[62] as well as two-thirds of the motets towards the end of fascicle 5.[63] At this point, one cannot know if there is any relationship among these unique collections, or whether they are unique for the same reasons. Perhaps most of these works were newly composed and the manuscript and its exemplars did not circulate much. Nevertheless, the uniqueness of fascicle 8's repertory is not an indicator of progressiveness. Although it may have been more recently composed, the music of fascicle 8 is no more advanced stylistically than that of the rest of the manuscript.

It is striking that fascicles 1 and 8 each begin with a different three-voice discant setting of the trope *Deus in adiutorium intende laborantium*.[64] In the thirteenth and fourteenth centuries polyphonic settings of this trope were most likely to introduce motet collections,[65] a circumstance that contributed to Rokseth's belief that fascicle 8 had been an independent manuscript.[66]

Aside from its initial piece, however, fascicle 1 is very different from fascicle 8. In addition to two hocket motets, fascicle 1 contains two short discants or clausulae and five lengthy organa tripla. Two of the organa have been attributed to Perotin,[67] and a third has

---

[61] Nos. 309, 313, 321, 326, 331, 336, 337, 340 and 341.

[62] The exception is no. 301, *Laqueus conteritur/Laqueus*, a two-voice motet attributed to Philip the Chancellor in London, British Library, Egerton 274, fol. 43.

[63] Of the thirty-one motets nos. 147–77, only seven pieces (nos. 149, 152, 165, 170, 173, 174 and 177) are preserved complete outside of Mo. Certain voices of two other motets (nos. 148 and 164) appear elsewhere.

[64] For an edition and commentary on the chant, see W. Arlt, *Ein Festoffizium des Mittelalters aus Beauvais in seiner liturgischen und musikalischen Bedeutung*, 2 vols. (Cologne, 1970), II, pp. 139, 252.

[65] Examples of motet collections beginning with this trope include Mo, fascicles 1 and 8; Turin, Biblioteca Reale, vari 42, fols. 4ᵛ–5ʳ (after the conductus *Parce virgo* and before the motet section); Darmstadt, Hessische Landes- und Hochschulbibliothek, MS 3471, fol. 1a; and, Brussels, Bibliothèque Royale Albert 1er, MS 19606. On the other hand, in Bamberg, Staatsbibliothek, Lit. 115, the *Deus in adiutorium* appears at the end of the motet collection, on fol. 62ᵛ. In Munich, Bayerische Staatsbibliothek, Cod. lat. 5539, it appears on fol. 31ᵛ, in the midst of a variety of polyphonic works. It also appears in a four-voice fourteenth-century version in a fragment belonging to Cambrai, Médiathèque Municipale; see U. Günther, 'Les versions polyphoniques du *Deus in adiutorium*', *Cahiers de Civilisation Médiévale*, 31 (1988), pp. 111–22.

[66] Rokseth, *Polyphonies du XIIIᵉ siècle*, IV, p. 26.

[67] *Alleluia, Posui adiutorium* and *Alleluia, Nativitas* are attributed to Perotin by Anonymous 4; see F. Reckow, *Der Musiktraktat des Anonymus 4*, 2 vols. (Wiesbaden, 1967), I, p. 46, ll. 12–14.

been hypothesised to have been by him, as well.[68] Of the last three organa in the collection, two belong to the Common of a Bishop Confessor (*Sancte Germane, O Sancte Germane* and *Alleluia, Posui adiutorium*), and the chant of the last piece, *Abiecto, Rigat ora lacrimis*, has been identified by Edward Roesner as the sixth responsory of Matins for the feast of Guillaume of Bourges (10 January), patron of the French nation of the University of Paris. The presence of two certifiable organa by Perotin and three pieces suitable for the feast of the Bishop Confessor Guillaume of Bourges hints at the fascicle's function both as an anthology of Perotinian organa and as a dedication to some individual or corporate body connected with the university.[69]

THE NOTATION OF THE MONTPELLIER CODEX

At the time of Mo's compilation there were various ways of ligating measured music. Melismatic passages were not written as single notes but were ligated as much as possible. In the earliest mensural systems, patterns of notes bound into ligatures corresponded with rhythmic patterns, or modes. The durational values of the notes constituting the ligatures were indicated by the mode in effect. The actual shapes of these ligatures had no rhythmic significance.

In later mensural theory, ligature shapes came to define the durations of the constituent notes. 'Propriety' denotes the appearance of the beginning of a ligature, 'perfection' (and 'imperfection') the appearance of the end. A ligature 'with propriety' has a downward stroke attached to the left side of the figure when the first two notes descend, and lacks such a stroke when the first two notes ascend. A ligature 'without propriety' has the opposite form. Perfection is indicated when the final note, if ascending, appears as a square attached to the ligature by its lower right corner; if descending, by its upper left corner. An imperfect descending

---

[68] See T. B. Payne, '*Associa tecum in patria*: A Newly Identified Organum Trope by Philip the Chancellor', *Journal of the American Musicological Society*, 39 (1986), pp. 238–9, 245–7. Payne speculates that the responsory *Sancte Germane, O Sancte Germane*, the duplum of whose respond also appears as a monophonic conductus with the text *Associa tecum in patria* by Philip the Chancellor, was also composed by Perotin.

[69] My thanks to Professor Roesner for communicating this information and sharing these ideas with me on the function of fascicle 1.

ligature ends with an oblique terminus; an ascending one with a square attached to the ligature by its lower left corner.

For Johannes de Garlandia the type of propriety indicates the rhythmic framework of the ligature. Propriety indicates that the final note of a perfect ligature is a long, the penultimate a breve, and all the notes preceding are equal to a long.[70] A figure lacking propriety has the opposite values.[71] Perfection is a sort of redundant indicator that affirms that the ligature is to end in the manner indicated by the type of propriety in effect. Imperfection indicates that the ligature has been interrupted just before the last note required by the propriety in effect.[72]

In the ligature system of Franco of Cologne, on the other hand, propriety and perfection govern only the first and last notes, respectively, of the ligature. Propriety indicates that the first note is a breve, lack of propriety a long. Perfection means that the final note is a long, imperfection a breve. All notes in the middle are breves.[73]

Lambertus does not espouse a logically consistent system.[74] Rather, he combines older modally contextual forms with some of the graphically representational practices associated with Franco and Garlandia. He adopts traditional ways of ligating first, third and fourth modes using ternariae with propriety and perfection, which is also Garlandia's practice, but he does not adopt Garlandia's theory of propriety and perfection. The sign of propriety does not indicate the value of the final note. As in Franco's system, perfection in Lambertus' ligatures indicates final longs, imperfection final breves, but with a striking exception. In a ligature without propriety, in which the penultimate is a long and the final note a breve, the last note is drawn perfect if descending, in the

[70] 'Omnis figura ligata cum proprietate posita et perfecta paenultima dicitur esse brevis et ultima longa. Si sint ibi praecedentes vel praecedens, omnes ponuntur pro longa' (E. Reimer, ed., *Johannes de Garlandia: De mensurabili musica*, 2 vols., Beihefte zum Archiv für Musikwissenschaft 10–11 (Wiesbaden, 1972), I, p. 50 (chap. III, 2–3)).

[71] 'Omnis figura sine proprietate et perfecta posita valet per oppositum cum proprietate' (*ibid.*, I, p. 50 (chap. III, 4)).

[72] 'Regula est: omnis imperfecta figura, si sit cum proprietate, extenditur usque ad primam longam sequentem, si sit sine proprietate, extenditur usque ad primam brevem sequentem' (*ibid.*, I, p. 51 (chap. III, 16–17)).

[73] 'Omnis ligatura cum proprietate primam facit brevem. Item omnis sine: longam. Item omnis perfectio longa, et omnis imperfectio brevis. . . . Item omnis media brevis. . . .' (Franco of Cologne, *Ars cantus mensurabilis*, ed. G. Reaney and A. Gilles, CSM 18 (n.p., 1974), p. 50 (chap. VII, 26–8, 30)).

[74] See F. Reckow, 'Proprietas und perfectio', *Acta Musicologica*, 34 (1967), p. 138.

manner of Garlandia, and imperfect if ascending, in the manner of Franco. Lambertus is roundly criticised for this by the St Emmeram Anonymous.[75]

There are also various philosophies concerning the notation of semibreves. Garlandia describes the breaking-up of the longs and breves of ligatures into notes of smaller value by means of 'reduction'. Ligatures exceeding three notes are reduced, or compressed, within the durational structure of the ternaria. In ligatures with propriety, all notes preceding the penultimate equal a long of two tempora.[76] Similar in principle to reduction is Garlandia's use of ligatures with opposite propriety, in which an upward stroke is attached to the beginning so that 'the last note is a long and all the preceding ones are put in place of a breve'.[77] If there are only two notes in the ligature, then both are semibreves.[78]

For Franco, opposite propriety indicates that the first two notes of a ligature are semibreves, although he does not explicitly reject more than two.[79] Otherwise, semibreves are written as individual rhombs grouped in combination with single longs, breves or ligatures. Franco maintains that these combinations, or conjuncturae, made of ligatures and single notes, or entirely of single notes, have no rules of their own, but are to be interpreted by the rules applicable to their constituent simple and ligated forms.[80] Lambertus provides a veritable glossary of semibreve forms which by and large follow Franco's rule,[81] and the St Emmeram Anonymous also offers a wide array of ligatures and conjuncturae similar to

---

[75] See C. E. H. de Coussemaker, *Scriptorum de Musica Medii Aevi*, 4 vols. (Paris, 1864–76), I, p. 274. For comments by the St Emmeram Anonymous, see J. Yudkin, *De musica mensurata: The Anonymous of St. Emmeram* (Bloomington, IN, 1990), p. 132, l. 43–p. 136, l. 19.

[76] 'Item omnis figura ligata ultra tres suo proprio modo reducitur ad tres per aequipollentiam' (Reimer, I, p. 63 (chap. VI, 8)).

[77] 'Omnis ligatura per oppositum cum proprietate et perfecta ultima est longa et omnes praecedentes ponuntur pro brevi, si sint ibi plures sive pauciores' (*ibid.*, I, p. 50 (chap. III, 6–7)).

[78] '. . . sed si sint duae tantum non valent nisi brevem . . .' (*ibid.*, I, p. 50 (chap. III, 7) ms. *P* only).

[79] 'Item omnis opposita proprietas facit illam semibrevem cui additur et sequentem, non per se sed consequenti, eo quod nulla sola semibrevis inveniri possit' (Franco, p. 50 (chap. VII, 29)).

[80] 'Sunt etiam quaedam coniuncturae simplicium et ligaturarum, quae partim participant ligaturas et partim simplices figuras. Quae nec ligaturae nec simplices figurae appellari possunt . . . De valore autem talium coniuncturarum non possunt aliae regulae dari quam illae quae de simplicibus et ligatis prius dantur' (*ibid.*, p. 53 (chap. VIII, 11–13)).

[81] See Coussemaker, *Scriptorum*, I, pp. 274–7.

those of Lambertus. These include figures that are said to follow the rules of propriety in their ligated parts.[82]

To a large extent, the various notational practices in Mo can be traced to known treatises and theorists. The scribe of fascicle 8 consistently employs Franconian notation. The scribes of Group 1 (fascicles 1, 7 and the supplements) employ Franconian notation tempered with elements from their own house style and those described by Lambertus. Koller believed that the non-Franconian elements were carried over from the exemplars.[83] This is certainly true in the organa of fascicle 1: in the lengthy, descending, ornamental conjuncturae, in the use of small strokes in the tenors to indicate short unmeasured rests or breaths,[84] and in the habit of elongating a note within a ligature to show it is exceptionally long.[85] However, certain idiosyncrasies appear so consistently in the Group 1 notation that it is clear they belong to the scribes' house style and are not derived haphazardly from models. One is the Lambertian practice of writing descending ligatures without propriety with perfect endings, and ascending ligatures with imperfect endings (see p. 292–3 above).[86] Another is the unusual notation of the second-mode ternaria (meaning BLB) with a stroke descending from the middle.[87]

The main scribe of fascicles 2–6 is the most eclectic in his use of notation. Commonly referred to as 'pre-Franconian',[88] his system combines a modally contextual system of ligatures and rests with graphically representational single notes and semibreve ligatures that are in accordance with descriptions of Lambertus, Franco and

---

[82] See Yudkin, pp. 166–82.
[83] O. Koller, 'Die Liederkodex von Montpellier: Eine kritische Studie', *Vierteljahrsschrift für Musikwissenschaft*, 4 (1888), pp. 27–32.
[84] E. Roesner, 'The Performance of Parisian Organum', *Early Music*, 7 (1979), pp. 175, 182–3.
[85] The elongated binariae on fol. 10, meaning duplex long–long, correspond to the description of the Karlsruhe Anonymous (Dietricus), edited in H. Müller, *Eine Abhandlung über Mensuralmusik* (Leipzig, 1886), p. 6.
[86] The scribes of Group 1 routinely follow this convention for binariae without propriety, except in the motetus of no. 50, in which scribe 1f uses an elongated binaria with propriety as described in the *Discantus positio vulgaris*, ed. in S. M. Cserba, ed., *Hieronymus de Moravia O.P.: Tractatus de Musica* (Regensburg, 1935), p. 190, ll. 13–15.
[87] See the tenors of nos. 3, 49 and 283, which follow Lambertus's practice for the final note of a ligature without propriety, although, as Koller (pp. 28–9) has shown, in other respects they do not follow any known rules.
[88] See W. Apel, *The Notation of Polyphonic Music 900–1600*, 5th edn (Cambridge, MA, 1953), p. 286.

the St Emmeram Anonymous. That this scribe employs both older and newer practices marks him as somewhat conservative, but knowledgeable about notational practices independent of the rhythmic modes. His treatment of rests and of ligatures with propriety and perfection follows customs that antedate Garlandia. The length of rests is not precisely indicated by the length of the strokes drawn through the staff, although strokes may be drawn longer or shorter to indicate the relative durations of the rests.[89] Most ligatures are drawn with propriety and perfection. Their meaning depends on the rhythmic mode in effect, and on whether the ligatures express modal patterns in longs and breves (as in a tenor), or are made up of two, three or four notes that must be reduced into durations of one or two tempora (as in an upper voice).[90] This scribe was possibly like Thomas de Sancto Iuliano of Paris, who did not notate in the contemporary way, according to Anonymous 4, but 'was good following the ancients'.[91]

Nevertheless, the main scribe does use more graphically precise features. He writes single notes in the forms of longs, breves or semibreves, and he writes some ligatures without propriety, with opposite propriety, and with imperfect endings. Binariae without propriety follow the Lambertian convention: the final breve is drawn perfect when descending, imperfect when ascending. The ascending form is sometimes found in interrupted first-mode ternariae, meaning long–breve (LB),[92] and the descending form is sometimes used to mean LB in upper voices.[93] The descending binaria also is used in the tenor at final cadences to mean LL or

---

89   As in the tenor of no. 178, in which rests of three tempora span the entire staff, while rests of one or two tempora are drawn somewhat shorter.

90   These two systems of writing ligatures are called the 'proper' and 'improper' manners, respectively, by Garlandia. The strict observation of propriety (or lack of propriety) and perfection 'is known in conductus or motets, when it is taken without text or with text, if they [the ligatures] are figured in the proper manner. If they are figured in the improper manner, almost all figures are accepted to be imperfect, and this is known in discant and wherever modal measure is accepted' ('. . . intelligitur in conductis vel motellis, quando sumitur sine littera vel cum littera, si proprio modo figurantur. Si improprio modo figurantur, omnes fere figurae accipiuntur imperfectae, et hoc intelligitur in discantu et ubicumque rectus modus accipitur' (Reimer, *Garlandia*, I, p. 51 (chap. III, 16–20), MS B). Lambertus alludes to the same situation; see Coussemaker, *Scriptorum*, I, p. 273b.

91   'Et tempore illo fuit quidam, qui vocabatur Thomas de Sancto Iuliano Parisius antiquus. Sed non notabat ad modum illorum, sed bonus fuit secundum antiquiores' (Reckow, *Der Musiktraktat*, p. 50, ll. 23–5).

92   In the tenors of Mo, nos. 21, 53, 82, 94 and 127.

93   See Mo, nos. 42, 57, 93, 95, 96, 135, 173, 181, 187 and 250.

duplex long–long.[94] Occasionally perfect ternariae and quatern-ariae without propriety are used in the third mode to indicate LBB (nos. 70 and 72) and LBBL (no. 73).

The main scribe uses the imperfect ending in the Garlandian manner to indicate that the ligature has been interrupted (by a change of syllable, a repeated note, a page-turn) before it could complete the rquirements of its propriety. Perfection indicates that the ligature is complete.[95] If a ternaria with propriety, meaning LBL, was interrupted after the second note, the binaria containing the first two notes would be written imperfect. Imperfect endings signifying interruption are found in tenor ligatures interrupted by page-turns[96] and by repeated notes.[97] In other cases imperfection indicates that the last note is no longer than the preceding ones. An imperfect ternaria with propriety means BBB and one with opposite propriety means SSS.[98] A perfect ternaria with opposite propriety, on the other hand, usually means SSB.

The most telling evidence that the scribe of Mo 2–6 was versed in more progressive notation lies in his versions of ligatures containing semibreves and in conjuncturae. In the mensural theory of Franco, Lambertus and the St Emmeram Anonymous, the rhythm of a conjunctura is directly indicated by the form of its parts. There is no questioning that the Franconian principles practically demon-strated by Lambertus and the St Emmeram Anonymous are to be applied to Mo, fascicles 1, 7 and 8. What has not been evident to previous editors of Mo is that these same principles should be applied to the conjuncturae of fascicles 2–6.

Table 4 compares some conjuncturae of Mo, fascicles 2–6, with descriptions of Lambertus and the St Emmeram Anonymous. Most

---

[94] See Mo, nos. 75, 81, 101, 102, 106, 156, 163, 166, 169, 178, 189, 210 and 218.

[95] This meaning of perfection is also found in motets in second mode, in which the last notes of phrases in the upper voice, which are properly breves, are nevertheless written as longs. These longs are not actual longs, but indicate that the phrase ending is perfect and complete, just as the final note of a second-mode ternaria is perfect and ends with a breve. G. Kuhlmann, *Die zweistimmigen französischen Motetten des Kodex Montpellier, Faculté de Médecine H 196 in ihrer Bedeutung für die Musikgeschichte des 13. Jahrhunderts*, 2 vols. (Würzburg, 1938), I, pp. 100–1, considers these final notes to be actually breves, while L. Dittmer, 'The Ligatures of the Montpellier Manuscript', *Musica Disciplina*, 9 (1955), pp. 49–50, considers them to be literally longs.

[96] Mo, nos. 35, 46 and 60.

[97] Mo, nos. 178, 225 and 228.

[98] The concept of imperfection as interruption may still apply here, if we view these imperfect ternariae as truncations of reduced quaternariae.

Table 4 *Conjuncturae of Mo 2–6 compared with descriptions of Lambertus and St Emmeram Anonymous*

Values	Figures		
	Mo 2–6	Lambertus	St Emmeram Anon.
1. SSS			
2. SS = Balt (BrBr)		allowed	not allowed
3. SSS = Balt (SSBr)		allowed	not allowed
4. SSSB			
5. BSS			
6. BSSS			
7 BSSB			
8. BSSSB			(sixth mode)
9. BBB (cf. box 2)		allowed	not allowed
10. with propriety BBSS(S) = BL			
11. without propriety BBSS(S) = LB			
12. LSS			
13. LSSS			
14. LBBB(L)			(third mode)
15. LSS(S)Balt			

of the conjuncturae fall under Franco's general instruction to perform them according to the rules of simple and ligated notes. There
are, in addition, some special cases. The lozenge-shaped
semibreves of the conjuncturae can take on values beyond right
measure, that is, they can become breves,[99] and this is acknowledged by approbation or rejection by various theorists. Lambertus
tells us that binarie with opposite propriety, that is, two ligated
semibreves, can be put in place of an *altera brevis*, that is, each
semibreve would equal a *recta brevis*.[100] Three semibreves may also
be placed for an *altera brevis*[101] and three semibreve lozenges may
even be put in place of a *recta* plus *altera brevis*, as he demonstrates in
Table 4, box 15.[102] Anonymous 7 concurs in putting three or four
semibreves (which he calls breves) in place of a *recta* plus *altera
brevis*, and provides a rule that is applicable to the conjuctura of
Table 4, box 15.[103]

Franco, however, objects that fewer than four or more than six
semibreves cannot be placed for an *altera brevis* and directs his
criticism pointedly against those who put two or three semibreves
for an *altera brevis* (see Table 4, boxes 2 and 3).[104] The St Emmeram
Anonymous also forbids the placement of two semibreves for an
altera brevis.[105] He criticises placing three semibreves for three
tempora, and maintains that it would be better to use an imperfect
ternaria with propriety.[106] However, as can be seen in Table 4, box

---

99 See E. H. Roesner, review of *The Earliest Motets (to circa 1270): A Complete Comparative
   Edition*, ed. H. Tischler, in *Early Music History*, 4 (1984), p. 373.
100 'Quod si aliquando pro altera brevi ponantur, tunc enim duo tempora compleantur'
   (Coussemaker, *Scriptorum*, I, p. 274a).
101 'Omnes semibreves equales et indivisibiles proferuntur, nisi in tertio loco quarti modi,
   pro altera brevi reperiantur; nam sicut altera brevis tenet affinitatem recte breves, sic
   etiam tales affinitatem inter se tam in forma quam proprietate tenebunt' (*ibid.*, I, p.
   275b).
102 *Ibid.*, vol. 1, p. 275b. The figure in Paris, Bibliothèque Nationale, f. lat. 11266, fol. 28,
   was originally a long followed by a ternaria with propriety and perfection, which was
   erased and changed to a long followed by two rhombs. In Siena, Biblioteca Comunale,
   L.V.30, fol. 28, it is a long followed by three rhombs, as represented in Table 4, box 15.
103 'In isto tertio modo datur talis regula: quod quando nos habemus multitudinem
   brevium, illa que plus appropinquat fini dicitur longior proferri. Ergo de duabus
   brevibus prima est unius temporis, reliqua vero duorum. Si vero tres vel quatuor
   inveniantur, pro duabus brevibus, ultima valet duo tempora et totum residuum non
   valet nisi unum' (Coussemaker, *Scriptorum*, I, p. 379a).
104 'Pro altera autem brevi minus quam quatuor semibreves accipi non possunt, . . . nec
   plures quam sex, . . . eo quod altera brevis in se duas rectas includit; per quod patet
   quorundam mendacium, qui quandoque tres semibreves pro altera brevi ponunt,
   aliquando vero duas' (Franco, p. 40 (chap. V, 25)).
105 Yudkin, p. 148, ll. 32–40; p. 166, l. 30–p. 168, l. 3.   106 *Ibid.*, p. 172, ll. 31–42.

14, he breaks his own rule by allowing the three middle semibreves of a third-mode conjunctura to equal three *rectae breves*.[107]

The scribe of Mo, fascicles 2–6, often places two or three semibreves for an *altera brevis* and three or four for a perfection (Table 4, boxes 2, 9, 14 and 15) in the manner of Lambertus. It would be reasonable to assume that he also accepted the common mensural practice of making paired semibreves unequal (minor and major, or vice versa).[108] This is not to say, however, that all the ligatures and conjuncturae of fascicles 2–6 can be interpreted according to the rules of the extant treatises. Generally the figures are quite flexible, expanding or contracting to fill the duration required by the mode. It is this curious mixture of pre-Garlandian, Lambertian and Franconian practices that belies the description of this scribe's notation as 'pre-Franconian'.[109] He was capable of notating the same sort of motets as those copied by his Franconian contemporaries in fascicles 7 and 8, for it can be argued that the motets of all the fascicles share the same rhythmic principles. While employing a modally contextual system, the scribe of fascicles 2–6 also drew on the graphically representative ligatures and conjuncturae of Franconian and Lambertian theory to resolve potentially ambiguous situations and to represent semibreves in places other than at the beginning of a ligature (as specified by the rules of reduction and ligatures with opposite propriety).

SOME IMPLICATIONS OF THE NEW DATING OF MO

It has been considered that Mo was notated in three stages that record the evolution of rhythmic notation and style. Fascicles 2–6 were notated in a modally contextual, or 'pre-Franconian' system, fascicle 7 in a nearly Franconian and fascicle 8 in an entirely Franconian way.[110] However, the accepted use of Mo for dating

---

[107] *Ibid.*, p. 176, ll. 31–4.

[108] See Franco, pp. 38–9 (chap. v, ll. 22–3); Coussemaker, *Scriptorum*, I, p. 272b. On controversies surrounding the ordering of unequal semibreves see Wolinski, pp. 114–20.

[109] Apel, *The Notation of Polyphonic Music*, p. 286.

[110] See E. H. Sanders, 'Sources, MS, § v, 2: Early Motet, Principal Sources', *The New Grove Dictionary*, XVII, pp. 655–7; G. Reaney, *Manuscripts of Polyphonic Music 11th–Early 14th Century*, RISM B/IV/1 (Munich and Duisburg, 1966), p. 272; and W. Apel, *The Notation of Polyphonic Music*, pp. 284–301, 315–18.

such systems and the theorists connected with them is invalid, first of all, because scribes regularly combined various systems in devising their own unique brands of notation. This can be seen in the work of the scribes of fascicles 1 and 7, and the scribe of fascicles 2–6. Secondly, the fact that at least the first seven fascicles were copied at the same time is further proof that several notations were used simultaneously.

The redating of fascicles 1–7 of Mo has implications for the dating of Franco of Cologne's *Ars cantus mensurabilis*, or, more importantly, the application of the theories he describes. Scholars' conjectures have placed the treatise anywhere from *c.* 1260 to *c.* 1280.[111] The dating of Mo posited above suggests that the Franconian notation of fascicles 1 and 7 dates from the late 1260s or 1270s. More importantly, however, Mo demonstrates that Franco's ligature rules were combined with those of Lambertus in fascicles 1 and 7, and that Lambertus's influence was felt in fascicles 2–6. This situation does not support the assumption that Lambertus preceded Franco, but shows rather that the teachings of both found credence at roughly the same time.

The dating of Mo has more striking ramifications for the dating of Petrus de Cruce, the composer credited by Jacques de Liège with writing motet tripla having more than three semibreves to a breve. Two of his motets appear at the beginning of fascicle 7 (see p. 288 above). Petrus, the motet composer, has been identified with 'Magister Petrus de Cruce de Ambianis', who compiled an *historia* of St Louis in 1298.[112] In addition, Petrus de Cruce of Amiens is cited as the owner of a 'liber organicus'[113] and the author of a tonary.[114] Whether Petrus the motet composer can be identified

---

[111] Heinrich Besseler placed Franco *c.* 1260, at the time Ludwig dated the motets central to Franco's treatise; see H. Besseler, 'Franco von Köln', *Die Musik in Geschichte und Gegenwart*, ed. F. Blume, 14 vols. (Kassel and Basle, 1949–68 and suppls.), iv, cols. 688–98. Wolf Frobenius believed that Franco's *Ars* appeared just after the St Emmeram Anonymous's treatise of 1279; see W. Frobenius, 'Zur Datierung von Francos *Ars cantus mensurabilis*', *Archiv für Musikwissenschaft*, 27 (1970), pp. 122–7. Michel Huglo redates Franco between 1260 and 1265, which he believes is after Lambertus supposedly flourished in 1250 to 1260, and before Jerome of Moravia transmitted Franco's *Ars*, which could have been as early as 1275; see M. Huglo, 'De Francon de Cologne', pp. 45–50, 60.

[112] See J. Viard, *Les journaux du Trésor de Philippe IV le Bel* (Paris, 1940), pp. 127, 144, 159.

[113] G. Durand, ed., *Ordinaire de l'église Notre-Dame, cathédrale d'Amiens, par Raoul de Rouvray (1291)* (Amiens and Paris, 1934), pp. xxiii–xxiv, lxx.

[114] Petrus de Cruce, *Tractatus de tonis*, ed. D. Harbinson, CSM 29 (American Institute of Musicology, 1976).

with these personages remains in doubt. The conservative Jacques de Liège's characterisation of Petrus de Cruce, as a composer 'who composed many good and beautiful measured songs and observed the practice of Franco',[115] places Petrus in the best tradition of the thirteenth-century *antiqui*. This is compatible with dating Petrus's motets in the 1260s or 1270s. At the same time, this new viewpoint contradicts the traditional appraisal of Petrus as a transitional composer who anticipated the Ars Nova minim.

The chronology of the late thirteenth-century motet has been closely linked with the dating of fascicles 7 and 8 of Mo, whose motets have been thought to provide a transitional link to the Ars Nova. Some of these motets are considered to display a more progressive rhythmic style marking the gradual breakdown of modal rhythm and prefiguring the new practice of the fourteenth century. However, the evidence that at least the first seven fascicles of the Montpellier codex were created as a unified whole some time during the 1260s or 1270s suggests a radically different view of the development of the motet in the second half of the century, a view that is supported by contemporary theorists. Garlandia, Lambertus, the St Emmeram Anonymous of 1279 and later writers referring to earlier practices describe a musical scene as rich and diverse as the content of Mo, including types of motets and hockets that historians have traditionally placed only at the end of the century. The use of more than three semibreves to a breve, of imperfect rhythmic modes and other deviations from normal modal rhythm can be understood as part of the Ars Antiqua and not as transitional features leading to the fourteenth-century Ars Nova. A discussion of the testimonies of the theorists with reference to the repertory goes beyond the present codicological study of Mo. Future articles will address this subject and the question of what actually did take place at the turn of the century.

University of Rhode Island

---

[115] '. . . qui tot pulchros et bonos cantus composuit mensurabiles et artem Franconis secutus est' (Jacobus of Liège, *Speculum musicae*, ed. R. Bragard, 7 vols., CSM 3 (American Institute of Musicology, 1973), VII, p. 36 (chap. XVII, 7)).

REVIEWS

DONATELLA RESTANI, *L'itinerario di Girolamo Mei: dalla 'Poetica'*
alla musica con un'appendice di testi. Florence, Leo S. Olschki, 1990.
218 pp.
GIROLAMO MEI, *De modis*, edited by Tsugami Eisuke. Tokyo,
Keiso Shobo, 1991. lvi + 247 pp.

After two aborted plans to publish Girolamo Mei's *De modis musicis*
of 1566–73 in the seventeenth and eighteenth centuries, two editions of the treatise have now appeared within a year of each other,
one of them limited to book 4, the other containing all four books.
The edition of book 4 is offered as an appendix to a study of Mei's
life and work by Donatella Restani. The other is a critical edition of
the entire treatise, with a preface in both English and Japanese.

Giovanni Battista Doni planned an edition of the treatise, as he
announced in his *Idea sive designatio aliquot operum*,[1] but he died
prematurely in 1647 before completing many of his projects. The
copy that would have served as the basis for Doni's edition, collated
by him with the autograph in the Vatican, is in the Biblioteca
Riccardiana in Florence. Padre Martini also contemplated a publication of the treatise, having had Doni's copy transcribed by
Lorenz Mehus, who in a letter of 13 June 1761 strongly urged
Padre Martini to pursue the edition of Mei's 'noble offspring'
('aureo parto').[2]

Restani's edition of book 4 provides much more than a critical
text. Exhaustive annotations account for the sources, mostly Greek,
that stand behind Mei's revelations about ancient Greek musical
theory and practice. Although Mei was careful not to transcend

---

[1] Bologna, Civico Museo Bibliografico Musicale, MS D32, quoted in my *Girolamo Mei:*
Letters on Ancient and Modern Music to Vincenzo Galilei and Giovanni Bardi (2nd edn, Neuhausen, Stuttgart, 1977), p. 38, n. 97.
[2] The letter is printed in Restani, *L'itinerario*, p. 92.

what he could document, he rarely cited the authors on whom he depended by book and chapter. Restani drew on a seemingly encyclopedic knowledge of the surviving writings on music, whether in treatises or fragments dedicated to music, or more general philosophical, historical or literary works, to document his sources. In effect she retraversed Mei's *itinerario*, studying all that he had read and also sources that he might not have seen which corroborated or would modify his conclusions. The annotations also refer the reader to pertinent modern literature.

Restani's book consists of a ninety-six-page chronological survey of Mei's career and scholarly production, closing with a consideration of the transmission and reception of his writings from the seventeenth century to the present. A 119-page appendix contains the edition of book 4 and excerpts or full texts of twenty-one letters, all in Italian, all addressed to Vettori except one to Niccolò del Nero. She chose book 4 to illustrate Mei's work for several reasons. It was the only one of the four books that Mei felt was sufficiently refined to present to his mentor Piero Vettori in 1573. Indeed, the autograph manuscript, Vat. lat. 5323, which appears to be Mei's final working draft, exhibits many more revisions in this book than in the others. It is the most historical of the four books, the others dealing with aspects of the theory of the Greek modes and of their differences from and ties to the church modes. Book 4 also has the greatest affinity with Restani's interest in classical literature and its echoes in the Renaissance. This book deals less with technical questions and more with the uses of music in antiquity, the ethos of the modes, the relevance to music of Aristotle's theories of catharsis and imitation, and the contrasting attitude of Plato and Aristotle towards the modes and their effects.

There is much that is new in her study of Mei's life and work. Restani utilised the considerable body of published research since 1960 to reconstruct the intellectual and social milieu in which Mei moved in Florence, Lyons, Padua and, during his several visits and final residence, in Rome. She sees his Florentine period, 1519 to around 1548, as one of apprenticeship with Piero Vettori and of adherence, as was traditional in Mei's family, to the politics of the Medici family, then headed by Cosimo as duke. Evidence of this is not only the fact that he was named a Magistrato dei Dodici Buonòmini in 1545 but that his treatises on Tuscan verse and prose address one of the chief aims – the advancement of the Tuscan vernacular – espoused by the Accademia Fiorentina, which he joined in 1541. She fleshes out the personalities and sketches the relationship to Mei of the many men whose names are dropped in the letters. It is a distinguished list. During his Florentine days they included Bartolomeo Barbadori, who with Mei helped Vettori prepare the *editio princeps* of Euripides' *Electra*, Niccolò del Nero, with whom he continued to correspond throughout his life, Piero del Nero, to whom he left his books and manuscripts when he left Florence, and associates in the Pianigiani academy – Bartolomeo Cavalcanti, Jacopo Pitti and Agnolo Guicciardini.

Restani explores the possible reasons for Mei's self-exile from Florence, pursuing my suggestion[3] that Mei may have had unorthodox religious views and that this may explain his position of leadership in the informal association of apparently dissident young men called the Accademia del Piano.

The first period of exile – 1547–59, before Mei established himself definitively in Rome – was one of job-seeking and cultivating influential friends of Vettori, such as in Rome Alessandro Farnese (Pope Paul III), Marcello Cervini (later Pope Marcellus II), Padre Ottavio Pacato, and in France Albizzo del Bene, legate to the Queen of France, who helped Mei get a position as companion to the young Guglielmo Guadagni, based in Lyons. Restani recalls that Tommaso Guadagni, one of the richest men of the time, built the chapel of Notre-Dame-de-Comfort in the church of St Domenique, which was a gathering-place of the Florentines and employed among other notable musicians Francesco de Layolle. Apparently the young Guadagni inherited Tommaso's musical inclinations. Mei credits Guglielmo Guadagni with encouraging his first musical researches. After his employment in France ceased in 1554, Mei avoided returning to Florence and instead spent the next five years in Venice and Padua, a period he lamented as his 'ozio padovano' (Paduan idleness), while waiting for a favourable papacy in Rome.

Taking advantage of recent studies concerning the university in Padua, Restani throws light on Mei's activity on behalf of Vettori's candidacy for a position as professor there. The large number of

---

[3] Palisca, *Girolamo Mei*, pp. 21–2.

students in Padua were organised in 'nations', and these national groups, through the election of councillors, could influence the appointment of their teachers. Besides attending lectures in Padua, Mei was active in the organisation of the Florentine *fuorusciti* in Venice, where he often stayed with Francesco Nasi.

Finally, there is the circle around Mei in Rome, where in his rooms, first in the palace of Cardinal Giovanni Ricci, later in that of Giovanni Francesco Ridolfi, he was host to a virtual academy. Among the frequenters, some resident in Rome, others visitors from abroad, were the German Johannes Caselius, Latino Latini, Giovanni Vincenzo Pinelli, Antonio Possevino, Niccolò del Nero, Niccolò Ridolfi, Baccio Valori, Federico Borromeo and Giovanni Battista Strozzi the younger. Conspicuously missing from his associations or mention in his letters were persons then active in Roman musical life, even those with Florentine links, such as Emilio de' Cavalieri, Luca Marenzio, or Vittoria Archilei. His letters never name musicians or speak of going to hear musical performances, but this may be due partly to Vettori's slight interest in music.

Mei is remembered today mostly because he inspired Galilei to promote a reform of music in the direction of monody and provided fuel for Bardi's critique of the current polyphonic method of composition. He earned this reputation in the twentieth century partly through Piero del Nero's posthumous publication of a brief treatise, *Discorso sopra la musica antica e moderna* (Venice: Gio. Battista Ciotti, 1602), which was reprinted in Milan in 1933.[4] In 1960 I showed that this treatise was almost identical with the core of Mei's first letter to Galilei of 8 May 1572. My publication of the six surviving letters from Mei to Galilei and Bardi reinforced the association of Mei with the Camerata movement.

But among the humanists of his own time Mei was remembered chiefly for his authoritative writings on Greek music. Restani's discussion of Mei's work complements mine because she plays down the connection with the Florentine Camerata and concentrates on Mei's production as a scholar, first as a commentator on the *Poetics* of Aristotle in his letters to Vettori, then on the history

[4]   This is discussed in, among other places, D. P. Walker, 'Musical Humanism in the 16th and Early 17th Centuries', *Music Review*, 2 (1941), pp. 1–13, 111–21, 221–7, 289–308; 3 (1942), 55–71, reprinted in *Music, Spirit and Language in the Renaissance* (London, 1985).

of the Greek modes, culminating in the fourth book of *De modis*, and lastly on early medieval music theory, bearing fruit in the unfinished treatise *De' nomi delle corde del monochordo*. Similarly, Tsugami's edition of the entire treatise complements my edition of the letters to Galilei and Bardi and Restani's of selected letters to Vettori bearing on music. Thus all that remain unpublished of the musical writings are the incomplete *Trattato di musica* that begins 'Come potesse tanto la musica appresso gli antichi nel commuovere gli animi degli ascoltanti' and *De' nomi delle corde*.

Restani gives a lively account of Mei's struggle to come to terms with his recalcitrant subject of the Greek modes. In a letter to Vettori, he compares the task to an ass that 'stumbles at every step, so closely sniffing the earth that I don't know how it keeps from breaking its neck'.[5] Each book occupied him about two years. The first, which was finished in January 1567, discusses the tonoi, tropoi, systemata and consonances, with particular attention to terminology. He presents the tuning schemes of the tetrachords that form the perfect system in the various genera, showing how some theorists followed the sense of hearing, others arithmetical reasoning. The systems of Aristoxenus, Ptolemy and Boethius are thus passed in review.

The second book concentrates on the consonances and their species, particularly the species of octave which he calls *diapasΩn formae*. The differences among Aristoxenus, Ptolemy and Boethius concerning these species are graphically represented in charts. The misinterpretations of the system of Ptolemy by Boethius, who wrongly attributed to him an eighth tonos, and by Glarean and Gaffurius are detailed with some contempt. Mei takes pains to show that the division into authentic and plagal modes had no basis in Greek theory. Mei finished the second book in 1568 and was eager to begin the third, but he encountered 'a thousand difficulties' with which he told Vettori he could have used some help, but most of all his occupation as secretary to a cardinal gave him little peace of mind, and books were not conveniently available. The manuscripts of the Vatican library had become less accessible with the reorganisation imposed by Pius V. Besides, in a letter of 1570, he wondered what use his treatise would be to anyone:

---

[5] Letter, Mei to Vettori, 22 March 1567, quoted in Restani, *L'itinerario*, p. 49.

In view of its slight usefulness, considering that it is a labour that will not serve anyone, I would not mind tearing myself away from it altogether. Nevertheless I don't see that I am much good for anything else; so to pass the time I resolved to get myself back on the tail of this ass and make him, just for my pleasure, go forward by force of the cudgel if he does not want to make headway otherwise.[6]

The third book was finished in 1571, and Mei had six copies made, evidently for his Roman circle. Here he traces the transmission of Greek theory by Boethius and its reception by Gaffurius and Glarean. A parallel theme is the gradual corruption of simple ancient song by the ambitious display of instrumentalists through which it lost its close alliance with poetry and its immediate affective expression.

Restani sees the fourth book as a convergence of the network of cross-references to Greek practices in the first three. Here historical perspective and philological acumen, learned in Vettori's school, come to the fore. Mei contrasts the Platonic 'republic of saints', which tolerates only the Dorian and Phrygian modes, with Aristotle's openness to any mode, whether ethically beneficial or simply enjoyable to various segments of the population. Restani recognises the synthesis in this book of Mei's study of the *Politics* with his penetration into the *Poetics*. He interprets the operation and benefits of catharsis in medical terms, a purification needed by the mind, oppressed with an excess of pity, fear or anger, analogous to the purgation sometimes needed by the body when it is suffering from a superfluity of blood, catarrh or bile. This purification may be brought about homeopathically by presenting artistic imitations of the passions that disturb the mind. Restani sees Mei's accomplishment in this context as having

rewritten for Aristotle that page on the relation *kátharsis–mousiké* 'missing' in the *Poetics*, freeing himself, in venturing this interpretation, from the philological rigour of Vettori that he otherwise methodically applied to the critical examination of texts. It is important to throw into relief in Mei's approach the profound influence exercised on this scholar by the music-theoretical literature regarding the two nodal points of the Aristotelian exposition, *kátharsis* and *mímesis*. (p. 55)

Mei applied the theory of imitation quite literally to music. Just as the actor in a tragedy imitated with gestures the behaviour of

---

[6] Mei to Vettori, 28 April 1570, in Restani, *L'itinerario*, p. 51.

someone calm or proud, so by means of the voice aimed at the low, high or median pitches, he imitated the states of the soul through the Hypodorian, Mixolydian or Dorian. Thus the pairing by Aristides Quintilianus of regions of the voice and poetic genres, comments Restani, is applied to Aristotle's mimetic theory. The Dorian, for example, Mei observed, was most suited to dramatic music, whereas the Lydian occupied the pitch space that best served nuptial songs. Restani sees this 'rewriting' of Aristotle as the application of a technical 'code' drawn from Greek music theory to the philologic–literary Aristotelian code. Mei's contribution is thus a 'transcodification', a term she borrows from D. Lanza's Italian translation of the *Poetics* (Milan: Rizzoli, 1987).

I translate below Restani's handy synopsis of the fourth book, which divides it into its component themes in terms of the paragraph numbers supplied in her edition (Tsugami's edition introduces paragraph indentations but does not number them).

The historical–political exegesis is based, in the first part (i–xx) on the diachronic reading of the changes in musical structures (transition from vocal music to instrumental, iv–vii; modes and ethos, viii–x; music in the tragedy, xi–xii; *nómoi*, xvii–xviii) and, in the second (xxi–xxv) on the interpretation of two different political models – Platonic (xxiii) and Aristotelian (xxiv) – observed through the role played by music and its circumstances. The other level of exploitation of the text is founded on the distinction between *usus* [usage, custom] and *utilitas* [usefulness, profit, ethical exploitation]. It proposes the 'sociological' analysis of different settings and contexts (symposium, theatre, religious holiday) in which music was practised, through the predominant attention to the *usus* in the first part (i–xx); counterpoised against and complementary to it is the analysis of the *utilitas* of music in the 'ideal' *pólis* [city-state], as theorised by Plato and Aristotle, developed in the second section (xxi–xxv). (p. 58; my interpolations are in square brackets.)

In the midst of this discussion (xi–xii, pp. 117–18) we meet the critical emendation of that key Aristotelian problem, number 48 of section 19, which deals with music in the theatre and which provided Mei with a crucial document for his theory that the ancient tragedy was sung throughout. In the traditional reading of the text, Hypodorian and Hypophrygian are said to be most suitable to tragic actors. Mei emended Hypodorian to Dorian and Hypophrygian to Phrygian, because the author of the problem, who he thought was Aristotle himself, goes on to say that the first is magnificent and stable, while the second incites to action. This is how the Dorian and Phrygian are characterised in the *Politics* (8.7), and, besides, Mei's research showed that the designation 'hypo' was not used before Aristoxenus. An unspecified mode – there is a lacuna in the text of this problem – is assigned to the chorus. In his Latin translation, Theodore Gaza, who may have had a better text, Mei thought, supplied Mixolydian, which Mei shows by his discussion (xi:1) that he accepted.[7]

Of signal importance in book 4 is also the discussion of the musical embellishment of different genres of poetry. Mei launched into the subject from the *Poetics* of Aristotle but bolstered that text with findings from many other authorities.[8] Here Mei proposed that tragic actors sang their parts, but not with the rhythm of dance, that the stationary chorus similarly had melody but not rhythm, and that the non-stationary chorus which represented the crowd sang with both melody and rhythm. It is interesting that Francesco Patrizi came to a similar conclusion in his *Della poetica: la deca istoriale* (Ferrara: Baldini, 1586) and that there is evidence that Patrizi had consulted Mei before publishing his treatise, though about what is not known. Latino Latini, writing to G. V. Pinelli on 10 August 1585, reported that Mei spent several solid days of work to satisfy Patrizi's requests.[9]

Donatella Restani is ideally qualified as an interpreter and editor of Mei's writings on ancient Greek music. She holds a *laurea* in classical philology, with a dissertation on musical-rhetorical terminology in selected Greek sources, and a post-*laurea* doctorate in musicology from the University of Bologna, with a dissertation on Mei that was revised to produce the present book. She observes the standards for scholarly editing in the field of classics, while focusing in her study and annotations on matters that are relevant

---

[7] On a folio that is apparently an appendix to Mei's letter to Galilei of 6 September 1581, an Italian translation of this problem is provided that shows the emendation to Dorian and Phrygian but in which Lydian replaces Mixolydian. See Palisca, *Mei*, pp. 178–9. Galilei also assigned the Lydian to the chorus, suggesting that he got this from Mei. It is possible that after completing *De modis* Mei rethought the question and decided that Aristotle's time was too early also for the name Mixolydian.

[8] For translations of sections xv 8–9 and xvi 1–5, see Palisca, *Humanism*, pp. 420–1.

[9] Milan, Biblioteca Ambrosiana, MS D 169 inf.: 'Il Mei stà assai commodamente; et ha hauuto da trauagliare alcuni di per sodisfare al Francesco Patritio.' However, the translation that Patrizi offered in his *Poetica* of problem 48 does not reflect either Mei's emendations or Gaza's translation. See the text in Patrizi, *Della poetica*, ed. D. A. Barbagli (Florence, 1969–71), I, pp. 331–2, and in Palisca, *Humanism*, pp. 413–14.

to the history of music. However she is uncompromising in not wishing to write down to the linguistic level of those unschooled or rusty in Greek and Latin. Thus Greek quotations, phrases and proverbs that speckle Mei's writings in both Italian and Latin are left untranslated, and the fluency in Latin and acquaintance with the conventions of editorial apparatus expected of users of standard editions of classical literary sources is assumed in the readers of this book. Yet it is obviously addressed to musicologists. Classicists, even those who have edited or translated musical treatises, have shown almost no interest in either Mei or Giovanni Battista Doni, to name just two scholars who were highly competent in the field of Greek music theory before von Jan. (Andrew Barker, for example, does not include them in his bibliography in *Greek Musical Writings*.) It may be idle to hope that this book will awaken classicists to the fact that there was serious philology in this field before Wallis and Meibom, indeed more critical and sympathetic than theirs.

In view of the centrality of music in Mei's scholarly output, Restani's reluctance to bend to the musicological readership's linguistic limitations is unfortunate. The reason she gives for not supplying a translation of book 4 (which she has confessed to preparing for her own use) is that the twenty-one letters and excerpts from letters of Mei which she presents in the appendix are themselves a bowdlerisation and exegesis of his treatise: 'To the edition of the text I have not attached a translation, considering it superfluous in the light of the thorough combing of the correspondence, which describes and justifies the poetics and methodology of the author in a way much more faithful than any other possible exegesis' (preface, p. 7). In presenting a Latin music-theoretical text without translation, she is following the footsteps both distant and near of Gerbert, Coussemaker, Smits van Waesberghe and her teacher F. Alberto Gallo. The Anglo-American tradition of parallel texts and translations exemplified by the Loeb Classical Library, the Heinemann series of Cambridge and Harvard, and the more recent series, Greek and Latin Music Theory, reflects not only a desire to broaden the audience of an ancient author but acknowledgement of the fact that commentary and interpretation must start with a clear understanding of precisely what an author meant, which the process of translation better than any other means often reveals. Restani's dissertation, and consequently the book, follows a convention common in Italy and Germany of assuming that those trained in the humanities are all literate in Latin, and to some extent Greek. Both Latin and Greek dictionaries should be kept handy when reading Restani's book and, for those not conversant with the standard abbreviations of classical sources, also a list such as that in *The Oxford Classical Dictionary*, because she gives no list of abbreviations. As with many Italian publications, there is no index of either names or subjects and also no index of classical *loci*, though there is a list of manuscripts.

The book is written in an exquisitely refined Italian style, with great economy and scholarly caution. Restani obviously resisted many opportunities to enlarge upon her favourite topics and kept strictly to her role as commentator and editor. One place where some expansion would have been desirable concerns Mei's role in the first edition of Euripides' *Electra*, published by Vettori (Rome, 1545) and Mei's contribution to the edition of the tragedies of Aeschylus (Paris: H. Stephanus, 1557). Also useful would have been a consideration, apart from the footnotes to the edition of book 4 and the letters to Vettori, of Mei's wide-ranging reading. How strong is the evidence that he knew all the places referred to in the footnotes? What Greek literature did he know beyond the list he gave in his first letter to Galilei, which is confined to works dealing exclusively with music?[10]

Tsugami's book does not raise any of these questions, because it is strictly a critical edition of the text of the entire *De modis*, with a preface limited to a description of the manuscript sources, particularly detailed with respect to the autograph in the Vatican, a stemma codicum, and a statement of editorial principles. Tsugami was able to consult Restani's published book and takes issue with her on some points. Their most significant disagreement concerns the stemma of sources. Restani posits the existence of two lost copies of the autograph, one of which would have served as an intermediate source for the copy made for Doni, another for a presumed lost codex on which the two existing Paris copies are based. Tsugami assumes that all the copies stemmed directly from the autograph except for that made by Mehus from Doni's copy

[10] See Palisca, *Mei*, pp. 118–21.

and the second of the two related Parisian exemplars. In favour of Restani's conjecture of an intermediate copy of the autograph as a base for the Paris manuscripts is her recognition of a Florentine rather than Roman provenance of the prototype of the Paris copies. This is founded on the presence in the parent Paris codex of Mei's treatise on Tuscan verse as well as the Italian music treatise 'Come potesse la musica . . .', of which there were no copies in the Vatican. On the other hand her assumption of an intermediate copy of the autograph for the manuscript once belonging to Doni is contradicted by Doni's own statement in *Idea sive designatio aliquot operum* which identifies his scribe's model as the autograph given to the Vatican library by Antonio Quaerenghi.[11]

Tsugami's edition is extremely accurate, as I was able to judge by comparing it with the autograph and with Restani's edition of book 4. He follows a conservative editorial policy, that of the *Oxford Latin Dictionary*. Tsugami's book is well supplied with indexes: Latin and Greek *indices verborum* (the former occupying 110 pages!), produced by computer through the *Oxford Concordance Program*, and an *index locorum*. The latter refers to parenthetical insertions in the text that precisely locate citations whenever Mei mentions his source. Unlike Restani, Tsugami does not try to identify the source when Mei is silent about it. The only discrepancies with the autograph are in several of the diagrams (pp. 46 and 66), in which Tsugami has failed to offset the solmisation syllables to show graphically the continuity of hexachords as Mei does in his autograph, and an incorrect fraction on p. 48 (third row, fifth column should be 1/27 instead of 1/23). Graphically the diagrams are beautifully executed, aside from the upper-case O's above the T's, where Mei abbreviated 'T[on]o' (whole tone).

Scholars and students are now well furnished with an authoritative text of Mei's major treatise, and the dream of Doni and Padre Martini – not to mention my own – has been realised beyond our wildest hopes.

Claude V. Palisca
Yale University

---

[11] See Palisca, *Mei*, p. 38, n. 97, or G. Gaspari, *Catalogo della Biblioteca musicale G. B. Martini di Bologna*, ed. N. Fanti, O. Mischiati and L. F. Tagliavini (Bologna, 1961), I, p. 234.

THOMAS FOREST KELLY, *The Beneventan Chant*. Cambridge,
Cambridge University Press, 1989. xvi + 350 pp.

We owe this splendid book to a particularly fortunate match of
subject matter and author. The Beneventan chant is a limited
enough subject to be manageable within one volume, while of
considerable importance because of its implications for the most
central questions of early chant history. The author, Thomas Forest Kelly, was the ideal scholar to undertake the project; in addition
to the more general run of musicological virtues, he has special
strengths in liturgy and palaeography as well as the presentational
ability to make a difficult subject come alive.

The text of the book is set out in five chapters: one each on the
general history of the Beneventan chant; its manuscript sources; its
liturgy; its musical style; and finally its relationship with other
chant families – Roman, Gregorian, Milanese and Byzantine. This
takes up some two-thirds of the volume; the rest is devoted to
bibliography, indexes and three invaluable appendices that present
the entire extant repertory, its concordances and sources in clear
and convenient layout.

It is generally known that Beneventan sources are late and fragmentary; the bulk of them are Gregorian manuscripts of the
eleventh century that contain a number of Beneventan chants. No
source devoted entirely to Beneventan chant has been preserved,
but palimpsest leaves do survive; they add a number of pieces to
the extant repertory and, just as important, suggest that the Beneventan chant was a self-sufficient body of ecclesiastical song,
presumably meeting the needs of the Beneventan church before the
imposition of Gregorian chant in the Carolingian era. Kelly, working in Italy for extended periods of time, has examined all the
previously known material and added significantly to it, even if
more often discovering new sources for already known chants
rather than entirely new items. Among the most important sources
are the two Gregorian graduals, Benevento 38 and 40, and the final
flyleaf of Benevento 35, from a lost Beneventan gradual; they
present all told some twenty Beneventan masses. Those in the
Gregorian sources are 'doublets', the term used by liturgical
historians to designate alternative items: each Beneventan Mass

follows immediately after a Gregorian Mass for the same feast. Kelly speculates about the reasons for this arrangement, wondering whether the Beneventan Masses were intended as genuine practical alternatives to the Gregorian, as second Masses for the same day, or merely as antiquarian souvenirs. (While much of the repertory is preserved in these three manuscripts, Kelly has identified a surprising total of about eighty-five, all of which are carefully described in appendix 3.)

Among his more important contributions is the demonstration that the Beneventan chant was indeed a complete liturgical repertory. The principal temporal feasts are represented in the preserved Masses as well as the most important sanctoral dates, although there is a gap in the sources from the feast of St Stephen to Palm Sunday. In view of what remains, one can safely assume the previous existence of at least the feasts of St John the Evangelist, the Holy Innocents, Epiphany and the Sundays of Lent. At the same time one does not have to imagine that the Beneventan liturgy approached the Roman in completeness. It seems unlikely, for example, that there would have existed formularies for most of the weekdays in Lent, or proper formularies for the ordinary Sundays of the year. On a related point Kelly observes that the existing formularies themselves appear not to have been fixed in their liturgical assignment in the manner in which we have become accustomed to think of Gregorian mass formularies. The ingressa may have been so assigned, but the other items display instability even within the closely related Benevento 38 and 40. Not only does one item, say a communion, appear at one festival in one manuscript and at another in the other, but the various liturgical genres, particularly offertories and communions, are themselves interchangeable. This creates the impression on Kelly that originally a proper ingressa was used at the celebration of Mass, the additional chants being chosen from a common repertory. He shrewdly observes that the arrangement of Benevento 38 and 40 is meant to imitate the Gregorian practice of fixed formularies.

An interesting characteristic of the Beneventan liturgy is the presence of antique features. We know from indirect evidence, for example, that the Lenten Sundays were named after the old Roman gospels *De Samaritana*, *De Abraham*, *De caeco* and *De Lazaro*; and there are traces of three readings at Mass and a great number of proper prefaces. One cannot help comparing it in this respect with the Milanese liturgy. It has the curiously contradictory appearance of new wine in old bottles, that is, an ancient liturgical framework filled with material that is in many cases more recent than the Gregorian. Another puzzling contradiction is that while the Beneventan liturgy shares several features of the ancient framework with the Milanese, and while its entrance chant shares its name ingressa, and its omission of psalm verses, the order of chant items within the Mass matches that of Rome rather than Milan – there are an ingressa, a gradual, an alleluia, an offertory and a communion. All this is grist for the comparative liturgical mill; certain of these liturgical features can be dated and thus may help eventually in sorting out the chronology of pre-Carolingian Italian chant. On matters liturgical, incidentally, Kelly displays a rare professionalism, unsurpassed, I would say, by any other non-clerical chant scholar.

The music of the Beneventan chant is copied in diastematic neumes that lack complete precision in the earlier sources. Larger intervals are less certain than smaller ones, and there can be difficulty in moving from the end of one line to the next. These conditions have created uncertainties for scholars who transcribed isolated chants, but in working with the entire repertory Kelly was able to arrive at reasonably firm conclusions by using strategies such as comparison with Gregorian chants in the same manuscripts and the recognition of stock formulas. In general Beneventan chant is characterised by its confinement to a limited pitch range, the use of melodic formulas and prolixity of surface detail; this last trait is frequently manifested in a repeated podatus figure that reminds one of Old Roman chant. Kelly sees the use of melodic formulas as an essential structural device. He isolates two formulas that are used at the end of phrases and pieces with great regularity, and two frequently employed opening formulas; internally used formulas are less clearly defined yet still recognisable. Large compositions are often constructed with the repetition on the same pitch level of surprisingly long phrases. As for tonality, there is less trace of a modal system than in any other of the Italian chant dialects. The use of two closing pitches, G and A, and the occasional transposition in later sources of A pieces down to D, has created the impression of a bi-modal system with authentic and plagal divisions. Kelly, however, finds that the G and A endings are incidental to the tonal substance of an entire chant, and concludes that 'we are in the presence of a sort of pre-modal music which operates within a single family of melodic procedures' (p. 155).

For those wishing to make comparisons with other chant families there are two melodic points of special significance. For one, there is no trace of the stylistic differentiation that characterises the various genres of Gregorian chant; all use roughly the style just described, and in fact, as indicated earlier, items such as offertories and communions are used interchangeably. Nor is there any uniformity in the general length of items; virtually all genres offer examples of extremely short chants and extremely long ones. There is an overlap here of musical and liturgical consideration, and the same is true of the second point. Kelly finds no trace in any of the chant genres – gradual, offertory or whatever – of a curtailed or stylised psalmody. In fact strikingly few Beneventan chants have psalmic texts; most use non-biblical texts or texts paraphrased from other books of the Bible, what Kenneth Levy calls 'librettos'.[1]

Kelly sets the liturgy and music in context with an excellent chapter (actually his first) on the historical background, both secular and ecclesiastical. It is difficult to say much about the origins of Beneventan chant beyond the likelihood that it could not have come into being before the conversion to Catholicism of the Beneventan Lombards in the later decades of the seventh century. Its flourishing and its spread to centres like Bari and Monte Cassino probably coincided with the mid eighth-century prominence of the duchy, climaxing in the reign of Arichis II (758–87). Just as suddenly it entered into its decline, as the northern Lombards fell to Charlemagne in 776 and the Beneventan Lombards began to experience a long period of political pressure from Franks, Greeks and Arabs, and of ecclesiastical pressure from Rome. The Gregorian chant (or more properly, Frankish–Roman chant) came to Benevento before the end of the eighth century; this is clear from numerous archaic features of Gregorian chant preserved in Beneventan sources, only the most obvious of which is the absence of the *Omnes gentes* formulary for the seventh Sunday after Pentecost. Nevertheless the Beneventan chant survived alongside the Gre-

---

[1] See for example 'Toldeo, Rome and the Legacy of Gaul', *Early Music History*, 4 (1984), pp. 49–99.

gorian until its suppression in the mid-eleventh century under Pope Stephen II (1057–8). It is, in fact, a matter of survival rather than continued development: the patronal feast of the Twelve Brothers, instituted in 760, has a unique Beneventan Mass, while the later patronal feast of St Bartholomew, instituted in about 838, has a Mass adapted from Gregorian chants. Kelly is at a loss to explain the precise mode of the Beneventan chant's survival. A plausible guess, for example, is that it 'was sung in the chapel of St Sophia, established by Arichis II himself, while Gregorian chant was sung in the cathedral. But this is only a guess, and we are left sharing the author's puzzlement with a phenomenon – the coexistence of two chant repertories in the same centre – that may be unique in the early history of ecclesiastical music.

While Kelly has shown us that the Beneventan chant is a fascinating subject unto itself, it may be his fifth and final chapter, where he compares it with the other chant dialects, that will be of the greatest interest to many. The most remarkable conclusion from this comparison is how little it has in common with either Milanese chant or Roman chant (I use the term Roman chant here and subsequently in the broad sense, to include pre-Carolingian Roman chant, Gregorian chant and Old Roman chant). While Benevento shares many texts with Milan and Rome, there are few cases where a text has the same liturgical assignment, and fewer still where such a text also has a related melody.

This is especially surprising of Milan. After all the Beneventan and Milanese chants represent, respectively, the principal ecclesiastical centres of the southern and northern Lombard principalities. That the two chants were associated in the minds of contemporaries is clear from the fact that what we call Beneventan chant is labelled 'Ambrosian' in the eleventh-century sources (a matter of some confusion to an earlier generation of chant scholars). And then there are the similarities of liturgical framework alluded to above like the use of the ingressa without psalm as an entrance chant. Yet Kelly fails to endorse the tempting notion of an original pan-Lombardic chant because of the general failure of formularies to match. He is forced to assume that 'the shared material, except where it is a late direct borrowing, must come from a time before its standardization, before texts were invariably fixed as to feast and liturgical function' (p. 166). These are only his most general conclusions; they result from a painstaking comparison of the entire Beneventan repertory with the cognate chants of the neighbouring liturgies. It is disappointing that the most tangible points of comparison, both textual and musical, tend to be instances of late borrowing, for example, the two Masses for the feast of All Saints from Gregorian chant, and the Office antiphons for the feasts of St Apollinaris and St Nazarius from the Ambrosian. There are, it is true, instances of shared chants in the Holy Week and Easter liturgies, but still fewer than one would have expected, and again these chants tend not to occupy the precisely analogous places in the different liturgies. So in the end one can only resort to the notion of a repertory of Italian chant existing at some time before the standardisation of the various liturgies, a necessary notion perhaps, but one in need of much refinement. One might ask, for example, when such a repertory might have existed; when were the historical circumstances in Italy favourable for its sharing? Was it a large repertory, meeting the needs of an entire liturgy, or a limited one, including only chants for special occasions such as the Holy Saturday Mass for the newly baptised described by Kenneth Levy?[2] Was it an equally shared (and created) repertory, or was it a repertory originating primarily at one centre and borrowed by others? These are questions, needless to say, that fall outside the limits of the book at present under consideration.

The comparison of Beneventan and Byzantine chant is of a different order. Here Kelly is able to isolate the Greek elements in the Beneventan chant with comparative ease and to work out a convincing historical scenario for their inclusion. This only serves to highlight the difficulties in constructing a similar comparative history of the principal Italian chant families. Kelly has gone as far as one can, I believe, within the limits of his subject. He set out to produce an overview of the Beneventan chant itself, and has done so with a degree of thoroughness, perception and elegance that must stand as a model in chant studies for some time to come. On the matter of comparison he starts from this composite view of Beneventan chant and makes comparisons only with cognate chants in the other liturgies, not with the liturgies as a whole. The latter procedure would properly be the subject of another book,

[2]   'The Italian Neophytes' Chants', *Journal of the American Musicological Society*, 22 (1970), pp. 181–227.

indeed several other books. Still the appearance of Kelly's volume makes it possible to hazard a few guesses about the way such a comparison might go with the Roman Mass in particular, utilising little more than the overview provided many years ago by Peter Wagner.[3] To say such a comparison would be tentative is of course an understatement; still it might be a useful exercise or at least an entertaining one.

It would have to begin with crystallising Kelly's overview of Beneventan chant, by catching up with him, so to speak. He has provided the means to do so with his appendices 1 and 2. The first of these lists the incipits of the entire repertory in liturgical order, giving first the chants of the Mass and then those of the Office. This is a simple enough accomplishment, but the second appendix is a genuine *tour de force*. It presents every Beneventan chant text (some 175) in alphabetical order, each followed by its biblical or non-biblical derivation and its concordances in Old Roman, Gregorian and Milanese chant. This is clearly the result of immense labour and a singular knowledge of the chant repertory and its sources. For one thing it could not have been accomplished by merely consulting indexes because many of the concordances, perhaps most, are not exact, frequently beginning with different words. For another it is remarkably free of typographical errors and similar mechanical lapses for so enormously detailed an effort; the only item of the sort I would consider mentioning is the puzzling contradiction of the alleluia *Hodie migravit* identified as that of St Peter in appendix 2, and appearing as the Ascension alleluia in appendix 1. In any case what one can do is simply to merge appendix 1 and 2, that is to add the text derivations and comparative results of appendix 2 to the outline of the liturgy provided by appendix 1. One then mulls over the results, now so visually comprehensible, in the hope of duplicating to some extent the knowledge of the

---

[3] *Introduction to the Gregorian Melodies*, part 1, translated by A. Orme and E. G. P. Wyatt (London, 1901), pp. 175–89, 280–97. Work along the lines indicated by Wagner has been carried out by a number of liturgical historians, most notably Antoine Chavasse; see, for example, 'Cantatorium et Antiphonale Missarum . . .', *Ecclesia Orans*, 1 (1984), pp. 15–55. The method employed in such work, the examination in sequence of chant texts and their derivation, is greatly promising, but frequently marred in execution by the tendency to see the hand of Gregory I at every turn. I attempt to use a similar method in my own work on communions presented in two recent papers: 'The Roman Post-Pentecostal Communion Series', Cantus Planus (Pécs, Hungary, September 1990); 'The Eighth Century Roman Communion Cycle', American Musicological Society (Oakland, CA, November 1990).

material that is second nature to Kelly from long familiarisation.

In turning to a comparison with Rome, one is struck first and foremost by the utter difference between the two repertories. The annual cycle of the Roman Mass is characterised by order: there is, for example, the numerical series of psalmic texts; programmatic sequences of chants following the liturgical seasons; and stylistic differentiation between chant genres. All this is absent from Beneventan chant so that at first one has the impression of chaos. If further acquaintance modifies this to an impression of something sophisticated enough in its own right, the Beneventan chant appears still never to have been subject to revision, perhaps not to have been quite completed. But however one may choose to characterise it, its difference from Rome remains little short of startling. Are we to look on this, then, as a matter of choice? Was the polished Roman liturgy ignored by the Beneventans for motives of, say, Lombard pride? Or might it be that the Roman liturgy was itself still in a state of flux and hence not available for copying at the very time the Beneventan was developing? That the latter came into being in a period of a century at most, and perhaps considerably less, suggests the possibility of a similarly brief flurry of Roman activity as opposed to a steady evolution over the centuries.

Another point of comparison is Roman fixity of liturgical assignment for its Mass chants as opposed to Beneventan fluidity. We tend to take this fixity for granted, but its absence in Beneventan chant reminds us that it is the result of a policy decision, not a natural phenomenon. An interesting facet of this Roman fixity is that it was imposed genre by genre, not festival by festival; that is to say, one can discern in individual chant items, especially communions, a compositional sequence beginning in Advent and extending throughout the year. This can only be the product of revision, not an outline that had been set up centuries in advance and then systematically filled in. Peter Wagner was already aware of this and attributed it to Gregory I. The purpose of our new-found knowledge of Beneventan chant serves here to make our sense of the Roman practice more vivid, to bring us to reflect on it anew, and to recognise it as something singular and chronologically determined. One asks, for example, whether it is likely that it already existed in the time of Gregory I, only to be ignored a century later in the composition of the Beneventan liturgy.

Perhaps the single most striking difference between the two chants is the paucity of psalmic texts in the Beneventan. Not much more than a tenth of the Beneventan texts are taken from the Psalms, with the rest about equally divided between other books of the Bible and non-biblical sources. The Roman Mass repertory, in contrast, is basically psalmic (Gregory I still refers to chant simply as *psalmos*[4]), with a later infusion of non-psalmic texts, most notably in the form of communions derived from the Gospels. The Beneventan preference for non-psalmic texts, manifested as it is in the late seventh century or earlier eighth, might be taken to suggest that the Roman gesture in the same direction is roughly contemporary.

While Beneventan texts, as pointed out above, very seldom have Roman concordances with the same liturgical assignment, the majority of them have concordances, either precise or approximate, somewhere in the Roman (and Milanese) liturgies. Of the twenty preserved Beneventan Masses only three have formularies that are for the most part indigenous Beneventan compositions with no echo at Rome; these are the Mass for the Twelve Brothers not surprisingly, the second Mass of the Holy Cross and the Mass for St Andrew. If the majority of Beneventan Mass chants, then, have concordances, textual at least, with Rome, is there any pattern in the relationship? At least one curious circumstance is immediately apparent: most of the chants are shared not with the Roman Mass but with Roman Office antiphons (and Milanese Office psallenda). Now if Kelly is right in his assumption that we are dealing with Italian chants before their fixity in the various liturgies, and if we take into account the late date of the Beneventan chant, then we must entertain some fairly radical proposals. The most extreme perhaps is that the Beneventans borrowed from a fund of chants used at Rome during the seventh century indiscriminately in both Mass and Office, and that the Roman Mass known at present was composed after this time and tightly sealed off from the Office. As startling a thought as this is, it seems no more implausible than its alternative, that the Beneventans decided to avoid in their borrowing a fixed and isolated Mass and turned instead to an unassigned Office repertory. (A curiously contradictory detail in all of this is

---

[4]   *Registrum* v, 57a; Monumenta Germaniae Historica, *Epistolarum* 1 (Berlin, 1891), p. 363.

that the one time of the year where the shared Beneventan chants appear with any frequency in the Roman Mass, Paschaltide, is the one time of the year when Roman communions are borrowed from Office responsories and antiphons.)

These thoughts are offered here not as conclusions, hardly even as serious hypotheses, but rather as lines of thought worthy of exploration. In the aggregate they suggest the proposition that the revisions which created the Roman chant repertory as we know it were later rather than earlier, perhaps as late as the time that Beneventan chant was coming into being. There are other categories of evidence that have led many of us to think in that way already, but Kelly's work offers an entirely fresh perspective. For the time being it is the textual and liturgical side of things that has been so greatly facilitated. What of the music? The author is at work now preparing a volume of facsimiles for publication in *Paléographie musicale*; one wonders if he and the editors of that series would consider a transcription volume also, after the model of the invaluable Ambrosian *pars hiemalis* in volume VI.

James W. McKinnon
University of North Carolina at Chapel Hill